# DISTINGUISHED ASIAN AMERICAN BUSINESS LEADERS

**Recent Titles in the
Distinguished Asian Americans Series**

Distinguished Asian American Political and Governmental Leaders
*Don T. Nakanishi and Ellen D. Wu*

# DISTINGUISHED ASIAN AMERICAN BUSINESS LEADERS

## Naomi Hirahara

*Distinguished Asian Americans Series*

**An Oryx Book**

GREENWOOD PRESS
Westport, Connecticut • London

**Library of Congress Cataloging-in-Publication Data**

Hirahara, Naomi, 1962–
    Distinguished Asian American business leaders / Naomi Hirahara.
        p.  cm.
    Includes bibliographical references and index.
    ISBN 1–57356–344–7 (alk. paper)
    1. Businesspeople—United States—Biography.   2. Asian Americans—Biography.   3.
Entrepreneurship—United States—Biography.   I. Title.
    HC102.5.A2H56   2003
    338.0973′092′395—dc21        2002067835

British Library Cataloguing in Publication Data is available.

Library of Congress Catalog Card Number: 2002067835
ISBN: 1–57356–344–7

First published in 2003

Greenwood Press, 88 Post Road West, Westport, CT 06881
An imprint of Greenwood Publishing Group, Inc.
www.greenwood.com

Printed in the United States of America

The paper used in this book complies with the
Permanent Paper Standard issued by the National
Information Standards Organization (Z39.48–1984).

Cover images used by permission.

10  9  8  7  6  5  4  3  2  1

# Contents

# Preface

The term "business leader" can be applied broadly. An attorney, an architect, or even a doctor with a thriving practice can be considered a business leader—in fact, any field may require some marketing, management, and financial skills in order to be a success. In this volume, *Distinguished Asian American Business Leaders*, I've identified the category in both narrow and unconventional ways to reflect the historic experiences of these ethnic minorities. For example, in the late 1800s, many Chinese immigrants, barred by discriminatory federal and state laws from owning land, becoming citizens, or even entering the country, found occupational niches as laundrymen. When their livelihood was threatened, it was a business leader—Yick Wo—who successful contested municipal and county laws that seemed to be targeted against Chinese Americans. As a result, among the 96 individuals profiled in this volume, I've included a wide variety of entrepreneurs and business persons, including a Chinese laundryman, who have had a significant impact on their profession and on the larger community from as long ago as the 1880s to the early twenty-first century.

The 96 individuals profiled here are not necessarily the wealthiest or even the most successful business leaders in the Asian American community. One, in fact, just recently launched a single restaurant, while another has a chain of more than 400 outlets. What was considered was the individual's situation and the hurdles that needed to be overcome. Philanthropy, in addition to ethnic and regional diversity, were other deciding factors.

Their personal philosophies in conducting business differ widely. As you read each individual profile, which presents basic biographical information, along with more information about their business, and the way they have conducted them, you will learn of one Internet entrepreneur who successfully negotiated a $400 million deal from Microsoft Corporation and of another who, along with his partner, gave away $100 million in bonuses to their employees after the lucrative sale of their company. Some are highly educated with law and doctoral degrees, while others never completed college. These stories reflect that there are multiple paths to succeeding in business—in that sense, business is rich in creative opportunities that cannot be easily limited to a single management theory.

Most of these profiles were compiled from secondary sources, which are referenced at the end of each profile. This enables interested students and readers to refer to these sources for more information about each business leader. The profiles are organized alphabetically; there is also an appendix that lists the individuals by broad category of business.

Most of the research was conducted from 1999–2001, a turbulent time in terms of the high-tech industry. Some contemporary business leaders have had to close their enterprises, but odds are the same individuals will create new ones in this twenty-first century. Determination and perseverance are the two qualities that seem apparent in the lives of all those profiled, whether they have had to flee political upheaval or rebuild after being held in an internment camp during World War II by their own U.S. government. Personal failures and setbacks have also not deterred these men and women from succeeding in their chosen fields.

Networking is another important part of the formula. Japanese immigrant gardeners learned from other immigrants in launching their small businesses, as did Cambodians in their domination of the doughnut industry in Southern California. The same principle applies to South Asians and Chinese Americans who have created their own organizations in Silicon Valley to obtain millions of dollars in venture capital for their high-tech ideas. Asian American women, who still lag behind their male counterparts but are making more inroads than ever before, are also creating their own formal and informal networks. Many couples also have effective business partnerships.

Special acknowledgments go to Judy Soo Hoo of the UCLA Asian American Studies Reading Room; J.D. Hokoyama of the Leadership and Education for Asian Pacifics (LEAP); Grant Ujifusa; Brian Niiya; and *The Rafu Shimpo* newspaper. Contributing writers were John S. Saito Jr., Takeshi Nakayama, and Joyce Nako. Donna Sanzone and Anne Thompson of Oryx Press were especially helpful in making this project a reality. Wes Fukuchi, as always, provided support in times of need.

This book has been written for any person interested in how some Americans, from recent immigrant to fourth generation, labored to realize their entrepreneurial and corporate dreams. Their life stories not only reflect individual triumphs but also the trials of families and ethnic groups to ensure that all have a chance to apply their skills and passions for economic prosperity.

# Profiles

# A

## C.K. Ai

**Full Name at Birth**: Chung Kun Ai.

**Born**: 1865, Saisan, China.

**Death**: 30 September 1961, Honolulu, Hawaii.

**Education**: Iolani School, Honolulu, Hawaii, c. 1880–82.

**Positions Held**: Owner of dry goods store and tailoring shop, Honolulu, Hawaii, 1883; clerk, store owned by James Isaac Dowsett, Honolulu, Hawaii, 1887–98; import business, Honolulu, Hawaii, 1898; founder and operator, City Mill Co., Honolulu, Hawaii, 1899–61.

**Summary**: C.K. Ai was one of the Chinese American business pioneers in Hawaii. Becoming involved in lumber importing, rice milling, and even pineapple canning, this man from Kwantung Province established the foundation of his 70-year career on the islands at the beginning of the twentieth century.

### Early Years

When Chun Kun Ai was three years old, his father traveled from South China to the islands of Hawaii to find work. Other men from his province had already made the trek to work as field hands on sugar plantations in the 1850s. Rather than join them, Ai's father instead established a store in Honolulu and began to bring his family members over. Ai finally sailed to Hawaii in 1879.

Ai, who did not speak any English at the time, enrolled in Iolani School, a Honolulu boarding school that was operated by Anglicans connected with the Church of England. (There he became friends with another Chinese classmate, Sun Yat-sen, the son of peasant farmers who eventually became a leader of modern China.) Ai's conversion to Christianity at this time was not supported by his father, who also thought Ai was not learning to speak English at a fast enough pace.

After two years, Ai was called home to Kona, Hawaii, but he eventually returned to Honolulu in 1883 to become a partner in a small dry goods store and tailoring shop. Meanwhile, on the mainland of the United States, the Chinese Exclusion Act, which prohibited the entry of Chinese immigrants, had gone into effect in 1882. Chinese laborers, however, continued to enter the islands, because Hawaii had not yet been annexed as a U.S. territory. By 1893, Chinese comprised 20 percent of the islands' population.

## Career Highlights

In 1887, Ai, then 21, became a clerk in the store of James Isaac Dowsett, who helped develop the whaling trade in Hawaii. Dowsett was apparently impressed with Ai; he allowed him to use part of a Dowsett warehouse to set up a small business of his own. Ai soon began importing tea, nails, and other items in his spare time. In 1895, he married Seu Shee; they went on to have 10 children.

When Dowsett passed away in 1898, Ai purchased some of his former employer's equipment and began working on his own enterprise fulltime. He organized a company to bore wells for the irrigation of sugar and pineapple plantations. With his associates, he launched City Mill Co., which specialized in lumber importing and rice milling. Located in the Chinatown district of Honolulu, City Mill Co. was in operation for two years, when a fire, set by authorities to destroy rats carrying bubonic plague, went out of control and practically wiped out the entire area. The incident left Ai thousands of dollars in debt, yet he did not give up on his business.

He rebuilt City Mill Co. only to suffer more losses due to a devastating fire in 1919. He remained optimistic and even began a pineapple canning enterprise, Honolulu Fruit Co. The pineapple venture faltered in the 1930s, yet City Mill Co. continued to flourish. Ai continued to go in to work daily until his death in 1961. He was 95 years old. At that time City Mill Co., with 200 employees, had total sales exceeding $5 million a year. Its headquarters was located on land purchased by Ai in 1916, the same year he led a group of investors to launch the Chinese American Bank.

Ai's children and other descendants continued to operate the business. It began retailing in 1955 and finally dropped the wholesale end of its business in 1980. The company, which has seven hardware and building-supplies retail stores throughout the island of Oahu, celebrated its 100-year anniversary in 1999.

Ai, a devout Christian, founded the Chung Kun Ai Foundation to promote Christian missions and churches and help the poor and needy. He was president of the Chinese Hospital and the Chinese United Society. He also received the Order of the Splintered Paddle from the Honolulu Chamber of Commerce.

Ai died on September 30, 1961, at the age of 95.

## Sources

Ai, C.K. 1960. *My Seventy-Nine Years in Hawaii*. Hong Kong: Cosmorama Pictorial Publishers.

Brady, Spencer. 1961. "City Mill Built Up from a Hard Struggle." In Robert M. Lee, ed., *The Chinese in Hawaii: A Historical Sketch*. Honolulu, HI: Advertiser Publisher Company, Ltd.

# Pauline Lo Alker

Pauline Lo Alker in 1986 © Roger Bessmeyer/CORBIS

**Full Name at Birth**: Pauline Leung.

**Born**: 1943, Canton, China.

**Education**: Arizona State University, Phoenix, Arizona, B.A. in mathematics and music, 1964.

**Positions Held**: Typist, General Electric, Arizona, 1965; programmer, General Electric, Arizona, 1965–c. 1970s; Amdahl Corporation (later acquired by Fujitsu), Sunnyvale, California, c. 1970s; software engineering manager, Four-Phase Systems (later acquired by Motorola), Cupertino, California, 1974–77; marketing manager, Intel, Santa Clara, California, 1977–80; vice president of marketing (later vice president and general manager of special products division), Convergent Technologies (later acquired by Unisys Corporation), California, 1980–84; cofounder, Counterpoint Computers, Inc. (later acquired by Acer, Inc.), San Jose, California, 1984–87; president of network computer division (later president of sales and marketing operations), Acer America Corporation, San Jose, California, 1987–94; president, chief executive officer, Network Peripherals, Inc., Milpitas, California, 1994–98; founder, chairman, president, chief executive officer, Amplify.net, Fremont, California, 1998– .

**Awards, Honors**: Outstanding Entrepreneur, Governor's California Conference on Women in Business Award, 1995; Award, Committee of 100, 1998.

**Summary**: Pauline Lo Alker, who entered the computer field in the 1960s, pioneered the way for Asian American women to excel in high technology. She went on to launch and lead numerous corporations in the Silicon Valley.

## Early Years

Alker was the only daughter and middle child of an entrepreneur in Canton, China.

When she was six, her family fled to Hong Kong to escape the 1949 Chinese Revolution. Alker had been active in church from a young age; her minister recognized her musical talent and gave her piano lessons. By her junior year of high school in Hong Kong, Alker was taking classes from a concert pianist. She contemplated teaching music and mathematics before she was given a full scholarship to attend college in Arizona, where her father's colleague had a gift shop.

## Higher Education

Both Alker and her older brother attended Arizona State University in Phoenix. The adjustment to the Southwest desert, in contrast to the crowded streets of Hong Kong, was challenging. To help defray their living expenses, they worked in the dorm cafeteria. Alker also worked after school as a sales clerk at the local Sears department store.

Alker decided to double major in mathematics and music. As part of her mathematics degree, she took classes in computer science. "I was fascinated by it," she told *Transpacific*. "It was extremely challenging, a combination of logic as well as art, mathematics, the discipline, as well as composition and creativity. Music and math are very similar, a lot of correlation, so somehow this just hit me."

## Career Highlights

The only job Alker could find after graduation was a bookkeeper position at Sears. After marrying a Chinese American man she met at college, she continued with her education and took computer classes at night. One of her classmates was an editor in the technical publication department at General Electric Company and advised Alker to apply for an entry-level position with the firm as a manuscript typist. Alker began that job, and within two months she became a programmer for the payroll department.

She later obtained some experience in systems programming at General Electric before being recruited by a high-tech startup, Amdahl Corporation, in Sunnyvale, California. Other engineering and marketing manager positions followed with then-fledgling Silicon Valley companies such as Four-Phase Systems and Intel. In 1980, a former supervisor recruited Alker from Intel to Convergent Technologies. As vice president of marketing, she negotiated more than $500 million in contracts with such major customers as AT&T, NCR, and Burroughs. Her performance led to a promotion to vice president and general manager of the company's special products division.

In 1984, the same year she married Steve Alker, Alker and the director of engineering of her division at Convergent, Frederick Kiremidjian, decided to launch their own enterprise, Counterpoint Computers, Inc., in San Jose. Counterpoint competed against Sun Microsystems, Apollo Computer, Digital Equipment Corp., and IBM in the expanding market for UNIX workstations used by engineers and scientists. As president and chief executive officer, she raised $19 million in venture capital. The company also formed alliances with AT&T, Japan's Kyocera, and Great Britain's Commonwealth Shipping to market a high-powered workstation that was able to be adapted with additional components for various applications. The Taiwanese company, Acer Inc., became one of Counterpoint's largest customers, and finally acquired the San Jose business in 1987. Alker remained as president of Acer's network computing division, and later became the president of Acer America's sales and operating division.

In 1991, Alker was recruited to become the president and chief executive officer of Network Peripherals, Inc., a networking company specializing in high-performance Ethernet switching solutions. At that time, business computer networks were slowed down by antiquated hubs that connected each personal computer to a network. Conventional switches, in contrast, enabled the user full access to the Ethernet's full capacity, 10 million bits, or units, of data per second. Network Peripherals offered FDDI (fiber distributed data interface technology), which raised a network's speed to 100 million bits per second.

Before Alker joined the company, Network Peripherals had only $246,000 in sales. By 1993, revenues had reached $10 million. In 1994, Network Peripherals became a public company with an initial public offering in June and a secondary offering in early November. More than $45 million was raised; Network Peripherals was named the Best IPO Performer by both *USA Today* and the *Wall Street Journal* in 1994. In subsequent years, the stock experienced some volatility; in 1995, its value dropped by 53 percent. Yet it continued to aggressively court value-added resellers through a nationwide education and marketing campaign, which included user seminars and heavily discounted units.

After eight years with Network Peripherals, Alker left the company in 1998 to organize another startup: Amplify.net. Alker, along with two longtime associates—Raymond Ho and Fred Kiremidjian—teamed up to raise $3.63 million in venture financing from Alpine Technology Ventures and Aspen Ventures. A second equity infusion of $6.1 million came from 3Com, Wi-LAN, and Kingston Technology Corporation. From its inception, Amplify.net, headquartered in Fremont, was designed to manage online traffic jams through the development of Internet Protocol (IP)-based technologies. Through developing software tools, Amplify.net enables service providers and telecommunications companies to measure customer use and guarantee Internet services.

Alker has fostered partnerships with companies like Harris Corporation and Interspeed, Inc., as well as cultivated inroads into the Asian market. In 2000, Amplify.net established a wholly owned subsidiary in Hong Kong after closing a $12.6 million deal for equity funding from a group of Asian institutional investors. A year later, the company announced the formation of an Asian Business Advisory Board featuring leaders from Japan, Korea, Hong Kong, and China.

"I'm a strong believer in global strategic partnerships," stated Alker to *The Business Journal* (23 April 1999). "Perhaps because I've been exposed to different cultures and my horizon is broader I see the benefits as well as the difficulty."

As a woman who has been the chief executive officer of three companies in Silicon Valley, Alker is certainly an anomaly. According to a 1996 Korn/Ferry study of senior corporate executives, only 14 percent of the women surveyed wanted to be CEO, while 46 of the men did. "We must have the courage to dream bigger dreams," Alker stated to *Chief Executive*. "We must look beyond the barriers and make our dreams come true."

Alker has a son, Kevin Lo, from her first marriage.

### Sources

Amplify.net, www.amplifynet.com [accessed November 19, 2001].

"Amplify.net Receives $6 Million in Funding." 17 December 1999. *The Business Journal*: 19.

Engstrom, Theresa. September 1986. "Starting Up in a Tough Industry." *Working Woman*: 47+.

Moltzen, Edward F. 20 February 1995. "Network Peripherals Plans New VAR Program." *Computer Reseller News*: 38.

Pipes, Sally. April 1996. "Glass Ceiling? So What?" *Chief Executive*: 16.

Rodriguez, Karen. 23 April 1999. "Talented, Aggressive CEO Leading Startup Amplify.net." *The Business Journal*: 16.

Schwalb, Stefanie H. 1 August 2001. "Wisdom of an Old Pro." *Internet World*: 9.

"Silicon Sister." *Goldsea*. www.goldsea.com/ww/Loalker/loalker.html [accessed November 19, 2001].

Wise, Deborah C. 3 February 1986. "IBM and Digital Equipment Don't Scare Pauline Alker." *Business Week*: 70A.

# Rioichiro (Ryoichiro) Arai

Rioichiro Arai. Photo courtesy of the Harvard University Archives

**Full Name at Birth**: Ryosuke Hoshino.

**Born**: 31 August 1855, Mizunuma, Japan.

**Death**: 9 April 1939, Connecticut.

**Education**: Takasaki Domain English School, Tokyo, Japan, graduate, 1871; Kaisei Gakko, Tokyo, Japan, 1874; Shoho Koshujo

(Short-Term Training School), Tokyo, Japan, 1875; Plymouth Institute, Brooklyn Heights, New York, circa 1880s.

**Positions Held**: Partner of Sato Arai Company, New York City, New York, 1878–81; New York representative of the Doshin Company, New York City, New York, 1880–93; founder of Yokohama Kiito Gomei Kaisha and Morimura Arai Company, New York City, New York, 1893–1939.

**Awards, Honors**: Medal (Order of the Sacred Treasure, Fourth Class), Japanese government.

**Summary**: Rioichiro Arai was one of the pioneers of the U.S.–Japan silk trade of the late 1800s. By firmly establishing himself as an honest and reputable trader, Arai helped to build the foundation of trade relations between the two countries before World War II.

### Early Years

Arai's name at birth was Ryosuke Hoshino. Born the sixth son of silk producer Yahei Hoshino, he was raised amidst the mulberry trees in a mountainous region just north of Tokyo. At the age of six, he was privately tutored, and two years later, he was trained in the Chinese classics by a former samurai who had become a Confucian scholar.

When he was 12 years old, Arai was adopted by Keisaku Arai, a large landowner and silk producer in the same area. This practice of adoption, called *yoshi*, was very common in Japan among families who had no male heirs to carry on the family name. Keisaku's son had died at an early age, and the two boys they had subsequently adopted had also passed away. Arai changed his name to Rioichiro Arai. (The more common English-language spelling of Arai's first name is Ryoichiro, but apparently he preferred Rioichiro.) Arai, however, continued his education with the Hoshinos, and never lived with his adoptive family.

Reflecting the general mood of his countrymen during the Meiji Era (1868–1912), Arai wanted to learn Western practices. At the age of 14, he made the 65-mile journey to Tokyo on foot, carrying only a small bundle of clothing and books of Chinese classics. In 1871, he enrolled in the Takasaki Domain English School and later the Kaisei Gakko, a government school for the teaching of English, which was to later become part of the revered Tokyo University. He continued his study of English at the Shoho Koshujo (Short-Term Commercial Training School) in 1875.

Meanwhile, his older brother Chotaro Hoshino saw the need for Japanese silk producers to establish their own trading companies in foreign countries. Until this time, excessive profits were going to unscrupulous foreign traders. As a result, in March 1876 six well-connected Japanese men, including Arai, were sent on the S.S. *Oceanic* for a three-and-a-half-week voyage to the United States.

### Career Highlights

Once Arai arrived in New York, he began work for Momotaro Sato, a pioneering Japanese expatriate who had established a store in New York City. Arai experienced anti-Asian sentiment firsthand as landlords refused to rent rooms to him, saying, "Chinaman, go away." However, Arai remained undeterred from his goal to establish an import-export business. He attended English-language classes at the Plymouth Institute in Brooklyn Heights and attempted to study conversational English as much as he could, even sitting in on sermons by preacher Henry Ward Beecher.

Probably the incident that served to launch his New York trade enterprise was his dealing with B. Richardson and Sons, leading importers of silk. Arai promised to provide 400-pound bales of Hoshino raw silk at $6.50 a pound for delivery in September 1876. As communications between the United States and Japan were extremely limited, Chotaro Hoshino did not receive the order for several weeks and when he finally did, he was shocked. By July, prices were close to 80 percent higher than what was quoted. Fulfillment of the order would leave the Hoshino family in terrible financial straits, yet Arai refused to renegotiate the contract. As his granddaughter, Haru Matsukata Reischauer, wrote in her memoir, *Samurai and Silk*, Arai had "staked his honor and the future success of his business on this order."

When the bales of silk arrived on September 21, they marked the first direct shipment of Japanese silk by Japanese merchants to America and the first time that Japanese silk was sent across the Pacific Ocean. Richardson and Sons voluntarily offered to increase the price one dollar per pound, but $2,000 was still lost in the deal. However, the long-term benefits outweighed the costs. Arai was now seen as an honest trader who could be trusted.

In 1878, he partnered with Momotaro Sato to establish Sato Arai Company, a raw-silk business in New York City. The following year he doubled sales to $41,000. By 1880, the demand for silk reached another high. With his new-found success and wealth, he returned to Japan to wed Tazu Ushiba, a sophisticated 18-year-old, in Tokyo, and together they traveled to America to make their new home in New York.

Arai's meteoric rise continued. He went on to form another partnership in 1893, the Morimura Arai Company, and began to expand into European and Chinese silks; the same year he and his family moved into a large Victorian-style home in Connecticut, which soon became a site for various social activities. In 1901, Arai was the first Asian to be elected to the board of governors of the American Silk Association. He also diversified into the cotton trade, and was the first to export American cotton to Japan.

Active in the Nippon Club and the Japan Society, Arai was awarded a Japanese medal, Order of the Sacred Treasure, Sixth Class, in 1928. (The award was later elevated to the Fourth Class.)

He died at the age of 84 on April 9, 1939, in Connecticut. He and his wife Tazu had two children, Yoneo and Miyo.

### Sources

Miyakawa, T. Scott. 1972. "Early New York Issei: Founders of Japanese American Trade." In Hilary Conroy and T. Scott Miyakawa, eds., *East Across the Pacific*. Santa Barbara, CA: American Bibliographic Center-Clio Press.

Reischauer, Haru Matsukata. 1986. *Samurai and Silk: A Japanese and American Heritage*. Cambridge, MA: The Belknap Press of Harvard University Press.

## George Aratani

George Aratani. Photo courtesy of George T. Aratani

**Full Name at Birth**: George Tetsuo Aratani.

**Born**: 22 May 1917, South Park, California.

**Education**: Keio University, Tokyo, Japan, 1935–40; Stanford University, Stanford, California, 1940.

**Positions Held**: General manager of Guadalupe Produce Company, Guadalupe, California, 1941; instructor, Military Intelligence Language School, Camp Savage (later Fort Snelling), Minnesota, and Monterey, California, 1944–46; president of All Star Trading (name later changed to American Commercial, Inc.), Los Angeles, California, 1946– .

**Awards, Honors**: Audio Hall of Fame, *Audio Times*, 1977; medal (Order of the Sacred Treasure, Gold Rays with Rosettes), Japanese government, 1988.

**Summary**: George Aratani used his bilingual and bicultural abilities to launch three successful international trade companies: Mikasa, which specializes in tableware; Kenwood, a seller of audio equipment; and AMCO, a supplier of medical equipment. Impacted by the incarceration of Japanese Americans during World War II, when his family lost their successful business and much of their fortune, he later became heavily involved in philanthropic efforts to aid the Japanese American community.

### Early Years

George Aratani spent his youth on California's farmland, as his father, a native of Hiroshima, Japan, was attempting to establish himself in agriculture since immigrating to America in 1905. Aratani was the only child of Setsuo and Yoshiko Aratani; his mother Yoshiko, however, had been widowed in Japan, where she left a son and daughter before remarrying and moving to America.

Two years after Aratani was born in a strawberry-growing area south of downtown Los Angeles, his family moved to the San Fernando Valley near a newly constructed aqueduct. Before Aratani was five, the family relocated again—this time to a coastal town called Guadalupe in Santa Maria Valley, about 170 miles north of Los Angeles.

It was in Guadalupe that Aratani made close friends who would later prove instrumental in the launching of his international trade business. Santa Maria Valley was also where his father Setsuo would build an agricultural empire, consisting of close to 5,000 acres of vegetables, as well as a chili dehydrating plant, hog farm, fertilizer and chemical factory, and finally an international trade company, All Star Trading.

His father was also an avid sportsman and encouraged Aratani to pursue golf, as well as baseball. Setsuo, in fact, had sent a multicultural baseball team to Japan to participate in exhibition games in 1928; Aratani, then only 11, accompanied the group as a bat boy.

As he grew older, Aratani excelled in athletics, and even had an opportunity to work out with the Pittsburgh Pirates baseball team coached by the legendary "Flying Dutchman," Honus Wagner, during the team's spring training in nearby Paso Robles. However, a serious football injury in 1933 foiled any consideration of pursuing a professional baseball career. After graduating from Santa Maria Union High School with honors, he was planning to attend Stanford University—until his parents persuaded him to study in Japan instead.

### Higher Education

In Japan, Aratani was under the guidance of a private tutor to learn Chinese characters and other aspects of the Japanese language necessary to study at one of the nation's elite colleges. Tragically, months after he and his parents arrived in Japan, his mother, who suffered from chronic asthma, died in December 1935. Although Aratani had not initially wanted to come to Japan, he wanted to fulfill his dead mother's wishes and gain a Japanese education. As a result of his diligent studying, Aratani was accepted at Keio University in Tokyo, where he majored in law. He even played for a brief time on the Keio baseball team before his former football injury sidelined him from any kind of athletic activity requiring the pivoting of his knee.

While at Keio, Aratani was befriended by the college president, Shinzo Koizumi. Aratani's father, in fact, helped sponsor the Keio judo team during an international exchange in California in the 1930s. Before Aratani could graduate from Keio, his father's bout with tuberculosis compelled him to return to California. When Setsuo died on April 16, 1940, Aratani decided not to return to Japan and instead enrolled at Stanford. However, with the pressing demands of the family farm, Aratani had to drop out to assume his role as the head of Guadalupe Produce Company.

## Career Highlights

Aratani was trained by his father's partners, also Japanese immigrants. After the bombing of Pearl Harbor, the corporate assets of the business were transferred to American-born executives; that way the business would be protected during the war, or so Aratani believed. However, with the forced removal of Japanese Americans from the West Coast in 1942, Aratani and other farmers in the area were forced to hand over their enterprises to trustees. Aratani, his stepmother Masuko, and Guadalupe friends were first sent to Tulare

Assembly Center, a former fairgrounds in central California, before eventually being sent to Gila River War Relocation Center in Arizona.

During the course of the war, the farm operation was sold at a low price that merely covered a year of income tax. Aratani, however, was determined to succeed to some kind of commerce after the war ended. At the time Japanese Americans were being drafted into the U.S. Army in 1944, Aratani joined the Military Intelligence Service (MIS) as a civilian language instructor at the school in Minnesota. The MIS Language School trained American soldiers to speak, write, and read Japanese to aid in the interrogation of prisoners and to break military codes in the Pacific.

Aratani served with the MIS Language School until 1946. He then decided to launch an international trade business in Los Angeles using his father's corporate moniker, All Star Trading. Later he changed the name to American Commercial, Inc. Aratani first intended to import Japanese foodstuffs to the United States, but quickly learned that Japan was in need of basic foods itself. One of the first businessmen to travel to Japan after World War II, Aratani went on an entrepreneurial expedition to Tokyo, Nagoya, and Hiroshima in March 1948. There he found a nation in ruins—but made some valuable contacts through his business colleague, Seiichiro Shigeyoshi "Shig" Kariya, and a Sumitomo Bank executive.

Mortgaging some personal property in Santa Maria Valley and securing a loan from Bank of America, Aratani was able to finance his business on a shoestring budget. American Commercial handled a variety of items during its early years: dried abalone from Mexico and shell buttons from Japan, which were sold in the garment district in New York City. To accommodate the two coasts of the United States, Aratani opened both Los Angeles and New York branches. The New York office was managed by Kariya, who had relatives involved in the ceramic trade in Nagoya.

It was not until American Commercial, Inc. began importing chinaware from Japan that the company began to establish a reputation strong enough to get its merchandise into top-notch department stores like Macy's. With the leadership of Al Funabashi, an experienced chinaware businessman from New Jersey, American Commercial, Inc. created a new image for tableware as being fresh, contemporary, and changeable. Bargain sets rather than open-stock chinaware were created. The brand, Mikasa, was officially launched in December 1957. The name, Mikasa, meaning "three umbrellas" in Japanese, referred to a three-peaked mountain in Japan's ancient capital of Nara.

Aratani also diversified into other markets. An old friend from Guadalupe, Tad Yamada, headed up the company's first Japanese division in an apartment in Tokyo in 1951. It grew to become a subsidiary, AMCO, specializing in export of U.S.-made medical and scientific equipment, beginning with nitrous oxide machines and including even a nuclear reactor for an exhibition in Tokyo in 1959.

Through another friend from the MIS Language School, Bill Kasuga, Aratani later became involved in the audio equipment business. Developing an agreement with the Japanese manufacturer of high-fidelity stereo equipment, Trio, Aratani founded the company Kenwood in 1961. At this time, the stereo world was dominated by U.S. manufacturers; Japanese-made products, on the other hand, were considered to be shoddy and badly constructed. In 1966, with the advent of the transistor, audio equipment created by companies like Kenwood and Sony rivaled more established counterparts.

While many other U.S.–Japanese trading companies could not survive in the competitive post–World War II environment, American Commercial thrived. In 1969, both Mikasa and Kenwood moved their West Coast administrative headquarters to a new $500,000 building in Gardena. Later the companies would relocate south to Carson, California. The New York operations of Mikasa, on the other hand, moved to the growing commercial community of Secaucus, New Jersey, with showrooms in Manhattan. The first factory outlet, in fact, began in a warehouse in Secaucus; hundreds of Mikasa outlets followed throughout the United States, Canada, and Europe.

Mikasa, Inc. went public on the New York Stock Exchange in 1994. It was doing approximately $400 million in sales when it was purchased by France-based J.G. Durand Industries, Inc. in 2000. Kenwood, on the other hand, was purchased by the Japanese manufacturers in the 1980s, yet Aratani is still connected to the company as the chairman of the holding company, Kenwood Americas. AMCO, with 10 branches and approximately 250, is also owned by the Japanese today.

Aratani's business motto was adopted from his father Setsuo: "Find good people and work as a team. You only have 24 hours a day. Treat your people well." And like his father, Aratani has given a large portion of his personal wealth to philanthropic projects in the Japanese American community. Among those receiving funds are the Japanese American Cultural and Community Center in Los Angeles, services for the elderly, Japanese American National Museum, Union Center for the Arts, and a national monument commemorating the patriotism of Japanese Americans during World War II.

Aratani and his wife Sakaye, who reside in Hollywood Hills, have two daughters, Donna and Linda.

## Sources

Hirahara, Naomi. 2001. *An American Son: The Story of George Aratani, Founder of Mikasa and Kenwood.* Los Angeles, CA: Japanese American National Museum.

Interviews with George Aratani (Naomi Hirahara, Japanese American National Museum, 1997, 1998, 1999).

Lifshey, Earl. 1 December 1980. "The Mikasa Story." *HFD: Retailing, Home, Furnishings*: 19–21.

Sano, Marilyn. 30 October–5 November 1995. "George Aratani: A Profile in Multicultural Harmony." *The Japan Times Weekly International Edition.*

# Larry Asera

**Born**: 15 July 1948, Vallejo, California.

**Education**: University of California, Berkeley, California, B.S. in civil engineering, 1970; Massachusetts Institute of Technology, Cambridge, Massachusetts, Sloan Fellows Program.

**Positions Held**: Assistant program manager, United States General Services Administration, 1966–c. 1970s; civil engineer, Federal Energy Regulatory Commission, c. 1970s; city council member, Vallejo City Council, Vallejo, California, 1973–77; chief legislative consultant, California State Senate and Assembly, Sacramento, California, 1974–76; Solano County Board of Supervisors, 1977–80; project manager, Southport Investors, Sacramento, California, 1980; president and founder, Asera West Corporation (later changed to Asera-Pacific Ltd.), Sacramento (later moved to Vallejo), California, c. 1980s– ; founder, Asera LLC, Vallejo, California; vice president, project development, PG&E Properties, 1990.

**Summary**: Engineer Larry Asera, a third-generation Filipino American, has parlayed his knowledge of alternative energy sources into successful international consulting enterprises. The first Filipino American to be elected in the mainland United States to political office in 1973, Asera has held numerous public positions, including serving as the "energy czar" in his hometown of Vallejo, California.

## Early Years

Asera was raised by his father, Henry, and his grandfather, Lorenzo, in the town of Vallejo, located northeast of San Francisco where the Sacramento River drains into the bay. At the time, Vallejo's Mare Island was home to a naval shipyard where Lorenzo began to work at a shipbuilding plant in 1927. Lorenzo and his wife Rufina had originally come to Hawaii from the Philippines in 1906. Engaged in agricultural labor, they moved to California in 1925 and eventually settled in Vallejo. Asera's father Henry became a naval architect technician at Mare Island shipyard.

As a child, Asera spent his time in the public library reading about math, physics, and other sciences. He told *Filipino Achievers in the USA & Canada*: "I was fascinated with technology, growing up in an era when radio, TV, rockets, and satellites were coming of age."

Not only a diligent student, Asera was also popular in school. In 1966 he became student body president of Vallejo High School. Receiving many awards and scholarships, including the Stafford Cox Scholarship, Asera was accepted to the University of California, Berkeley.

## Higher Education

At UC Berkeley Asera majored in civil engineering. In addition to pursuing his interest in computers, he also was exposed to a new field called photovoltaics, in which silicon semiconductors are used to convert sunlight into electricity.

While attending school, Asera also served as an engineering trainee on Mare Island, where he was part of a team designing components for high-profile projects like the *Nautilus*, America's first atomic submarine, according to *Filipinas* magazine (October 2001).

## Career Highlights

After graduating from college, Asera secured a position with the United States General Services Administration (GSA), which was preparing to erect nine new federal buildings in the western United States. As assistant program manager, Asera supervised the $150 million project and went on to oversee other governmental building plans.

Asera, however, established himself in the field that would mark his career when he became a chief consultant to the Assembly Committee on Energy. While participating in politics himself as a member of the Vallejo City Council (he became the first Filipino American to be elected to public office on the mainland in 1973), Asera also wrote legislation that shaped the state's policy on solar energy and helped to create the state Solid Waste Management Board, a major advocate of alternative energy. He also was named as California governor Jerry Brown's chairman of the state's Building Standards Commission.

During the next decade, Asera devoted his life to electoral politics. In 1976 he was elected to the Solano County Board of Supervisors and even made a run for State Assembly in 1980. After his failed attempt, he left public office to pursue his entrepreneurial interests, which focused on real estate development and alternative energy technology. He became involved in real estate projects in Yolo County, and even established his own company in the Sacramento area, Asera West Corporation. As the project manager for Southport Investors, he oversaw the use of a large parcel of commercial land in West Sacramento in the 1980s. He also launched two other enterprises: Pacific Rim Consortium (Primcon), a development company in Vallejo and San Francisco with projects in California and the Philippines, and Solarize, Inc., an international alternative energy company. He later specialized in helping companies relocate through his company, Asera-Pacific, a property management and research firm, and he created Asera, LLC, to provide consulting services in energy resources.

Asera was responsible for the installation of solar energy systems at Travis Air Force Base in Fairfield, California, and Dixon City Hall in Solano County—the latter site being the first city hall to be "solarized" in the nation. He also worked through the U.S. Agency for International Development and the United Nations to create solar photovoltaic "eco-villages" in developing nations like Mexico, the Philippines, and Malaysia. In 1990 he was elected vice president of project development of PG&E Properties, a wholly owned subsidiary of PG&E Enterprises.

The closure of the Mare Island Naval Shipyard in 1996 resulted in a loss of 50,000 jobs for Vallejo, but marked a new opportunity for Asera, who worked in his hometown to attract different kinds of businesses to the area. And in 2001 he was named Vallejo's first "energy czar," responsible for developing alternative energy production to reduce the city's reliance on the state's electrical grid, as well as natural gas production. Vallejo's efforts were recognized in July 2001 when the city was approved to receive a $2.5 million grant from the California Energy Commission for the construction of a solar microutility. Once in operation, the microutility is expected to generate $500,000 to $1.5 million in revenue a year.

Also a professor of engineering technology at California State University's Cal Maritime Academy, Asera believes that businesses will be able easily to integrate solar energy into their building design, which will eventually lead to financial savings. This may take the form of traditional rooftop solar collectors or the blending of silicon chips into roofing material. In the future, even office windows, with the addition of cadmium telluride and gallium arsenide, can become photovoltaic cells used to generate power, according to *East Bay Business Times* (5 March 2001).

Asera is also investigating other alternative energy sources, including wind and co-generation plants, as well as seeking to maximize the potential of Mare Island's dormant power plant. Such efforts may be part of a larger trend, as the city of San Francisco prepares to build solar plants that will generate 50 megawatts within three years.

A member of the Solano County Board of Education, Asera has served on the Board of Trustees of the University of California, Davis Foundation. He married Lilibeth De Fiesta.

### Sources

Bautista, Veltisezar B. 1996. "Larry Asera: Noted Engineer, Entrepreneur and Public Servant." In Crisostomo, Isabelo T., ed., *Filipino Achievers in the USA & Canada: Profiles in Excellence*. Naperville, IL: Bookhaus Publishers.

Bolling, David. Winter 2001. "Wind Power." *Whole Earth*: 26.

Doyle, Alan. 23 February 2001. "Vallejo to Make Asera Its First Energy Czar." *East Bay Business Times*: 7.

Overholt, Charles. 27 July 1987. "West Sacramento Ripe for a Development Boom." *The Business Journal–Sacramento*: 18.

Yr, Ed. October 2001. "He's Electric." *Filipinas*: 51–52.

## Ramani Ayer

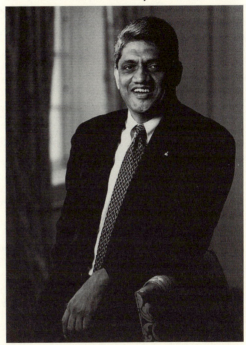

Ramani Ayer. Photo courtesy of Debbie Bennett for Ramani Ayer

**Born**: c. 1947, India.

**Education**: Indian Institute of Technology, Bombay, India, B.S., c. 1969; Drexel Institute of Technology, Philadelphia, Pennsylvania, M.S. and Ph.D. in chemical engineering, c. 1973.

**Positions Held**: Researcher, Hartford Financial Services Group, Hartford, Connecticut, 1973–79; assistant secretary and staff assistant to the chairman and chief executive, The Hartford, Hartford, Connecticut, 1979–83; vice president, HartRe (The HartFord's reinsurance subsidiary), Hartford, Connecticut, 1983–86; president, Hartford Specialty Company, Hartford, Connecticut, 1986–89; senior vice president, The HartFord, Hartford, Connecticut, 1989; executive president, The HartFord, Hartford, Connecticut, 1990; president and chief executive officer, Hartford Fire Insurance Company, Hartford, Connecticut, 1991–97; chairman, president, and chief executive officer of The HartFord, Hartford, Connecticut, 1997– .

**Summary**: Ramani Ayer, a native of India, is a leader in the insurance and financial services industry. The chairman and chief executive officer of The HartFord, Ayer has pioneered innovative programs in an era of changing technological needs and corporate consolidation.

### Early Years

Like many successful East Indians of his generation, Ramani Ayer was educated at the Indian Institute of Technology in Bombay. After graduation in 1969, with a trunk of clothes and a few books in hand, he headed for New York. Once in the United States he continued to pursue a higher education—gaining his master's and doctoral degrees in chemical engineering from Drexel University in Philadelphia, Pennsylvania.

### Career Highlights

Ayer secured an entry-level position with The HartFord Financial Services Group in 1973. Little did he know that he would someday be at the helm of this multibillion-dollar insurance and financial service company founded in Connecticut in 1810.

In six short years, Ayer was elected assistant secretary and staff assistant to the chairman and chief executive of The HartFord. The analytical skills gained as an engineering student were paying off. "Engineers very much are taught the capacity for thinking, and how to think in business models," he told *Independent Agent Magazine*. "I love this business—the art of risk-taking."

His success in both the business and the company continued. In 1983, he was named vice president of HartRe, and in three years he was promoted to president of Hartford Specialty Company. He was elected senior vice president of The HartFord in 1989 and executive president in 1990. A year later he was appointed president and chief operating officer of Hartford Fire Insurance Company. On February 1, 1997, he became the ninth chairman of The HartFord and its president and chief executive officer.

In his present position, Ayer has overseen the phenomenal growth of his company. The HartFord's North American operations are the eighth largest in the United States with revenues of more than $6.3 billion, and its international operations generates revenues of $1.6 billion. Under Ayer's leadership, The HartFord has instituted unique programs to capture a larger percentage of the highly competitive property/casualty market. While working with 11,000 various independent insurance agencies, the company markets directly to members of the American Association of Retired Persons (AARP), as well as customers of automobiles and household goods. In 1999, The HartFord forged the largest marketing alliance to date between an automobile manufacturer and insurance company. Through an affinity marketing agreement with Ford Credit, The HartFord offers personal lines of insurance through the Ford Motor Company Vehicle Insurance Program. A similar agreement has been established with Sears.

Ayer has also incorporated technology into a traditional "bricks and mortar" company. The HartFord has an Electronic Business Center (EBC), a secure Web portal site which facilitates communication between the company and independent agents.

Viewed as a passionate leader in his field, Ayer is chairman of the American Insurance Association, a board member of the American Institute for Chartered Property Casualty Underwriters/Insurance Institute of America, and a board member of the Insurance Information Institute. He is also a member of the Business Roundtable and the board of directors of Hartford Hospital, and a trustee of the Mark Twain House in Hartford, Connecticut.

Although working 13- to 14-hour days, Ayer still finds time to attend his children's activities and pursue various hobbies, including drawing, travel, learning Spanish, and reading. "I'm Eastern, so I do love Eastern philosophy," said Ayer to *Independent Agent Magazine*.

The course of Ayer's life is best exemplified by the slogan of his company: "Whatever Life Brings You, Bring It On."

## Sources

The HartFord. "The HartFord's Management Team," http://www.thehartford.com/corporate/about/management.html. [accessed Novermber 23, 1999].

"Revenge of the Nerds. Tomorrow: The Empire Strikes Back." November 2000. *Independent Agent Magazine*.

# B

## Kavelle R. Bajaj

**Born**: 15 June 1950, New Delhi, India.

**Education**: University of Delhi, Delhi, India, B.S. in home economics.

**Positions Held**: Avon saleswoman, Bethesda, Maryland, c. 1980s; founder, chief executive officer, I-Net Inc., Bethesda, Maryland, 1985– .

**Awards, Honors**: Women of Enterprise Award, Avon Products and Small Business Administration, 1990; Top 50 Woman-Owned Businesses, *Working Woman* magazine and National Foundation for Women Business Owners, 1994.

**Summary**: Kavelle R. Bajaj, an Indian woman who came to the United States with her husband, launched a computer networking systems corporation from the basement of her Maryland home—which eventually grew to support $327 million in revenue and 3,000 employees. The privately held company, I-Net, was sold to Wang Laboratories for $167 million in 1996.

### Early Years and Higher Education

Bajaj and her two siblings were raised in a traditional household in India. Her mother was a homemaker, while her father had his own construction company. Bajaj received her bachelor's degree in home economics from Delhi University in Delhi, India. As was the custom, Bajaj's parents then arranged for her to be married. Bajaj had only met her future husband, Ken S. Bajaj, a few times prior to their wedding in 1973. Ken, a computer engineer who held a doctorate in system sciences from Michigan State University, was working as a professor at Wayne State University in Detroit.

"I came [to the United States] as a bride," Bajaj said to *Nation's Business* (June 1991). "I just had stars in my eyes, and the only dream I had at that time was to set up house and home with my husband." They eventually had two sons.

### Career Highlights

In the late 1970s, the family relocated to the Washington, D.C., area, where Ken got a new job with Ross Perot's Electronic Data Systems (EDS) Corp. After winning a $656 million contract with the U.S. Army, he became vice president of the company. Bajaj, meanwhile, took care of the children, while considering various work options. She became an "Avon lady" and considered designing her own jewelry and leather purses. After taking some computer courses, she set up a personal computer in the basement of their Maryland home to do word processing. But she began to acknowledge the larger opportunities in computer networking and telecommunications on the horizon. "I had a gut feeling that the computer networking industry was going to take off," Bajaj stated to the *Washington Post* (2 May 1994).

With an initial $5,000 from her husband, and assistance from a former EDS marketing manager, Bajaj officially launched her own company, which specialized in computer networks in 1985. She originally intended to call her enterprise Information Networks, Inc., but discovered that name had been taken. As a result, she chose an abbreviated version, I-Net. At that time, General Motors had taken over EDS and had asked Ken to transfer to its Detroit branch. This time, Bajaj refused to make the move. As a result, Ken went to Detroit by himself, flying back to Maryland on the weekends for two years to see his family.

Bajaj, meanwhile, began to build her company. She applied for the Small Business Association's "set-aside" program in which a number of governmental contracts are set aside for minority-owned businesses. After first being denied for the certification, Bajaj appealed and finally won her case. "I had to overcome some cultural barriers," she told the *Washington Post*. "I came from a very protected environment where you live life in a shell. For me, the concept of going out and networking to establish business contacts was difficult, but I realized it was a necessity."

Their first governmental contract was for $130,000 to help the National Oceanic and Atmospheric Administration (NOAA) transition from word processors to personal computers. The contract enabled Bajaj to hire some part-timers to work in the makeshift basement office. That opportu-

nity led to a larger four-year contract with the agency, followed by many other governmental jobs.

In spite of I-Net's growth, Bajaj was unable to obtain a line of credit with a bank for two years. "Finance still seems to be a big challenge for women—for any small business owner—but especially women," said Bajaj to the *Washington Business Journal* (11 March 1991). "They kept asking me, 'Is this a hobby? Are you going to stick with it? Are you serious?'"

I-Net's early entry in telecommunications systems integration and its diversification into fields such as optical-disc conversion led to phenomenal growth. In 1988, the company had 100 professional employees and $500,000 in profits on annual revenues of $8 million. By this time, Ken had rejoined his family in Bethesda. He had left EDS and a $250,000 salary to work for a new startup, Perot Systems, in Virginia. When the company started to have problems, Bajaj offered her husband a job at I-Net. He agreed to take another pay cut to become executive vice president of his wife's company.

"Hiring Ken away from Perot was a coup that gave people we were trying to hire confidence that we are here to stay," Bajaj told *Computerworld* (9 September 1991). "We are complementary: He has the operations and marketing skills." Ken later was promoted to chief operating officer and then president. Another important recruit was William Hooton, who oversaw I-Net's optical-disc integration development after having worked in the field for the National Archives and Records Administration.

Most of the stock holdings, however, remained in Bajaj's name. In 1995, I-Net was the twenty-third largest woman-owned company in the nation. By this time, the company had 2,700 employees in 50 offices and $230 million in annual revenue. In addition to managing computer operations for the White House and Department of Defense, I-Net was also parlaying its reputation to gain commercial clients, including British Petroleum Co. Ltd., LSI Logic Corp., Shell Oil Co., and Enron Corp. While other companies also offered similar services, I-Net rose above its competitors in its comprehensive management of computer systems as well as securing networks against hackers.

A year later, in 1996, I-Net was sold to Wang Laboratories, Inc. for $167 million. At that time, it became a wholly owned subsidiary of Wang, and Ken remained president. He later founded AppNet Inc., a company that created online stores for retailers. AppNet was then acquired by Commerce One for approximately $2 billion.

## Sources

Corcoran, Elizabeth. 25 July 1996. "Wang Laboratories to Buy I-Net of Bethesda." *Washington Post*: D15.

Estrada, Louie. 2 May 1994. "Recognizing an Emerging Market: Early Move into Computer Networking Boosts I-Net to Prominence." *Washington Post*: F9+ .

Girishankar, Saroja. 27 March 1995. "Integrator's Road to Success." *Communications Week*: 120+ .

Horwitt, Elisabeth. 9 September 1991. "I-Net Soars by Capturing Fledgling Niches." *Computerworld*: 69.

Love, Alice. 11 March 1991. "Business Journal Ranks Area's Top Women-Owned Businesses." *Washington Business Journal*: 17+ .

McMenamin, Brigid. 8 November 1993. "Yes, Dear." *Forbes*: 344+ .

Meer, Aziza K. 21 October 1991. "I-Net's Bajaj Built Company from Basement Up." *Washington Post*: F8.

Murray, Kathleen. May 1995. "Kavelle Bajaj." *Chief Executive*: 32+ .

Nelton, Sharon. June 1991. "How an Indian-Born Entrepreneur Found the 'Tiger' Within Herself." *Nation's Business*: 10+ .

Savage, David G. 2 April 1995. "Plan to Boost Firms Owned by Minorities Is Assailed Affirmative Action." *Los Angeles Times*: 14.

Walker, Sam. 14 April 1995. "Women Business Owners Go around Glass Ceiling." *Christian Science Monitor*: 3+ .

# Dado Banatao

Dado Banatao. Photo courtesy of Tallwood Venture Capital

**Full Name at Birth**: Diosdado P. Banatao.

**Born**: 23 May 1946, Iguig, Cagayan, Philippines.

**Education**: Ateneo de Tuguegarao, Cagayan, Philippines, graduate, circa 1962; Mapua Institute of Technology, Manila, Philippines, B.S. cum laude in electrical engineering, 1966; Stanford University, Stanford, California, M.S. in electrical engineering, 1972.

**Positions Held**: Design engineer, National Semiconductor Corp., Santa Clara, California, 1972–75; design engineer, Commodore International, 1976–78; design manager, Intersil, 1978–80; engineering manager, director of engineering, Seeq

Technology, Fremont, California, 1981–84; cofounder of Mostron, 1984; cofounder and vice president of engineering, Chips & Technologies (now owned by Intel), 1985–97; cofounder, chief executive officer, and chairman, S3, Inc. (now Sonic Blue), Santa Clara, California, 1989–97; venture partner, Mayfield Fund, 1998–2000; managing partner, Tallwood Venture Capital, Palo Alto, California, 2000– .

**Awards, Honors**: Ellis Island Medal of Honor, National Ethnic Coalition of Organizations, Inc., 1993–94; Distinguished Asian Leadership Award, Asian Business League of San Francisco, 1993; Pamana Ng Filipino Award, President Fidel V. Ramos; Master Entrepreneur of the Year Award, Ernst & Young, *Inc. Magazine*, and Merrill Lynch Business Financial Services, 1997.

**Summary**: A scientific pioneer in chip technology, Philippine-born Dado Banatao left established computer companies in California to launch three high-tech enterprises of his own in the state's Silicon Valley. He now is active as a philanthropist and venture capitalist, while also continuing to develop new technologies in computing and communications.

### Early Years

The son of a farmer, Banatao was raised in the town of Iguig in Cagayan Province in the northern part of the Philippines after World War II. According to *Asiaweek* (21 July 2000), he walked threadbare to school along dirt roads. "In the summer, we [his sister, three brothers, and himself] worked on the farm, but once school started, my father made sure we were in school," he stated to *Red Herring* (25 April 2001). "He understood the value of education."

In high school at Ateneo de Tuguegarao in Cagayan, Philippines, Banatao excelled in math and physics. His counselor recommended that he pursue engineering, so he applied to Mapua Institute of Technology in Manila, known as the best engineering school in the Philippines, at that time.

### Higher Education

While studying at Mapua Institute of Technology, Banatao was first exposed to an IBM computer. "I was hooked," he told the University of the Philippines' Teresita G. Maceda in an interview. "That was it. We made all kinds of programs, and toggled over through tests, and I thought, this was fun."

After graduating with honors, Banatao applied for engineering jobs but was discouraged by his limited options. He then began training with Philippine Airlines to become a commercial pilot, but eventually returned to engineering when Boeing recruited him to work in Seattle, Washington, in 1968. While in the United States, Banatao realized that his academic training had been inadequate, and began taking classes at the University of Washington. He eventually pursued a master's degree in electrical engineering at Stanford University, where he also studied computer science. He graduated from Stanford in 1972.

### Career Highlights

Banatao interviewed with three companies involved in computer microprocessor development in California's fledgling Silicon Valley region: Intel, American Microsystems, Inc., and National Semiconductor. (A microprocessor is a central processing unit, or CPU, on a single silicon chip that powers a computer.) Impressed with National's microprocessor design capabilities, he joined National's technical staff and was soon writing software for the team. However, since Banatao was not given the responsibility to design an entire CPU at National, he left the company to join start-up company Commodore International in 1976. At that time, there were only four engineers, and Banatao had the opportunity to design a CPU chip for a calculator. Whereas Hewlett Packard and Texas Instruments' calculators sold for hundreds of dollars, Commodore's machine, designed by Banatao, was priced at $20. Commodore thus became a household name in the mid-1970s, and it further elevated its reputation when the company released a ground-breaking personal electronic transaction (PET) computer, an early version of the home computer, at the Consumer Electronics Show in 1978.

Commodore continued to focus on the consumer market, but Banatao saw the potential in the business arena. After three years, he went to another company, Intersil, where he designed his first microprocessor—the CMOS 8048—with electronically programmable read-only memory (EPROM). Unfortunately his design could not be replicated in the fabrication factory, and in 1981 he went to work at Seeq Technology in Fremont, California. Collaborating with the inventor of the Ethernet, or the local area network (LAN) that connects computers together, Banatao was able to design the first Ethernet controller semiconductor chip in the early 1980s. This development eliminated the need for large bulky boards—thereby revolutionizing and streamlining the design of computers and improving network capability. By 1984, Banatao realized the potential of the personal computer and with Francis Siu as his partner, launched a high-tech company, Mostron, with $500,000 of capi-

tal, mostly from friends. Within eight months, they hired an executive from Intel, Ron Yara, who was originally from Hawaii.

Mostron was launched as a manufacturer of computer boards. Banatao devised a five-chip set; companies seemed to be more interested in his semiconductor chips than the board itself. As a result, Banatao cofounded Chips & Technologies in 1985. He developed the first enhanced graphics adapter and system logic chip set for the IBM PC/AT, and within 22 months, Chips & Technologies went public. After selling the graphics chip set for only one quarter, the company boasted revenues of $12 million.

"I've done tremendous things for the industry from the technical point of view," stated Banatao in *Asiaweek* (21 July 2000). "But what drove me first was the business side. For every success there are 100 or 200 failures. A main component of that is, the technical guys didn't take care of business."

Banatao continued to launch companies. In 1989, he and Yara started S3, Inc., an acronym for "third start-up," in Santa Clara, California. S3 focused on enhancing the graphics capabilities of personal computers through a graphics accelerator chip. Key would be Banatao's invention of a local bus, which would move data much faster within a personal computer. The company had an initial public offering of $30 million. In 1996, S3 became the leader in the graphics-chip market, beating out the previous leader, Cirrus Logic Inc. Also that same year, Intel Corp. purchased Chips & Technology for $300 million.

Banatao went on to become a venture capitalist in high-tech start-up companies. Typically investing $1 million or more in seed funding, he became a significant shareholder of the Marvell Technology Group before it went public in 2000. He became a venture partner at the Mayfield Fund for two and a half years before investing $100 million into his own venture-capital firm, Tallwood Venture Capital in Palo Alto, California, near Stanford University in June 2000. In February 2001, *Forbes* magazine named Banatao among its Midas 100 top investors.

"Dado defines what we look for in an entrepreneur—a market-sensitive technologist," stated Andy Rachleff, a general partner at Benchmark and a former lead investor for S3, in an interview with *Red Herring* (25 April 2001). "He has the ability to understand customers' problems and draw upon his deep technical understanding to create innovative solutions."

Banatao, who still is an avid pilot, has been honored with multiple awards, including the National Ethnic Coalition of Organizations' Ellis Island Medal of Honor, an award to honor an outstanding U.S. citizen who contributes significantly to an ethnic group or country. He also has been recognized by his birth country: former Philippine President Fidel V. Ramos presented him with the Pamana Ng Filipino Award for his efforts in preserving and promoting the Philippines heritage.

He and his wife are also involved in philanthropy: they gave a large sum of money to the University of California, Berkeley for the Center for Information Technology Research in the Interest of Society.

### Sources

Aragon, Lawrence. 25 April 2001. "VC P.S.: The Tao of Dao." *Red Herring*.

Crisp, Penny, and Antonio Lopez. 21 July 2000. "Making Good in Silicon Valley." *Asiaweek*.

Diosdado Banatao's biography, provided by the Asian American Federation in New York.

Interview with Diosdado Banatao, Teresita G. Maceda, University of the Philippines.

# Sabeer Bhatia

Sabeer Bhatia. Photo courtesy of Bhatia Enterprises

**Born**: 1968, India.

**Education**: Bishop's School, Pune, India; St. Joseph's College, Bangalore, India, graduate; Birla Institute of Technology, Pilani, India; California Institute of Technology, Pasadena, California, B.S. with honors in electrical engineering; Stanford University, Stanford, California, M.S. in electrical engineering.

**Positions Held**: Engineer, Firepower Systems, Inc., Menlo Park, California; systems integrator, Apple Computers, Cupertino, California; cofounder, president, and chief executive officer, Hotmail Corporation, Fremont (later moved to Sunnyvale), California, 1996–97; general manager, Hotmail division, Microsoft Corporation, Mountain View, California, 1998–99; cofounder, president, and chief executive officer,

Arzoo.com, Fremont, California, 2000–01, chairman, Televoice Corporation.

**Awards, Honors**: Entrepreneur of year, Award by Deeper Fisher Jurvetson, 1998; MIT's TR100 Award, 1999; Indians of the Century, *Times of India*, 2001.

**Summary**: India-born Sabeer Bhatia made history when he and his partner sold their two-year-old free Web-based e-mail company, Hotmail Corporation, to Microsoft for reportedly more than $400 million at the end of 1997. Hotmail's method of capturing new customers through a simple Internet link popularized the term "viral marketing."

## Early Years

Bhatia spent much of his youth as an only child in the southern Indian city of Bangalore. His father, Baldev Bhatia, was a captain in the Indian Army, while his mother Daman worked as an accountant at the Central Bank of India. A serious student, Bhatia also exhibited an entrepreneurial streak: he devised a plan to sell sandwiches to students at a nearby college.

For his secondary education, Bhatia attended Bishop's School, located in the city of Pune, and then St. Joseph's School & College in Bangalore. Regarding his teachers at St. Joseph's College, he told *India Today*: "They gave me a great education while I was there, which enabled me to come to the U.S.A., and compete with the best ... and further my education—the foundation was very strong." While in college, Bhatia also played field hockey.

## Higher Education

From St. Joseph's, Bhatia enrolled in the Birla Institute of Technology at Pilani, India. He then entered in a competitive process to transfer to the renowned California Institute of Technology (Caltech) in Pasadena, California. To receive a transfer scholarship, he had to pass a rigorous exam; in 1988, he was the only person in the world to receive a passing score.

Bhatia arrived in California to study electrical engineering at Caltech in September 1988 with only $250, the legal limit allowable by the Indian government. "I felt I had made a big mistake," he said to *Asiaweek* (25 June 1999). "I knew nobody, people looked different, it was hard for them to understand my accent and me to understand theirs. I felt pretty lonely."

Yet he persevered and graduated with honors. He then entered a master's program in electrical engineering at Stanford University. Before going on for his doctoral degree, Bhatia worked a short time at a high-tech company, Firepower Systems, in Menlo Park, California, before getting a job with Apple Computers as a systems integrator.

## Career Highlights

While working at Apple Computers, Bhatia also attended sessions of The IndUS Entrepreneurs, also known as TIE, to network with older business leaders from India. Learning about their entrepreneurial success, Bhatia brainstormed with a colleague from Apple, Jack Smith, to create their own venture. Their idea: free e-mail that could be accessed from any computer with an Internet connection. It would be called Hotmail.

Although the idea was simple, it was entirely original. To protect their concept from being stolen, they first approached venture capitalists to fund an Internet-base personal database called JavaSoft. In this way, Bhatia and Smith would get a sense of the thought processes of these potential investors—if they felt they could trust and respect them, they would pitch the Hotmail idea. After being rejected at least 19 times, they approached Steve Jurvetson of the venture capital company, Draper Fisher Jurvetson. After an hour, Bhatia casually mentioned the Hotmail idea—more as a marketing tool than a stand-alone venture. Jurvetson quickly understood its potential. "He [Bhatia] had hallucinogenic optimism," Jurvetson told writer Po Bronson in the book, *The Nudist on the Late Shift*. "He had an unquenchable sense of destiny."

Jurvetson and third-generation venture capitalist Tim Draper offered to provide $300,000 for 30 percent ownership on a $1 million valuation. But Bhatia was a tough negotiator. He wanted $2 million of valuation—with the venture capitalists receiving a reduced rate of 15 percent. This was a bold move, especially since the entrepreneurs' only other option was using $100,000 raised through friends and relatives. When Draper refused to capitulate, Bhatia walked out of the negotiations. "I still sometimes can't believe he had the guts to walk out of that room," Smith said (quoted in Bronson's *The Nudist on the Late Shift*).

A day later, Draper Fisher Jurvetson agreed to the deal—on Bhatia's terms. Bhatia and Smith opened a small office in Fremont, California, with 15 employees. Still fully aware that their nascent idea could be stolen at any time, they used the name JavaSoft. One month before the launch day, Imperial Bank approved $100,000 in unsecured loans.

Key to the Hotmail approach was a built-in advertisement for Hotmail at the end of each e-mail message. Upon receiving a message from a Hotmail user, a person could easily subscribe to the service by clicking on a direct Internet link. As a result, when Hotmail was officially launched on July 4, 1996, 100 subscribers were signed up within the first hour. In 18 months, Hotmail had 11 million users. This strategy, referred to as "viral market-

ing" in that advertisement for a product spreads from one user to another like a virus, was eventually emulated by many other Web-based corporations.

Because the e-mail service was free, Hotmail had to generate income from another source—news services and other companies that would pay money to have links and advertisements on the Hotmail site. Partnerships were formed, with Hotmail always receiving money for content. Apparently these partnerships formed a strong foundation for income, as Menlo Ventures agreed to contribute additional funding.

In two years, Hotmail, later headquartered in Sunnyvale, California, had 22 million subscribers—gaining more subscribers than any other media company in the world in that time span. In 1997, Microsoft Corporation approached Hotmail about acquiring the company, thereby beginning a round of high-powered negotiation discussions. As was the situation with the venture-capital funding, Bhatia held his ground. He demanded $500 million—an offer that was immediately rebuffed by Microsoft. Microsoft returned with $350 million, but Bhatia still was not satisfied. Finally on December 31, 1997, Bhatia and Smith sold their company to Microsoft for approximately 2.7 million shares of Microsoft, then worth more than $400 million.

Bhatia stayed on with the company as the general manager of Microsoft's Hotmail unit, which at the time had about 140 employees. Hotmail's headquarters moved from Sunnyvale to Mountain View, California. Bhatia had a three-year contract, but in March 1999, he left Microsoft to again participate in a startup. This time, the venture, called Arzoo.com (meaning "heart's desire" in the Urdu language), was a business-to-business portal designed to offer information-technology consulting services over the Internet. For a flat fee, customers could receive unlimited assistance from 2,000 technology experts—30 percent of whom were based in India. The venture was funded by both Bhatia and Softbank Corporation of Japan, and headquartered in Fremont, California, where Hotmail also had its early beginnings.

Arzoo.com was officially launched in September 2000 to much fanfare. Unfortunately, the enterprise shut down after nine months. "Once again, we strongly believe in this model but, unfortunately, this is just not the right time to introduce such a service to our corporate partners—all of whom are engaged in what some call a 'ruthless cost-cutting' exercise," stated a message on Arzoo.com Web site signed by Bhatia in 2001.

Bhatia, however, was not deterred from future entrepreneurial efforts. He and his former partner, Jack Smith, invested funds into IronPort Systems, Inc., an e-mail management system based in San Bruno, California.

Regarding the success of Indians in Silicon Valley, Bhatia commented to *India Today Plus*'s Raj S. Rangarajan: "I think the best and the brightest are allowed to use their intellect and their mind, there is no dearth of capital, you don't have to have connections, you don't have to have super-influence in the government or banking system. Labor and capital are freely available for anyone. If you have a good idea, you can make it over here."

Bhatia is known for his affinity for sportscars; he owns a Porsche, BMW, and Ferrari, as well as a luxury apartment in the exclusive Pacific Heights neighborhood in San Francisco.

## Sources

Bronson, Po. 1999. *The Nudist on the Late Shift and Other True Tales of Silicon Valley*. New York: Random House.

"Fremont Web Venture Arzoo.com Shuts Down." 20 June 2001. *East Bay Business Times*.

"Health & Technology: Web-Messaging Pioneers, Dell Form Firm That Hopes to Alter E-Mail Management." 27 November 2001. *Wall Street Journal*: B7.

Rangarajan, Raj S. January–February 2000. "The Hot Male." *India Today Plus*.

Silicon India Web site. www.siliconindia.com [accessed, November 29, 2001].

Walker, Andrew. 22 June 2001. "Sabeer Bhatia: Things Go Cold for Mr. Hotmail." *BBC News*.

Whitmore, Stuart. 25 June 1999. "Driving Ambition." *Asiaweek*.

# Amar Bose

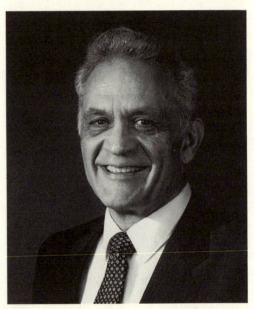

Amar Bose. Photo courtesy of Bose Corporation

**Full Name at Birth**: Amar Gopal Bose.

**Born**: 2 November 1929, Philadelphia, Pennsylvania.

**Education**: Massachusetts Institute of Technology, Cambridge, Massachusetts, B.S. and M.S. in electrical engineering, 1952; Ph.D. in electrical engineering, 1956.

**Positions Held**: Professor of electrical engineering and computer science, Massachusetts Institute of Technology, Cambridge, Massachusetts, 1956– ; founder and chairman of Bose Corporation, Framingham, Massachusetts, 1964– .

**Awards, Honors**: National Inventor of the Year, Intellectual Property Owners Association, 1987.

**Summary**: Scientist Amar Bose, a professor at Massachusetts Institute of Technology, revolutionized sound technology while successfully launching his own audio equipment company, Bose Corporation. Bose, whose father was originally from India, still owns a majority of his Framingham, Massachusetts–based corporation.

### Early Years

Bose was born and raised in a predominantly white suburb of Philadelphia, Pennsylvania, during the Great Depression. His father, Noni Gopal, was an importer, originally from India, while his mother, Charlotte, was a European American. Bose, being of mixed race, experienced discrimination by both his peers and adults. Neighborhood boys often terrorized Bose and some restaurants in Philadelphia refused to serve his family. At first, Bose's father told him, "Never, never fight." However, after Bose came home beaten up one day, his father talked about racism and then taught him to box—admonishing him never to start a fight but never to lose one, either.

"I would not trade being brought up like that for anything," Bose told *USA Today* (22 September 1992). "Because anything that people teach people in college or anything in courses about prejudice, they never reach inside you. You've got to be in it, and unless a person has experienced that, he can never know it."

In addition to his academic pursuits, Bose also studied the violin for seven years during his childhood. He also was a teenage entrepreneur: in 1943, he opened a radio repair shop after many young engineers had been sent overseas during World War II.

### Higher Education

Bose gained his undergraduate and graduate degrees from the Massachusetts Institute of Technology (MIT) in Cambridge, Massachusetts. After he completed his doctorate in electrical engineering in 1956, he joined the faculty as a professor. To celebrate, he purchased a new high-fidelity stereo system, but when he and his friends played music on it, shrill strains of the violin resounded from the speakers. While scientifically advanced for the time, the speakers were still far from able to reproduce sounds heard in concert halls. Both troubled and challenged by the speakers' performance, Bose set out to create a better system—first in his living room after work, and later in an MIT laboratory.

### Career Highlights

Bose's passion to create a better speaker system after hours soon led to a research project in psychoacoustics sponsored by MIT. The project investigated how people perceive sound versus how sound can be measured by electronic equipment. MIT allowed Bose to patent his discoveries, but no existing manufacturers seemed to be interested in adopting his new audio technologies. A colleague, MIT professor Y.W. Lee, then suggested that Bose launch his own company to integrate his research into audio products. Lee himself was willing to invest his life savings, $10,000, toward the realization of this proposal. So, at the age of 34, Bose launched Bose Corporation in

1964, with the help of Lee and four other scientific colleagues. His first hire was a former student, Sherwin Greenblatt.

The company's first product release, the Bose 2201 speakers, delivered high-quality sound but were a failure in terms of aesthetic design—the speakers were too large and obtrusive for consumer tastes. During its first four years, Bose Corporation was able to obtain contracts with the U.S. military and NASA, yet the mass market still seemed out of reach until the release of the 901 Direct/Reflecting loudspeaker in 1968. The 901, which was designed to reflect 89 percent of sound off walls, revolutionized the industry.

While Bose speakers continued to prosper in the domestic arena, the company faltered internationally, specifically in Asia. In fact, from 1970 to 1973, it sold fewer than 100 pairs of speakers in Japan. However, as the Japanese audio market was significant—worth $126 billion—Bose did not give up. He opened a Tokyo office in 1975, and for the next five years, it struggled, only attracting $300,000 in revenue. Bose then tenaciously recruited a Japanese businessman, Sumi Sakura, who eventually agreed to lead Bose Asia Ltd., Japan Branch. Together they traveled across Japan to woo local distributors and dealers. The speaker's walnut casings were altered to better suit Japanese tastes. In four years, sales rose to $16 million. Bose speakers are now bestsellers in Japan; in fact, many Japanese automobiles arrive in the United States with Bose audio systems.

Marketing and advertisement have also been key to Bose's growth. By 1999, 35 years since its founding, Bose Corporation had $950 million in sales; revenues exceeded $1 billion a year later. Overseeing the administration of the company is Bose's first paid employee and former student, Sherwin Greenblatt, who is now president and chief operating officer.

Instead of always depending on orthodox sales strategies, Bose Corporation has been creative. For instance, when its top-of-the-line Wave radio was first introduced in 1993, Bose Corporation opted to sell the product directly to customers rather than through retailers, who at the time did not know how to promote an expensive high-end radio. The strategy was successful, and within five years, approximately 200,000 Waves were sold.

Research, however, has remained Bose's foremost priority. One hundred percent of its profits are reinvested into product development. When it came time to enter the car stereo market, Bose invested $13 million and four years in the project. By 1992, car audio components made up 25 percent of revenue for the company; automobile manufacturers also embraced the product. Bose Corporation has also kept abreast with new trends, recently introducing a Wave/PC Interactive Audio System which provides easy access to Web radio and MP3 music files.

Much of this attention to research is possible because Bose, who still teaches at MIT, remains a majority stakeholder of this private company. "My interest in this company is as a machine for research," he said to *The Economist* (15 January 2000). This is in keeping with its motto: "Better Sound through Research." Moreover, the firm's headquarters, called "The Mountain," as it stands on a hill overlooking Boston, has 600 engineers, many of them MIT alumna, on staff. In addition to "The Mountain," Bose Corporation has seven other manufacturing sites throughout the United States, Ireland, Canada, and Mexico, and many wholly owned international subsidiaries.

Bose, as a majority shareholder, is also very wealthy. In 1999, *Forbes* named him the sixty-ninth richest man, with $650 million of personal wealth; a year later, he was reported to have $720 million. Bose, who resides near the Framingham headquarters, has a son and daughter.

## Sources

*Bose Corporation*. www.bose.com [accessed 12 November 2001].

"Face Value: Vox Populi." 15 January 2000. *The Economist*: 71+ .

Kotkin, Joel. December 1984. "Going through Customs." *Inc.*: 180+ .

La Franco, Robert. 9 August 1999. "Loudspeaker Envy." *Forbes*: 68+ .

"A Man and His Stereo: Setting Out to Solve the Great Puzzle of Better Sound." 17 June 1993. *Christian Science Monitor*.

"Manufacturers." 11 October 1999. *Forbes*: 338+ .

Walker, Blair S. 22 September 1992. "Bose Learned Hard Way to Fight Back." *USA Today*: 4B.

Walker, Blair S. 22 September 1992. "Revenue Growth Music to Bose's Ears." *USA Today*: 4B.

# C

## Phyllis Campbell

Phyllis Campbell. Photo courtesy of Phyllis Campbell

**Full Name at Birth**: Phyllis Jean Takisaki.

**Born**: 25 July 1951, Spokane, Washington.

**Education**: Washington State University, Pullman, Washington, B.A. in business administration.

**Positions Held**: Management trainee, Old National Bank of Spokane, Spokane, Washington, 1973; executive vice president and manager of the distribution group, U.S. Bank, Washington; president and chief executive officer, U.S. Bank of Washington, Washington, 1989–2000.

**Awards, Honors**: Human Relations Award, American Jewish Committee, 2000.

**Summary**: Phyllis Campbell, undergirded by her Japanese grandfather's principles, has risen through the ranks of bank management in her home state of Washington. As the former president and chief executive officer of U.S. Bank of Washington, Campbell is viewed as a leader in her region and among financial executives.

### Early Years

Born the oldest of five children in Spokane, Washington, Phyllis Campbell helped to take care of her siblings and also assisted in the family's dry cleaning business during the 1950s, the resettlement period for Japanese Americans forcibly removed from the West Coast during World War II. While her father, Raymond Takisaki, had served in the U.S. Army, the rest of his family had been interned in North Dakota after having to leave the family business.

Campbell's paternal grandfather, Tomotsu Sebastian Takisaki, remained optimistic about the United States and opened a small grocery and antique store after the war. A collector of fine art, he often was observed meditating on an art object for hours. He served as an influential figure in Campbell's life—both in terms of work and philosophy. In one documented incident, he advised a musician to refrain from practicing so much and instead concentrate on helping others. The result: his music performance improved. "The story became a metaphor for me," Campbell says, as quoted in *The Inner Work of Leaders: Leadership as a Habit of Mind*. "Because I am so task oriented, I tend to lose the forest for the trees. When I can step outside of myself, like in the story, and see there is a lot more out there, things happen the way they need to happen."

Another role model was Campbell's mother Marion, who worked as a medical technologist while raising her large family. Aspiring for a corporate career, Campbell worked her way through both undergraduate and graduate studies. After gaining her master's degree in marketing at Washington State University she was hired as a management trainee by Old National Bank of Spokane.

## Career Highlights

At Old National, Campbell rose quickly through the ranks to become senior vice president of all the branches in Spokane—in spite of a battle with cancer at age 32.

Radiation therapy was completely effective in beating the disease, yet more changes were ahead for Campbell during the 1980s, the height of bank deregulation. In 1987, Old National was acquired by U.S. Bank, headquartered in Portland. "You feel you have this stable career, and then things change with one announcement," she said, as quoted in an article in *Washington CEO* magazine. "It was quite a shock."

Campbell, however, adjusted well and in fact, continued her career ascent. First promoted to senior vice president and area manager for eastern Washington, she was elevated to executive vice president and manager of the distribution group for U.S. Bank in 1989. In 1989, she was named president and chief executive officer of its Washington operations, U.S. Bank of Washington. In this capacity, she was responsible for more than 190 bank branches.

In March 1997, Campbell experienced her second bank merger when U.S. Bank was purchased by Minneapolis-based First Bank System, Inc. in a $9 billion deal. Campbell continued as president of the Washington state operation until May 2000, when she stepped down from her position after nearly to 30 years of service.

Throughout her banking career, Campbell has remained faithful in her philanthropic pursuits and forays in community leadership. She has served on the boards of the Greater Seattle Chamber of Commerce, the Association of Washington Business, the Washington State University Board of Regents, the Pacific Science Center, and the Seattle Symphony Foundation. As the chair of the United Way of King County, she was able to raise a record-breaking $6.8 million; Campbell also led U.S. Bank's involvement in a nonprofit housing development, Noji Gardens, the former site of a plant nursery operated by a

Japanese American family who were interned during World War II. In 2000, she received a Human Relations Award by the American Jewish Committee.

Campbell continues to be connected to U.S. Bank as chair of the company's Seattle bank board; she also works to retain and train employees and represents the bank on several community boards.

As she has learned from her grandfather, as stated in *The Inner Work of Leaders*: "Get out of yourself for awhile, and see there is a lot more out there. Maybe the essential work of a leader is to expand the pie. The more we concentrate on giving back, whether it is giving a compliment or doing different things for different people, more is available for everybody else."

### Sources

Enbysk, Monte. June 1997. "Changes Loom, But U.S. Bank to Keep Its Name and a Familiar Face." *Washington CEO*.

Mackoff, Barbara, and Gary Wenet. 2000. *The Inner Work of Leaders: Leadership as a Habit of Mind*. New York: AMACOM.

Nelson, Robert T. 27 May 2001. "Campbell Leaves U.S. Bank with Deposit of Goodwill." *Seattle Times*.

"U.S. Bank Names New Washington President." 1 March 2001. *Puget Sound Business Journal*.

# F. Chow Chan

**Full Name at Birth**: Fung Chow Chan.

**Born**: 3 April 1910, Canton, China.

**Died**: 29 January 2001, Los Angeles, California.

**Education**: Canton Christian College, Canton, China, circa 1920s; University of Southern California, Los Angeles, California, 1933.

**Positions Held**: Cofounder, Phoenix Bakery, Los Angeles, California, 1940; co-founder and chairman, Cathay Bank, Los Angeles, California, 1962–71; cofounder, East West Federal Savings and Loan, Los Angeles, California, 1972.

**Summary**: F. Chow Chan, an entrepreneur and banker, was instrumental in addressing the financial needs of the growing Chinese American population in Los Angeles. He helped organize the first Chinese American bank in Southern California and later one of the first federally chartered savings and loan associations.

### Early Years

Chan's grandfather was a successful silk merchant from Canton, China, who traveled on a clipper ship to San Francisco in the late 1800s. Chan himself was born in Canton, a southern port city about 75 miles northwest of Hong Kong. Canton, also known as Guangzhou, was a center of political change: both the Opium War of the mid-1800s and leaders like Sun Yat-sen can be traced to that region.

### Education

According to a Southern California Chinese American Oral History Project interview (1979), Chan attended Canton Christian College. In 1933, he immigrated to the United States to join his father and to study business at the University of Southern California in Los Angeles. The 1882 Chinese Exclusion Act had barred the immigration of Chinese laborers, but had allowed for merchants, students, travelers, teachers, and government officials.

### Career Highlights

In 1938, Chan, his wife, Wai Hing, and his brother, Lun, launched their own enterprise, Phoenix Bakery, in a new development called New Chinatown between North Broadway Avenue and Castelar

Street in Los Angeles. (The old Chinatown had been destroyed by fires.) Lun was able to use skills learned at Los Angeles Trade Technical College, and key to the success of the bakery were family recipes from China.

Phoenix Bakery continued to grow throughout World War II and the postwar years. Because there were no banks within Chinatown, Chan had to travel outside the Chinese community to manage his financial affairs. In the 1960s, he approached his bank for a loan to expand his business but was denied. This incident became the impetus for him to organize a group of five investors to begin a bank in Chinatown. Using Phoenix Bakery as the original incorporator, the group filed a request for a charter from the state banking department. The department initially did not see a need for a bank serving the Chinese community, but after some time had elapsed, the charter was finally approved.

With only $550,000 in capital and seven employees, Cathay Bank opened its 1,000-square-foot office in Los Angeles' Chinatown in 1962. It was the first Chinese American–owned bank in Los Angeles.

The same year Chan also broke racial barriers in his personal life. He moved his family into the Silver Lake district of Los Angeles, an area in which Asians had been barred from buying homes until the late 1950s. Recognizing the importance of home ownership and the financing required to buy real estate, Chan then partnered with Betty Tom Chu, then an attorney for the Los Angeles Unified School District, to apply for a charter for a savings and loan association in the mid-1960s. Again, as in the case of Cathay Bank, the road for approval was difficult. The application was first denied. For several years Chan and Chu appealed to the chairman of the Federal Home Loan Bank Board—Preston Martin, a former USC

professor whom Chu was familiar with from her college days. This time the application was accepted: East-West was officially chartered in 1972.

One of Chan's sons, Kellogg, an attorney with the Los Angeles County district attorney's office, served on East-West board of directors; in 1976 he was appointed chairman. He eventually left law to pursue a career in banking.

Chan was very active with various community and civic groups. He served as president of the Chinatown Chamber of Commerce, Chinese American Citizens Alliance, and the Gee How Oak Tin Family Association.

Chan passed away in Los Angeles in January 2001. In addition to Kellogg, he was survived by two other sons, Kelly and Kenneth, and a daughter, Kathryn.

### Sources

Hamilton, Denise. 9 April 1995. "Banking on the Family Name." *Los Angeles Times* (City Times): 12–14.

Jean Wong's interview with F. Chow Chan, 5 July 1979, Southern California Chinese American Oral History Project, UCLA Asian American Studies/Special Collections.

Woo, Elaine. 7 February 2001. "Obituaries; Fung Chow Chan; Founded L.A.'s Phoenix Bakery." *Los Angeles Times*: B6.

# Roger H. Chen

**Born**: c. 1952, Taiwan.

**Education**: National Taiwan University, Taipei, Taiwan, B.S. in business and agriculture, c. 1970s.

**Positions Held**: Founder, Man Wah Supermarket, Westminster, California, 1984– ; founder and chief executive officer, Tawa Supermarkets Inc., Buena Park, California, 1985– .

**Summary**: Roger Chen, who came to the United States from his native Taiwan in his thirties, was able to build an innovative supermarket chain, 99 Ranch Market, specializing in Asian foodstuffs. Since opening his first market in 1984 in California, he has become involved in the manufacture of food products and real estate development. Through independent license agreements, many 99 Ranch Markets have been established in other states and even overseas.

### Early Years and Higher Education

Chen was raised in Taiwan in the 1950s and 1960s—a time in which there was much turmoil between Taiwan and mainland China. Chen studied business and agriculture at National Taiwan University, an elite educational institution in Taipei, Taiwan.

### Career Highlights

Chen eventually became involved in international trade, and came to Southern California regularly to import American cars for the Taiwanese market. In the 1970s, he became acquainted with Frank Jao, a real estate developer who had started the company, Bridgecreek Development Co., in Westminster, California, to build the Vietnamese community of Little Saigon.

During these trips, Chen began to believe that California would be a good place for him and his wife to raise their three children and eventually immigrated to the United States in 1983. At that time, Chen was already in his thirties. He and his family first settled in Fountain Valley, California, and later nearby Anaheim Hills.

Chen first attempted to continue in the international trade business, exporting cars and computers to Taiwan, but could not compete with already established exporters. Because he spoke little English, he was unable to secure a job at a large company. Observing the numerous "mom-and-pop" grocery stores serving the Vietnamese community in the Orange County region of Southern California, Chen seized on the idea of opening a Western-style supermarket that sold Asian food products. He identified a warehouse in a light industrial park in Westminster as an ideal site, but could not convince bankers to loan him the capital to lease and develop it. As a result, Chen and his partner gathered $1 million from their savings and investments to open Man Wah Supermarket in 1984.

Because Chen and his partner were not familiar with the operation of a supermarket, they had to learn on the job. Chen quickly learned about the various regulations issued by the Food and Drug Administration (FDA) and the local health department. For example, in Taiwan, meat, fish, and eggs were often stacked in ice; In the United States, however, those items must be refrigerated. Chen was also assisted by his wife, who worked as cashier, accountant, and administrator. The store imported about 40 percent of its inventory; the rest was from local vendors.

The supermarket, with its wide, gleaming aisles and expansive Asian inventory was an immediate hit. Within five months, Chen bought out his partner's share in Man Wah. In a year, the store grossed more than $2 million.

In 1985, Chen incorporated his company under the name Tawa Supermarkets, Inc. and even began developing his own food products. A year later, he approached Union Bank about a loan to open a second store. This time, with the success of Man Wah Supermarket, Chen was able to easily secure adequate funding for his 99 Price Market. (That number—99—would become the brand name of Chen's other supermarkets; 99 is considered a lucky number among Taiwanese.) Establishing a strong development strategy that would be emulated in later projects, Chen anchored 99 Price Market in a new retail development created in partnership with Bridgecreek's Frank Jao in a 100,000-square-foot industrial park in Westminster. The two men would collaborate on future developments, including the two-story Asian Garden Mall, completed in 1987. That same year, Chen opened the doors of another 99 Price Market in the city of Montebello, east of downtown Los Angeles. This community, unlike Westminster, was more multicultural, with Chinese, Latino, and Anglo American residents.

In 1988, Chen embarked on another ambitious project with Taiwanese investors: a retail complex able to accommodate 32 restaurants and stores and a 36,000-square-foot supermarket. The development project would be established on the site of an abandoned 110,000-square-foot Gemco Department Store in Rowland Heights, a suburb east of the well-known Chinese American community of Monterey Park. This time Chen would call his store, "99 Ranch Market," which became the new brand name for his entire chain.

Key in the Chen expansion throughout southern California would be alliances with businesses like the Chinese restaurant chain Sam Woo. As anchors for new developments in such areas as Irvine and Van Nuys, 99 Ranch Market and Sam Woo together would help attract foot traffic and a steady stream of native Chinese customers, according to the *Los Angeles Times* (5 December 1995). The two enterprises are the central focus of the San Gabriel Shopping Plaza in San Gabriel, a massive 250,000-square-foot development spearheaded by Chen and four partners.

In 1990, the privately owned Tawa Supermarkets, Inc., established a management consulting program to connect out-of-state investors with property owners in developing their own 99 Ranch Markets through license agreements. A store opened in Doraville, Georgia, in August 1993, with more following in Honolulu, Hawaii; Las Vegas, Nevada; and Phoenix, Arizona. In 1994, Tawa acquired Welcome Market Inc., which operates six 99 Ranch Market stores in northern California. Another store was launched near Seattle, Washington.

Tawa Supermarkets has also been active in releasing new food products. It markets more than 300 products under the brand names Kimbo, 99, Sinbo, I-Pin, and Flying Horse on Earth.

Chen is also taking his concept overseas: a 99 Ranch Market was opened in Jakarta, Indonesia. He expects further interest to come from Hong Kong and Taipei. "More than half the people in Asia still shop in traditional stores, not supermarkets, but it's changing day by day as the younger generation is converted," Chen stated in an interview with the *Los Angeles Times* (27 April 1997).

Tawa Supermarkets is headquartered in Buena Park, California.

### Sources

Hamilton, Denise. 27 April 1997. "99 and Counting." *Los Angeles Times*: D1, D12.

La Ganga, Maria. 11 December 1988. "Asian Lure for Anglos Growing." *Los Angeles Times* (Orange County Edition): 7.

"Our Organization." *Tawa Supermarkets*. http://www.99ranch.com. [accessed September 20, 2001].

## Andrew Cherng

Andrew and Peggy Cherng. Photo courtesy of Panda Restaurant Group, Inc.

**Full Name at Birth**: Jin Chan Cherng.

**Born**: 1948, Shanghai, China.

**Education**: Baker University, Baldwin, Kansas, B.S. in mathematics, 1970; University of Missouri, M.S. in mathematics, c. 1972.

**Positions Held**: Founder, Panda Inn, Pasadena, California, 1973– ; president, Panda Express, South Pasadena, California, 1983–94; chairman, Panda Management Company, South Pasadena, California, c. 1994– , Founder and Chairman, Panda Restaurant Group, South Pasadena, California, c. 2001– .

**Summary**: Andrew Cherng and his wife, Peggy, lead the largest Chinese quick-service chain in the United States, Panda Express. First opening a restaurant in Pasadena in 1982, Cherng is the founder and chairman of Panda Restaurant Group

(PRG), which includes more than 400 Panda Express branches throughout the United States, Puerto Rico, and Japan. PRG is also the parent company for Panda Inn, Hibachi San, and Orleans Express.

### Early Years

Cherng's father, Ming-tsai Cherng, had been a master chef in Shanghai, where Cherng was born. The family then moved to Hong Kong and then Taiwan. Ming-tsai served as the head chef at the Taipei Grand Hotel in Taiwan before taking a position in Yokohama, Japan. Cherng spent his formative years in Yokohama, a large city with a sizable Chinese community, and graduated from an international high school there.

### Higher Education

From Japan, Cherng traveled to the midwestern United States, specifically Baldwin, Kansas, for his undergraduate education. He gained his bachelor's degree in mathematics from Baker University in 1970. He went on to earn a master's degree in mathematics at the University of Missouri, where his wife-to-be, Peggy Tsiang, a Chinese native of Burma who emigrated to the United States via Hong Kong, would eventually obtain her master's degree in computer science and a doctorate in electrical engineering.

### Career Highlights

In 1972, Cherng's cousin, who lived in southern California, recruited the mathematics scholar to manage a restaurant in Hollywood. After Cherng's father, Ming-tsai, secured proper papers to reside in the United States, the father and son opened a Mandarin and Szechuan Chinese restaurant in Pasadena, California. That enterprise, Panda Inn, which became more upscale and larger over time, would serve as the flagship site of Cherng's quick-serve food empire. While other eateries in southern California offered more traditional Chinese food, the 130-seat Panda Inn served fresh dishes better suited to the American palate in a comfortable family atmosphere.

According to the *Los Angeles Times* (5 October 1993), Cherng would even chase after customers who were discouraged by the long lines. "We had a new guest sitting at a table by the time the previous customer had paid his bill and reached the door," he told reporter Karl Schoenberger. "The food was good, and it came out on time. We executed well."

An opportunity in a large suburban mall near Pasadena, Glendale Galleria, led Cherng to open his first Panda Express quick-service outlet in 1983. His wife, Peggy, who had just given birth to their third daughter, wrote the company's first software programs and handled administrative duties. The freshness and quality of the food—as well as the operation's efficiency—made the venture a success. Over the next decade, the Cherngs would open more than 100 Panda Express outlets nationwide with revenues exceeding $100 million. Under their parent company, Panda Restaurant Group (PRG), headquartered in South Pasadena, California, they would open additional Panda Inns and diversify into a Japanese fast-food enterprise, Hibachi San. PRG employed more than 2,600 individuals in 1993.

Up to this time, PRG had expanded predominantly in shopping mall food courts, as well as in supermarkets, airports, and universities. (PRG chairman Cherng, in fact, had opened the first quick-service restaurant in a Vons supermarket in 1988.) But by 1995, Panda Express began opening street stores, primarily in Los Angeles, Las Vegas, and Denver. Peggy, who became president and chief executive officer in 1998, continued Panda Express' phenomenal growth. With the expansion into stand-alone street stores, the Cherngs saw the need for television commercials to attract customers and embarked on broadcast advertising in 1999. That same year, sales for Panda Express alone reached $224 million, and in 2000, revenues increased to $283 million. By 2001, there were close to 400 Panda Express outlets; PRG had also launched a new venture, Orleans Express, a quick-service Cajun cuisine restaurant, in Honolulu, Hawaii.

To help facilitate Panda Express' continued growth and quality control, the Cherngs have instituted management training and employee incentive programs. The company remains family-owned; limited shares are also earmarked for employees. "I think that the spirit and the culture within Panda—we have a very strong learning spirit, and that's really carried us to this level," said Cherng in an interview with Mario Machado for asianconnections. com. "And I think every day when you try to grow more, that's the fundamental power of growth. It's the people, it's the culture, it's the belief that we are very good and we can do it and we can get better."

The Cherngs have also been very active in philanthropy. Panda Express donated $100,000 to different nonprofits after the 1992 Los Angeles riots, and in 1999, the company held its inaugural Panda Care Open Golf Tournament, which raises funds for various charitable groups. In 2001, the couple donated $1 million to the Collins School of Hospitality Management at California State Polytechnic University in Pomona via the United Way.

### Sources

"Andrew Cherng." Asian Connections. http://www.asianconnections.com [accessed January 16, 2001].

"Building a Panda." *Panda Management Company.* http://www.pandamgmt.com [accessed September 11, 2001].

Schoenberger, Karl. 5 October 1993. "Expatriate Entrepreneurs: Well-Educated Chinese Pour Their Energy into Businesses." *Los Angeles Times*: D1, D10.

Spector, Amy. 25 September 2000. "Peggy Cherng." *Nation's Restaurant News*: 174+ .

# David Chu

**Born**: c. 1954, Taiwan.

**Education**: Fashion Institute of Technology, New York City, New York, graduate, c. 1977.

**Positions Held**: Cofounder Nautica A.W.O.L., New York City, New York, 1983–84; president of Nautica Apparel Inc., New York City, New York, 1984–2001; chief executive officer, president, and designer, Nautica International, New York City, New York, 1984– ; executive vice president and head designer, Nautica Enterprises Inc., New York City, New York, 1984– .

**Summary**: Taiwan-born David Chu has combined his sense of design with business know-how to sustain his company, Nautica, through the competitive cycles of the apparel industry. Key to Nautica's success is its transition from an independent company to its tremendous growth as a subsidiary of a public company.

## Early Years

The oldest of three children, Chu was born in Taiwan. When he was 15 years old, his family relocated to the United States. Talented in drawing, Chu enjoyed sketching members of his family and dreamed of someday becoming an architect. While taking a summer drawing course at the Fashion Institute of Technology in New York City, Chu began to consider another career path: fashion design.

## Higher Education

Chu went on to gain his bachelor's degree from the Fashion Institute of Technology. Graduates usually worked as assistant designers for large firms or stylists working on the runway of fashion shows.

## Career Highlights

After graduation, Chu designed for Catalina Sportswear. While working as a designer and merchandiser for Cresco, then the outerwear division of Kayser-Roth, he noticed a lack of colorful jackets in the apparel market, which led him to create six designs for functional pieces that were inspired by the sport of sailing. With a partner who provided $160,000 in capital, Chu launched the company, Nautica A.W.O.L.—the name from the Latin word for ship, *nauticus*—in 1983. His original logo was a spinnaker in full sail.

The jackets made a definite splash in a season of tan, subdued fashions. "They were very functional in very powerful, bold, classical colors. I think I sold them to Barneys New York, Saks, and Bloomingdale's," stated Chu to *Daily News Record* (6 February 1995).

In the first year, sales reached $700,000; in the next year, revenues multiplied to close to $3 million. To continue growing, Nautica needed more capital. In 1984, State-O-Maine, Inc., a publicly owned company led by Harvey Sanders, bought out Chu's partner for a small amount of cash and assumption of around $1 million in liabilities, according to *Forbes* (25 November 1991). Chu later received State-O-Maine stock for his share of the company.

Until the 1984 acquisition of Nautica, State-O-Maine was mainly known as a bathrobe manufacturer and seller. The bathrobe business provided the cash flow for Nautica to expand its line of jackets. The Nautica line was sold only to select retail stores—only one or two department stores in each market, except in New York, according to *Forbes*. Key to both Sanders' and Chu's strategies was that department stores should maintain the clothing's retail price, aside from certain sale seasons, such as after-Christmas, not only to uphold the line's image, but also to gain a good full-price sell-through rate (the percentage of clothing sold for the retailers' original markup).

Within five years, Nautica sales comprised two-thirds of State-O-Main's $95 million in revenues. Also in 1989, Nautica introduced a line of women's sportswear, but this expansion apparently came too early. The first year of sales generated $11 million, yet the line was losing money. Revenues for Nautica rose to $95 million, yet the net income slipped to $2.2 million from $5.8 million. By 1991, the company had abandoned the line—at least temporarily.

Nautica continued to aggressively pursue advertising campaigns, spending 6 percent of revenues for advertisements in glossy monthly magazines such as *GQ*. By 1991, the Nautica collection contained 400 pieces, including men's and children's sportswear and various licensed products. It still maintained a high full-price sell-through rate—85 percent—while other men's sportswear companies averaged only 55 percent. In 1992, in-store shops expanded from 180 to 350, while sales increased 40 percent from the previous year. Under a licensing agreement with Revlon, the first Nautica men's fragrance was launched.

Chu continued to make innovations in casual wear. In 1994, he introduced Nautex, a special textile for street or boat wear, which was incorporated in uniforms for PACT 95, a sailing team participating in the America's Cup competition. Nautica

hit a record year of earnings: profits jumped 60 percent to $16.8 million while sales rose 27.8 percent to $192.9 million. That year Chu earned $7.85 million by exercising options on 526.708 shares of Nautica stock. Chu now owned only 4.5 percent of his original company.

In 1995, Nautica decided to make a second attempt to launch a women's wear collection for the 1996 collection. Bernard Chaus, Inc., was licensed to manufacture and market the line. By this time, Nautica had 15 menswear licensees, as well as various licensing agreements with car manufacturers (Ford Motor Co.'s Lincoln Mercury) and watchmakers (Timex Corp.). In addition to opening free-standing stores, Nautica also pushed to expand its presence within department stores. In 1996, the company had 850 in-store shops throughout the world.

1997 was a milestone year with the introduction of a women's fragrance, Nautica Women, a new jeans line, and a home furnishings collection. Chu also announced the establishment of Nautica's own international distribution and marketing arm. A year later, Nautica Enterprises had teamed up with a banking firm, Financo Global Marketing, to create Nautica Europe and open sales offices overseas.

Nautica also diversified into sports-oriented clothing with its Nautica Competition collection, and in 1999, the company debuted its (NST (Nautica Sport Technology) label aimed for younger consumers. Committed to this sports market, Chu hired a new president of Nautica Apparel, Christopher Heyn, who had served as the senior vice president of global merchandising for the National Basketball Association.

Pivotal to Nautica's success is the teamwork between Sanders, a former basketball player for the University of Maryland, and Chu. "David has sensational taste, and he's a fantastic marketer. What I do well is manage a business," Sanders reported to *Forbes* (25 November 1991).

Chu also has expressed the importance of the business side of fashion. "To me, design is not just about fashionable clothes," Chu explained to *Crain's New York Business* (16 December 1996). "I have to design the proper infrastructure first, the proper systems. It's all in the planning."

Chu, who is married and has children, maintains a close relationship with his family.

## Sources

Cannon, Paul Lee. 4–10 October 1996. "Captain of Fashion." *Asian Week.*

Gault, Ylonda. 16 December 1996. "At Nautica, Lots to Chu On; Founder Prudently Expands Brand Name." *Crain's New York Business:* 1.

Walsh, Peter. 6 February 1955. "Nautica's Ship Came In." *Daily News Record:* 38–39.

Weisman, Katherine. 25 November 1991. "Kismet on Seventh Avenue." *Forbes:* 152–53.

# James Chu

James Chu. Photo provided by View Sonic Corporation

**Born**: 23 October, 1957, Pingtong, Taiwan.

**Education**: Tong Hai University, Tai Chung, Taiwan.

**Positions Held**: President, BTC USA, Fremont, California, 1986–87; founder, Keypoint Technology Corporation (later renamed ViewSonic Corporation), Santa Fe Springs (later moved to Walnut), California, 1987– .

**Summary**: James Chu is founder, chairman, and CEO of ViewSonic Corporation, a privately held company in Walnut, California, that has become a leading provider of high-performance computer display technologies.

## Early Years

The fifth of six children of an enlisted man in the Nationalist China Air Force and a housewife with a second-grade education, Chu was an indifferent student who left high school in the eleventh grade for life in Taipei. A shy and quiet youth afflicted with a stuttering problem, Chu finished high school but failed the examination to gain entrance to a top university.

In December 1977, the 20-year-old Chu joined the Taiwan Army paratroopers for a two-year tour. A few months after leaving the army, he was hired by Duplo Enterprises to sell mimeograph machines.

## Higher Education

While at Duplo, he enrolled at Tong Hai University, a private second-tier college, and also supported himself by working in the evenings selling Chinese-English dictionaries to classmates during classroom breaks. Chu, admittedly not a good student, dropped out of college after three years.

In order to become a good salesman, he overcame his shyness by forcing himself to be outgoing and talkative on the job, and conquered the speech problem by reading aloud to train himself to speak without stuttering.

## Career Highlights

Chu held a variety of sales positions before immigrating to the United States in 1986 for Behavior Technology Corporation (BTC), a Taiwanese keyboard manufacturer. In 1984, Chu had convinced BTC's owner to make keyboards as part of an inexpensive Apple-clone system to sell to Taiwanese companies exporting to Europe and the United States. By August of that year, super-salesman Chu was selling so many orders that BTC could only fill about half of them for the next three years.

In 1986, Chu moved to Fremont, California, to become president of U.S. operations for BTC. The company was so successful that it was selling $1.1 million by its third month of operations. Due to differences in marketing strategy, Chu decided to eventually leave the company and start his own enterprise, specializing in computer keyboard sales. With $50,000 in savings and an additional $50,000 from relatives, he launched Keypoint Technology Corporation in Santa Fe Springs, an industrial city outside of Los Angeles, in 1987. In his first month, Chu sold $1 million in keyboards. Later, he and two other employees targeted mail-order companies, who were in need of quality products at reasonable prices. In time, he moved his company's headquarters to the city of Walnut in East San Gabriel Valley in Southern California.

In 1990, Chu decided to specialize in computer monitors, "the product he felt customers could relate to best," according to the *Los Angeles Times* (27 March 2000). Working with an advertising company, he chose a logo that features three colorful finches, and named the brand View Sonic. He collaborated with a Japanese manufacturer and then advertised his new product in *PC Magazine*.

By 1993, sales of View Sonic monitors were so high that Chu dropped all other products and renamed his company ViewSonic Corporation. ViewSonic's new mission and focus: to develop and deliver advanced visual technology at an affordable price.

Monitors slowly increased in display size throughout the 1990s. In addition to 17-inch monitors, ViewSonic introduced 20-inch displays that were targeted at the computer-aided design and desktop publishing markets.

In 1997, *Computer Reseller News* ranked ViewSonic first among the top 10 brand monitor manufacturers with $708 million in revenue. "We attribute a very large portion of our growth in 1997 to our relationships with resellers," Chu told *Computer Reseller News* (20 April 1998). ViewSonic has since diversified into flat panel displays, projectors, and the latest in SuperPDA, Tablet PC, and HDTV technology for business, education, entertainment, Internet, and professional markets.

In total, ViewSonic products have won more than 1,000 awards from such publications as *PC Magazine*, *PC World*, and *VAR-Business*, as well as many European, Asian, and Latin American publications. Additionally, the company—which continues to be privately held by Chu and his family—is ranked as the leading noncaptive monitor brand in the United States and many countries worldwide and has been named one of America's fastest-growing companies by *Inc.* magazine.

Rather than adopting traditional, slower processes, ViewSonic developed a business model that allows the company to quickly match advanced technologies from research laboratories around the world to market demands. That model has resulted in a series of technology innovations from ViewSonic, such as the series of Tablet PCs, and the latest liquid crystal display (LCD) monitors.

Moreover, customer service has always been preeminent to ViewSonic. A special interactive Web site was established so that customers could provide feedback to the sales staff. "I saw that to be successful ultimately in the U.S. you needed a more customer-oriented approach," Chu told the *Los Angeles Business Journal*.

Today, ViewSonic is the fifth largest seller of computer monitors in the country. Chu has set his sights on replacing the personal computer with the Internet as the preferred mode of communication, according to a report in the *Los Angeles Business Journal*, and plans to launch new devices, including a Web "pad" with a 10.4-inch screen and a Web-compatible phone with a 3-inch monitor. The *Los Angeles Business Journal* also reported that Chu plans to enter the market for digital television monitors, which can be used for both TV viewing and Web access.

ViewSonic Corporation reports that its annual sales have risen from $4 million in the company's first year to more than $1.3 billion in 2000.

But ViewSonic is not just about making lots of money. In a campaign to become "good corporate citizens," under Chu's leadership the company sponsors the Starlight Children's Foundation's Journey of Hope, and has committed $400,000 to the campaign. The Starlight Children's Foundation grants wishes and provides diversionary activities for children who are critically, chronically, or terminally ill.

Chu and his wife, the former Lily Huang Lee, have two children.

—By *Takeshi Nakayama*

### Sources

Bickford, Jim. 2002. *The American Dreams Collection*. Las Vegas, NV: American Dreams.

Howle, Amber, and Joseph Kovar. 20 April 1998. "Branded Monitors." *Computer Reseller News*: 120+ .

Kagy, Tom. January–February 1996. "A View From the Top." *Transpacific*: 52+ .

Kaplan, Karen. 27 March 2000. "For ViewSonic Chief Constant Monitoring Pays Off." *Los Angeles Times*: C1+ .

Pettersson, Edvard. 21 August, 2000. "Quiet Computer Powerhouse Takes Next Step." *Los Angeles Business Journal*: 3.

Torres, Vicki. 18 December, 1996. "A Hidden High-Tech Hot Spot." *Los Angeles Times*: A1.

ViewSonic Corporation Web site. www.viewsonic.com [accessed December 15, 2001].

# Ellery J. Chun

**Full Name at Birth**: Ellery Joe Chun.

**Born**: 17 April 1909, Honolulu, Hawaii.

**Death**: 16 May 2000, Honolulu, Hawaii.

**Education**: Yale University, New Haven, Connecticut. B.A. in economics, 1931.

**Positions Held**: Proprietor, King-Smith Clothiers, c. 1930s–45; director and vice president, American Security Bank, 1945–66.

**Summary**: Hawaiian businessman Ellery J. Chun trademarked the "aloha shirt" during the depths of the Great Depression, thereby cashing in on a fashion trend that continues today.

## Early Years

By the time Chun was growing up in Hawaii during the early 1900s, several forms of the islands' "aloha shirt" were already in existence. Filipinos sported *barong tagalog*, relaxed shirts that are worn untucked, while missionaries had introduced a plain, solid-color work shirt called the *palaka* to Hawaiian men. Japanese immigrant mothers also sewed silk tops for their children out of left-over kimono material. And, after American tourists began to arrive in cruise ships, Hawaiian tailor shops began making custom prints on shirts to sell as souvenirs.

Chun, the son of Chinese merchants in downtown Honolulu, graduated from Punahou School in Hawaii in 1909. He then decided to leave the islands for his college education at Yale University. But he would return home—and his future success would be directly linked to Hawaii's aloha shirt.

## Career Highlights

After earning his degree in economics in 1931, Chun worked in the family business, a Chinese dry goods store called King-Smith Clothiers on North King Street in Honolulu. Attempting to keep the business afloat during the Depression, he was the first to mass produce the Hawiian "aloha" shirts. He and his sister, Ethel Chun Lum, designed a few dozen styles in silk with Hawaiian motifs of palm trees, hula girls, and pineapples. His tailor sewed three or four dozen at a time, according to the *New York Times*.

Chun placed the shirts in the window of his store with a sign that said, "Aloha Shirts." By 1933 Chun was producing shirts designed by his sister from cloth imported from the mainland United States, Japan, and Tahiti. "He was very creative," said

Chun's wife Mildred in an article by the Associated Press. "I'm sure he had a good business instinct."

In 1936 Chun registered the "aloha shirt" trademark. He furthered the image of Hawaiian style by sponsoring a radio talent show in the late 1930s that was broadcast from Waikiki Beach. The program helped launch local musical performers, including the popular local singer Emma Veary.

Chun eventually left the world of retail merchandising for banking. In 1945 he closed his clothing store and became a director of American Security Bank. He retired in 1966 as a vice president but continued to serve on the bank's board until 1980.

The aloha shirt trend has continued to make its mark on Hawaii and the mainland United States. Popularized by entertainers and even politicians, the aloha shirt also played a role in the concept of "casual Friday" in which casual dress is encouraged in the workplace. The Honolulu Board of Supervisors passed a resolution in 1947 that city workers should wear sports shirts from June 1 through October 31. By the mid-1960s all workers had adopted the practice of wearing aloha shirts on the last day of the workweek.

Chun contributions in popularizing the aloha shirt have been remembered. In 1991 the Hawaii Senate honored Chun on the sixtieth anniversary of the year he released his version of the aloha shirt.

In 2000, officially proclaimed as the year of the aloha shirt, Chun passed away at the age of 91.

## Sources

"Aloha Shirt Creator Chun Dies at 91." 8 June 2000. Associated Press.

Carlson, Peter. 8 June 2000. "Aloha to the Man with Fashion's Brightest Idea." *Washington Post*: C1, C10.

Hoover, Will. 11 July 2000. "Aloha Shirts Unplugged: Unraveling Some Rumors and Fabrications." *Honolulu Advertiser*.

Hope, Dale. 2000. *The Aloha Shirt: Spirit of the Islands*. Hillsboro, OR: Beyond Words.

Lum, Curtis. 6 June 2000. "Ellery J. Chun, Aloha Shirt Pioneer, Dead at 91." *Honolulu Advertiser*.

Martin, Douglas. 8 June 2000. "Ellery Chun, 91, Popularizer of the Shirt That Won Hawaii," *New York Times*.

# Lilia Clemente

Lilia Clemente. Photo courtesy of Lilia Clemente

**Full Name at Birth**: Lilia Calderon.

**Born**: 21 February 1941, Philippines.

**Education**: University of the Philippines, Manila, Philippines, B.A. in business administration, 1960; University of Chicago, Chicago, Illinois, M.A. in agricultural economics and international trade, 1962.

**Positions Held**: Investment analyst and portfolio manager, CNA Financial Corporation, Chicago, Illinois, 1966–69; director of investment research and assistant treasurer, Ford Foundation, New York City, New York, 1969–76; founder, chairwoman, chief executive, Clemente Capital, Inc., New York City, New York, 1976– ; chairwoman, Clemente Global Growth Fund (later Clemente Strategic Value Fund) New York City, New York, 1987–2000; president, director, chief executive officer of the First Philippine Fund, New York City, New York, 1989– .

**Awards, Honors**: Pamana Ng Filipino award, Philippine President Fidel V. Ramos, 1996.

**Summary**: Lilia Clemente, the first woman to serve as an officer with the Ford Foundation, founded her own New York-based investment consulting firm, which was later reorganized to launch closed-end mutual funds specializing in the Pacific Rim, including the country of her birth, the Philippines.

### Early Years

Clemente's roots lie in the Philippines, where her grandfather was the first mining engineer in the country. Her father, Jose Calderon, was a well-respected attorney who worked primarily in the mining trade. He later became involved in politics within the Philippines; after allying himself with Benigno Aquino against dictator Ferdinand Marcos, he was imprisoned for a period of time in 1972. He also assisted Aquino's widow, Corazon Aquino, in drafting the Philippines' new constitution.

Clemente's mother, Belen Farbos Calderon, also had a distinguished career. She was a psychology professor at the University of the Philippines, a provincial governor, and the first woman to hold a seat on the Manila Stock Exchange. "My mother was a real role model," Clemente said to *Transpacific* (October 1996). "I thought it was natural for women to go into business and politics."

Clemente was the oldest of seven children. The family lived on an estate in Nueva Viscaya in northern Luzon and traveled frequently within Asia to large cities such as Tokyo, Jakarta, and Seoul. Clemente became interested in the mining and financial world at a young age; in fact, on her tenth birthday, she requested stocks instead of cake and traditional presents. She also regularly visited her father's mines and learned how precious metals were traded.

When Clemente was 15, she met Leopoldo M. Clemente Jr., who would eventually become her husband and partner in business.

## Higher Education

Clemente attended the University of the Philippines in Manila, where she was active in school politics and was editor of the college newspaper. After gaining her bachelor's degree in business administration, she headed for the United States, at the age of 19. Before she began her graduate studies at the University of Chicago, Clemente went on a cross-country bus trip to Miami for an international conference for Asian studies. In Mississippi, a restaurant refused to serve her, citing their "no colored allowed" policy. Clemente was incensed, telling the proprietor how Filipino soldiers had died defending the United States during World War II. Moments later, after she returned to the bus, the proprietor reemerged, with an apology and Clemente's food.

Clemente was one of only seven women out of 400 students in her academic department at the University of Chicago. In 1962, she graduated with a master's degree

in agricultural economics and international trade.

## Career Highlights

After graduate school, Clemente returned to Manila, where she married her teenage sweetheart, Leopoldo, who was working as an economist in the Office of the President of the Philippines. Together they resettled in Chicago, where Leopoldo worked on his master's in finance and marketing and later a doctorate at Northwestern University in Evanston, Illinois.

Clemente, meanwhile, secured a position at CNA Financial Corporation, an insurance holding company. "It was very boring. Gold was fixed. The dollar was fixed. You could throw a dart and make money," she said in an interview with the *Wall Street Journal* (16 August 1991).

However, it was at CNA that she was able to become an investment analyst and portfolio manager responsible for covering metals, steel, retailing, and consumer industries. Here, her past experiences in the mining trade helped open doors. In 1969, when her husband Leopoldo had completed his doctorate, Clemente was managing a $300 million portfolio of steel company stocks and copper futures, according to *Transpacific*. Leopoldo's new job as a senior security analyst with Merrill Lynch took the couple to New York City, where Clemente, at age 28, made history by becoming the first woman investment manager and youngest officer of the esteemed Ford Foundation. As director of investment research, assistant treasurer, and manager of the research staff, she oversaw a staff of 14 analysts and a $3 billion portfolio. Sitting at the same table with the legendary Henry Ford, who began the fund with his brother Edsel with Ford Motor Company stock, Clemente was able to convince the organization to begin investing in international stocks, beginning with the Japan Fund, which was trading on the New York Stock Exchange. Within two years, she had funneled $150 million into the Pacific Rim.

In 1976, Clemente decided to go independent and launched her own consulting company, Clemente Capital, Inc. in New York City with $25,000 of her own savings. While publishing a monthly newsletter on Asian business affairs, she also consulted for her former employer, the Ford Foundation, and other corporations. A year later, American Family Corp., which had just entered the Japanese insurance market, provided Clemente with additional startup funds for 30 percent of the company.

In 1983, Mitchell Hutchins, a subsidiary of financial giant PaineWebber, Inc., contracted Clemente Capital to launch a global fund, PaineWebber Atlas. Two years later, the fund had grown from $66 million to $206 million, ranking first of all global funds. At this time, Clemente Capital was reorganized and five partners joined the team. With this new infrastructure, Clemente and her husband Leopoldo decided to introduce their own publicly traded mutual fund while also continuing to manage fund for other groups and corporations. Leopoldo left his position as vice president and portfolio manager of Van Eck Management, and together they created Clemente Global Growth Fund, Inc., designed as a closed-end fund specializing in undervalued stocks in Malaysia, Thailand, Korea, and Japan. (In a closed-end fund, unlike an open-end mutual fund, only a limited number of shares is issued. As a result, the shares' value may be more or less than the value of the securities held by the fund.) In 1987, with additional funding from a source in Japan, Clemente Global

Growth Fund (CLM), was listed on the New York Stock Exchange (NYSE). Two years later, Clemente was able to list another closed-end fund, First Philippine Fund (FPF), on the NYSE. This fund was created primarily for investments in equity securities of Philippine securities, and was the only non-Filipino investment company allowed to invest in "A" shares of Philippines companies.

In 1989, CLM faced a hostile takeover by Thomas B. Pickens III and his Sterling Grace group, who purchased 19 percent of the fund. However, due to Clemente's close ties with her Japanese and European investors, the takeover attempt was foiled. The following year was marked by an important milestone: her autobiography was released in Japan by a women's publisher—Shufunotomo. Later, the company would be selected to manage both the California state pension fund and the New York City pension fund.

The next decade, however, would prove to be a challenge for Clemente Capital's own mutual funds. Their performances in the 1990s reflected the downturn of the Asian markets, particularly in Japan and the Philippines. In 1991, CLM, with $67 million in assets, was ranked fourth among the seven Big Board-listed global funds tracked by Lipper Analytical Services, Inc., according to *The Wall Street Journal* (16 August 1991). In 1997, investments were at $63 million and due to shareholder pressure, the portfolio was restructured to consist of at least 85 percent of U.S. equities. In 1997, returns increased to 37.6 percent, and then 36.4 percent (1998) and 40.7 percent (1999). The fund was renamed Clemente Strategic Value Fund. In May 2001, the fund was renamed again—this time to Cornerstone Strategic Value Fund—and during the same year,

Clemente Capital officially relinquished management of the fund.

The First Philippine Fund, on the other hand, performed well in the mid-1990s. In September 1997, it had $126 million in assets; share prices had increased by 22.6 percent. In fact, it was ranked as the top fund in closed-end fund performance by Lipper Analytical Services. However, with the weakening of the Philippine currency, declining import growth, and political instability, the fund's net asset value dropped to more than 40 percent in 2000. As a result, Clemente reduced its Philippines corporate holdings and invested 13.3 percent of the fund's assets into U.S.-traded global leaders, including Coca-Cola and Citibank, both of which conduct business in the Philippines.

In addition to the Philippines and Japan, Clemente also has a presence in China. In 1992, she began the Cathay Clemente Holdings Ltd. Fund, which invests in Chinese corporations. Also, with $150,000 seed money from Clemente Capital, she founded the Asian Securities Institute, which trains security industry professionals in Manila and Beijing.

### Sources

Bautista, Veltisezar. 1998. *The Filipino Americans: From 1763 to the Present.* Farmington Hills, MI: Bookhaus Publishers.

Clemente Capital, Inc. web site www.clementecapital.com [accessed November 3, 2001].

MacDonald, Lawrence. 16 August 1991. "A Philippine Fund Manager's Recipe: Blend Connections With Global Outlook." *The Wall Street Journal.*

Pizzani, Lori. 1 October 2001. "Two Fund Groups Exit Fund Business." *Mutual Fund Market News.*

"Transpacific 100: Asian American Entrepreneurs." October 1996. *Transpacific.*

# Donna Fujimoto Cole

**Full Name at Birth**: Donna Fujimoto.

**Born**: 9 June 1952, Denver, Colorado.

**Education**: Southwest Texas Junior College, Uvalde, Texas, 1970–71; The Amos Tuck School, Dartmouth College, Hanover, New Hampshire, Minority Business Executive Program.

**Positions Held**: Stenographer, Lone Star Gas Company, Houston, Texas, 1972; assistant to the president, Goldking Chemical International Ltd., Houston, Texas; vice president of sales, Del Rey Chemical International, Houston, Texas, 1976–79; founder, president, and chief executive officer, Cole Chemical & Distributing, Inc., Houston, Texas, 1980– .

**Honors and Awards**: Women on the Move, *Houston Post* and Texas Executive Women, 1987; U.S. Pan Asian Excellence 2000 Award, 1993; Entrepreneur of the Year, Houston Asian Chamber of Commerce, 1995; Top 100 Chemical Distributors in the U.S., *CPI Magazine*; Gold Pentastar Award, Chrysler Motors

**Summary**: Unusual for a woman of Japanese ancestry, Donna Fujimoto Cole has made her mark in the chemical trading industry. She is the head of a multimillion-dollar petrochemical distributor based in Houston, Texas—Cole Chemical & Distributing—which she began in 1980 at the age of 27.

### Early Years

Born in Denver, Colorado, in 1952, Cole moved to McAllen, Texas, with her family when she was six months old. Her father farmed while her mother worked in the high school cafeteria. Cole and her two older brothers were among only a handful of Asian children in the small town and at times experienced racial taunts.

## Higher Education

Cole graduated from high school in McAllen, Texas, in 1970. She dropped out of the junior college in Uvalde, Texas, after less than a year. According to an article in the *Houston Post*, Cole stated: "I regret not buckling down and studying, and finishing college. I regret not listening to Dad and Mom." She then received training as a computer operator and took a job with an accounting firm. Discovering that field was not a good fit, she quit in three months. Next was a position with Lone Star Gas in Houston, her entry into the petrochemical field.

## Career Highlights

First hired as a stenographer, Cole rapidly moved up through the company to office manager and then to secretary to the director of gas purchases and sales. She eventually left the company and got married. She returned to Houston, where she worked for a small chemical trading company, Goldking Chemical International Ltd. Her wide range of duties included secretarial, accounting, customer service, and sales. After two years, she took a job as vice president of sales at another Houston distributor, Del Rey Chemical International, Inc.

Although Goldking did well, Cole yearned for something more. In 1980, at the age of 27, she set out to launch her own chemical trading distribution company, first working out of her friend's real estate office. Recently divorced, she had a four-year-old daughter and had purchased a house. She only had $5,000 as seed money. "I was so young when I started the company—there was no thought of failure," she reported to the *Houston Post*.

The company, Cole Chemical, quickly found its niche. Four years later in 1984, Cole began another company, Cole Distribution, a warehousing and customer service corporation to complement the expansion of Cole Chemical. These enterprises eventually combined to become Cole Chemical and Distributing, Inc., which specializes in distributing chemicals used by the food, electronic, plastic, oil, chemical automotive, coatings, beverages, paper, textile, gas, and personal care product industries. The independent distributor operates nationwide from its Houston facilities and leased warehouses across the country in conjunction with its suppliers' plants, terminals, warehouses, and exchange agreements.

The company now employs more than 20 people and has annual sales of more than $25 million. And although Cole had dropped out of college in the 1970s, she has continued her advanced education with Minority Businesses Executive Program (MBEP) offered through Darmouth College's Tuck School of Business. Cole has participated in five-day intensive workshops with the school several times and also has served as the Tuck MBEP Alumni Association president. She's been associated with the National Federation of Independent Businesses and the Association of Chemical Industries of Texas and has been on the boards of numerous organizations, including the National Association of Women Business Owners, Houston Business Council, and Asian Pacific American Chamber of Commerce.

Such opportunities have enabled Cole to keep abreast of her field and grow her company. "Our core competency is giving great customer service, being responsive to customer needs while being a logistics

*Donna Fujimoto Cole*

provider," she explained in an interview with Tuck's MBEP.

Cole has also been recognized as one of the top minority and women-owned businesses in Houston. In 1991, she was chosen by President George Bush to serve on his Export Council.

Philanthropy has also been an integral part of Cole's life; she has served as a Girl Scout leader and a volunteer with the Small Business Administration, the American Heart Association, and the American Cancer Society.

## Sources

"Donna Cole: Leveraging Her Formula for Success." *Tuck Minority Business Executive Programs.* http://www.tuck-mbep.org. [accessed June 5, 2001].

"History." *Cole Chemical & Distributing, Inc.* Web site http://www.colechem.com/history.htm [accessed June 5, 2001].

Roberts, Raequel, and Erika Fiske. November 22, 1987. "Donna Fujimoto Cole." *Houston Post:* 11G.

"Transpacific 100: Asian American Entrepreneurs." October 1996. *Transpacific:* 22+ .

*49*

# D

## Yen Ngoc Do

Yen Ngoc Do. Photo by Eugene Garcia/*The Orange County Register*

**Born**: 1940, Vietnam.

**Positions Held**: Reporter, Saigon, Vietnam, c. 1960s–70s; founder of *Nguoi Viet* newspaper, San Diego, California (later moved to Santa Ana, California, and then Westminster, California), 1978– ; publisher, *Nguoi Viet Daily News*, Westminster, California, 1994–2001.

**Awards, Honors**: Sky Dunlap Award for Lifetime Achievement, Orange County Press Club, 1999; Lifetime Achievement Award, Asian American Journalists Association, 2001.

**Summary**: Yen Nguoc Do, known for his balanced journalism practices, launched the first Vietnamese-language daily newspaper in the United States from his home with $4,000 in savings in 1978. The former Saigon journalist, who was once on a death list by an unidentified political group, has overseen the growth of the company, which has $1 million in assets and 18,000 subscribers.

### Early Years

Do was raised in Vietnam during and immediately following World War II. When he was 12 years old, he worked for an underground high school student newspaper. Shortly thereafter, he participated in student protests demanding that the government improve school conditions and provide more scholarships. As public dissent was outlawed in Vietnam at the time, Do was arrested and suspended from school.

## Career Highlights

Although he was drafted, the military rejected Do because of his extreme near-sightedness. Do went on to work as a war correspondent for newspapers in Saigon in the 1960s. He also served as an interpreter for U.S. and French journalists.

In 1975, Do, his wife, and three children were part of the first wave of Vietnamese refugees fleeing to the United States. They landed in Camp Pendleton, Orange County, where Do worked as a dishwasher at a local fast-food restaurant before relocating to Texas. Three years later, he read about the upcoming second wave of refugees—100,000 of them due to arrive in Orange County—and realized that there would be [a] large demand for news in the Vietnamese language. "The boat people are starting over with nothing," he explained in an interview with the *Los Angeles Times* (13 April 1997). "This was an opportunity to chronicle history. I decided to get back into journalism. I left Texas with the intention of starting [a] newspaper."

Do moved his family, which now included a fourth child born in Texas, to San Diego, California. Borrowing a Western-style typewriter from a colleague who owned a Vietnamese monthly magazine, Do translated stories from mainstream newspapers; he had to add Vietnamese accent marks by hand. On December 6, 1978, he launched the first issue of *Nguoi Viet*, or *Vietnamese People*, with the banner headline announcing that 100,000 refugees would be airlifted from Southeast Asia. Two thousand issues of the weekly were printed with an initial investment of only $4,000. Two months later, the Do family moved to Santa Ana in Orange County. They shared a two-bedroom apartment with 10 other newspaper colleagues, who worked out of the garage to create more issues of *Nguoi Viet*.

The newspaper's popularity and circulation continued to grow. In the beginning, the newspaper featured stories aiding immigrants in acclimating to American life, in addition to profiles about Vietnamese Americans. By 1993, *Nguoi Viet* was published six days a week for 12,000 subscribers. The company, which now supported 30 employees, established its headquarters in Westminster, the core of the Vietnamese community in Southern California. As the newspaper's editor-in-chief since its inception and publisher since 1994, Do was known for his balanced approach to covering controversial issues, specifically the normalization of U.S. trade relations with Vietnam's communist government. "To write news, to chronicle events, is to have power, and with power comes responsibility," Do said to the *Los Angeles Times*.

In spite of its neutral position, *Nguoi Viet* still found itself the target of right-wing protests. When a television station connected with the newspaper inadvertently broadcast an image of Vietnam's communist flag, extremists firebombed one of the *Nguoi Viet* delivery trucks in 1989. In 1994, Do resigned as editor-in-chief after comments he made regarding a Vietnamese American doctor's controversial trade mission to Hanoi brought out 200 demonstrators to the newspaper's offices in Westminster. Boycotts were also threatened. Do continued as publisher, however, and by 2000, *Nguoi Viet* was stronger than ever with a daily circulation of 15,000 and a Sunday issue of 48 pages.

When Do officially retired in 2001 for health reasons, the newspaper had 18,000 subscribers with the largest classified ad sections among all Vietnamese newspapers in the world. Do's company is associated with a radio station, as well as other Vietnamese newspapers in Canada, Australia, France, Seattle, San Jose, Boston, San

Diego, Dallas, Orlando, and Houston. It also has a branch office in San Gabriel in Los Angeles County.

Observers have said that *Nguoi Viet* has inspired the launching of at least 50 other Vietnamese periodicals, radio stations, and television stations in the United States. One of Do's four children, Anh, has followed in her father's footsteps—an experienced journalist, she is a columnist on Vietnamese issues for the *Orange County Register*.

### Sources

Dizon, Lily. 13 April 1997. "On Neutral Ground." *Los Angeles Times* (Orange County Edition): 1+ .

Gittelsohn, John. 7 August 2001. "Local Vietnamese Editor Honored." *Orange County Register*.

Hong, Binh Ha. 8 December 2000. "Vietnamese Fete Paper's 22 Years." *Orange County Register*: 1+ .

Lait, Matt. 30 September 1994. "Readers' Ire Spurs Editor's Resignation at *Nguoi Viet*." *Los Angeles Times* (Orange County Edition): 1+.

*Nguoi Viet Daily News*. www.nguoi-viet.com [accessed November 13, 2001].

# Kanetaro Domoto

**Born**: c. 1860s, Tanaka, Wakayama, Japan.

**Education**: English studies, San Francisco, California.

**Positions Held**: Partner, Domoto Brothers, Oakland, California (later moved to Hayward, California), 1885–1930s, president, California Flower Market, 1917–19.

**Awards, Honors**: Commercial Award, American Horticultural Society, 1975.

**Summary**: Kanetaro Domoto, an immigrant from Wakayama Prefecture, Japan, was among a group of brothers who pioneered both the flower-growing and nursery industries in the United States. The
Domoto Brothers' "New Ranch," established in 1902 in Oakland, California, was the first large-scale Japanese nursery in the United States. They also introduced flowers such as the Coral Bells azalea to America as early as 1917.

### Early Years

Domoto was the third son of Kaichiro Domoto, a large landowner in Tanka, Wakayama Prefecture, located in southeastern Japan. In 1884, his second oldest brother, Takanoshin, traveled to the United States with an Englishman who wanted to export fruit trees from Japan. At the time, there were only 100 Japanese nationals in the San Francisco area. A year later, in 1885, Domoto followed his older brother to America.

### Career Highlights

Domoto first began working as a "schoolboy" for a European American family. A schoolboy attended classes while also serving as a domestic helper. His brother, on the other hand, secured a position at the Golden State House, a boardinghouse, where he stayed for 15 years.

Domoto left his position as a schoolboy to try his hand in a lumber mill in Seattle, Washington. Later he returned to San Francisco and became an assistant to the head gardener of an estate owned by the Sutro family. In late December 1885, the Domoto brothers pooled their money and rented a piece of land in Oakland, California, and began a small nursery. Domoto held a part-time job while growing carnations and chrysanthemums and selling them on street corners. Also living in Oakland was Hiroshi Yoshiike, an immigrant from the Nagano prefecture who had been the first Japanese in America to commercially grow chrysanthemums.

Other Domoto brothers—Motonoshin and Mitsunoshin—came over from Japan to help with the nursery enterprise. Finally, in 1892, they purchased two acres of land—perhaps the first agricultural land owned by Japanese in the Bay Area, perhaps anywhere in the United States. Two years later, the Domoto brothers had expanded by another two acres. The Domotos not only produced cut flowers; they also imported ornamental plants from Japan, Australia, and Europe. World Fairs and the Japanese Tea Garden in San Francisco's Golden Gate Park further fueled interest in exotic plants.

The Domotos were also influential in supporting other Japanese immigrants to enter the trade. From 1892 and particularly every year following, Domoto traveled to his hometown of Tanaka, Wakayama, and brought back a young man who would join the nursery business. Soon the Domoto Brothers Nursery was known as "Domoto College" because they trained so many Japanese immigrants in the ins-and-outs of rose production, plant-growing cultural practices, viruses, and pests. Another aspect of the nursery business was, of course, sales. Domoto sold flowers in his dry goods store, Domoto Shokai, in San Francisco. More important was the open air market for wholesalers. Every Wednesday and Friday, the Domotos sent out a wagon filled with not only their flowers, but also the products of other Oakland-based growers.

Eventually, the Domoto Brothers' steady stream of business convinced an Oakland bank to give them a loan. In November 1902, they purchased an attractive piece of land at the foot of the Oakland Hills. Referred to as "New Ranch," the 35-acre operation was the first large-scale nursery in the United States. At the time, the Domoto Brothers offered 230 varieties of chrysanthemums and 50 types of ever-blooming tea roses, which were shipped all across the country and marketed through their own publication, *Descriptive Catalogue of Novelties.*

By 1906, after the San Francisco earthquake, it became evident to the Domoto brothers that an indoor wholesale market should be established. Organizing the California Flower Growers Association, they finally located a storefront in an alley in San Francisco in 1909. Joining with Chinese and Italian growers, the Japanese quickly outgrew their space and finally, in 1912, incorporated as the California Flower Market. The corporation's first president was the oldest Domoto brother, Motonoshin. Domoto became president in 1917 and served in that capacity for two years.

The 1915 Panama-Pacific Exposition in San Francisco led to the Domoto Brothers' involvement with Kurume azaleas. This type of azalea was introduced to the United States for the first time at the exposition. In 1917, the Domotos traveled to the village of Kurume in southern Japan and began to import the plants for the American market. The Domotos named one of the Kurume pink azaleas "Coral Bells," which is also known as "Daybreak." The brothers were also the first in Northern California to commercially raise camellias, wisterias, spear flowers, and lily bulbs, all imported from Japan.

After World War II, the Domoto Brothers Nursery moved to Hayward, California. In 1975, the nursery was honored with the American Horticulture Society's Commercial Award.

## Sources

Kawaguchi, Gary. 1993. *Living with Flowers: The California Flower Market History.* San Francisco, CA: California Flower Market, Inc.

Yagasaki, Noritaka. 1992. *Ethnic Cooperativism and Immigrant Agriculture: A Study of Japanese Floriculture and Truck Farming in California.* Doctoral dissertation in geography, University of California, Berkeley.

# F

## Eddie Flores Jr.

**Born**: 19 December 1946, Hong Kong.

**Education**: University of Hawaii, Manoa, Hawaii, B.A. in business administration, 1970; University of Oklahoma, Tulsa, Oklahoma, M.A. in liberal studies, 1987.

**Positions Held**: Loan officer, Bank of Hawaii, Honolulu, Hawaii, 1970–73; founder, president, Sun Pacific Realty, Honolulu, Hawaii, 1973– ; president, L&L Franchise, Inc. Honolulu, Hawaii, 1991– .

**Awards, Honors**: Hawaii Small Business Person of the Year (with partner Kwok Yum Kam), U.S. Small Business Administration, 1998; Distinguished Alumni Awards, University of Hawaii, 1999; Entrepreneur of the Year Award, Filipino Chamber of Commerce of Hawaii.

**Summary**: Pedro Flores Jr. and his partner were one of the first restaurateurs in Hawaii to incorporate the local concept of "plate lunches" into a chain operation. L&L Drive-Inn, which offers combination meals of Asian-style meats, rice, and macaroni salad, has franchises throughout Hawaii, California, and Oregon.

### Early Years

Flores was born in Hong Kong to a Chinese mother, Margaret Lum, and a Filipino father, Eduardo Flores. At the age of 16, he came to the mainland United States and attended high school in San Francisco before moving to Hawaii. During high school, Flores was influenced by a book written by a real estate executive. "It convinced me that money is made in real estate," he told *Hawaii Business* (1 February 1997).

### Higher Education and Career Highlights

Flores studied business administration at the University of Hawaii at Manao. After graduating in 1970, he participated in a two-year management training program at the Bank of Hawaii. However, his early interest in real estate inspired him to obtain a license to sell properties, and by 1973, he had already opened his own business, Sun Pacific Realty, in Honolulu.

While Flores toiled to make his brokerage business successful, his mother, Margaret Flores, was working hard at a local Island eatery, Patti's Chinese Kitchen Ala Moana. In 1975, Flores purchased a restaurant, L&L Drive-Inn, located on Liliha

Street in Honolulu, only a block from the Flores home, for his mother for $22,000. The original L&L was a hamburger stand established in 1959 at the end of the Honolulu Trolley route from downtown Honolulu. The landowner at that time was L&L Dairy, hence the name of L&L.

In time, Flores' mother needed help during the night shift, and Flores recruited his soccer buddy, Kwock Yum "Johnson" Kam, a native of Macao, who was working for Kaiser Foundation Health Plan and operating a lunch-catering truck. From its inception, L&L offered "mini-plates" and a variety of mixed plates—including chicken *katsu* (Japanese-style fried chicken) and barbecued short ribs, along with two scoops of rice and a large scoop of macaroni salad—a popular combination among Hawaiians. However, according to *Hawaii Business* (1 February 1997), neither Kam nor Flores' mother knew how to cook for mass consumption. They needed to learn how to buy in volume, budget, and manage employees. By 1979, the operation was grossing $600 a day in sales, and another L&L Drive-Inn was opened. A third location was launched shortly thereafter.

Margaret eventually retired in 1980, and Kam bought Flores' share of the business for $40,000. During the 1980s, Kam continued to hone L&L's menu and open new locations. Flores, meanwhile, had gotten married to Elaine Soohoo and was pursuing his master's degree in liberal studies from the University of Oklahoma while also building his real-estate empire in Hawaii. He wrote books, including *How to Buy and Sell Business Opportunities* (1987), and taught real estate, investments, management, travel, and business appraisal courses throughout the University of Hawaii educational system.

In 1988, Kam approached Flores about reestablishing his connection to L&L. The restaurant needed capital and real estate expertise to expand to the next level. As president of L&L Franchise, Inc., Flores was able to implement both an effective financing and marketing campaign, while Kam continued to be in charge of operations.

According to *Hawaii Business*, "L&L Drive-Inns began sprouting like mushrooms after a rainstorm." By 1993, there were 14 restaurants and four year later, that number grew to 26 with an expanded menu of seven types of plate lunches, 40 hot entrees, and 10 different sandwiches.

Sales had also steadily risen an average of 28 percent a year through the 1990s; in 1995, the company had $6.2 million in revenue. The highest grossing outlet was the Airport Trade Center with annual sales of $1 million that year.

L&L's franchise structure is unique. Each franchise is a separate corporation with a special ownership structure, lease agreements, and management responsibilities. Franchises are only sold to employees, and some employees have even purchased restaurants outright. Such sales help finance further expansion of the business. "Take care of your employees, and your employees will take care of you," Flores said to *Small Business Magazine* (Volume XII). "The key is decentralization. When employees run the restaurants on their own, they make them successful."

Shared are the menu, brand name, and marketing expenses. As part of the franchise agreement, independent outlets pay L&L Franchise one percent of gross receipts.

Limited growth opportunities in Hawaii forced Flores to offer new concepts and to expand in the mainland United States. In 1997, he opened the first L&L Steak and Pizza location in Pearl City, Hawaii, and an Italia Café at the Airport Trade Center in

Honolulu. He has also diversified into Chinese food with Chopsticks Express restaurants. In October 1999, he established the first L&L Hawaiian Barbecue in the City of Industry in southern California, followed by more mainland outlets, including one in Hillsboro, Oregon. By 2001, L&L had more than 50 restaurants throughout the nation.

Doing business in Hawaii has not been trouble-free for Flores. In 1999, 11 federal lawsuits, initiated by disabled-rights attorney Lunsford Dole Phillips, were filed against L&L for violations of the Americans with Disabilities Act (ADA). Four of the cases were dismissed, but Flores was ordered to pay for repairs at his restaurants to comply with the ADA and to compensate Phillips for large legal costs. As most of ADA lawsuits are settled out of court, this case generated widespread publicity in both Hawaii and the restaurant business community. "Our intent was to fully comply and not fight," Flores, who maintained that lawyers were unfairly targeting small businesses, said to *Restaurant Business* (15 August 2000). "Yet, when you have people trying to get you for money, what choice do you have but to fight? That's ambulance chasing."

Flores has been very active in philanthropy and civic service in Hawaii. He has served on the boards of the Goodwill Industries of Honolulu, American Red Cross Hawaii chapter, and Aloha United Way. He has also assisted the Filipino Community Center in Honolulu, which serves the large yet neglected Filipino population in Hawaii. Regarding philanthropy, Flores was quoted in *Pacific Business News* (10 December 1999): "Unless you're successful, making money, and being profitable, you can't do that. That's very important, how much you pay back to the community."

Flores and his wife Elaine have two daughters, Elisia and Ellice.

## Sources

Campos, Frellie. 18 May 1998. "L&L Owners Take Top SBA Honor." *Pacific Business News*: B8.

Engle, Erika. 10 December 1999. "L&L's Eddie Flores: Mover, Shaker, Newsmaker." *Pacific Business News*.

Gomes, Andrew. 10 October 1997. "L&L Drive-Inn Testing Pizza & Steak Concept." *Pacific Business News*.

L&L Drive-Inn Web site. www.lldriveinn.com [accessed November 30, 2001].

Salkever, Alex. 1 February 1997. "Feeding Frenzy." *Hawaii Business*: 31+ .

"Top Level Advice on Improving Your Bottom Line: Your Profitability Strategies from the Owners of Some Exceptionally Successful Small Businesses." *Small Business Success* (Volume XII).

University of Hawaii press release. 13 April 1999. "UH Announces 1999 Distinguished Alumni Awards, Recipients to be Honored at Dinner May 26."

# Pedro Flores

**Born**: c. 1899, Vintar, Philippines.

**Death**: Unknown.

**Education**: High School of Commerce, San Francisco, California, 1919–1920; University of California at Berkeley and Hastings College of Law, San Francisco State University, law studies, c. 1920s.

**Positions Held**: Founder of Yo-Yo Manufacturing Company, Santa Barbara, California, 1928; founder of Flores Yo-Yo Corporation, Hollywood, California, c. 1929; cofounder of Flores and Stone, Los Angeles, California, c. 1929; promoter of yo-yo contests, Duncan Yo-Yo Company, c. 1930s; cofounder, Chico Yo-Yo Company, c. 1950; and founder, Flores Corp. of America, 1954.

**Summary**: Pedro Flores, an immigrant from the Philippines, adopted a toy from his native land for the American market, calling it a "yo-yo"—Tagalog for "come-come." After establishing yo-yo factories in the late 1920s in California, Flores eventually sold his interest in his companies to Donald Duncan Yo-Yo Company for, reportedly, $250,000 during the depths of the economic depression.

## Early Years

Flores was from Ilocos Norte province in the Philippines. In the era in which Flores was born, relations between the United States and Philippines were in turmoil. As a result of the Spanish-American War, the islands of the Philippines were ceded to the U.S. government in 1898. A war of resistance against U.S. rule, now referred to as the Philippines-American War, broke out in 1899. By 1901 the resistance had largely died out, and the United States maintained civil rule.

As a result of governmental reorganization, Flores' hometown of Vintar, which had been struggling financially, was annexed to another city. In 1909, however, this agricultural city was able to declare its independence as a municipality.

In 1915, during these political and economic transitions, Flores emigrated to the United States and enrolled in San Francisco's High School of Commerce.

## Higher Education

Flores studied law at the University of California at Berkeley and Hastings College of Law in San Francisco. He did not, however, complete his studies and instead dropped out to move to Santa Barbara, California.

## Career Highlights

In Santa Barbara, Flores worked at various odd jobs. He was working as a bellhop at a hotel when he was demonstrating a toy that he had carved out of wood during his lunch break. It was fashioned in the style of a toy popular in the Philippines and commonly called a *yo-yo*, or "come-come" in the Filipino language of Tagalog. This toy—round disks attached to string—can be traced back to the ancient Greek culture. In the United States, before the impact of Flores, it was only known by its French name, *bandalore*, or return wheel.

After hearing a story about a man who made a million dollars by selling a ball attached to a rubber band, Flores began considering the potential market for the yo-yo. According to *Lucky's Collectors Guide to 20th Century Yo-Yos: History & Values*, Flores had said, "I do not expect to make a million dollars, I just want to be working for myself. I have been working for other people for practically all my life and I don't like it."

He solicited financing for his project, and was first met with skepticism, especially from his friends. That did not deter him from applying for a business certificate to produce yo-yos. On June 9, 1928, at the age of 29, he was officially certified to conduct business as the Yo-Yo Manufacturing Company in Santa Barbara. He carved a dozen yo-yos by hand and began selling them to neighborhood children. By November 1928, his company had sold 2,000 yo-yos. With capital from two Los Angeles investors, James and Daniel Stone, Flores was able to mechanize his factory. Four months later, his company had produced more than 100,000 yo-yos.

Employing Dorothy Carter as his chief designer, Flores released various versions of his product. Some of his yo-yo strings were made of silk. Prices ranged from 15 cents to $1.50. By November 1929, Flores had established two additional factories: Flores Yo-Yo Corporation in Hollywood, and Flores and Stone in Los Angeles.

Instrumental to the success of his company were yo-yo spinning contests, which heralded the Flores Yo-Yo as "The Wonder Toy." It was at this time that the slogan, "If it isn't Flores, it isn't a yo-yo," was used. These contests, which were held in theatres, gave prizes to the entrant who could either continuously spin a yo-yo for the longest duration or throw a yo-yo the farthest distance with complete return.

Although the concept of a yo-yo had already been patented as an "improved bandalore" by two men from Ohio in 1866, Flores did register the Flores Yo-Yo as a trademark on July 22, 1930. Shortly thereafter entrepreneur and inventor Donald F. Duncan, who had first become acquainted with the yo-yo while on a business trip in California, bought Flores' business for a reported $250,000, considered a fortune during the depths of the depression. (Duncan had invented the Eskimo Pie, originated the Good Humor ice cream truck, and successfully marketed the first parking meter.)

Flores stayed on with the Duncan company to promote the product through demonstrations and contests. A number of Filipinos, including Joseph Radovan, Flores' childhood friend from the Philippines, were hired to perform yo-yo tricks on tour throughout the United States, Europe, and Latin America. In the 1930s Radovan opened his own enterprise, Royal Tops Manufacturing Company, in Long Island, New York, which eventually produced the Royal Yo-Yo.

After World War II Flores assisted Radovan to launch a new line of yo-yos, the Chico Yo-Yo before founding Flores Corporation of America in 1954. Not much is known of Flores after this time, but the name, "yo-yo" became a legal issue in the 1960s when Donald F. Duncan, Inc. sued Radovan's Royal Tops Manufacturing for trademark infringement. In 1965 it was decided that "yo-yo" was indeed a generic term and could be freely used by any company.

Yo-yo aficionados remember Flores' contributions to the development of the yo-yo; a genuine original Flores Yo-Yo from the 1920s can command up to $1,000.

### Sources

"Duncan Yo-Yo History." *Official Duncan Yo-Yo Website.* http://yo-yo.com/history/duncan_history_2.html. [accessed August 26, 2001]

Meisenheimer, Lucky J. 1999. *Lucky's Collectors Guide to 20th Century Yo-Yos: History & Values.* Orlando, Fl.: Lucky J.'s Swim & Surf, Inc.

"Royal Story: Joseph T. Radovan." *Royal Yo-Yo.* http://royalyo-yo.com/royalpages/royalhist.html. [accessed August 27, 2001]

# Fritz Friedman

**Full Name at Birth**: Edwin Fritz Friedman.

**Born**: 23 March 1950, Manila, Philippines.

**Education**: Vassar College, Poughkeepsie, New York, B.A. in East Asian Studies, 1974; University of Pennsylvania, Philadelphia, Pennsylvania, M.A. in communications, 1982.

**Positions Held**: Managerial assistant, Columbia Artists Management Company, New York City, New York, 1976–79; production manager, Dick Young Productions, New York City, New York, 1979–80; marketing executive, Columbia Pictures Home Entertainment (later RCA-Columbia Pictures Home Entertainment), New York City, New York (later transferred to Burbank, California), 1980– ; vice president of publicity, RCA-Columbia Pictures Home Video, Burbank, California, 1989– ; senior vice president of worldwide publicity, Columbia TriStar Home Video, Culver City, California, 1992– ; senior vice president of worldwide publicity, Columbia Tristar Home Entertainment, 1998–.

**Awards, Honors:** Executive of the Year, Asian American Legal Defense Organization, 1998: Corporate Leader Award, *Filipinas Magazine*, 1999.

**Summary:** Fritz Friedman is one of the highest ranking Filipino Americans in the corporate entertainment industry. As the senior vice president of worldwide publicity for three divisions of Sony Pictures Entertainment, he oversees the publicity campaigns of the divisions, theatrical releases, video products, corporate communications, and special events.

### Early Years

Friedman was born in Manila, the Philippines. His father, Dr. Frederick Friedman, was an anesthesiologist of Austrian and Filipino descent. (Frederick's father, originally from Austria, had been drafted during the Spanish American War after moving to New York and was subsequently sent to the Philippines where he remained after the war.) Friedman's mother, Catalina Cornista, was a registered nurse from the town of Jaro in the Philippines. When Friedman was a child, the family moved to Massachusetts, where Frederick had accepted a position at Boston University Medical Center. Friedman attended the Cathedral School in Boston and then Boston College High School, a Jesuit educational institution. After graduation, Friedman returned to Manila for two years.

### Higher Education

Friedman entered the first male class at the previously all-women's school, Vassar College, in Poughkeepsie, New York, and eventually majored in East Asian Studies. In 1974, he was the first Asian American man to graduate from Vassar. He later pursued graduate studies at the Annenberg School of Communications at the University of Pennsylvania, where he eventually submitted a master's thesis on messages within disco music.

### Career Highlights

One of Friedman's first jobs after college was as an usher at Carnegie Hall in New York City. He was soon elevated to a position backstage, in which he took care of visiting artists, such as Leonard Bernstein and opera star Pavarotti. His connections led to a job at Columbia Artists Management, the largest classical music management company in the United States. As an assistant manager from 1976 to 1979, Friedman handled prominent artists such as Yehudi Menuhin and the Royal Ballet of Flanders. After this position he worked temporary jobs and also served as a production manager with Dick Young Productions.

In 1980, Friedman was offered a job in the marketing division of the newly created Columbia Pictures Home Entertainment in New York City, which would herald the beginning of Friedman's illustrious career with the company. After his first year, he was transferred to the office in Southern California. His duties as a marketing and public relations executive ranged from promoting a video documenting the recording of the popular "We Are the World" single, a fund-raiser for USA for Africa, to leading innovative campaigns for video releases of films that might have performed poorly in the theater.

From 1980 to 1989, Friedman rose steadily through the studio's marketing ranks and helped to expand its home video division, a profitable unit that netted nearly $700 million in 1990. During this time, the corporation also went through changes—becoming RCA-Columbia Pictures Home Video in 1983. In 1989, Friedman was promoted to vice president of publicity. Two years later, the company was renamed Columbia TriStar Home Video when Columbia's parent company, Sony Corporation, acquired NBC's interest in the RCA-Columbia joint venture.

In 1992, Friedman became vice president of worldwide publicity for Columbia TriStar Home Video (CTHV), and in 1997, its office moved to the new Sony Pictures home office in Culver City, California. In this position, Friedman has been responsible for all worldwide publicity activities for the company's theatrical releases, video products, corporate communications, and special events, such as the Academy Awards galas.

With the rising popularity of DVDs in the early twenty-first century and the importance of "sell-through," or direct sales, the home video market has been undergoing a transformation. Popular titles, such as *Jerry Maguire*, *Men in Black*, and *My Best Friend's Wedding*, were instrumental in catapulting the company, now known as Columbia Tristar Home Entertainment (CTHE) to the position of one of the top four distributors of home video products in 1997. Also important was the sell-through release of the family movie, *The Indian in the Cupboard*, which was specially packaged with a toy figure, in 1995. The company further strengthened its children's offerings by forging a five-year distribution agreement with Jim Henson Pictures, the creators of the Muppet movies.

One example of his creative publicity campaigns involved the 2000 release of the classic movie, *Mr. Smith Goes to Washington*. CTHE and *George* magazine cosponsored a special screening at the Palace Theater in Manchester, New Hampshire, in conjunction with the presidential primaries being held there. A second screening was held in Washington, D.C., for 550 press secretaries of current U.S. senators and congressmen.

Friedman is also involved in philanthropy and community service. He has been active in AIDS Project Los Angeles, the second largest AIDS organization in the United States, and the Asian American AIDS Committee in Los Angeles. Friedman has a personal connection to the disease because his mother become contaminated with the HIV virus during her nursing duties at Boston University Hospital. She died in 1989.

In 1998, Friedman was named to the newly created position of senior vice president of worldwide publicity. In addition to overseeing all publicity for CTHE's activities in its 13 operating territories and 60 licenses, he also heads worldwide publicity for two other divisions of Sony Pictures Entertainment: Sony Pictures Releasing, and Sony Digital Studios. While conceiving campaigns for *Crouching Tiger, Hidden Dragon* and *Charlie's Angels* for CTHE, Friedman has also been involved in promoting the Japanese animation film, *Metrop* and the re-release of Barbra Streisand's classic, *Funny Girl*.

Friedman, a board member for the L.A. Independent Film Festival and a Jesuit film company called Loyola Productions, also helped to organize the Coalition of Asian/Pacifics in Entertainment (CAPE), a network of 600 Asian Americans in film, television, and music. In 1993, some 40 to 50 young Asian Americans were estimated to be working in junior executive positions in studios and at production companies. "Our early successes are proof that your ethnicity does not necessarily hold you back," Friedman stated to the *Los Angeles Times* (13 May 1993). "At the same time, there certainly are not enough Asian Americans and other ethnic groups in management."

He also has been involved with groups seeking American citizenship and veterans' benefits for Filipino American soldiers who fought on behalf of the United States in World War II. Chairman emeritus of the Asian American Alumni of Vassar College, Friedman is also president of the Filipino American Library.

## Sources

Biography provided by Fritz Friedman, March 2002.

Crisostomo, Isabelo T. 1996. *Filipino Achievers in the USA & Canada: Profiles in Excellence*. Naperville, IL: Bookhaus Publishers.

"Fritz Friedman." *ABC Flash*. www.abcflash. com/template/apaent/apaent5.html [accessed November 26, 2001].

Goodridge, Mike. 5 June 2001. "Equal Opportunity?" *The Advocate*: 48–50.

Hunt, Dennis. 28 June 1985. "New 'We Are the World' Cassette Likely to Be Hit." *Los Angeles Times*: 17.

Iwata, Edward. 13 May 1993. "Asian Movies Take Flight; Filmmakers Making Move into the Mainstream." *Los Angeles Times*: 1+ .

Wilson, Wendy. 7 February 2000. "Columbia TriStar, George Partner for Mr. Smith Promo." *Video Business*: 25.

# G

## Sue Ling Gin

**Born**: 23 September 1941, Aurora, Illinois.

**Education**: Aurora College, Aurora, Illinois, 1959; DePaul University, Chicago, Illinois, circa 1960s.

**Positions Held**: Copartner and cofounder, Urban Search Corp., Chicago, Illinois, c. 1968–78; investor and copartner, Café Bernard, Chicago, Illinois; 1972– ; cofounder, owner, chief executive officer of New Management Ltd., Chicago, Illinois, c. 1978– ; chairman and chief executive officer, Flying Food Fare (parent company Flying Food Group, Inc.) Chicago, Illinois, 1983– .

**Awards, Honors**: Women of Achievement Award, Anti-Defamation League, 1994; Infinitec National Leadership Award, Infinitec, 2001.

**Summary**: Sue Ling Gin, the daughter of Chinese restaurateurs in Illinois, launched a successful airline catering business that now has customers in Shanghai. The widow of the late William G. McGowan, the founder of MCI, Gin also is involved in real estate development in the Chicago area.

### Early Years and Education

Born in the Chicago suburb of Aurora, Illinois, Gin was the youngest child of two immigrants from Canton who had started a Chinese restaurant called the Paradise Inn. The Gin family was one of the few Chinese households in the area in the 1940s. When Gin was 10, her father died unexpectedly, so her older brother Richard had to take over the restaurant business at the age of 19. Eventually the Paradise Inn was sold and Richard was drafted into the U.S. Army during the Korean War. As a result, Gin had to work after school and on the weekends, but she still managed to be active at East Aurora High School. She was a member of the Junior Red Cross and a cheerleader.

Her brother Richard first involved Gin in real estate when she was 17 years old. They purchased a house that was set for demolition and moved it to a lot about three miles away. The house was converted into a six-unit apartment complex, which Richard continued to own and manage more than 30 years later.

After graduating from high school, Gin enrolled in the local college, Aurora College. After a semester she dropped out to pursue work in Chicago.

## Career Highlights

In Chicago Gin began a job as a waitress at the Chicago Playboy Club. Being a Playboy Bunny enabled Gin to gain capital for future investments, build business networks, and sharpen her administrative skills. While working for the club, Gin trained other waitresses and even wrote training manuals. After four years, Gin wanted to pursue other professional opportunities and worked for an insurance broker selling life insurance while taking courses at DePaul University for a year and a half. She then segued to real estate as a condominium salesperson for Dunbar Builders. At that time, in the 1960s, the concept of a condominium was new, yet Gin became the company's top salesperson.

In the late 1960s, Gin entered a partnership with other former employees of Dunbar to begin Urban Search Corp., a Chicago-based company which specialized in developing, managing, and buying condominium conversions. Around 1978, Gin sold her share of the partnership and started her own independent enterprise, New Management Ltd., intended to manage and develop Gin's personal properties. Among Gin's investments in the 1970s was a building at 2100 N. Halstead in the gentrifying Lincoln Park area for $40,000. Partnering with chef Bernard LeCoq, Gin invested in a French restaurant at the location, Café Bernard.

A breakfast meal on Midway Airlines in the early 1980s changed the course of Gin's future. Biting into a sweet roll, Gin discovered that it was still partially frozen. She then wrote a letter to the chairman of Midway Airlines, telling him that she could provide better food than his present caterers. She was later invited to give a presentation and submit a bid on the airline's total food contract. "I managed to convince him that it would be to his advantage to use a Chicago-based company to serve

his Chicago-based airline," stated Gin (*Chicago Tribune*, 14 November 1993).

The million-dollar contract was Gin's entry into the in-flight catering business. In 1983 she founded Flying Food Fare; she also continued to invest in new restaurants and development projects. Her personal life also went through a major transition: in 1985, Gin married William G. McGowan, the founder of MCI, who had been embroiled in an anti-trust lawsuit against AT&T.

In 1988, Gin forged an alliance with tenants in Chicago's LeClaire Courts housing project, who had formed a small company that prepared meals, mostly for local day-care centers, to bid on a $38-million food-and-beverage contract for Chicago's secondary airport, Midway. The partnership was successful—and Flying Food Fare was now positioned to take over a major share of the 22 snack concessions. By 1990, Flying Food Fare had expanded to O'Hare International Airport, as well as to airports in Seattle and Minneapolis. Among Gin's clients were Air France, Belgium's Sabena, Spain's Iberia, and American-European Express trains operating from Chicago to New York and Washington. Midway Airlines, however, still comprised 80 percent of Flying Food Fare's business.

As a result, the bankruptcy of Midway Airlines in 1991 was sure to affect Flying Food Fare. Gin, who was owed $1.2 million from Midway Airlines, had to reduce her staff from 250 to 25. "The first week was devastating," she told the *Chicago Tribune* (5 December 1993). "Everyone was dealing with first things first, like their anger and placing blame. Some people jumped ship. We were seeing a lot of negative feelings. I thought I grew warts all over my body. I didn't want to see anybody, talk to anybody."

Tragedy continued for Gin, this time on a personal front. Her mother died in February 1992, followed by the death of her husband William McGowan in June 1992. Nonetheless, Gin was determined to keep Flying Food Fare financially afloat, without selling off her $40 million of real estate investments.

The company was restructured to be divided into three corporate entities to handle diverse clients: governmental agencies, jails, Amtrak, and foreign airline carriers. In addition to a facility near Midway Airport, kitchens were established near O'Hare International Airport and Seattle International Airport. By 1993 business had been restored to its pre-1991 level—$20 million in revenues.

"People say you can't learn to be an entrepreneur," she stated to the *Chicago Tribune* (5 December 1993). "But it's a process, like learning to walk. Our staff had a little success, so they'd try again. And again. And it worked. It was their company, and they made it work."

In the 1990s and early 2000s Gin continued diversifying her business, while also becoming more involved in philanthropy and civic affairs. She became a partner in a venture investigating the possibility of Chicago riverboat gambling, while also participating in special business meetings at the White House and with the governor of Illinois. She has also served on boards of various organizations, including De Paul University and Commonwealth Edison Co.

"I learned long ago never to put all my eggs in one basket," she stated to the *Chicago Tribune.*

While the in-flight catering industry is now dominated by two companies—Gate Gourmet and LSG Lufthansa Sky Chefs, Flying Food Fare continues to expand and compete. Its joint venture with Servair now provides catering services to Shanghai's new Pudong International Airport. In 2000, the Flying Food Group Inc., the parent company of Flying Food Fare, did $107 million in sales with 1,712 employees producing 45,000 meals a day for 80 largely international airlines from nine U.S. kitchens and additional catering units in China. Both Flying Food Group and New Management are headquartered in Gin's building on Sangamon Street in Chicago.

## Sources

Moore, Patricia. 5 December 1993. "Sky's the Limit for Entrepreneur Sue Ling Gin; Mellower Gin Keeps Her Edge." *Chicago Sun-Times*: People Plus, 1.

Novit, Mel. 14 November 1993. "Sue Gin; Chicago Has Truly Been the Land of Opportunity." *Chicago Tribune Sunday Magazine*: 8.

"Transpacific 100: Asian American Entrepreneurs." October 1996. *Transpacific*: 22+

# Rajat Gupta

Rajat Gupta. Photo courtesy of McKinsey & Company

**Born**: 12 December 1948, Calcutta, India.

**Education**: Indian Institute of Technology, New Delhi, India, B.S. in mechanical engineering, 1971; Harvard University, Cambridge, Massachusetts, M.B.A., 1973.

**Positions Held**: Consultant, McKinsey & Company; New York, New York, 1973; junior partner, McKinsey & Co., 1980; manager of Scandinavian operations, McKinsey & Co., Copenhagen, Denmark, 1983; manager of operations, McKinsey & Company, Chicago, Illinois, 1989; managing director, McKinsey & Company, New York City, New York, 1994–

**Summary**: In March 1994, Rajat Gupta became the first non-Western managing director of McKinsey & Company, the world's largest management consulting firm whose client list includes 100 of the 150 largest global companies. Gupta is in his third three-year term with the consulting firm.

### Early Years

Born the second of four children, Gupta was five years old when his family moved from Calcutta to New Delhi, where his father was an editor and active in India's independence movement. His father died in 1964 when Gupta was 15, and his mother, a Montessori teacher, died four years later.

By then, Gupta was studying mechanical engineering at the Indian Institute of Technology (IIT), the country's elite institution of higher learning whose graduates have gone on to become some of the most prominent chief executives, entrepreneurs, and inventors in the world. He also took part in school theater productions, where he met his future wife, Anita, an electrical engineering student.

### Higher Education

After graduating from IIT in 1971, Gupta earned a scholarship to the Harvard Business School, and was remembered as being exceptionally gifted. "Things came easily to Rajat," said one former Harvard classmate in a *New York Times* interview (22 May 1994). "He reviewed cases very easily. Even if we had tests, he would study for a time and then sit down without fail every day to write a letter to his girlfriend."

Before completing his graduate degree, Gupta was already putting his business skills into practice, helping the father of a Harvard classmate run his company more efficiently. "We packed products for private label manufacturers and ran into a very complex scheduling problem," said David Manly, owner of the Red Wing Company, which makes preserves, jellies, and condiments, in a May 1994 interview with the *New York Times*. "Rajat turned up an outstanding system that is still in use. It is called the Rajat system."

Years later, Gupta would characterize his experience integrating into the mainstream as a positive one. "You know, often people have asked me about the glass ceiling and whether I was able to assimilate well," he said in a May 2001 interview with the *Academy of Management Executive*. "I believe most of this glass ceiling is actually in our minds, and I've never truly experienced that."

### Career Highlights

Harvard M.B.A. in hand, Gupta began his job hunt in 1973. He applied for a position at McKinsey & Company, the largest and perhaps most prestigious management consulting firm in the world. McKinsey's primary mission is to help clients achieve substantial, lasting improvements in strategy, organization, and operation. Its clients include dozens of the largest global companies as well as governments, institutions, and nonprofit organizations.

When he first applied, Gupta was rejected due to a lack of experience. He then asked one of his Harvard professors to write a letter of recommendation for him. Mc-Kinsey reconsidered and hired him. One of Gupta's first assignments was to conduct a performance improvement study for a company planning to invest in a new plant. His analysis showed that the company had already underutilized capacity, although the company president did not agree with Gupta's findings. He asked Gupta to meet with all six of the plant managers, and after Gupta did, the company decided not to build the plant.

By 1980, Gupta had become a junior partner at McKinsey. A year later, he was sent to Copenhagen, Denmark, to help manage McKinsey's foothold in Scandinavia. In 1983, he became the head of Scandinavian operations, which came as a surprise to many industry leaders because such a job normally would be given to one of the firm's senior partners.

Within three years, operations grew from about 25 consultants to 100. Gupta returned to the United States in 1989 to manage the firm's Chicago practice, and drew rave reviews from clients such as Chicago's Sara Lee and the May Department Stores Company in St. Louis. All the while, Gupta, who became a U.S. citizen in 1981, was making a name for himself as a leader with an international background and the skills as a consensus builder.

He characterized his leadership qualities as an empowering one: "We have senior partners who are very much like tenured faculty; they are leaders in their own right," Gupta said in an interview with the *Academy of Management Executive* (May 2001). "One of the things I'm very fond of saying is, our firm is a firm not of leaders and followers, it's a firm of leaders. It's the quality of people we hire and how we develop them.

"That implies that the task of the managing partner is to create the right set of values, the right culture, the right environment to motivate people, and let them do what they are best at. If you can give them that kind of freedom, then I think they will do extraordinary things."

In 1994, the firm's 148 senior partners voted to name Gupta the next managing director. It put him in charge of expanding McKinsey's international reach with a staff of 3,000 consultants in 31 countries and producing revenues of $1.3 billion in 1993. "I know a number of people in McKinsey who have better records than me," Gupta told the *New York Times* in 1994. "The reason my partners picked me was because they trusted me."

During his tenure, he has steered a decentralized private partnership that has grown to 7,000 consultants worldwide, including some 900 partners. His vision for global expansion has seen the opening of nearly 50 of the firm's 84 offices while rebalancing McKinsey's client base to include leading companies of the new Internet economy. In July 2000, Gupta began his third three-year term as managing director.

Outside of McKinsey, Gupta has played a key role in establishing the Indian School of Business in Hyderabad, India, which was opened in July 2001. Along with President Bill Clinton and others, Gupta also helped set up the American India Foundation, which was formed to provide aid to the victims of the tens of thousands killed during the devastating Gujarat earthquake in January 2001.

He and his wife have four daughters.

—*By John Saito Jr.*

## Sources

Kripalani, Manjeet, with Pete Engardio, and Leah Nathans Spiro. 7 December 1998. "Whiz Kids: Inside the Indian Institutes of Technology's Star Factory." *Business Week*: 116.

Pandya, Mukul. 22 May 1994. "Triumph of the Quiet Man at McKinsey & Company." *New York Times*: 7.

Singh, Jitendra, V. May 2001. "McKinsey's Managing Director Rajat Gupta on Leading a Knowledge-Based Global Consulting Organization." *The Academy of Management Executive*.

# Vinita Gupta

Vinita Gupta. Photo courtesy of Quick Eagle Networks

**Born**: 1950, India.

**Education**: University of Roorkee, Roorkee, India, B.S. in engineering, 1973; University of California, Los Angeles, Los Angeles, California, M.A. in electrical engineering, c. 1974.

**Positions Held**: Engineer, GTE Lenkurt, San Carlos, California, 1974–78; engineering manager, Bell Northern Research (later became Nortel Semiconductors), 1978–85; cofounder, chairperson, Digital Link Corporation (later became Quick Eagle Networks), Palo Alto, California (later moved to Sunnyvale, California), 1985– .

**Awards, Honors**: Philanthropy Award, Asian Pacific Fund, 1994; Great Corporate Teams Award (Quick Eagle Networks Executive Team), Growth Leadership Center, 2001.

**Summary**: Vinita Gupta became the first East Indian American woman to launch a publicly traded company in the United States when her Silicon Valley-based telecommunications enterprise, Digital Link Corp., opened on NASDAQ in February 1994. Later she reversed her strategy and reprivatized the company, which currently operates as Quick Eagle Networks.

## Early Years

Gupta was raised in New Delhi, India in the 1950s and 1960s. Her parents encouraged her to excel in school so that she could eventually get a good job. "Instead of investing in my dowry, my parents chose to invest in my education," Gupta said, quoted in the Web site, siliconindia.com. "When it came to math and science, my parents would push and push. Even though my mother was a housewife, she would always insist on a career."

## Higher Education

Gupta studied communications and electronics at the University of Roorkee in India. The same year she graduated with a bachelor's degree in engineering, her parents introduced her to a young man, Narenda "Naren" Gupta. Naren was also well educated: he had degrees from the India Institute of Technology and California Institute of Technology in Pasadena, and was working toward his doctorate in engineering at Stanford University. Yet Gupta was not interested. "At that time I was not in a frame of mind to get married," she told *Forbes* (18 November 1996). "I was a career person."

Gupta attended graduate school at the University of California, Los Angeles. Naren, meanwhile, continued to romance Gupta and in 1974, they were married in a traditional Indian ceremony in southern California.

## Career Highlights

After gaining her master's degree in engineering, Gupta worked as an engineer for GTE Lenkurt, a division of the telecommunications giant. She remained with the company until 1978, when she joined the engineering management team at Bell Northern Research, a research and development wing of Northern Telecom. At this time, the telecommunications industry was undergoing a technological revolution. Digital lines were quickly replacing existing analog telephone lines, thereby increasing data transmission speed fourfold.

Gupta understood the vast applications of this new technology. She was eventually able to obtain two U.S. patents: one for "solid state relay" and another for the "square root circuit." In 1985, she and another colleague left Bell Northern Research to form an independent startup, Digital Link Corporation, in Palo Alto, California, adjacent to Naren's alma mater, Stanford University. "AT&T was just breaking up, and for the first time, telecommunications was wide open for firms like this," she was quoted in an article in *Working Woman* (March 1996).

Digital Link Corp. was created to design, manufacture, and market high-speed digital-access products for computer networks within telecommunications companies. Naren, who had already established his own software company, Integrated Sys-

tems, five years before, was one of Digital Link's primary financial backers and a member of the board. (Gupta, in turn, sat on the board of Integrated Systems.)

After six months, Gupta's partner quit. The staff was small; when Gupta hired her first employee, an engineer, he had no idea that he would be the only employee at Digital Link. The company's first customer immediately returned a purchased product, and for the first eight months, Digital Link lost $10,000. Yet Gupta was determined to make her fledgling venture a success. She went back to the dissatisfied customer to remedy the problem. Slowly, but surely, Digital Link began to make a profit, 20 percent of which went directly toward research and development. Soon Digital Link was working with other vendors to introduce cutting-edge equipment and standards.

"An entrepreneur faces a million challenges in growing a business," said Gupta to siliconindia.com. "The supreme test of an entrepreneur's leadership and managerial acumen is in how he/she reacts to a challenge and in the kind of decision he/she makes under pressure."

Another major test came in November 1992, when Gupta was pregnant with her second child at the age of 42. Her husband, Naren, was in a business crisis. His publicly traded company, Integrated Systems, was performing poorly compared to its years of phenomenal growth in the 1980s. As a result, a campaign had been launched to remove him from his position as chief executive officer. As one of the board members, Gupta argued in support of Naren—then her water broke. While Gupta wanted to remain in the meeting, Naren convinced her to go with him to the hospital. "Her clothes were all wet, everyone was concerned," Naren stated to *Forbes* (18 November 1996). "They hadn't seen that in a boardroom before."

Gupta's second daughter, Serena, was delivered later that evening. Several days later, Gupta had returned to an Integrated Systems board meeting, in which Naren was retained as the head of the company.

In 1994, Gupta made history by taking Digital Link public at $14 a share in February 1994. Digital Link's stock was listed on the NASDAQ, the electronic stock exchange operated by the National Association of Securities Dealers. (In the mid-1990s, the NASDAQ listed significantly more women-run companies than either the New York Stock Exchange or the American Stock Exchange.) By launching this initial public offering (IPO), Gupta became the first East Indian American woman to own a publicly traded company in the United States.

Subsequent years, however, proved to be rocky. The release of a highly heralded product, the Gateway switching system, was delayed, and the new president and chief operating officer resigned after seven months on the job, leaving Gupta to assume the position of president, as well as chief executive officer and chairperson. The value of Digital Link's stock plunged 36 percent, or $9, to close at $16.25 per share in October 1995. A year later, the company faced an insider trading class action lawsuit filed by attorney Bill Lerach.

Yet Digital Link, which remained debt-free and cash rich, continued to flourish despite these challenges. A new president and CEO was appointed in 1996, and the company began to shift its attention to wide area network (WAN) circuit management devices.

In 1997, the Guptas experienced a more personal setback—Naren developed health problems and suffered a heart attack. Both their companies—Integrated Systems and Digital Link—lost money during this period. However, Naren was able to overcome his illness, and the corporations regained their health as well. By 1998, Digital Link had 222 employees in its headquarters in Sunnyvale with $66 million in annual revenues. Xerox Corp.'s Semaphone unit was also acquired by the company to help it corner the WAN/Internet security market.

In 1999, Gupta, a 50 percent shareholder of Digital Link, offered to buy the remaining shares of the company. After successfully reprivatizing the company, making it 100 percent employee owned, she renamed it Quick Eagle Networks, Inc. The company's executive team, led by Gupta, was awarded the 2001 Great Corporate Teams Award by the Growth Leadership Center in 2001.

Gupta has also been active with the IndUS Entrepreneurs and Maitri, a San Jose, California-based support group for South Asian American women. "I view my husband, kids, and career as three legs of a stool—you have to learn to balance them or the whole thing will collapse," she told *Working Mother* (December 2000/January 2001).

## Sources

"25 Mothers We Love." December 2000/January 2001. *Working Mother.*

Digital Link Web site. www.dl.com [accessed on December 13, 2001].

Espe, Erik. 24 September 1999. "Investors Claim Digital Link Trying to Sell Itself to Founder." *Business Journal [San Jose]:* 10+ .

Marsh, Ann. 18 November 1996. "The Day Vinita Gupta's Water Broke." *Forbes:* 91–98.

Marsh, Ann. 22 March 1999. "Keeping the Faith." *Forbest:* 24+ .

"Vinita Gupta-Hi-Tech Woman Power." 16 June 2000. Silicon India Web site. www.siliconindia.com [accessed November 29, 2001].

# H

## Supenn Harrison

Supenn Harrison (left). Photo courtesy of Supenn Harrison

**Full Name at Birth**: Supenn Supatanasinkasem.

**Born**: c. 1945, Thailand.

**Education**: Thailand, B.A. in education; University of Minnesota, Minneapolis, Minnesota, M.A. in art education, 1974.

**Positions Held**: Founder/proprietor of Siam Café, Minneapolis, Minnesota, 1979–83; founder and chief executive officer of Sawatdee chain of restaurants, St. Paul, Minnesota, 1983– .

**Awards, Honors**: Minnesota Small Business Person of the Year, 1999; Asian Pacific Endowment for Community Development (APECD) Donor of the Year, 1999.

**Summary**: Restaurateur and philanthropist Supenn Harrison, a native of Thailand, has been instrumental in popularizing Thai food in the Minnesota area. Beginning with a booth at the state fair, Harrison's chain of restaurants has grown to include catering services.

### Early Years and Education

Harrison grew up in Thailand in the 1950s. She studied education in Thailand and taught biology before moving to the United States to earn a master's degree at the University of Minnesota. In 1973, while a graduate student in art education, she met and married Bruce Harrison, originally from Iowa. After graduation in 1974, the couple traveled to Thailand but soon realized that job opportunities there were limited.

### Career Highlights

Returning to Minnesota, Harrison obtained a temporary position in a hospital in Minneapolis. From time to time, she brought homemade Thai delicacies to share with her coworkers. They were so taken with her food, especially the egg rolls, that they encouraged her to secure a Thai food booth at the Minnesota State Fair in 1976.

Harrison did so for three years. Realizing the potential for a flourishing restaurant, Harrison searched for an appropriate location. In 1979 she took over the site of a former coffee shop in Minneapolis and opened Siam Café, the first authentic Thai restaurant in the Twin Cities. With her husband Bruce as her partner and business manager, she continued to operate the successful eatery until 1983, when she sold it for a tidy profit. Her next foray into the restaurant business would affirm Harrison's skills to lead a small franchise when she established the first Sawatdee restaurant on Washington Avenue in Minneapolis. Menu highlights included chicken satay appetizers, chicken with peanut curry sauce, Thai noodles, and, of course, fresh spring rolls.

With her sister she opened a Sawatdee in St. Paul and with another sister, Sawatdee in St. Cloud. The dynasty was rapidly expanding: in 1993 Sawatdee Bar and Café opened in the Twin Cities' Warehouse District, followed by Sawatdee on the Mall. To facilitate this pace of growth, Harrison approached the U.S. Small Business Association's Minneapolis District Office for a loan. She was awarded $100,000, and then $175,000 in 1998.

In 1999 the Small Business Association (SBA) selected Sawatdee for the Minnesota Small Business Person of the Year Award. "The best business tip I can give is to continually invest in your company and employees," she stated to the SBA. "It is important to update equipment, implement new marketing strategies, and change with the times. In addition, and perhaps most importantly, give your employees adequate compensation."

Harrison reiterated to *City Business* (November 13, 2000) the importance of good management, especially because her restaurant empire has grown to nine locations, including a venture that offers both Thai food and sushi. Regarding managers, Harrison stated: "You have to give them authority and trust that they will do a good job—and you have to pay them well."

Harrison reported that she visits about three of her restaurants a day. Her sister continues to manage one location, while some are franchised. Throughout all this business activity, the Harrisons have raised two daughters—Jenny and Cynthia—both of whom were educated at Macalester College in Minnesota. Harrison has also authored a book, *Cooking the Thai Way* (Lerner Publishing Group, 1986).

"You have to schedule time for your love, your husband, your family," she stated to *City Business in* an article on December 11, 2000. Harrison is also notable because of her commitment to her local community. In 1981, the Sawatdee Thai Two on 5K Run/Walk was launched to benefit the American Lung Association of Minnesota. She also has been active in the National Association of Women Business Owners and other philanthropic efforts.

## Sources

"Global Appetite." *Pioneer Planet*. www.pioneerplanet.com/justgo/dining/1116face.htm. [accessed January 15, 2001]

Harris, Phyllis Louise. 15–30 April 2000. "Sushi Sawatdee." *Asian Pages*. St. Paul, Minnesota: 5.

Michalski, Patty. 4 May 1999. "Sawatdee." *Minneapolis St. Paul Magazine*. *Sawatdee Thai Restaurant*. www.sawatdee.com [Accessed July 22, 2001].

"Supenn Harrison." SBA Online Women's Business Center. www.onlinewbc.org/docs/success_stories/ss_SupennHarrison.html. [accessed July 23, 2001]

# Helen Young Hayes

Helen Young Hayes. Photo © Ray Ng Photography, Inc.

**Full Name at Birth**: Helen Young.

**Born**: 11 July 1962, Oakland, California.

**Education**: Mississippi State University, Mississippi State, Mississippi, communications major; Yale University, New Haven, Connecticut, B.A. magna cum laude in economics, 1984.

**Positions Held**: Research analyst, Fred Alger Management, New York City, New York, 1984; analyst, Janus Capital Corporation, Denver, Colorado, 1987–1991; portfolio manager, Janus Worldwide Fund, Denver, Colorado, 1992– ; and portfolio manager, Janus Overseas Fund, Denver, Colorado, 1994– .

**Awards, Honors**: Excellence 2000 Award, U.S. Pan Asian American Chamber of Commerce, 2000.

**Summary**: Helen Young Hayes, a daughter of Chinese immigrants, is considered one of the top mutual fund managers in the United States. In 2000 she managed $60 billion in assets.

## Early Years

Hayes was born in Berkeley, California, but was raised in Starkville, Mississippi, where her father taught physics at Mississippi State University and her mother pursued her doctorate. When she was 7, she joined a swim club and swam competitively until age 18. In high school she was also a member of the cross-country track team.

## Higher Education

Interested in electronic journalism, Hayes majored in communications at Mississippi State University. One day her father came home with an application from Yale University and encouraged Hayes to apply. Hayes did; she was accepted and eventually graduated magna cum laude in economics.

## Career Highlights

Hayes had intended to pursue a career as a college professor, but a research analyst position at Fred Alger Management in New York changed the course of her life. There she worked with fund manager Tom Marsico. In 1986 Marsico left Alger to take a position with Janus Capital Corporation in his home town of Denver, Colorado. At that time Janus was a relatively new company with only 23 employees and $800 million in assets. Marsico nonetheless was able to recruit Hayes to join Janus the following year. "I was ready to leave New York," Hayes stated to *Worth Online* in 1997. "And ready to work with a small organization where I could hopefully be a big contributor."

Success was not immediate. According to *Mutual Funds* magazine, it took some time before she became a money manager; eventually she was assigned to manage a $250,000 scholarship fund for disadvantaged children in Vail. She then assisted with Janus Worldwide Fund before being named as the fund's manager in October 1992.

"She was probably the most hard-working person to ever work here," Alger commented to *Money* magazine. "I don't think she ever went home."

Her investment skills led to instant results. In 1993 the global fund gained 28.4 percent. From 1993, to 1996, it returned a compound annual average of more than 20 percent, more than other similar funds. In May 1994 another new fund—Janus Overseas—was assigned to Hayes. Soon Hayes was at the top of Best Buy funds list in *Forbes* magazine; in 1998 *Smart Money* magazine ranked Hayes as the eleventh most important person in the mutual fund industry.

Her strategy from the beginning was to approach investments creatively, and not as a "technical exercise." Janus Worldwide Fund, for example, is highly diversified. Working with multiple research analysts, she identifies undervalued corporations that are managed well. She also travels frequently—spending 12 weeks out of the year in other U.S. cities or overseas.

"While many international fund managers focus on geographic regions or economic conditions, I invest in one company at a time, regardless of country. Although this approach is much less prevalent in foreign investing, I have found it very effective," Hayes says, as quoted on the Janus Web site.

After the downturn in technological stocks in 2000 led to a fall in the fund's return, Hayes and her comanager reduced their investment in high-tech companies, but continued to hold onto shares of companies like China Telecom, which, as of 2000, served more than 30 percent of wireless customers in China. At one point before the downturn, Hayes was overseeing assets of more than $60 billion.

Hayes, whose parents are both from China, has opened the door for other Asian American money managers, including her sister Claire, another Yale alumnus who joined Janus in 1992 and is now a fund manager.

Frequently mentioned is her participation in triathlons, in which she competes in bicycling, swimming, and running. Hayes also speaks French, Spanish, and Mandarin Chinese.

## Sources

Clash, James M. 23 September 1996. "Worldwide View: Janus Worldwide Fund Manager Helen Hayes." *Forbes*: 228.

"Fund Manager Credits Dad for Success." 2 June 2000. *Denver Business Journal*: 3A.

Janus Funds Web Site. http://www.janus.com [accessed May 1, 2001].

O'Shaughnessy, Lynn. August 1997. "Triple Threat." *Mutual Funds*.

# Chinn Ho

**Born**: 26 February 1904, Honolulu, Hawaii.

**Died**: 12 May 1987, Honolulu, Hawaii.

**Education**: University of Hawaii Extension, 1925–26.

**Positions Held**: Staff, Bishop Bank (now First Hawaiian Bank), Honolulu, Hawaii, 1924; various positions, Duisenberg, Wichman and Company (later Dean Witter & Company), Honolulu, Hawaii, 1924–43; founder, chairman, Capital Investment Company, Honolulu, Hawaii, 1944–87.

**Awards, Honors**: Citizen of the Year in Hawaii award, 1974; Distinguished

Achievement Award, National Association of Chinese Americans, 1983; Hawaii Business Hall of Fame, Junior Achievement, 2001.

**Summary**: Chinn Ho, referred to as the "Chinese Rockefeller of Hawaii" and reportedly the model for an enterprising character in James Michener's novel, *Hawaii*, built a multimillion-dollar empire comprising international real-estate holdings, stock investments, and newspaper interests. Breaking racial barriers in the corporate boardrooms of Hawaii, he was the first Asian American to sit on the board of directors of a "Big Five" firm and to serve as president of the Honolulu Stock Exchange.

## Early Years

Ho was the son of a storekeeper who supplemented his income by raising ducks. Ho's grandfather had originally come to Hawaii in 1875 from China to serve as a caretaker for a coconut grove; he later farmed rice on the island of Oahu.

Ho exhibited an entrepreneurial spirit early in life. While in school, he sold pencils, thermometers, and pennants and later purchased penny stocks with his $150 in earnings. Ho also played the piccolo in the band at McKinley High School alongside classmate Hiram Fong, who went on to become a U.S. senator and successful businessman.

According to the *Los Angeles Times* (14 May 1987), Ho learned early not to be overly greedy: "If you bought something for 15 cents and it went up 10 cents, that was almost doubled. . . . That was good."

Later his business mottos would be "Kill them with kindness in competition" and "Achieve success by contributing to the success of others."

## Higher Education

After graduating from high school, Ho took correspondence courses through the University of Hawaii Extension. Although he never graduated from college, he did provide funds for his friend Hiram Fong to attend Harvard Law School in the 1930s.

## Career Highlights

Ho's first job was with the Bishop Bank, which later became First Hawaiian Bank. After a year, he worked as an office boy at the securities company, Duisenberg, Wichman and Company, which later merged with Dean Witter & Company in 1929. Ho rose through the company to become an expert on sugar plantation stocks. At the age of 30, Ho purchased his first piece of property, a lot in Honolulu with three cottages on it, for $5,000. He sold it a year later for $16,500.

The capital enabled Ho to expand his property holdings, according to the *Los Angeles Times* (14 May 1987). But he faced barriers in the lending market, which was closed to nonwhites. He then launched his own discount house, offering installment credit to Asian Americans and other ethnic minorities, and acquired property in Waikiki and downtown Honolulu. In 1943, he left Dean Witter to begin his own enterprise. Pooling his own assets with his friends', Ho was able to collect $150,000 to $200,000 to form Capital Investment Company in 1944.

Three years later, the company outbid Castle & Cooke to purchase $1.2 million in stock for 9,000 acres of the defunct Waianae Sugar Company in Makaha Valley in Oahu. At the time, this was the largest land acquisition made by an Asian in Hawaii. By 1951, Capital Investment Company had already made approximately $4 million by subdividing 40 percent of the land and selling the property to small farmers.

Ho was daring in his real-estate development decisions. In the late 1940s, he leased some beachfront property and constructed the first commercial high-rise building on Waikiki in 1948. Retaining the land lease, he eventually sold the building for $850,000 and continued to receive $50,000 a year for rental of the land. In 1959, he built the Ilikai, the largest condominium apartment-hotel complex in Hawaii at the time with more than 1,000 units. (He eventually sold the building to United Airlines, Inc., in 1974 for $35 million.)

Ho also expanded into overseas development projects. In 1958, he began constructing luxury homes able to accommodate 16,000 people on 2,200 acres outside San Francisco in the exclusive Marin County. He also built the 166-room Empress Hotel in Hong Kong and purchased an interest in the 1,000-room Great Wall Hotel in Beijing, China. He was one of the first prominent Asians to urge recognition of mainland China.

Ho was also breaking racial barriers in corporate boardrooms in Hawaii, which had, until the 1960s been dominated by European Americans. He became the first Asian American to sit on the board of directors at a "Big Five" firm, Theo H. Davies & Company; the first to manage a land holding, the Robinson Estate; the first to serve as president of the Honolulu Stock Exchange; and the first to lead the Hawaii Visitors Bureau. As president of the Honolulu Stadium, he brought the Pacific Coast League, Class AAA baseball, to Hawaii.

While on the board of the Hawaii Advertising Publishing Company, Ho learned that their competing newspaper, the *Honolulu Star-Bulletin* was up for sale in 1961. He organized a group of multiethnic buyers and successfully raised $11 million. When he contacted a New York newspaper broker regarding the purchase, the broker reportedly asked: "Who the hell is Chinn Ho?" Ho then made history as the first Asian American to be the principal owner of a major daily newspaper. In 1971, his group

sold the *Star-Bulletin* to the Gannett chain for $33 million, and Ho eventually became chairman of the Gannett Corporation.

As a developer in Hawaii, Ho faced opposition from low-growth proponents and environmentalists who wanted to retain the natural beauty of the Islands. His plan to develop Diamond Head on Oahu was foiled by a movement that resulted in the area being named a National Natural Landmark. He responded to criticisms by pointing out that he restored sacred temples in isolated valleys, the same valleys that he has visited on a regular basis. "I am not a religious man," he told a reporter in 1982, according to the *Los Angeles Times*. "But sometimes I go to a mountaintop and ask, 'Mr. Ho, how will they remember you?'"

Ho, who served as a civilian aide to the Secretary of the Army from 1965–71, received honorary degrees from the University of Guam in 1980 and the University of Hawaii in 1983. He also was recognized with numerous awards, including the Citizen of the Year in Hawaii award in 1974.

When James Michener traveled to Hawaii to conduct research for his novel *Hawaii*, he spent time with Ho. Ho "took me under his wing," Michener told *USA Today* (14 May 1987). "He was one of the most important men in my life." Ho invited various young Asian American political leaders, including future U.S. senators Daniel Inouye and Spark Matsunaga, to participate in discussions at Michener's apartment. Michener later based a character, Hong Kong Kee, on Ho.

Ho died on May 12, 1987 at the age of 83 in Honolulu. A year before his death, Capital Investment Company had $17.4 million in assets. The company continues to this day; in 2000, it became private after operating as a small public company.

Ho and his wife Betty had six children: Stuart, Dean, Karen, John, Robin, and Heather.

## Sources

Beeissert, Wayne. 14 May 1987. "Man of Many Firsts Dies; Hawaii's Ho Built Empire, Inspired Novelist." *USA Today*: 2A.

"Chinn Ho: Office Boy to Multi-Millionaire." 1961. Robert M. Lee, ed. *The Chinese in Hawaii: A Historical Sketch*. Honolulu, HI: Advertiser Publisher Company, Ltd., 116.

"Deaths Elsewhere." 14 May 1987. *Washington Post*: D6.

Folkart, Burt A. 14 May 1987. "Known as 'Chinese Rockefeller' of the Islands, Hawaii Multimillionaire Chinn Ho Dies." *Los Angeles Times*: 1.

Jokiel, Lucy. June 1988. "The House of Fong." *Hawaii Business*: 18+ .

Lynch, Russ. 4 January 2000. "Capital Investments Opts for Private Status." *Honolulu Star-Bulletin*.

Shapiro, Treena. 8 October 1999. "Chinn Ho: From Rice Fields to High Finance." *Honolulu Star-Bulletin*.

## Benjamin B. Hong

**Born**: South Korea, 1932.

**Education**: Seoul University, Seoul, South Korea, B.A.; University of California in Los Angeles, Los Angeles, California, M.B.A.

**Positions Held**: Trainee, First Interstate Bank, Los Angeles, California, 1972; senior vice president, First Interstate Bank, Los Angeles, California, circa 1970s; head of Asian operations, First Interstate Bank, Los Angeles, California, c. 1980–88; president and chief executive officer, Hanmi Bank, Los Angeles, California, 1988–94; president and chief executive officer, Nara Bank (formerly United Citizens Bank), Los Angeles, California, 1994– .

**Summary**: Benjamin B. Hong, a leader in the banking community, has assisted many Korean immigrants and businesses to survive and prosper in the United States. After working for First Interstate Bank for 16 years, Hong transferred his skills to lead Korean American banks headquartered in Los Angeles.

### Early Years and Education

Hong was raised in South Korea in the 1930s and 1940s. He gained his bachelor's degree from the prestigious Seoul University in South Korea. He later traveled to the United States to gain his M.B.A. from University of California in Los Angeles.

### Career Highlights

After graduating with his M.B.A., Hong secured a trainee position with First Interstate Bank in Los Angeles. He quickly rose through the ranks and was elevated to vice president and then head of Asian operations. After 16 years with that financial institution, he accepted the top position with Hanmi Bank, a Korean American bank that had been established in Los Angeles in 1983. In 1988, Hanmi's assets were at $130 million; it also became the first Korean-oriented bank to be publicly traded.

Under Hong's leadership, Hanmi began offering Small Business Administration loans to Korean businesses. In addition to the creation of a mortgage banking department, Hong also innovated a new financing plan modeled after Korean rotating credit groups, or *kye*. Each member of a *kye* commits to contributing a small amount of money to a general fund and takes turns receiving the pool of money. In order to attract Korean immigrants to use its banking services, Hanmi introduced an installment savings and loan plan structured like a *kye*.

"We're trying to build a bridge between the Korean community and mainstream American financial world," Hong was quoted in an article in the *Los Angeles Times* (5 October 1988).

During the next six years under Hong's tenure, Hanmi, the largest Los Angeles-based Korean community bank, would open three additional branch offices and centralize and expand its automobile loan production. What would prove the largest challenge, however, would be to survive the economic devastation of the Los Angeles riots in 1992.

According to Radio Korea, 2,000 businesses in the Koreatown district of Los Angeles suffered some sort of damage during the days of arson and looting in April; losses were estimated at $360 million. In response, Hanmi introduced a reconstruction initiative in which interest and principal payments were deferred for certain affected borrowers. Moreover, the institution also provided a $1.4 million construction loan to the Korean Youth Center in August of that year to spur low-income housing development in the Koreatown district.

As Hong established his reputation as a banking leader in the Korean American community, he made a pivotal career decision in 1994. He agreed to become president of the ailing Nara Bank, another Korean American financial institution in Los Angeles, but one that was just three weeks shy of being closed by the Federal Deposit Insurance Corp. (FDIC). Nara, which had been operating as United Citizens Bank since 1989, had only $369,000 while holding $55 million of assets. It had lost $3.1 million the previous year.

As president, Hong devised a plan to raise capital: he sold stock to the public at $3 per share with $1,200 the minimum investment. "My catch phrase was, 'For $1,200, you can be the owner of a bank,'" Hong stated to *American Banker* (30 December 1997). Within two weeks, he had raised $2 million. By the end of the year, Nara had an additional $1 million and then $3.5 million a year later. In November of Hong's inaugural year, he also received the title of chief executive officer.

During this campaign, Hong also solicited new customers, specifically small business owners. By the end of 1995, Nara had $86 million in assets and its net income rose to $1.5 million. Key to Hong's success, observers say, were his relationship skills. Even his employees from his former institution wanted to follow the charismatic leader to his new base.

"Ben Hong could drop his hat anywhere, and people would want to work for him," said Robert J. Gallivan Jr. of the Bank Compensation Strategies in San Diego in an article in *American Banker* (19 November 1999). "Ben is Mr. Korea."

Nara Bank continued to grow throughout the 1990s. In 1996, it had $2.6 million in profits and $122 in assets from a second public offering. Branches were opened in downtown Los Angeles, Silicon Valley, and southern California suburbs, while loan production offices were launched in Seattle and Chicago. In 1998, Nara listed its stock on the NASDAQ and also acquired Korea Exchange Bank's bank in Flushing, New York. With this move, Nara became the first Korean American bank to have branches on both coasts. In 2000, Nara deepened its presence in New York City, the home of the nation's second largest Korean American population, with the acquisition of Seoul-based Korea First Bank Ltd. Now the bank had a total of four branches in the city.

Nara's performance continued to be strong. In 2001, CIBC World Markets gave it a Strong Buy rating, citing Nara's strong financial track record. Nara Bank, which was reorganized as a subsidiary of the newly created Nara Bancorp., Inc., was also ranked first among the 300 largest community banks by *American Banker* in its July 2001 issue. As of the end of 2000, the bank had $602 in assets and a 147.50 percent growth rate.

"I want to be the catalyst of Korean immigrant success stories," Hong told *American Banker* (19 November 1999).

### Sources

Andrejczak, Matt. 19 November 1999. "L.A.'s Dealmaking Nara Bank Pursues a National Ambition." *American Banker*: 22+ .

Frantz, Douglas. 5 October 1988. "Hanmi Bank Uses Ancient Asian Lending Practice to Help Koreans." *Los Angeles Times*: 4(1).

"Hong Makes Magic in L.A." July 2001. *US Banker*: 42.

Kline, Alan. 30 December 1997. "Korean Bank in California Battles Back from the Brink." *American Banker*: 6.

Nara Bank Web site. http://www.narabankna.com [accessed October 2, 2001].

# Mercedes del Rosario Huang

**Full Name at Birth**: Mercedes del Rosario.

**Born**: c. 1950, Philippines.

**Education**: Philippine Women's University, Manila, Philippines, B.S. in food technology; University of Massachusetts, Amherst, Massachusetts, M.S. in food science, 1972.

**Positions Held**: Research analyst, University of Massachusetts, Amherst, Massachusetts, 1972–74; quality control manager (later elevated to plant foods manager), Ready Foods, Denver, Colorado, 1981–83; proprietor, Goldilocks, Lakewood, Colorado, 1984; founder, Rocky Mountain Food Factory, Englewood, Colorado, 1985– .

**Honors and Awards**: Asian Woman of Achievement Award, Asian Pacific Women's Network of Colorado, 1994.

**Summary**: Mercedes del Rosario Huang applied her expertise in food science into launching a successful food manufacturing business in Colorado. Her company, Rocky Mountain Food Factory, produces frozen, canned, and fresh food products that are sold throughout the state and even overseas.

### Early Years

Huang was born in the Philippines, where her father, Luis del Rosario, worked as an attorney. An uncle's food canning business in her hometown exposed Huang to the world of food technology and manufacturing, a field that would later play a large role in her professional life.

### Higher Education

Huang studied food technology at Philippine Women's University in Manila, Philippines. The institution was founded in 1919 by women who dreamed of creating a college that "morally edifies, academically instructs, and socially empowers Asian women."

After working for a brief time as a food technologist in Manila, Huang came to the United States to work on her master's degree in food science at the University of Massachusetts in Amherst. She studied under Professor Irving Fagerson, who specialized in sophisticated methods of food analysis involving glucose and protein products.

### Career Highlights

Huang stayed on at the University of Massachusetts after graduation as a research assistant on flavor chemistry and food analysis. In 1972, she married Whittack Huang, an engineer, and from 1974 to 1980, she devoted all her time to raising her young daughters, Sophie and Gemma, in their new home in Colorado. She returned to work in 1980 as a quality control manager and then plant manager at Ready Foods in Denver, but left the high-pressure job in 1983 to start her own bakery, Goldilocks, in the city of Lakewood in Colorado.

A year later, she sold the business to explore other opportunities. That opportunity was found in Rocky Mountain Food Factory, Inc., opened in 1985 with $22,000 from a second mortgage on the Huang's house. By this time, Huang saw the potential for the ethnic food market and began to develop recipes for Mexican, Italian, and Chinese goods—either fresh, frozen, or canned—predominantly for restaurant use. Their first food manufacturing facility was located on Santa Fe Drive in Denver, thereby inspiring her Mexican food brand name, Santa Fe.

A year later, Huang obtained additional financing from a $40,000 Small Business Administration loan. She was able to clear her debts within two years, reflecting her philosophy for steady but controlled growth.

In 1990, the company had sales of $750,000. A year later, revenues increased to $1.2 million. At that time, Huangs' profit margin varied between 15 to 20 percent. By 1992 Rocky Mountain Food Factory had 10 employees and a new facility in Englewood, Colorado, purchased through a $225,000 loan from the Colorado Development Corporation. Huang invested another $300,000 to expand the building from 7,000 to 9,000 square feet. And, to address the need for a canning facility, Huang spent $200,000 for specialized equipment.

At this time, Rocky Mountain Food Factory offered its 25 fresh and frozen products to restaurants like Colorado Café and Jackson's Hole. Ten percent of Rocky Mountain's products were sold to more than 200 grocery stores, including Safeway, which sold Huang's burritos in store delicatessens in Colorado, Wyoming, Nebraska, South Dakota, and New Mexico.

Canning made it possible to ship products to distributors throughout the nation. One of Huang's first distribution agree-

ments for its canned sauces was with Topco Associates in Skokie, Illinois, which at the time was the second largest wholesale grocery cooperative in the nation.

In 1994, Huang, in recognition of her achievements as an entrepreneur, was given an Asian Woman of Achievement Award by the Asian Pacific Women's Network of Colorado.

## Sources

Crisostomo, Isabelo T. 1996. *Filipino Achievers in the USA and Canada: Profiles in Excellence.* Naperville, IL: Bookhaus Publishers.

Sands, Lee. 17 July 1992. "Food Maker Is Hotter Than Its Chili." *Denver Business Journal*: 3.

# Rose Hwang

Rose Hwang. Photo courtesy of Rose Hwang

**Full Name at Birth**: Rosalina Hwang.

**Born**: 1959.

**Education**: California State University at Fullerton, Fullerton, California, B.A. in music, 1982; University of California, Los

Angeles, Los Angeles, California, M.D.E. in business management, 1996.

**Positions Held**: Cofounder, president, and chief executive officer, Alpha Systems Lab, Irvine, California, 1990– .

**Awards, Honors**: Honoree, National Association of Women Business Owners, Orange County Chapter, 1997; Pioneer Woman, National Association of Women Business Owners, 1997. Top 500 Women-Owned Businesses, *Working Woman*, 1998, 1999, 2000, 2001.

**Summary**: Rose Hwang, who successfully escaped from Vietnam after a harrowing incident at sea in 1976, cofounded a computer hardware company with her engineer husband in 1990. The company, Alpha Systems Lab, has since grown to become a leader in personal computer-based surveillance and digital video systems used for security purposes.

## Early Years

Hwang, who is of Chinese heritage, was raised in a wealthy household in Vietnam. Her grandfather was a business consultant to the French, while her father owned textile factories and publishing companies. The oldest child in her family, she attended a Catholic school, where she underwent a rigorous schedule involving both academic and music studies. At this time she was already multilingual—not only could she speak Vietnamese, but also Chinese and French.

The Vietnam War changed the course of Hwang's life. The fall of Saigon to the North Vietnamese communists forced Hwang's family and others to flee the country for Hong Kong. Dressed like fishermen, they and approximately 90 others left Vietnam by boat in June 1976. Eventually running out of drinking water and gas, they were captured by a patrol ship manned by communist soldiers. The refugees, however, failed to give up and concocted a plan to subdue their captors.

Hwang, who was 17 years old at that time, began her own surveillance operation. "I think they underestimated women, because I was allowed to move around, although everyone else had to sit in one place," she was quoted in an article in the *Orange County Register* (11 July 1994). "So I gave information on how many guards there were and where. I felt no fear. I don't know if I was numb or if determination overpowered fear. My first thought was, 'I don't care what happens, I will not go back.'"

The refugees, after killing or imprisoning the crew, were able to seize the ship and steer it into a port at the border of Thailand and Malaysia. Two months later, Hwang's aunt sponsored the family to come to Mission Viejo, California, in Orange County.

## Higher Education

Hwang eventually enrolled in the University of California, Los Angeles (UCLA) and gained her degree in music. While in college, she met Mitchell Phan, who had also escaped from Vietnam. He had traveled to the United States on one of the last flights out of Saigon in 1976.

## Career Highlights

Hwang taught piano and then received certification as one of the first Vietnamese court interpreters, later she joined the marketing department of a small high-tech company. In the early 1980s, she married Phan, who was working as a design engineer for Triconex Corporation, a manufacturer of computerized control systems in Irvine, California.

The couple bought a video rental store in Mission Viejo, which Hwang operated while Phan continued his engineering work at Triconex. When their first of three children was born, Hwang moved a playpen into the store. In spite of her hard work, the video rental business was sluggish. At Phan's suggestion, they invested half of their savings into computer inventory and officially launched Alpha Systems Lab (ASL) in 1990.

Phan left his job at Triconex to become a full-time computer consultant. He had designed an affordable circuit board that could upgrade the processing power of personal computers. With the economic downturn of the 1990s, Phan saw a niche for his product: instead of purchasing expensive new equipment, corporations could upgrade their existing hardware with his invention, the Transformer.

As president and chief executive officer of the fledgling company, Hwang took on the sales and administrative duties. She made cold calls to major corporations. Their slogan was, "Is your computer a wimp?" In a year, ASL had $1.2 million in sales. The following year, sales tripled to $3 million, and its staff expanded to 20 employees. Customers included Boeing, Mc-Donnel Douglas, Eastman Kodak, and PaineWebber.

More success came when Electronic Data Systems (EDS), the multibillion-dollar computer service firm started by Ross Perot, sought ASL's help in fulfilling a multi-million-dollar federal government contract.

The project was big—yet ASL was too small to secure sufficient financing from their bank. As a result, Hwang convinced EDS to pay cash on delivery, rather than through the typical 30-day billing cycle. "When we got the government contract, we had to decide whether to focus on doing our best on that one contract or not do our best on a lot of contracts. We focused on one and because of our delivery and faith in our product, we have succeeded," said Hwang (*Orange County Register*, 11 July 1994). In 1993, sales jumped to $40 million.

The reliance on one large customer also had its down side: in 1994, EDS's order was much smaller than the 1993 one, thereby greatly impacting ASL's sales. (By the middle of 1994, a total of 150,000 Transformer units had been delivered.) Fortunately, by this time, ASL had entered a new market: digital video technology for surveillance and technology applications.

In November 1993, ASL introduced its new MegaMotion video capture board. Invented by Phan, the add-on circuit board had the capability to transform an ordinary personal computer into a remote video surveillance and teleconferencing machine. This board, again an inexpensive alternative to similar kinds of equipment, enabled users to monitor different sites of their businesses and homes. Digital files could be accessed later to help solve crimes such as burglaries.

The invention of the MegaMotion formed the foundation of the ASL's new entry into the security field. In May 1994, another groundbreaking product—the RemoteWatch video telesurveillance system—because the first product of its kind to transmit live video over standard telephone lines anywhere in the world.

In May 1995, the U.S. Coast Guard and Northrop Grumman Corporation selected MegaMotion for sophisticated video surveillance systems for both domestic and international missions. A year later, the U.S. Customs and Immigration and Naturalization Service was using an upgrade of RemoteWatch to monitor the border between the United States and Canada. With the rise of crime at ATMs, ASL introduced ATM-Watch, a video and data storage system, in 1998.

Demand for ASL products was seen even in overseas markets. International versions (Spanish, Portuguese, Italian, and French) of RemoteWatch were released in 1997. A new modular digital recorder, DigiSaver, was popular among bank customers in South America. In 2000, ASL entered into a strategic alliance with TEAC Corporation's Information Products Division to distribute the ASL product lines to the Japanese market.

Response to ASL products has been good. In an article in *Security Management* (October 2000), executives with Switzerland-based Novartis Pharmaceuticals explained how they wanted to centralize security operations at three facilities in the United States. Through the installation of RemoteWatch, the company was able to easily transmit video signals from one U.S. site to another through a local area network (LAN). Moreover, the use of digital technology proved to be far superior to analog video.

ASL's achievements have not gone unnoticed. In 1998, 2000, and 2001, *Working Woman* magazine named ASL as among its Top 500 Women-Owned Businesses. In 1999, ASL had $23.4 million in sales; in 2000, revenues went up to $24.3 million. Forty people currently work for the company; its corporate headquarters is in Costa Mesa, California.

## Sources

Alpha Systems Lab. http://www.aslrwp.com [accessed August 17, 2001].

Lee, Cristina. 23 October 1991. "Souping Up Computers for Extended Mileage." *Los Angeles Times* (Orange County Edition): O.C. Enteprise, 4.

Norman, Jan. 11 July 1994. "She Left Fear Behind, Aboard Refugee Ship." *Orange County Register*: D3.

"Transpacific 100: Asian American Entrepreneurs." October 1996. *Transpacific*.

# I

## Paul Isaki

Paul Isaki. Photo courtesy of Liberty Studio

**Full Name at Birth**: Paul Shigemi Isaki.

**Born**: 6 June 1944, Topaz, Utah.

**Education**: University of California, Berkeley, B.A. in economics, 1965.

**Positions Held**: Staff, California Rating and Inspection Bureau, 1965; social worker, California, circa 1966–71; staff, Seattle Opportunities Industrialization Center, Seattle, Washington, 1971–73; program director, City of Seattle, Seattle, Washington, 1973; real estate developer, Seattle, Washington, 1979–85; special assistant for international trade and economic development, Governor's Office, Olympia, Washington, 1985–90; department director, Washington Department of Trade and Economic Development, Olympia, Washington, 1990–93; vice president for business development, Seattle Mariners, Seattle, Washington, 1993–99; special state trade representative, Olympia, Washington, 1999–2001; chief of staff, Washington Governor's Office, Olympia, Washington, 2001; special assistant for business, Governor's Office, Olympia, Washington, 2001– .

**Summary**: Paul Isaki became the first Japanese American vice president of a major league baseball league when he was appointed to the front office of the Seattle Mariners in 1993. By representing the team's interest in the new construction of Safeco Field, he contributed to keeping the ball club in the city. Isaki, who was involved in the public sector and community service since graduating from college, has returned to government work, now encouraging trade and business development with and in the state of Washington.

## Early Years

Isaki was born on June 6, 1944—D-Day—inside an American internment camp in Topaz, Utah, where 10,000 Japanese Americans were incarcerated during World War II. "I guess I've always found it ironic how, on the same day our troops landed in Normandy in the name of freedom, my mom was giving birth in a camp in Topaz, Utah, because her rights had been taken away," he later told the *Northwest Asian Weekly* (20 June 1997).

Isaki's father Shigeyoshi was originally from Oakland, where he had established a trucking business before the war. When he and his wife Haru, along with all other Japanese Americans along the West Coast, were ordered to pack only what they could carry and be forcibly removed into the nation's interior, the business had to be abandoned. Within the confines of camp, Haru had a miscarriage before eventually giving birth to Isaki in 1944. Isaki's father had smuggled in an 8-millimeter home movie camera into Topaz, so footage of Isaki as an infant was recorded.

After Japanese Americans were allowed to return to California in 1945, Isaki's family returned to Oakland. Although the Teamsters union barred the membership of Isaki's father because of his ethnicity, he perservered to rebuild his trucking business, K&F Drayage.

## Higher Education

After graduating from high school in Oakland, Isaki attended the University of California, Berkeley, in the 1960s, the height of the civil rights and free speech movements. He eventually gained a bachelor's degree in economics in 1965.

## Career Highlights

Influenced by the times, Isaki then embarked on a career of public service. He worked briefly for the California Rating and Inspection Bureau, a government agency that handled the state's Workman's Compensation claims, before joining an anti-poverty program designed for migrant farm workers as part of the nation's "War on Poverty" program. He worked in the San Joaquin Valley for three years before returning to California's Bay Area to participate in a jobs program in North Richmond called "Neighborhood House."

In 1971, Isaki relocated to the state of Washington, where he joined the Seattle Opportunity Industrialization Center, an agency that organized social programs for disadvantaged youth and adults. After two years, he became a director of a job training center in the inner city for the City of Seattle. A position with an economic development project followed before Isaki began his own real estate consultation business. When his company was acquired by a national commercial real estate company in 1981, Isaki stayed on to oversee the company's business development and acquisitions.

Isaki's ability to work and excel in both the private and public sectors was apparently being noticed: in 1985, Isaki was named Washington Governor Booth Gardner's special assistant for international trade and economic development. Five years later, he was appointed to direct the state's Department of Trade and Economic Development, a department responsible for the state's export trade promotion, business development, and tourism programs.

During his tenure with the Gardner administration, Isaki was instrumental in the development and expansions of the Washington State Trade and Convention Center; the development of the Washington State Technology Center program at the University of Washington; and the environmental clean-up program at the Hanford Nuclear Reservation. He spearheaded the establishment of the Everett Navy Homeport and even the 1985 King County Kingdome lease with the Seattle Mariners baseball team. He also established the state's first trade office in Europe in conjunction with the Port of Seattle and Port of Tacoma.

He created initiatives that expanded international exporting in various state industries, including wood products, processed foods, software, biotechnology, and aerospace. He devised an innovative partnership, Washington Village Program, between the state of Washington, its sister-state in Japan, Hyogo Prefecture, and a nonprofit, Evergreen Partnership. The program advocated the use of Washington wood products and Western home-building technology as an attractive alternative to traditional Japanese construction. The program successfully sealed trade agreements involving wood products with Japan, and in 1992, it was selected as a finalist in the Innovations in State and Local Government Awards Program.

In the same year, 1992, a Japan-based company, Nintendo, which had established a subsidiary in Redmond, Washington, announced that it would buy 60 percent of the Seattle Mariners professional baseball team for $75 million. (Minority owners were Microsoft and McCaw.) The news of a Japan-affiliated company buying an American baseball team sent shockwaves through the nation. The transaction would have a direct effect on Isaki's career, as he would be offered a specially created position, vice president of business development for the Mariners. Assuming the

position in 1993, Isaki became the first Japanese American vice president of a professional baseball team.

Isaki's responsibility was to raise more fan support in other regions, including Portland, Oregon; Vancouver, British Columbia; and even in Japan. In 1994, he secured the Mariners' first regional cable television agreement, before a larger project awaited him in 1995: the construction of a new baseball stadium, Safeco Field. Isaki, who represented the team's participation in the development of Safeco, met with countless politicians to convince them to support the project, which later faced expensive cost overruns. As one of seven members of a panel to select the architect, Isaki supported the team's choice, HOK Sport of Kansas City, but was outvoted by opponents in favor of a locally based company. Four years and $517 million later, Safeco Field was unveiled. Although the stadium was highly criticized throughout various stages of its construction, supporters claim that it ensured the retention of a professional baseball team in Seattle.

Regarding the effort it took to make Safeco a reality, Isaki commented to the *Seattle Post-Intelligencer* (2 April 2001), "It was almost as though I was supposed to do that job. That's the way I felt about it at the time, because I understood how that [stadium deal] was supposed to be done. It was tough. It was very difficult and yet there was almost an inevitability about it. I had a sense no matter how difficult it was, it was going to happen. You can't let up. That goes back to my dad."

The stress of the project apparently took its toll on Isaki, who already suffered from high blood pressure. Kidney failure led to self-dialysis treatments. In 1999, Isaki left the Mariners to become the special trade representative for Washington Governor

Gary Locke. During the next two years, he assisted Washington farmers to settle disputes regarding exporting apples and potatoes to Mexico. Through negotiations between the state and the Japanese government, he also was able to get the Japanese to accept U.S. standards for organic food exports to Japan.

In 2001, Isaki was appointed chief of staff by Governor Locke. In this top advisory position, Isaki directed the cabinet and had authority to act on behalf of the governor. At the time of the appointment, Locke called Isaki "a special blend of public servant and entrepreneurial businessman," according to the Associated Press. After a year, Isaki stepped down to become special assistant for business.

Isaki's wife Lucy also has ties to the government; she is the assistant state attorney general.

## Sources

Ammons, David. 10 January 2001. "Locke Names Former M's Executive." *Associated Press*.

Awanohara, Susumu. 23 December 1993. "Major-League Gambit: the Seattle Mariners Hope to be Japan's Baseball Team." *Far Eastern Economic Review*: 50.

Fryer, Alex. 2 April 200. "Mariners, Still Seeking Money, Target Stadium Builders." *Seattle Times*.

Gorlick, Arthur C. 9 March 1999. "Locke Names Isaki Special Trade Rep." *Seattle Post-Intelligencer*.

Lim, Paul. 22 January 1993. "Paul Isaki Lands Front Office Job." *Asian Week*: 4.

Vecsey, Laura. "Play Ball Has a Very Personal Meaning for Paul Isaki." 2 April 2001. *Seattle Post-Intelligencer*: B1+ .

Wilhelm, Steve. 26 January 2001. "Trade Representative Sought." *Puget Sound Business Journal*: 21.

Wong, Erik. 20 June 1997. "Mariners' VP Sees Greater Community Spirit." *Northwest Asian Weekly*: 10.

# Robert Iwamoto Jr.

Robert Iwamoto Jr. Photo courtesy of Robert Iwamoto Jr.

**Born**: c. 1938, Hawaii.

**Positions Held**: Franchisee, Budget Rent A Car, Lihue, Hawaii, 1960–67; executive vice president, Ilima Tours, Inc. (now Roberts Hawaii), Honolulu, Hawaii, 1964–85; owner and chief executive officer, Roberts Hawaii, Honolulu, Hawaii, 1985– ; president, Roberts Hawaii, Honolulu, Hawaii, 1985–2001.

**Awards, Honors**: Entrepreneurial Success Award, State of Hawaii, U.S. Small Business Administration, 1997.

**Summary**: Robert Iwamoto Jr. has been instrumental in making the family business, Roberts Hawaii, the largest tour and transportation operator in Hawaii. In addition to a past investment in a short-lived regional airlines, Iwamoto also possesses significant real estate holdings on the Islands.

## Early Years

When Iwamoto was a child on the island of Kauai, his father Robert Iwamoto Sr. founded a one-man taxi service based in the small town of Hanapepe in 1941. First targeting his business to U.S. servicemen stationed on Kauai, he expanded into the rental car business and purchased five automobiles. (He also was a salesman for the Chrysler/Plymouth dealer on Kauai.)

Iwamoto Jr., the oldest of five children, joined the enterprise in 1953. Only 15 years old, he washed and repaired cars and occasionally worked as a driver. At this time the transportation company began offering tours in limousines; after its first bus purchase, the whole operation was moved near the Lihue Airport and organized into two divisions: Roberts Tours, Inc. and Roberts Rent A Car, Inc. The tour company acquired the Island's first air-conditioned motor coach in the mid-1950s, which became popular with Hollywood production crews who were shooting the films *Blue Hawaii* and *Donovan's Reef*, according to *Hawaii Business* (September 1997).

After graduating from high school, in 1956 Iwamoto joined the Air Force. He returned to Kauai four years later.

## Career Highlights

Before becoming involved in the family business again, Iwamoto began his own car rental business at the Lihue Airport. It eventually became a Budget Rent A Car franchisee; in 1967 it was sold to Transamerica Corporation.

Roberts Tours, meanwhile, continued to expand, this time into "Room and Car" packages in cooperation with the Prince Kuhio hotel in Poipu Beach. Roberts was one of the first in Kauai to offer these innovative package deals: by 1964, the operation included two buses, five stretch sedans, and 25 rental cars. Iwamoto had rejoined the company, which now comprised 15 staff members.

In 1964, Roberts made a major move. Understanding that most of the tourist business was centered around Waikiki, they relocated to the island of Oahu with only $4,000 of seed money. They eventually purchased a used 49-passenger bus and five minibuses. Iwamoto became executive vice president of the newly named Ilima Tours, Inc., while his father was president.

The next decade was a key building time. Working from 3 a.m. to 9 p.m., Iwamoto wore many hats as a dispatcher, bus driver, and mechanic. Their line of vehicles grew to include six buses, 12 minibuses, and 12 stretch sedans. With the additional purchase of five trucks, luggage handling services for tour groups were offered. A partnership in the catamaran, Hula Kai, enabled the offering of sunset cruises off Waikiki. The company, now with the new moniker of Roberts Ilima Tours, expanded into Maui and the island of Hawaii. Roberts Rent A Car followed suit soon after.

The acquisition of four luxury Motor Coach International buses, worth $60,000 each, catapulted Roberts into the big leagues. Now directly competing against Greyhound Bus Lines, Roberts adopted a mascot and new logo of a yellow running rabbit, a reference to a dog race Iwamoto once witnessed in Mexico. The message behind the mascot: greyhounds never caught the rabbit, and in the tour business, the company, Greyhound, would never catch Roberts.

By 1976, Roberts Hawaii was the third largest transportation company in Hawaii, yet it still needed more cash flow in the competition for tourist dollars. Iwamoto Sr., however, was adamantly opposed to mergers or going public, citing quality control as the company's "No. 1 weapon." To remain a family business, Roberts had to explore additional markets. In 1981, the company exploited its existing base yards and pool of drivers and mechanics to service Oahu's 45 school-bus routes. The same year it acquired the Alii Kai, a catamaran that held 1,000 passengers, for $2.5 million. Although the competition expressed doubts that such a costly endeavor would succeed, the Alii Kai—the world's largest ocean-going twin hulled ship—was quickly booked by tourists attracted by its nightly dinner show. Three years later, Roberts acquired Captain Bean's Cruises, a Kailua company that operated sunset cruises on a 600-passenger motorized catamaran.

In 1984, the company went through a formal shift of leadership when Iwamoto Sr., who had been battling cancer for some time, passed away in October. His widow and Iwamoto Jr.'s mother, Florence, officially took over as president. Roberts Hawaii, at this time, had annual revenues of $20 million with 500 employees. The following year Iwamoto Jr. bought out his family's interest and became sole owner of the enterprise.

As Roberts' new president and chief executive, Iwamoto oversaw the company's next level of growth. With a renewed focus on the tourist industry, Iwamoto shed its rental car division in 1987, while also beginning to acquire Hawaii real estate properties. He cultivated partnerships to create "Magic of Polynesia," a Waikiki entertainment show, and to purchase Voyager Submarines, which had two 48-passenger submarines at Waikiki. He also invested close to $5 million in Mahalo Airlines, an interisland carrier.

By 1994, sales reached $89 million with 1,500 employees. Two years later Roberts had $105 million in sales, 2,000 employees, and a deal with Gray Line Worldwide, Inc. The company, with $35–$40 million in real estate holdings, was also developing a man-made island ocean water adventure park off Keehi Lagoon in 1997, which later was named Hawaiian Ocean Thrills' HOT Island.

Not all the ventures have been successful. Some of the real estate developments succumbed to Hawaii's recession in the 1990s, and in July 1997, Mahalo Airlines filed for bankruptcy protection, permanently suspending its flights later that year. Ground transportation services still remain the heart of Roberts' business. In 1999, the transportation division added 30 $400,000 luxury motorcoaches; a year later, a fleet of sightseeing trolleys, "Rainbow Trolleys," was launched on the streets on Oahu. The company now has more than 250 buses among its 600-plus transportation vehicles.

In 2001, Iwamoto made room for the next generation of Roberts' leaders. His son Troy, formerly the company's executive vice president, became president and chief operating offier, while Iwamoto continues as chief executive officer.

## Sources

Salkever, Alex. September 1997. "Robert's Road Trip." *Hawaii Business*: 11–17.

# J

## Frank Jao

Frank Jao. Photo courtesy of Frank Jao, President, USPAACC West Coast Chapter

**Full Name at Birth**: Trieu Chau.

**Born**: c. 1949, Haiphong, North Vietnam.

**Positions Held**: Vacuum salesman, The Kirby Company, Garden Grove, California, 1975; founder, Bridgecreek Development Company, Westminster, California, 1978– .

**Awards, Honors**: Outstanding Citizen Award, Golden West College, Huntington Beach, California, 1992.

**Summary**: Real estate developer Frank Jao, a native of North Vietnam who is of Chinese descent, served as a catalyst in establishing Little Saigon as a viable economic center in Orange County, California, in the late 1970s. He is taking his model into northern California, while also exploring business opportunities in Asia.

### Early Years and Education

The seventh of 11 children, Jao was born and raised in Haiphong, a port city north of Hanoi in North Vietnam. His father worked as a clerk for the government, but Jao became interested in business at a young age. By the time he was 14, he was distributing newspapers with the help of four employees and earning as much as his father.

After graduating from high school, Jao went to Saigon, now called Ho Chi Minh City, where he enrolled in night school. He also worked as an interpreter for the U.S. government.

## Career Highlights

Jao later secured a position with Xerox Corporation in Saigon. Because of his various business and governmental contacts, he and his wife Cathie were able to leave Saigon before the city fell to the communists in 1975. Arriving in Camp Pendleton in California with only $50, the Jaos did not waste any time beginning their new lives in America. Jao began work as a traveling salesman for The Kirby Corporation, a distributor of vacuum cleaners, while he and his wife settled into an apartment in Garden Grove, California. As Jao made his way through Orange County, he could see the potential of Bolsa Avenue in the city of Westminster. Real estate along the run-down thoroughfare was affordable and accessible to the growing Vietnamese immigrant community in the Camp Pendleton area. A trip to Los Angeles' Chinatown, more than 30 miles away, further confirmed a need for a nearby center specializing in Southeast Asian goods.

Jao, served a stint in a real estate office, then launched his own business, Bridgecreek Development Company in 1978. A year later, he purchased his first property with funds from a Chinese investor in Indonesia: a 21,000-square-foot mall on Bolsa Avenue, a remnant of a failed development project. This was the beginning of a burgeoning ethnic enclave. By 1984, according to the *Los Angeles Times* (16 March 1987), more than 200 stores and restaurants were operated by Southeast Asians in Westminster.

Jao envisioned harnessing this entrepreneurship and capital into a planned development. In concert with other business leaders and politicians, he began implementing plans for a huge commercial and cultural complex along Bolsa Avenue that would span 20 acres and house 440 retail shops. In 1985, Jao launched the first phase—Asian Village—with 160 shops and restaurants. He followed that development with Asian Garden Mall, a 150,000-square-foot pagoda-like building designed to hold 200 stores and cafes and four large 4,000- to 16,000-square-foot restaurants. In 1997, he opened the New Saigon Mall, a $4 million shopping center and cultural court featuring 124 marble and concrete statues and bas reliefs from China and Vietnam.

Not all of Jao's ideas for Westminster have materialized. Seeking to create a landmark for Little Saigon, Jao proposed a $2.4 million, 500-foot pedestrian bridge to be constructed over Bolsa Avenue. Community members, however, protested the bridge's roof design, which they felt contained too many Chinese influences and not enough Vietnamese representations, and Jao withdrew his plans. In 2000, Jao's proposal for a 270-unit senior apartment complex in Westminster near Asian Village was also halted after facing opposition from residents in the neighborhood expressing congestion concerns.

While operating multiple malls in Orange County, Jao has expanded into other markets, both domestic and foreign. He is developing International Marketplace, a 600,000-square-foot ethnic-themed mall in San Pablo, a city outside San Francisco with large Latino, African American, and Asian populations. With the normalization of U.S.–Vietnam relations, he was able to revisit his homeland and open an office in Ho Chi Minh City to investigate real estate opportunities in Vietnam. Another Bridgecreek Development Company project includes a 1.1-million-square foot, $300 million shopping center in a city in China bordering Hong Kong.

Jao and his wife, who reside in Huntington Beach, a coastal community in Orange County, have two daughters. He belongs to the exclusive Lincoln Club, a powerful Republican organization in Orange County.

## Sources

Le, Thuan. 12 January 1992. "Plaza Would Enshrine the Ambience of Saigon." *Los Angeles Times* (Orange County Edition): 11.

Lee, Don. 5 August 1997. "One Man's Vision for Little Saigon." *Los Angeles Times*: A1+ .

Mariano, Willoughby. 25 March 2000. "That L.A. Phenomenon, the Asian Mall, Spreads Across U.S., Canada." *Los Angeles Times*: C1+ .

Nguyen, Tina. 12 July 1995. "Vietnam's Promising Market: Many in O.C. Predict Bright Future, But Obstacles Remain." *Los Angeles Times* (Orange County Edition): A1+ .

Reyes, David. 16 March 1987. "Asiantown." *Los Angeles Times* (Orange County Edition): 1+ .

# Josephine Jimenez

**Born**: 6 June 1954, Lucena, Philippines.

**Education**: New York University, New York, New York, B.S., 1979; Massachusetts Institute of Technology, Cambridge, Massachusetts, M.S. in management, 1981.

**Positions Held**: Securities analyst of U.S. equities, Massachusetts Mutual Life Insurance Company, Springfield, Massachusetts, 1982–84; investment officer, Shawmut National Corporation, Boston, California, 1984–87; portfolio manager of investment in Latin America, Emerging Markets Investors Corporation, Washington, D.C. (later moved to Arlington, Virginia), 1988–91; money manager (later elevated to managing director), Montgomery Asset Management, San Francisco, California, 1991– ; founding partner, Montgomery Emerging Markets Fund, 1992– .

**Summary**: Josephine Jimenez is one of the nation's leading fund managers specializing in emerging markets of developing countries. As the founding partner of Mont-gomery Emerging Markets Fund, Jimenez travels regularly to Mexico, Latin America, Asia, Eastern Europe, and Africa to analyze new corporations as well as the economic and political climate of developing areas.

### Early Years

Josephine Jimenez was born in the town of Lucena in Quezon Province, Philippines. She spent her early childhood in her birthplace and in a village called Olongapo. According to *The Filipino Americans: From 1763 to the Present*, a family hardship required Jimenez to live in an orphanage, Hospicio de San Jose, between the age of 10 and 13. The institution, which houses both youth and elderly who are considered abandoned and homeless, was established in Manila, Philippines, in 1778 and has been continuously operated by the Daughters of Charity of St. Vincent de Paul since 1865.

Jimenez was quoted in *The Filipino Americans: From 1763 to the Present* as likening her three years at Hospicio de San Jose as being "happy days at a fine finishing school." She eventually attended St. Joseph's School in Olongapo and graduated from high school at the University of the East in Manila in 1970.

In 1972, at the age of 18, Jimenez immigrated to the United States.

### Higher Education

Jimenez financed her undergraduate education by working full-time. She eventually acquired enough money to pursue her bachelor's degree at New York University in New York City. Graduate studies at the Massachusetts Institute of Technology's prestigious Sloan School of Management immediately followed. Jimenez's thesis advisor was the legendary Franco Modigliani, a leading authority on economic theories involving interest, saving motivations, inflation, and international finance. (Dr. Modigliani would become a Nobel Prize laureate in economics in 1985.)

## Career Highlights

After gaining her master's degree in 1981, Jimenez worked for Massachusetts Mutual Life Insurance Company as a securities analyst of U.S. equities for two years. She then moved to Shawmut National Corporation, where she worked as an investor from 1984 to 1987. During this time, Jimenez was continuing her independent academic pursuits. In 1985, under the guidance of her former professor, Dr. Modigliani, she developed a proprietory stock valuation model for inflationary economies in such countries as Argentina and Brazil.

She become more involved in this area in her next position at the then Washington, D.C.-based Emerging Markets Investor Corporation. As the portfolio manager of investments in Latin America, Jimenez oversaw a fund worth $300 million. In 1989, she also received her chartered financial analyst designation.

In 1991, Jimenez left EMI for Montgomery Asset Management in San Francisco, California. In 1992, she and Montgomery partner Bryan Sudweeks cofounded the Montomery Emerging Markets Fund, the seventh such fund to be created in the United States By the mid-1990s, it had become one of the best-performing no-load emerging-markets funds. In 1997, assets reached $1 billion with investments in such countries as Brazil, Russia, Hong Kong, and China. However, bets on Brazil, rich in iron ore, and Russia, rich in oil, did not materialize and the fund's value dropped dramatically during the next two years.

Investments in emerging markets require in-depth quantitative analysis, Jimenez explained in an article she wrote in *Bloomberg Personal Finance* (November

1997). "At the outset, we examine a country's economic and political activity as well as its market fundamentals and investor sentiment," she wrote. "We also measure each market's historical volatility and its correlation with other emerging and developed markets."

This analysis is then complemented with fieldwork, for which emerging-markets analysts spend half of their time overseas. "Firsthand visits to the companies are an essential counterbalance to the conventional wisdom we may be hearing in the market," she wrote.

For example, in 2000, Jimenez attended a high-level conference in Moscow, where the newly elected president, Vladimir Putin, was the featured speaker. In 2001, she met with members of Thailand's ruling party, Thai Rak Thai, as well as the leaders of nine companies representing 50 percent of the Thai stock market, during a business trip to Bangkok.

As a managing director of Montgomery and senior portfolio manager, she currently directly oversees the Montgomery Emerging Markets Fund (MNEMX) and Montgomery Emerging Markets Focus Fund (MNEFX), which was launched in December 1987. As of 2001, MNEMX had assets of $141 million and MNEFX, $8 million.

In 1996, she was elected to serve a five-year term on MIT's board of trustees.

## Sources

Bautista, Veltisezar. 1998. *The Filipino Americans: From 1763 to the Present.* Farmington Hills, MI: Bookhaus Publishers.

Brown, Ken. 7 April 2000. "Longtime Manager Sudweeks Departs Montgomery Emerging Markets Fund." *Wall Street Journal*: 18.

Jimenez, Josephine. November 1997. "Silk Road Markets." *Bloomberg Personal Finance.*

Montgomery Funds Web site. www.montgomeryfunds.com. [accessed February 21, 2001]

# Andrea Jung

**Born**: 1959, Toronto, Canada.

**Education**: Princeton University, Princeton, New Jersey, B.A. magna cum laude in English literature, 1979.

**Positions Held**: Management trainee, Bloomingdale's, New York City, New York, 1979; general merchandising manager and then senior vice president, I. Magnin, San Francisco, California, 1987–91; vice president responsible for women's apparel, accessories, cosmetics, intimate apparel and children's apparel, Neiman Marcus, Dallas, Texas, 1991–94; president of Product Marketing Group, Avon Products, Inc., New York City, New York, 1994–96; president of Global Marketing, Avon Products, Inc., New York City, New York, 1996–97; executive vice president and president, Global Marketing and New Business, Avon Products, Inc., New York City, New York, 1997–98; chief operating officer, Avon Products, Inc., New York City, New York, 1998–99; president, Avon Products, Inc., New York City, New York, 1998–2001; chief executive officer, Avon Products, Inc., New York City, New York, 1999– .

**Awards, Honors**: Marketer of the Year, *Brandweek* magazine, 1996; Tenth in list of Most Powerful Women, *Fortune* magazine, 2001.

**Summary**: Andrea Jung is the first female chief executive officer of the world's oldest and largest direct-sales cosmetic company, Avon Products, Inc., known as "The Company for Women." Her leadership is key in instituting structural changes to aid the $5.3-billion company to remain internationally competitive.

## Early Years and Education

Jung was born in Toronto, Canada, but raised in Wellesley, Massachusetts. Her father, an immigrant from Hong Kong, worked as an architect; he gained his master's degree in that field from Massachusetts Institute of Technology. Her mother, a native of Shanghai, has worked as a chemical engineer and a concert pianist.

Jung excelled in school and studied Mandarin Chinese and classical piano. She attended Princeton University and in 1979 graduated magna cum laude with a degree in English literature.

## Career Highlights

Although she considered going to law school after graduation, Jung instead entered the world of retail sales. After completing an executive training program at Bloomingdale's in New York, she received promotion after promotion, and later went on to I. Magnin in San Francisco, where she became the department store chain's senior vice president and general merchandising manager. Later she worked as executive vice president for Neiman Marcus in Dallas, and while responsible for women's apparel and other related departments, she cultivated close relationships with designers and other fashion leaders, including Donna Karan. After marrying Michael Gould, Bloomingdale's chief executive officer, in 1993, she moved to New York City and eventually joined Avon Products, Inc., the largest and oldest direct-sales cosmetics company in the world. Since its founding in 1886, Avon, which calls itself, "The Company for Women," has distributed its products through independent representatives, known as "Avon Ladies," a term made popular in the 1960s.

Jung first joined the company as president of the products marketing group. Her strong marketing skills quickly led to other promotions: she became president of global marketing in July 1996, the same summer in which Avon was named an official sponsor of the Olympics in Atlanta, Georgia. The next year she was promoted to executive vice president and president of global marketing and new business. In this capacity, she oversaw Avon's research and development, strategic planning, and joint ventures; she was also responsible for the operations of Avon Canada and Discovery Toys, Inc., one of Avon's subsidiaries.

In 1998, she was elevated to Avon chief operating officer and president. This position gave her operating responsibilitiy for all of Avon's global business units, and she directed a more strategic and coordinated approach to global marketing. As part of this strategy, she created global brands such as Avon Color, a line of cosmetics, to replace regional brands.

In November 1999, Jung made history, becoming Avon's first female chief executive officer. However, the challenges she faced were considerable: sales growth had slowed to only 1.5 percent and a lagging four-quarter sales and earnings report had led to a 50 percent drop in the value of Avon stock. Moreover, the company was at a crossroads—what was the role of direct-sales marketing in an era dominated by the Internet and retail sales?

To address these concerns, Jung has been sensitive not to alienate Avon's 3.4 million sales representatives in 139 countries. She is committed to include her sales force as local "eRepresentatives" in the $60-million revamping of Avon's Web site–avon.com. New Avon kiosks in shopping malls, the company's initiation into traditional retail stores, are franchised to representatives. A separate line of cosmetic products has been developed for mass retailers, while an agreement with pharmaceuticals manufacturer Roche Holding Ltd. has enabled representatives to also sell nutritional supplements and vitamins. A program, Beauty Advisor, also trains representatives to become personal beauty advisors to their customers.

Also key has been the international market, which accounts for two-thirds of Avon's business. As one of her early milestone CEO events, Jung made her first-ever visit to China to speak to Avon factory workers. Multilevel marketing and showrooms have been opening in Taiwan to great success.

Jung's ascent in the business world has not gone unnoticed. In 2001, *Fortune Magazine* ranked Jung tenth in its list of "Most Powerful Women." Ninth was Martha Stewart; Oprah Winfrey was fifteenth.

Jung serves on the boards of directors of the General Electric Company and the Zale Corporation. In December 2000, she was named to the International Advisory Council of Salomon Smith Barney, the global investment bank and securities brokerage firm. She is the first woman to join this council, which comprises the world's foremost business, financial, and former government leaders. She is also a member of the Princeton University Board of Trustees and chair of the Cosmetic, Toiletry, and Fragrance Association.

Jung has a daughter from her first marriage and an adopted son from her second marriage to Michael Gould, chief executive officer of Bloomingdale's.

## Sources

"Andrea Jung, Chief Executive Officer." *Avon Products, Inc.* http://www.avoncompany.com/ investor/seniormanagement/ jung.html. [accessed July 16, 2001]

"Avon: The New Calling." 18 September 2000. *Business Week*: 136.

# K

## Charles Kim

**Full Name at Birth**: Ho Kim.

**Born**: c. 1884, Korea.

**Death**: January 1968, Los Angeles, California.

**Positions Held**: Owner-operator of Kim Brothers Company, 1921–65.

**Summary**: Ho "Charles" Kim and his partner Hyung-soon "Harry" Kim were pioneering Korean American farmers in California's Central Valley. Establishing the company Kim Brothers in the early 1900s, they are known for inventing the fuzzless peach, today known as the "Le Grand" or "Sun Grand" nectarine.

### Early Years

Korean immigrants to Hawaii and the mainland United States in the early 1900s worked as manual laborers in plantation fields or service-type industries in the cities. During World War I, Koreans began to lease farm lands as family businesses. Kim moved to the United States in 1914.

### Career Highlights

Seven years later in 1921, Kim became partners with Hyung-soon "Harry" Kim, and together they began a wholesale trucking business in Reedley, located in California's San Joaquin Valley. They first sold fruit from the valley to various outlets, including a Korean American produce market in Los Angeles.

The company, officially named Kim Brothers, eventually expanded to include large orchards, fruit-packing sheds, and nurseries, requiring an average of 200 employees—400 during harvest time. Boardinghouses were made available by the company for the workers, which included Korean Americans, Mexicans, and European Americans. Many Korean American students worked there during their summer vacations. The average wage was low—50 to 75 cents per hour—and the work hard, as described by one worker (Choy 1979, 127):

> It is very hot and dry in the fields of the San Joaquin Valley. The day starts out around 70 to 80 degrees and by noon time the temperature reaches a 105 and 110 degrees. In the Valley there is not breeze whatsoever. The heat makes that job difficult because you have to lift heavy things in the hot sun. By the end of the day your arms and legs feel very heavy and your back really aches.

While the Kim Brothers operation grew, other Korean American agriculturalists during the Depression did not fare as well. Rice growers struggled as the price of rice plummeted. Some farmers even declared bankruptcy. Weathering this uncertain financial time, the two Kims were exceedingly enterprising. They began to develop new varieties of fruit trees, working predominantly with peaches and nectarines. They are credited with inventing the fuzzless peach, also known as the "Le Grand" and "Sun Grand" brands and patented more than a dozen other hybrid fruits. Saplings of these varieties were shipped to orchards across the United States.

By the mid-1960s, Kim Brothers had six farms comprising 500 acres with an annual gross of $1 million. When they finally retired in 1965, their total operation—including farms, packing plants, and nursery facilities—was worth approximately $1.5 million. Kim Brothers was one of the largest businesses within the Korean American community.

The two Kims used their resources to contribute to the Korean independence movement and philanthropy in the Korean American community. During World War II they attempted to form a Korean American Air Force to fight against the Japanese. Establishing one of the first Korean churches in Reedley, they also were leaders of the Korean National Association of North America.

In 1957, the two Kims, leader Warren Kim, and others founded the nonprofit group, the Korean Foundation, to provide scholarships to needy students in Korea. The Kim Brothers company donated $500,000 of real estate to the foundation; more than $300,000 of scholarships were awarded to more than 200 students to attend Korean universities. The foundation eventually dissolved in 1968.

The Kims also attempted—without success—to reform the Korean National Association in the late 1950s. They then turned their efforts to establish Hanin-hoe (Korean Association) of California in 1965 and contribute funds to purchase the Korean Center building in Los Angeles. The organization is now known as the Korean Association of Southern California.

Kim died in January 1968 in Los Angeles.

### Sources

Choy, Bong-youn. 1979. *Koreans in America.* Chicago: Nelson-Hall.

Hurh, Won Moo. 1998. *The Korean Americans.* Westport, Connecticut: Greenwood Press.

Kim, Warren. 1971. *Koreans in America.* Seoul: Po Chin Chai.

# James J. Kim

**Full Name at Birth:** Joo Jin Kim.

**Born:** 8 January 1936, Seoul, Korea.

**Education:** Wharton School, University of Pennsylvania, B.A. in economics, 1959; University of Pennsylvania, M.A. in economics, 1961.

**Positions Held:** Assistant professor, economics department, Villanova University, 1962–68; founder, chairman, and chief executive officer, Amkor Technology, Inc., West Chester, Pennsylvania, 1968– ; co-founder and chairman of Electronics Boutique Holdings Corporation, West Chester, 1977– ; and chairman of Anam Semiconductor, Inc., South Korea, 1990– .

**Summary:** By launching a U.S. base of operations from his garage in Pennsylvania in 1968, James J. Kim has led the phenomenal growth of two corporations—Amkor Technology, which was closely linked to his father's semiconductor business in South Korea—and Electronics Boutique Holdings Corporation, a chain of video game stores that operate under various names.

## Early Years and Higher Education

Kim's father, Hwang Soo, operated an electronics factory in Seoul, Korea. Kim, who was the eldest son, left Korea for the United States in 1955 at the age of 19. While living with a friend, he spent a year studying English in Colorado before enrolling in the University of Pennsylvania.

While at the University of Pennsylvania, Kim gained both his bachelor's and master's degrees in economics. He accepted an assistant professorship at Villanova University in Villanova, Pennsylvania, earning only $8,000 a year.

## Career Highlights

In the late 1960s, Kim's father needed help when his partner in the electronics factory quit. Kim reluctantly resigned from academia and set up a makeshift office in his garage in his home in Paoli, Pennsylvania. According to an article in the *Philadelphia Inquirer* (1 April 2001), Kim then consulted with American engineers regarding the future of the factory, Anam Industrial, and sent telex messages to his father at night. In 1968, he launched Amkor Electronics, Inc. (AEI) to serve as the U.S. marketing and sales arm of his father's company.

Anam was one of the first Korean corporations to introduce a semiconductor packaging business. The company grew steadily, and in 1977, Anam Semiconductor listed its stock on the Korean stock market. In the same year, Kim's wife Agnes began selling digital watches, calculators, and small radios from a 10- by 13-foot kiosk at a mall in King of Prussia, a Philadelphia suburb. Originally named The Electronics Boutique, the business expanded into about 25 malls and boasted revenue of $13 million by the early 1980s.

Amkor and Anam Semiconductor, Inc. also flourished in the next two decades, buoyed by South Korea's economic growth and a strong clientele base, which included Texas Instruments, IBM, Intel and Lucent. In 1996, Anam, which was now one of South Korea's elite conglomerates, opened a semiconductor wafer fabrication foundry in the Korean city of Bucheon in a strategic relationship with Texas Instruments. U.S.-based Amkor, meanwhile, had also expanded in semiconductor packaging and testing while also managing three of Anam's packaging operations in the Philippines.

A year later, the Asian financial crisis struck: Anam was now facing possible seizure by Korean banks unless it could repay its huge loans. Amkor, with 68 percent of its 1997 revenue originating from Anam's products, was also at risk with debts of $514 million. Kim, seeking to save his family's company, decided to take Amkor public at $11 a share in May of 1998. With the additional floating of bonds, he was able to raise $3 billion. The debts were covered; Anam saved.

"There were a lot of personal guarantees given by me and my father," Kim reported to the *Philadelphia Inquirer* (1 April 2001). "In many ways, everybody was lucky. I vindicated myself to the Korean banks."

In July 1998, Electronics Boutique Holdings Corporation, with 500 electronic games stores, also went public: 5 million shares were issued at $14 per share. Approximately $70 million was raised.

In 2000, Forbes ranked Kim—with $2.7 billion in assets—ninety-fourth among the nation's 400 wealthiest people and listed him alongside Dell Computer's Michael Dell and Apple Computer's Steven Jobs in terms of high-tech influence. Through the wild fluctuations of the stock market, Kim has been able to retain his family's control over his companies. As of 2001, Kim's family owns 48.2 percent of Amkor's stock and

61.5 percent of Electronics Boutique's stocks.

Both companies are headquartered in West Chester, Pennsylvania, but Amkor's base of operations has since shifted to a suburb of Phoenix, Arizona. As of 2001, Amkor had 21,000 employees and 15 factories, mostly located in Asia, which produce computer chips for cellular telephones, personal computers, digital cameras, and air bags. In 2000, sales were at $2 billion.

Electronics Boutique, on the other hand, has more than 790 stores worldwide that sell video games, PC entertainment software, and video game hardware under the names Electronic Boutique, EBX, Stop-N-Save, BC Sports Collectibles, and EBKids. An online store—www.ebworld.com—has also been launched. In 2000, the company had sales of $768 million.

Kim is also a member of the board of managers of Vis.align LLC, a West Chester-based company which provides information technology services, and a director of Mattson Technology, Inc., a supplier of high productivity semiconductor processing equipment.

Kim, who serves as a trustee of the University of Pennsylvania, has given $3 million to the Wharton School for a new academic center and an endowment for the James Joon Jin Kim Professorship in health economics. He also supports the Gesu School, an independent Catholic school, and Young Scholars Charter School, both in North Philadelphia.

He and his wife Agnes, who make their home in Gladwyne, Pennsylvania, have three children: Susan, David, and John. Their daughter Susan is a director of Electronics Boutique, and her husband, John R. Panichello is the company's senior vice president and chief financial officer.

Kim became a naturalized citizen in 1971.

## Sources

Amkor Technology. http://www.amkor.com. [accessed July 26, 2001]

Anan Semiconductor. http://www.amkor.com [accessed July 26, 2001]

"Bytes & Boxes." 9 October 2000. *Forbes*: 185.

Electronics Boutique. http://www.ebholdings. com. [accessed July 23, 2001]

Fernandez, Bob. 1 April 2001. "Amkor Founder's Relentless Push." *Philadelphia Inquirer*: C1.

Steffora, Ann. 20 April 1998. "Amkor's Dilemma–IPO or Sell." *Electronics News*: 48–49.

# Jeong H. Kim

Jeong H. Kim. Photo courtesy of Jeong H. Kim.

**Born:** 1961, South Korea.

**Education:** Johns Hopkins University, Baltimore, Maryland, B.S. in electrical engineering and computer science, c. 1982; Johns Hopkins University, Baltimore, Maryland, M.S. in technical management; University of Maryland, College Park, Maryland, Ph.D. in reliability engineering, 1991.

**Positions Held**: Officer, U.S. Navy, c. 1982–89; senior project engineer, Allied Signal Inc., Morris Township, New Jersey, c. 1991; founder, chief executive officer, and president, Yurie Systems Inc., Lanham, Maryland, 1992–98; president of Broadband Carrier Networks, Lucent Technologies, Murray Hills, New Jersey, 1998; chief executive officer of the Optical Networking Group, Lucent Technologies, Murray Hills, New Jersey, 2000; president of Optical Networking Group, Lucent Technologies, Murray Hills, New Jersey, 2000; advisor, Lucent Technologies, Murray Hills, New Jersey, 2001– .

**Awards, Honors**: Emerging Entrepreneur Award, Ernst & Young; High Tech Entrepreneur Award, Liberty Award, Institute for Corean-American Studies, Inc., 1998.

**Summary**: Jeong H. Kim, a former officer in the U.S. Navy who earned a doctorate in engineering from the University of Maryland, taught himself communications technology at the height of the Internet revolution and launched his own company, Yurie Systems, Inc. In 1998, he sold the company for $1 billion.

## Early Years

Kim, who was born in South Korea, came to Glen Burnie in Anne Arundel County in Washington, D.C., with his parents when he was 14 years old. His acculturation into American society was difficult at times, because classmates teased him about his accent and Asian heritage. However, these difficulties only strengthened Kim's resolve to try harder. "People who are successful are often those who feel they have something to prove," he said in an interview with the *Washington Post* (28 April 1998). During the day, Kim attended high school; in the evenings, he worked at a 7-Eleven convenience store to save money for college.

## Higher Education

Receiving a scholarship to attend Johns Hopkins University in Baltimore, Maryland, Kim majored in electrical engineering. During his freshman year, he befriended Kwok L. Li, a relationship that would prove invaluable in the future. Kim invested in Li's computer startup, which remained in operation until 1985.

After obtaining both his bachelor's and master's degrees in three years, Kim joined the U.S. Navy. He served as an officer on a nuclear submarine for seven years and then went on to get his doctorate in reliability engineering from the University of Maryland in 1991.

## Career Highlights

Kim worked as a contract engineer for a subsidiary of AlliedSignal at the Naval Research Laboratory. Up to this point, Kim had no formal training in communications technology, according to *Business Week* (26 May 1997), yet he was able to devise a system for the military so that multimedia communications could take place on the battlefield. The laboratory's associate director, Herbert Rabin, also a former administrator with the University of Maryland engineering school, encouraged Kim to further develop his idea. In 1992 Kim left AlliedSignal and then, with $400,000 raised from mortgaging his home and from credit cards, he started Yurie Systems, Inc. in Landover, Maryland. Named after Kim's older daughter, the company specialized in selling asynchronous transfer mode (ATM) access equipment in which voice, video, and data are transmitted over phone lines and satellite and wireless networks.

With Rabin's contacts, Kim was able to attract high-profile individuals for his board of directors, including former Central Intelligence Agency head R. James Woolsey, according to the *Washington Post* (28 April 1998). Kim's college friend, Li, eventually joined the company's management team. Soon Yurie was gaining governmental contacts: its products were used to monitor elections in Haiti in 1995 and action on the warfront in Bosnia. Soon AT&T Corporation's equipment division, which later became part of Lucent Technologies, approached Yurie with an exclusive sales agreement which gained Kim's company $6 million in revenues.

After the exclusivity deal ended, Yurie also provided products to Bay Networks Inc., Ericcson Inc., and Lucent. The company reportedly led both in worldwide and Northern American sales for ATM wide area network (WAN) access equipment for 1996 and 1997. Among its offerings were the LDR200 ATM access concentrator (which won Data Communications Hot Product Award for WAN equipment) and the LDR5 for small-office applications.

By 1997, Yurie, with more than 240 employees, was ranked first on *Business Week*'s Hot Growth list, with revenues growing an average of 385 percent over three years to $21.6 million in 1996. Revenues had increased to $51 million in 1997, the same year Yurie completed its initial public offering. In the following year, Kim again attracted national attention when he sold his company to Lucent Technologies, Inc. for $1 billion. Under the provisions of the acquisition, Kim, who would become the president of Lucent's carrier networks division, received $510 million, making him among the 100 richest high-tech executives in the nation.

"People can look at someone like me," Kim said in an article in the *Washington Post* (28 April 1998). "They see someone who looks different, who speaks with a funny accent. And maybe they'll say, if I set my goals high, maybe I can succeed like that, too."

Kim did not waste any time in giving away some of his fortune. He pledged $5 million to the University of Maryland to establish the Jeong K. Kim Information Technology Endowment Fund for student scholarships, faculty research, and a new building (the first on campus to be named after an Asian American). Kim also donated $1 million to Johns Hopkins University, where he gained his bachelor's and master's degrees.

Hope was high for fiber-optic technology networks. In an article for *Telephony* magazine (9 October 2000), Kim explained the merits of such technology. "In the coming years, optical networks will make the Internet faster, smarter, easier to use, and more ubiquitous by enabling carriers to transmit information at the speed of light, while reducing power consumption and equipment and operational costs."

However, the economic downturn in early 2000 hit high-tech companies hard. The market for fiber-optic equipment diminished, and Lucent Technologies underwent a serious corporate downsizing and reorganization. In July 2001 Kim resigned from his latest position as Optical Networking Group president, but continued on as an advisor for Lucent.

Kim is married and has two daughters.

### Sources

Barrett, Amy. 26 May 1997. "Yurie Systems: High-Tech Hot Rod." *Business Week*.

Berselli, Beth. 11 August 1997. "Cutting Communications Data to Size." *Washington Post*: F5.

Henry, Shannon. 10 December 1998. "Millionaire Is True to His School." *Washington Post*: B1.

Kim, Jeong. 9 October 2000. "Lighting the Way." *Telephony*: 48–56.

Leibovich, Mark and Mark Mills. 28 April 1998. "For Immigrant, A Billion-Dollar High-Tech Deal." *Washington Post*: A1+ .

# Kija Kim

Kija Kim. Courtesy of Harvard Design & Mapping

**Born**: c. 1942, South Korea.

**Education**: Seoul National University, B.A. in geography, 1965; Clark University, Worcester, Massachusetts, M.A. in geography, 1967; Babson College, Wellesley, Massachusetts, Executive Management Program, 1992, 1994; The Amos Tuck School, Dartmouth College, Hanover, New Hampshire, Business Executive Program, 1995; The Amos Tuck School, Dartmouth College, Hanover, New Hampshire, Advanced Business Executive Program, 1996.

**Positions Held**: Cofounder, president, and chief executive officer, Harvard Design and Mapping Company, Inc., Cambridge, Massachusetts, 1988– .

**Awards, Honors**: Academy of Women Achievers Award, YWCA, Boston, 1995.

**Summary**: Trained cartographer Kija Kim has taken map-making to the next level: she leads her own Cambridge-based company that provides the high-technology expertise to chart transportation systems, municipal utility services, and even toxic-waste sites.

## Early Years and Higher Education

Kim was born in South Korea during World War II. Her father owned his own construction business; Kim had early aspirations to become a lawyer, but she instead decided to pursue a career as a professor.

Kim majored in geography at Seoul National University, one of the top educational institutions in South Korea. She graduated at the top of her class in 1965, and traveled around to the United States to continue her geography studies at Clark University in Massachusetts.

## Career Highlights

Although Kim originally intended to return to South Korea and teach at Seoul National University, her life took a detour when she got married in America. While raising a son and a daughter, she worked as a consultant to engineering firms. Working as a cartographer in 1970s, Kim used a compass, slide rule, paper, and pens. However, with the advent of the personal computer in the 1980s, computer-aided design (CAD) technology soon became the industry's standard. In the late 1980s she managed the computer-aided mapping division of a Boston-based engineering firm. There she met Jim Aylward, a former city manager. The two saw the potential for a company that specialized in geographic information systems (GIS) to produce computerized maps for analysis and display of information. With $15,000 borrowed from relatives, Kim and Aylward launched Cambridge Design and Mapping, Inc. in 1988. At that time, very few GIS firms were in existence, and even fewer were being led by women.

These computerized maps had many advantages over traditional ones. As explained by reporter Maria Shao in the *Boston Globe* (11 December 1994), "Information such as the location of pipelines, household incomes, or soil types is overlaid onto maps displayed on computer screens. The result: A visual database that can be more precise, detailed, and easier to manipulate than cumbersome paper maps."

Kim soon took her company into the international arena. In 1991, with only seven employees, she participated in an Asian trade mission with Massachusetts Governor William F. Weld. As a result, she was able to forge a partnership with a Japanese company, NS Environmental Science Consultants of Japan, to help map toxic waste disposal sites in Japan. Within a year she was involved in two multimillion-dollar projects.

Kim also attended the MIT Enterprise Forum in 1991 to network with potential investors. Her client roster grew steadily to include Boston Edison, Massachusetts Water Resources Authority, and Raytheon Engineers and Constructors. By 1994, Harvard Design and Mapping was embarking on the largest mapping and GIS project in New England. Through its work with Boston Edison, the company provided technical services and application development toward creating a database that maps wires, poles, manholes, and other equipment in 40 communities throughout the greater Boston area. Three years later, Harvard Design and Mapping had formed a strategic alliance with the utility company to design, develop, and implement GIS that could be used to assist land and facility use.

Harvard Design and Mapping grew to become a $2 million enterprise with 20 employees. In 1994, Kim married Jim Aylward, the company's vice president. (Her first marriage ended in divorce.) They subsequently opened another office in Washington, D.C., to serve their many governmental clients, including the United States Postal Service, U.S. Coast Guard, Smithsonian Institution, and Federal Emergency Management Agency.

Kim has been active in public service. She is on the Clark University Board of Trustees board of the Bentley College Graduate School of Management, Massachusetts Asian American Commission, and Massachusetts Women's Commission. She also has volunteered her time with the Korean American Citizens League of New England and the Asian Task Force Against Domestic Violence.

## Sources

Harvard Design and Mapping. http://www.hdm. com. [accessed August 22, 2001]

Kija Kim. http://www.kijakim.com. [accessed August 21, 2001]

Lopez, Julie Amparano. 16 October 1992. "Small Business: Foreign Flights—Going Global: Many Small Firms Think It's a Good Route to Expansion; Perhaps, But It Can Be a Bumpy Journey." *The Wall Street Journal*: R20.

Shao, Maria. 11 December 1994. "Mapping Up in Computers: Cambridge Firm Offers Custom Cartography." *Boston Globe*: 96.

# Steve Y. Kim

Steve Y. Kim. Photo courtesy of Rising Tiger Ventures, LOC.

**Born**: 1950, Seoul, South Korea.

**Education**: California State University, Los Angeles, California, M.S. in electrical engineering.

**Positions Held**: Engineer, Burroughs Corp., Los Angeles, California, c. 1980s; engineer, Litton Data Systems, Woodland Hills, California, c. 1980s; engineer, Phalo Optical Systems Division, Southern California, c. 1980s; founder, president, chief executive officer, Fibermux, Chatsworth, California, 1984–91; cofounder, chief executive officer, chairman, Xylan Corporation, Calabasas, California, 1993–99; managing partner, Alcatel Ventures, Los Angeles, California, 1999– ; chairman of the board, Mockingbird Networks, Cupertino, California, 2001– .

**Summary**: Steve Y. Kim, an engineer originally from South Korea, built one of the fastest-growing companies in southern California in the 1990s. As one of the managing partners of Alcatel Ventures, he works to fund the efforts of other emerging entrepreneurs.

## Early Years and Higher Education

Kim's father was involved in the publishing business in Seoul, South Korea. When Kim was a small boy, the business went bankrupt and the family struggled financially during the years of the Korean War.

Kim attended college in South Korea. After gaining his undergraduate degree, he, like other young men in his country, served in the military for a mandatory period of two years. Unhappy with the prospect of working in a Korean conglomerate with little chance of early promotion, Kim left for the United States in 1976 at the age of 26, with only $2,000 in his pocket.

## Career Highlights

One of Kim's first jobs was as a stock boy in an auto-parts warehouse. He later was able to secure positions with the Burroughs Corporation, a computer networking company that was eventually acquired by Unisys, and Litton Data Systems, an electronic and information systems firm, which is now under defense contractor Northrop Grumman. At night, Kim pursued his education and obtained a master's degree in electrical engineering from California State University, Los Angeles.

It was his next job with a fiber-optics modem company that inspired Kim to begin his own enterprise. Kim began Fibermux Corporation, a fiber-optic data networking company, in his garage in 1984. For the next seven years, Kim was able to spur Fibermux's phenomenal growth. When it was acquired by ADC Corporation for $54 million in 1991, the company had more than 300 employees and $50 million in revenues.

Kim's entrepreneurial spirit spurred the creation of another high-tech company in August 1993: Xylan Corporation. In the 1990s, a premium was placed on high-speed data routing for networks of personal computers and workstations, referred to as local area networks (LANs). Until this time, conventional hubs and routers were used to transfer information from one user to another within corporations. In response, Xylan had developed a new, powerful, and inexpensive switch shaped like a pizza box (thus earning it the name Pizza-Switch) so that personal computer users could share files of large volumes with minimal glitches.

Xylan's switches met the needs of large corporations and within three years, the Calabasas, California-based company was doing $30 million of sales a year. In March 1996, Xylan went public to much fanfare.

The stock's opening-day performance broke records: from its initial price of $26 a share, the stock jumped up as high as $75. The *Los Angeles Times* named it as one of the state's fastest growing high-technology companies—by 1999, Xylan had revenues of $348 million with more than 4,000 customers and approximately 1,000 employees. In spite of its phenomenal growth, the stock price did not increase accordingly, thereby frustrating Kim. "Today's investors are favoring the large companies," he said in an interview with the Associated Press (2 March 1999). "They sees us as still small."

As a result, in March 1999, French-based telecommunications company Alcatel, which already owned 6.5 percent of Xylan, announced its acquisition of the entire Calabasas corporation for $2 billion in cash. Before the sale, Kim himself owned 30 percent of Xylan.

Kim continued his relationship with the buyer, Alcatel, first as head of a consolidated U.S. networking division, and later as a managing partner of Alcatel Ventures, a venture capital fund in Los Angeles. The fund was established from a $60 million investment from Alcatel and another $60 million raised by Kim and his associates. In 2001, he was also named chairman of the board of Mockingbird Network, a switching company in Cupertino, California.

Kim and his wife Jung have a son and a daughter.

### Sources

Darlin, Damon. 4 November 1996. "A Need Import: Entrepreneurial Spirit." *Forbes*: 210+

"Team." Alcatel Ventures. http://www.alcatelventures.com/team.html [Accessed September 15, 2001].

Vrana, Debora. 3 July 2000. "Entrepreneur Turns His Talents to Venture Fund." *Los Angeles Times*: C1, C6.

# Gennosuke Kodani

**Born**: January 1867, Nemoto, Japan.

**Died**: 1 July 1930, Whalers Cove, California.

**Education**: Keio University, Tokyo, Japan, degree in marine biology, 1893.

**Positions Held**: Partner, Point Lobos Canning Company, Whalers Cove, California, 1898–1930.

**Awards, Honors**: Kodani Village, Historical Site, California Department of Parks and Recreation, 1994.

**Summary**: Gennosuke Kodani, called the father of the California commercial abalone business, parlayed his expertise in marine biology in the creation of a fishery and cannery on the Monterey Peninsula in the 1890s. He partnered with his landlord, Alexander M. Allan, to operate the Point Lobos Canning Company while pioneering diving techniques for the harvesting of abalone.

### Early Years and Higher Education

Kodani, the eldest son of Seisaburo and Tayo Kodani, was born in the village of Nemoto, located in Chiba Prefecture, north of Tokyo, Japan. He was born a year before Emperor Meiji took over Japan, signaling the end of the nation's isolationist policy. The Meiji government stressed the role of education in the modernization of Japan. Kodani took advantage of this policy and enrolled in Keio University, one of Japan's elite educational institutions in Tokyo. He gained his college degree in marine biology in 1893.

### Career Highlights

About the time Kodani was studying at Keio, another Japanese national, Otosaburo Noda, had come to the United States. Working as a labor contractor in communities near Monterey, California, he eventually established a base to fish for salmon in the Cannery Row area. It was in 1895 that Kodani noticed the proliferation of red abalone beds. Called *awabi* in Japan, abalone was considered a valuable delicacy throughout Asia. Abalone had been previously harvested in Monterey by Chinese immigrants in the 1880s, but the number of Chinese had been greatly reduced by discriminatory immigration laws.

Excited by his discovery, Noda informed the Agricultural Ministry of Japan of this new supply of the much-desired abalone. Because Keio University was asked to investigate this report, the university dispatched Kodani, then a recent graduate. According to family documents, Kodani left the port of Yokohama on September 14, 1897, aboard the *Doric*. He eventually reached Monterey in October of the same year.

Upon his arrival, Kodani's mission became an entrepreneurial one. Verifying the rich supply of abalone in rocky coves along the Monterey Peninsula, Kodani identified a site for a base for harvesting and processing the mollusk. This would be Whalers Cove at Point Lobos, five miles south of Monterey. Not only supporting a good environment for the harvesting of abalone, Whalers Cove was also close to steamship transportation for shipments to San Francisco and Asia. In late 1897, Kodani rented the cove and neighboring area from the Carmel Land and Coal Company. The following year, the property was sold to Alexandar M. Allan, who quickly identified the marketability of Kodani's future enterprise. The two men formed a partnership in 1898 to launch the Point Lobos Canning Company.

While Allan provided the capital, Kodani was able to recruit the appropriate personnel and adapt Japanese diving methods to conditions in Monterey. Joining his enterprise was his younger brother, Nakajiro, who was involved in the marine industries in their home prefecture of Chiba in Japan. Because Chiba was facing declining abalone levels and recovering from a debilitating fire, divers were open to traveling across the Pacific to be part of the Point Lobos Canning Company. However, diving techniques needed to be altered as the water near Point Lobos was considerably colder than that in Japan. Instead of donning just shorts and lightweight shirts, the divers had to be equipped with deep-sea suits and metal helmets. The divers rode in boats powered by a single sculling oar, according to *The California Abalone Industry—A Pictorial History*. Crewmen were required to stay on board the boat to monitor the pump that would provide air through a hose connected to the diver's suit. When the diver had filled a net bag with two or three dozen abalone, he would pull on a line and the crewmen would haul the catch into the boat. The net bag, consisting of a circular top made from bamboo or sake barrel hoops, was developed in Japan; the design is still used today.

After the abalone was harvested, the canning process began. The fresh abalone was packaged under the label, "Monterey Brand Deep Sea Shell Fish." Featured on the label was the company logo consisting of a diver, diving boat and crew, and Whalers Cove in the background, as well as recipes for abalone salad, chowder, and fritters. Forty-eight 16-ounce cans would be contained in one case.

According to a Report of the Commissioner of the U.S. Commission of Fish and Fisheries published in *The California Abalone Industry—A Pictorial History*, the Point Lobos Canning Company was quite productive in 1904: 60 cases of abalone had been packed for local use, 200 cases for the Japanese market, and 400 cases for the Chinese market. Moreover, the company had dried 48,000 pounds of abalone and prepared 44,000 pounds of shells for jewelry.

Kodani and Allan did not limit their operation to Whalers Cove. Kodani, suspecting that another good source of abalone could be found farther south, traveled 115 miles down the coast to Cayucos, a small town with a deep-water pier and a level shore that would be ideal for the drying of abalone. By 1903, Kodani and Allan had established an additional site for abalone harvesting and drying in Cayucos. A cannery followed, and in 1916, approximately 6,000 cases or 288,000 pounds of abalone were shipped. It was estimated that the Point Lobos Canning Company accounted for 75 percent to 80 percent of the total California abalone market.

During the course of his abalone business, Kodani faced many governmental regulations. In 1913, the exportation of abalone was prohibited. Two years later, the drying of abalone was prohibited. Ordinarily, this would have led to the demise of a seafood industry, but the introduction of the abalone steak in California sparked a new demand for the mollusk.

Kodani operated the abalone fishery and cannery at Whalers Cove for 30 years. (The Cayucos cannery eventually closed before 1920.) He and his wife, Fuku Tashiro, raised their nine children in the Monterey area. Kodani died on July 1, 1930, at the age of 63. The Point Lobos Cannery closed a year later, due to the economic depression and the state's plans to convert the area into a park.

In 1994, Kodani Village was officially dedicated as a historical site by the California Department of Parks and Recreation.

## Sources

Lundy, A.L. 1997. *The California Abalone Industry—A Pictorial History*. Flagstaff, AZ: Best Publishing Company.

Yamada, David T. and the Oral History Committee, Monterey Peninsula Chapter, Japanese American Citizens League 1995 (JACL). *The Japanese of the Monterey Peninsula: Their History and Legacy 1895–1995*. Monterey, CA: Monterey Peninsula Chapter, JACL.

# Lata Krishnan

**Born**: 1961, Palghat, India.

**Education**: London School of Economics, London, England, B.S. with honors in economics, 1982.

**Positions Held**: Auditor, Arthur Andersen & Company, London, England; tax accountant, Hill Vellacott & Company, London, England; financial analyst, Montgomery Asset Management, San Francisco, California, 1986–88; cofounder and chief financial officer (later vice president of business development, vice president of human resources and administration), SMART Modular Technologies (later acquired by Solectron), Fremont, California, 1988– ; member, Angels' Forum, Los Altos, California, 1999– .

**Awards, Honors**: Women of Vision Award, Career Action Center, 2000.

**Summary**: Lata Krishnan, who cofounded a computer memory company with her husband and a family friend, became the highest-compensated woman executive among publicly traded firms in Silicon Valley in 1998 with an annual salary of $3.9 million. Krishnan and the two other cofounders of SMART Modular Technologies represent East Indian Americans who lived in East Africa in the 1960s and 1970s before resettling in the United States.

## Early Years and Education

Krishnan's father, Gopal, was a bank executive who was assigned to such faraway posts as Africa and England. As a result, Lata and her brother spent their childhood years in Kenya; Jamshedpur, India; and London. "My mother, even though she comes from a very conservative family, raised me to be independent, to stand on my own feet," Krishnan said in an interview with *India-West* (30 July 1999). Krishnan attended the prestigious London School of Economics.

## Career Highlights

After graduating with honors in the 1980s, Krishnan attained accounting positions with the London-based firms of Arthur Andersen and Hill Vellacott & Company. At this time, she became a member of the Institute of Chartered Accountants in England and Wales. In 1986, at the suggestion of her father, Krishnan joined her brother in Houston, Texas, to explore opportunities in the United States. A call to a headhunter led to a position with Montgomery Asset Management in San Francisco. While living in northern California, Krishnan dated Ajay Shah, a young East Indian man originally from Uganda. The two had earlier met in England, and Shah, a graduate of the University of Baroda in India and Stanford University, was now working as an engineer and manager at Advanced Micro Devices in Sunnyvale, California. Within months, they were married in a ceremony in London.

Returning to California, the couple pursued their independent business interests. "He's very supportive of what I want to do, of letting me make my own decisions," Krishnan spoke about her husband to *India-West*. Shah had moved from Advanced Micro Devices to Samsung Semiconductor, Inc., where he was responsible for new semiconductor memory product development and the managing of Samsung's leading line of memory products. Krishnan, meanwhile, was developing a small semiconductor business.

While working at Samsung, Shah saw the potential for high-density memory modules, a product that would enable computer manufacturers to design personal computers with different levels of memory. "At the time, there were only a couple of module companies that had started up, and it was a very small, undefined, unrefined, Wild West marketplace. But I could see the trend," he said, quoted in *Electronic Buyers' News* (22 December 1997).

He pitched the concept to the company, but management was not interested. Krishnan, experienced in the finance world, suggested that they create a business plan and seek outside investors for an independent enterprise. Joining the team was a friend and Shah's colleague at Samsung, Mukesh Patel. Patel shared a similar family history as Krishnan and Shah: he had lived in East Africa during the 1960s and 1970s, before Ugandan President Idi Amin expelled South Asians from the region.

The team approached venture capitalists, but in the 1980s, Silicon Valley was not as receptive to new ideas as it would be in the 1990s. As a result, Shah turned to their retirement funds, as well as family and friends, to raise approximately $100,000. In 1988, SMART Modular Technologies was officially launched in Fremont, California. (SMART is an acronym for surface mount and reflow technology.) In the beginning, it focused primarily on manufacturing independent memory modules, and it had approximately 30 employees. With the demand for DRAM (dynamic random-access memory) high, SMART Modular Technologies was able to attract large original equipment manufacturers (OEMs) such as Apple Computer, Inc. In 1995, SMART acquired Apex Data, Inc., a manufacturer of wireless and wireline data/fax modem and connectivity devices in Pleasanton, California.

As the company's first chief financial officer, Krishnan's key role was assisting in the launch of the initial public offering (IPO) in November 1995, which, according to *Forbes* (4 November 1996), created at least 20 new millionaires. The decision to go public, according to observers, was to finance the company's growth and establish more credibility with OEMs. Three million shares of common stock were sold at $8.66 per share; by July 1997, the stock had soared to $43 per share. Sales in 1997 doubled from the previous year to $695 million with a $45.4 million profit.

After the IPO, Krishnan's responsibilities changed to vice president of business development and then vice president of human resources and administration. Both Krishnan and Shah placed a premium on low overhead, and even purchased used furniture for their offices. In 1998, Krishnan made an annual salary of $3.9 million, thereby making her the highest paid woman executive in Silicon Valley—an accomplishment that was heralded in regional and business publications.

SMART continued its high-growth path. The company offered more than 500 products focused on three areas: quick-turn DRAM modules; communications devices; and embedded system products. In terms of memory modules, fast turnaround was key: manufacturing cycles were reduced to less than 48 hours. Additional factories were created in Puerto Rico, Scotland, and Malaysia, with design centers and sales offices throughout the world. Employees, including those in offshore offices, reached 1,900. After 11 years of consistently growing profitability, the company had $1 billion in revenues.

SMART's success did not go unnoticed. In September 1999, Milipitas, California-based Solectron Corporation agreed to purchase $2 billion in stock to acquire SMART. The transaction was the largest to date in the electronics manufacturing services industry. The three original partners—Krishnan, Shah, and Patel—who collectively owned 35 percent of the outstanding shares all voted in support of the merger. Shah stayed on as the CEO and president of Solectron's Technology Solutions division, while Krishnan became more active in personal entrepreneurial projects. She is a member of Angels' Forum in Los Altos, California, which provides seed money for Silicon Valley and Bay Area startup companies.

Krishnan is also a fellow of the Silicon Valley chapter of the American Leadership Forum. She serves on the boards of the Tech Museum and the Children's Discovery Museum in San Jose, as well as on the advisory board of Narika, a Berkeley-based support group for battered women, and the board of trustees of the Indian Business and Professional Women.

She and Shah have a son and daughter and reside in Fremont, California.

## Sources

Angels' Forum Web site. www.angelsforum.com [accessed December 17, 2001].

Chopra, Sonia. 4 September 1999. "The Rise of a Silicon Valley Role Model." *Rediff.*

Damon, Darlin. 4 November 1996. "A Needed Import: Entrepreneurial Spirit." *Forbes*: 210+.

Donahue, Sean. 23 February 1998. "Ajay Shah." *Forbes*: 54–56.

"Journey to Success Began in Flight from Africa." 18 July 1999. *San Jose Mercury News.*

MacLellan, Andrew. 22 December 1997. "Ajay Shah—Helped Create a Market and Runs

Leading DRAM Module Maker." *Electronic Buyers' News*: 86+ .

Rao, Janhavi. June 1999. "SMART Modular Technologies: Staying Smart in the High-Tech World." *Indzine*.

SMART Modular Technologies Web site. www.smartmodular.com [accessed December 17, 2001].

Sundaram, Viji. 30 July 1999. "Smart Woman Goes Far." *India-West*.

Thurm, Scott. 14 September 1999. "Solectron Agrees to Buy Smart Modular, Posts Better-Than-Expected Earnings." *The Wall Street Journal*: A3.

# L

## Tri La

**Full Name at Birth**: Tri Minh La.

**Born**: c. 1953, Vietnam.

**Education**: University of Houston, Houston, Texas, B.A.

**Positions Held**: Vice president of marketing, Kim Son restaurants, Houston, Texas.

**Awards, Honors**: Entrepreneur of the Year Award, Asian Chamber of Commerce, 1996; Outstanding Young Houstonian, 1998.

**Summary**: Tri La and his family created a chain of successful Vietnamese restaurants in Houston after escaping from Vietnam on a wooden ship in 1979. The La family has been instrumental in introducing Vietnamese cuisine to the Houston area, which has the third-largest Vietnamese community in the United States.

### Early Years

La's parents, Son and Kim La, were successful restaurateurs in their native Vietnam. Their business, Kim Son, was in fact the largest restaurant in the city of Vinh Long. In 1975, seven years after its opening, Kim Son was closed after the communist government took over Vietnam. Intent on someday leaving the country, the family survived economically by buying and selling goods in the black market for several years.

When La was 16 years old, the family was finally ready to make their journey across the South China Sea. On June 12, 1979, 10 family members, including La's six siblings and grandmother, left Vietnam on a crowded refugee ship. They had paid $3,000 in gold bars for each person's passage.

Within two days, the ship had been captured by a Malaysian naval vessel. The refugees were robbed; the boat was then towed to a remote island in Indonesia, where the La family were forced to fend for themselves in a desolate camp for eight months. A United Nations relief team then helped the Las to relocate to a more established refugee camp on the island of Gelang. Relatives in Houston agreed to sponsor the family, and immigration visas were prepared. The Las would finally make it to the United States. (Between 1980 and 1991, 327,183 Vietnamese entered the United States as refugees, according to Larry Hajime Shinagawa in his article "The Impact of Immigration on the Demography of Asian Pacific Americans.")

## Education

Arriving in Houston on August 16, 1980, Tri La and his family had only $2,500. Living in a two-bedroom apartment, the family shared two used cars while La and the other adult children worked alongside their parents for U-Totem convenience stores seven days a week. In spite of this demanding work schedule, Tri was able to gain his bachelor's degree from the University of Houston.

## Career Highlights

Within two years of arriving in Houston, the La family had saved $10,000; with another $10,000 borrowed from relatives, they were able to open their first restaurant in the United States, also named Kim Son, in 1982. La and his family members all worked at the restaurant without drawing salaries. Sales totaled $280,000 in the first year and reached $1 million by 1985. By 1986, enough money was saved to open a second restaurant in west Houston.

In 1992, La and his eldest brother Tan embarked on building an expansive new restaurant in the Chinatown in downtown Houston. When the two-story, 22,000-square-foot Kim Son was completed in February 1993, it was the largest Asian restaurant in the state of Texas. Loans from the Houston-Galveston Area Local Development Corporation and the Small Business Development Corporation help fund the $1.9 million enterprise.

More restaurant locations have followed. By 2000, nine Kim Son restaurants were operating in the Houston area. A Little Kim Son eatery was even opened at the University of Houston, La's alma mater. The family has actively supported various philanthropic efforts, including the city's Business Arts Fund and a "Thank You, America!" celebration commemorating the twentieth anniversary of the Vietnamese refugee re-settlement program. "One chopstick is easy to break," he said in an interview with the *Houston Chronicle* on November 26, 1995. "But a bunch of chopsticks together, no one can break. If you always stay together, you will always succeed. But if you separate, if you divide, always you will fail."

La is married to Teresa Bo. They have two children, Thomas and Tessie.

## Sources

Rodriquez, Lori. November 26, 1995. "Appreciation for America: La Family Leads Vietnamese Community in Giving Thanks." *Houston Chronicle*: A1.

Schindeler, Janice. February 24, 1993. "Immigrant Family Finds Success after Perilous Voyage to Freedom." *Houston Post*: F1.

Shinagawa, Larry Hajime. 1996. "The Impact of Immigration on the Demography of Asian Pacific Americans." In Bill Ong Hing and Ronald Lee, eds., *Reframing the Immigration Debate*. Los Angeles: LEAP Asian Pacific American Public Policy and UCLA Asian American Studies Center.

Vip, Pamela. March 21, 1993. "Houston's Asian Entrepreneurs Reshaping Adopted Home." *Houston Chronicle*: B1.

# David K. Lam

David K. Lam. Photo courtesy of David Lam Group

**Born**: 1943, China.

**Education**: University of Toronto, Toronto, Canada, B.S. in engineering physics; Massachusetts Institute of Technology, M.S., Ph.D. in chemical engineering.

**Positions Held**: Engineer, Semiconductor Division, Texas Instruments; engineer, Xerox Corporation; engineer, Hewlett-Packard Company, 1976–79; founder, Lam Research Corporation, Fremont, California, 1980–85; cofounder, president, chief executive officer, Expert Edge, Palo Alto, California, 1988–97; founder and chairman of David Lam Group, 1997– ; chairman, Tru-Si Technologies, Palo Alto, California, 1999– ; board of directors, IteX, Santa Clara, California, 1999– .

**Summary**: Engineer David K. Lam began his own semiconductor processing equipment company after he felt that he had hit the glass ceiling at established high-tech corporations. Integrating pioneering research he had begun while a doctoral student, Lam introduced the first fully automated plasma etching system for semiconductor manufacturing. A former member of the Presidential Commission of Minority Business Development, he is also devoted to helping Asian Americans gain leadership positions in both the private and public sectors.

## Early Years

Lam was born in China during World War II, but raised in Cholum, South Vietnam. He had six brothers and one sister; his father was a businessman. Although his parents fled to South Vietnam to escape the war, they soon found themselves in another military battle. "We had learned to duck under the bed when we heard machine guns in the streets because of some insurgencies within the country," said Lam in an interview with high school student Sandra Ledbetter (www.thetech.org/revolutionaries/lam).

Teenage boys could be drafted into the military, so when Lam was in junior high (around 1956), he and his siblings were sent to Hong Kong while their parents stayed in South Vietnam. Lam learned to be independent and adjust to his new surroundings. After graduating from high school, he took a 21-day voyage across the Pacific to attend college in Canada.

## Higher Education

Lam gained his bachelor's degree in engineering physics from the University of Toronto. From there, he moved to the United States, where he obtained both his master's degree and doctorate in chemical engineering from the Massachusetts Institute of Technology (MIT). His dissertation centered on plasma chemistry, or etching, in which selected portions of metal and oxide film are removed from a silicon wafer so that a chip's circuitry pattern can be revealed.

## Career Highlights

After graduating from MIT, Lam began work at Texas Instruments, developing experimental chip-making processes based on plasma chemistry in its recently established semiconductor division. His first order of business was to walk the production line rather than seclude himself in a laboratory. "I walked in with a Ph.D., but I didn't know a damn thing," Lam stated to *The Business Journal* (8 August 1994). "I was so humbled. I talked with the line workers—they were my teachers."

After Texas Instruments, Lam worked with Xerox Corporation and then Hewlett-Packard in Silicon Valley in California. During his three years at Hewlett-Packard, he became a leader of one of its small engineering groups, but was passed over for promotion in favor of a European American man who had recently graduated from college. This corporate decision disillusioned Lam, who wanted to prove that he could be a good manager. Seeing a great potential in the use of plasma etching in production, he began making plans to launch his own enterprise. He created a business plan and approached potential investors for startup funds. His mother was the first investor, followed by his brothers. After securing a large commitment from venture capitalists, Lam officially launched Lam Research Corporation in Fremont, California, in 1980.

In the beginning, Lam was involved with the technical side of the business, including design, prototype production, and testing. A year and a half later, the company made its first sale, introducing the industry's first fully automated plasma etching system for semiconductor manufacturing.

Because the United States was in the middle of an economic recession in the early 1980s, Lam Research found the competition stiff. In 1982, Lam hired industry veteran Roger Emerick as chief executive officer and together they cornered the market for "dry etch" in which ionized gases remove film from semiconductor chips. A strategic partnership was also developed in Japan at that time.

In 1984, the company went public. A year later, Lam left the corporation, and then became involved in the reorganization of Link Technologies, a computer-terminal company that was sold to Wyse Technology in 1987. In 1988, he founded another high-tech venture, Expert Edge, with Stanford University professor Erlison Tse and $2.5 million from a Hong Kong-based family. Expert Edge, based in Palo Alto, was established to create user-friendly software compatible with either Macintosh or Windows platforms for the control of robotics manufacturing equipment. It began shipping products in 1992 and posted $2 million in sales the following year. At that time, 20 percent of sales originated from Southeast Asia.

Lam, meanwhile, continued to advance his personal mission to see more Asian American representation in corporate boardrooms. In 1990, he was named to serve on President George Bush's newly formed Commission on Minority Business Development. He has also been active with the Asian American Manufacturers Association and is a senior fellow of the American Leadership Forum and a member of the board of governors of the National Conference for Community and Justice.

In the mid-1990s, Lam launched his own consulting company, the David Lam Group in Campbell, California. He and his wife Eppie have two sons.

## Sources

Anonymous. 9 April 1990. "Lam Tapped to Serve on Presidential Commission." *The Business Journal-San Jose*: 27.

David Lam Group Web site. www.davidlam.com [accessed June 4, 2001].

Matsumoto, Craig. 8 August 1994. "David Lam: Asian Immigrant Presses Quest for Leadership Diversity." *The Business Journal*: 12.

The Tech Web site. "The Revolutionaries." www.thetech.org/revolutionaries [accessed June 17, 2001].

Yu, Winifred. 11 September 1985. "Asian Americans Charge Prejudice Slows Climb to Management Ranks." *The Wall Street Journal*: 1+ .

# Joanna Lau

**Born:** 1959, Hong Kong.

**Education:** State University of New York (SUNY) at Stony Brook, New York, B.S. in computer sciences and applied mathematics, Massachusetts, 1981; Old Dominion University, Norfolk, Virginia, M.S. in computer engineering; Boston University, Boston, Massachusetts, M.B.A., 1991.

**Positions Held**: Programmer, General Electric, Binghamton, New York, 1981–89; Digital Equipment Corporation, Massachusetts, 1989–90; Founder, chief executive officer, chairman, Lau Technologies, Acton (later Littleton), Massachusetts, 1990– .

**Awards, Honors**: First Annual Leadership to Women in Business, New England Council, 1993; Turnaround Entrepreneur of the Year, *Inc.* magazine, 1995; Pinnacle Award for Achievement in busienss, Boston Chamber of Commerce, 1997.

**Summary**: Joanna Lau took over a beleaguered defense contractor in Massachusetts and transformed it into a leading provider of military systems and digital imaging for the commercial market. Lau is the first Asian American woman to head a high-technology corporation involved in the defense industry.

## Early Years

Lau was raised with her three sisters and four brothers in Hong Kong. Her father, who had been involved in the bulldozer business, died from a stroke when Lau was only 16. Two of Lau's sisters had already left Hong Kong for New York and Toronto, so Lau's mother, Hing Fong Chui, moved the rest of the six children to New York City in 1976.

In the United States, Lau's mother become a garment worker to support the family. Lau realized the difficulty of such labor, and committed herself to her studies while working after school at Barnes & Noble and Carvel Ice Cream. Lau had previously con-

sidered becoming a schoolteacher, but with the advent of computer technology, she instead pursued science and mathematics.

## Higher Education

Lau received a full scholarship to attend State University of New York (SUNY) at Stony Brook in Long Island, where she double majored in computer science and mathematics. She went on to gain a master's degree in computer engineering from Old Dominion University in Norfolk, Virginia.

## Career Highlights

Lau joined General Electric in Binghamton, New York, where she met her future husband, Denis Berube. Lau initially worked as a programmer for the commercial aerospace department before being transferred to Virginia and then to Lynn, Massachusetts, where she worked on GE's Factory of the Future. This project involved both computing and manufacturing. "I kind of like the hands-on aspect of just making widgets—the feel, the touch, that people really use it—it really is a turn-on for me," she said to *CommonWealth* magazine (Winter 2000). "I like writing software because it's like putting a puzzle together."

After eight years with GE, where she also worked on defense projects, Lau left for Digital Equipment Corporation (DEC). At DEC, Lau oversaw the production of disk drives under the goal of "six-sigma," or only six failures per thousand units. She also studied interrelationships between various cultures and technologies from around the world.

While working, Lau also took classes at Boston University toward her M.B.A. degree. It was a class on operations management that connected Lau to the company, Bowmar/ALI, a defense-industry subcontrator in Acton, Massachusetts, which became the topic of her paper. Bowmar/ALI had been struggling; it had lost $1.5 million a year on $7 million of sales with only two customers remaining. Nonetheless, Lau was impressed with the staff and its niche, which was building electronics for the Bradley armored fighting vehicle. She also discovered that the parent company, Arizona-based Bowmar Instrument Corporation, was in the middle of post-bankruptcy reorganization and not interested in retaining the facility.

In spite of her past history with established companies like GE, Lau was ready to take a risk. She and her husband Denis mortgaged their house; in addition, Lau cashed in her pension, yet she was still short of capital necessary to purchase Bowmar/ALI. She then went to the 60 employees, including managers, purchasers, and production-line workers to join her in acquiring the company. Twenty-three agreed to invest $10,000 to $20,000 each. With a $750,000 minority-targeted Small Business Administration loan and $1.2 million in another bank loan, Lau was able to raise a total of $3.1 million for the buyout. The company, renamed Lau Technologies, became independent in March 1990, with Lau holding 56 percent ownership. Husband Denis joined the company as chief operating officer.

Lau did not waste any time in reestablishing relations with its customers—FMC Corporation, GE-Pittsfield, and the U.S. Army—and ensuring them that Lau Technologies would be producing products at new higher standards. In five months, a test came: the Persian Gulf War had started and both FMC and the Army requested that their order for the Bradley personnel carrier be met in one year instead of five. Seventy temporary assembly workers were hired to meet the deadline. Lau Technolo-

gies also assisted FMC in correcting a circuitry problem on the Bradley that affected operation of a gun turret. The problem was solved in 45 days, rather than the normal 270 days. Lau Technologies' phenomenal performance was recognized with one of the Army's 11 Supplier Excellence Awards a year later.

Within two years, the company had paid off its debts. A subsidiary devoted to military products manufacturing, Lau Defense Systems, was organized, and later Andrew Davis, formerly of FMC, was named its chief executive officer. In spite of the company's strong reputation in this area, Lau knew that she could not depend entirely on the defense industry for business.

"A company has got to have the will to change," Lau said in an interview with *Inc.* (December 1995). "You have to say, 'OK, I'm going to walk out of this comfort zone and into a totally unknown black hole.'"

In 1992, she committed $300,000—35 percent of Lau Technologies' retained earning—toward establishing new civilian markets. Nearly 100 percent of profits were devoted to research and development the following year. Five employees worked exclusively on researching new opportunities and, in the end, digital imaging was identified as a strong area. In 1994, Lau Technologies launched its Viisage Technology subsidiary to advance and develop facial recognition capabilities.

Digital imaging has a number of applications: driver license and other ID programs, including voter systems; fraud deterrence; and security improvement. For instance, Viisage developed in conjunction with ImageWare Software of San Mateo, California, a Face ID package for the Los Angeles Sheriff's Office in which a composite sketch of a criminal suspect is compared against a database of digital mugshots for possible matches. Another client was the

Electoral Office of Jamaica, who ordered a new voter ID system consisting of long-life secure identification cards and electronic collection stations.

Viisage has seen its economic performance go up and down. Although its revenues grew $11.9 million in the first six months of 1996, sales fell in subsequent years. Its initial public offering raised $18.7 million, of which $8.8 million was used to pay off its debts. Revenues fell again in 1998 to $16 million, $13 million less than the previous year. The value of the stock, 70 percent of which is owned by Lau Technologies, has also seen severe shifts from $20 to 63 cents. With the renewed demand for face recognition systems in airports and other public areas, however, Viisage has strong possibilities in the future. The Lau Security Systems division, formed in 1997, markets products and services based on this facial recognition technology.

In 1999, Lau Technologies acquired Vista Controls Corporation, the major U.S. supplier of electronic control systems and subsystems for the defense industry. For the next two years, Vista, together with Lau Defense Systems, offered electronic equipment for such powerful U.S. Army combat vehicles as the Bradley armored fighting vehicle, Abrams M1A2 tank, and the Brigade armed vehicle. They also provided flight control computers used on the U.S. Air Force Global Hawk, as well as electronics for F-16s, the Space Shuttle, and Navy submarines.

By 2000, Lau Technologies was doing $60 million in business. A year later, it entered an agreement with Curtiss-Wright Corporation to sell both Lau Defense Systems and Vista, headquartered in Santa Clarita, California, for $41 million in cash and the assumption of certain debt. Curtiss-Wright, based in Lydhurst, New Jersey, also became a licensee for Lau Technologies' lat-est patented "Face in the Crowd" facial recognition product line for certain U.S. government and industrial markets.

Lau is a board member of various institutions, including the BostonFed Bancorp, Inc., Concord-Assabet Family and Adolescent Services, Kennedy Library Foundation, and Massachusetts Taxpayers Foundation. She is also a member of the International Women's Forum, Committee of 200, and Young President's Organization. She, her husband Denis Berube, and their family reside in Massachusetts.

### Sources

Ahern, Nichole Bernier. Winter 2000. "Turning Heads and Profits." *CommonWealth*.

Anonymous. December 1995. "Cutbacks, Layoffs, Plant Closings." *Inc.*: 90+ .

Anonymous. December 1995. "The Hottest Entrepreneurs in America." *Inc.*: 35+ .

Brokaw, Leslie. December 1995. "Case in Point." *Inc.*: 88+ .

Lau Technologies. www.lautechnologies.com [accessed November 19, 2001].

Mulqueen, John T. 25 November 1996. "Viisage Helps Agencies Eyeball the Bad Guys." *CommunicationsWeek*: 78.

Star, Mark. January–February 1996. "Image Is Everything." *Transpacific*: 68+ .

Strother-Vien, Leigh. January 1998. "Mugshot Recognition Meets Witness Composite Sketches in L.A." *Advanced Imaging*: 22.

# Chris Lee

**Full Name at Birth:** Christopher Lee.

**Born:** 30 October 1956, New Haven, Connecticut.

**Education:** Yale University, New Haven, Connecticut, B.A. in political science, 1980.

**Positions Held:** Entertainment segment producer, *Good Morning America*, New

York City, New York, 1980–82; first assistant director and assistant editor, *Dim Sum*, San Francisco, California, 1983; assistant story editor, TriStar Pictures, Burbank, California, 1985–87; director of creative affairs, Tristar Pictures, Burbank, California, 1987–88; senior vice president of motion picture production, TriStar Pictures, Culver City, California, 1989–97; president of motion picture production, TriStar Pictures, Culver City, California, 1997–98; president of motion picture production, Columbia Pictures, Culver City, California, 1998; producer and president, Chris Lee Productions, Culver City, California, 1999– .

**Awards, Honors**: Justice in Action Award, Asian American Legal Defense and Education Fund; Visionary Award, East West Players; Legacy Award, Museum of Chinese in the Americas; Business Person of the Year, Asian Business League of Southern California.

**Summary**: Chris Lee was the first Asian American to head the production arm of a major Hollywood movie studio. With his experience in the traditional motion-picture studio system as a foundation, he has launched his own media enterprises, which range from the production of computer-generated films and music videos to comic books.

### Early Years and Higher Education

Born to a Chinese American father and a Scottish American mother, Lee spent his early years in Hawaii, a place known for its ethnic diversity, and attended Iolani School in Honolulu. However, when it came time for Lee to go to college in 1975, he returned to his birthplace, New Haven, Connecticut, to attend Yale University, his father's alma mater. While his ancestors had originally come to the United States as railroad workers, Lee, a fifth-generation Chinese American, was free to explore all professional fields, including those previously closed to ethnic minorities.

### Career Highlights

After graduating with a degree in political science, Lee went to New York City to attempt to break into the television industry. His first job was as an entertainment segment producer for ABC's *Good Morning America*. In 1983, he gained more hands-on experience in the film industry as first assistant director and assistant editor on the feature film, *Dim Sum*, directed by Wayne Wang. Here Lee was able to merge his interest in his Asian American heritage with the entertainment field.

Determined to one day produce his own projects and movies, he began work as a free-lance script analyst for TriStar Pictures in 1985 and quickly segued into a position as an assistant story editor. His success in recruiting talented filmmakers for the studio, including John Woo, Gus Van Sant, and Cameron Crowe, gained him successive promotions—from director of creative affairs to vice president of production to finally president of motion picture production for TriStar Pictures. Among the award-winning films under Lee's care were *Philadelphia*, *As Good as It Gets*, and *Jerry Maguire*. Lee was in his position as president of production at TriStar Pictures for less than a year when Sony Pictures Entertainment named him president of production at Columbia Pictures, where he had been instrumental in putting together *The Patriot*.

In spite of his success within the studio system, Lee aspired to become an independent producer. In 1998, he left Columbia to begin his own independent ventures—Chris Lee Productions and SuperMega Entertainment, the latter with a partner, Joseph Kahn. In 1999, he signed a two-year, first-look production deal with Sony Pictures Entertainment for movies drawn from new computer technologies. Chris Lee Productions set up shop on the Sony lot on the old MGM studios in Culver City, California.

"The focus of the company is going to be what I call 'boy popular culture,'" Lee said to the *Hollywood Reporter* (20 January 1999). "There is a wonderful need for movies like that on the slate, and I intend to fill it."

Lee made history in 2001 when a movie he coproduced with Square USA, *Final Fantasy*, was released in July. It was the first feature-length animation created entirely with computer graphics technology. Based on the computer game of the same name, *Final Fantasy* featured the Asian American character Aki Ross, a digitally created actress who is expected to appear in other film projects. Approximately 200 computer technicians worked on the movie, which involved the building of a $45-million studio in Honolulu, Hawaii. "*Final Fantasy* is the first time animators have tried to create humans as lifelike as possible," said Lee to the *Boston Globe* (29 July 2001). "We want the audience to forget that they're watching a cartoon."

The film, however, opened to mixed reviews and the box-office returns fell short of expectations. Video rentals, on the other hand, seem to be posting strong results. Lee has moved on to a variety of other projects, which include the production of new action films involving Asian directors, music videos with SuperMega Entertainment, and even comic books with Dreamwave Productions. Lee is also a member of the Committee of 100, founder of the Coalition of Asian Pacifics in Entertainment (CAPE), and a board member of the National Asian Pacific American Legal Consortium.

"I think the lesson here is that you can build new businesses, and you can work outside of traditional businesses that perhaps were not always willing to let us become involved and to run them," said Lee in an interview with Mario Machado. "And that's what I'm doing. I'm building my own company basically and I'm doing it within the structure of Hollywood."

## Sources

"2001 Gala: Chris Lee's Bio." Asian American Federation. www.aafny.org/special/gala2001/lee.asp [accessed March 15, 2001].

Galloway, Sephen. 20 January 1999. "No Idle Hands: Lee in SPE Deal." *The Hollywood Reporter*. 1, 79.

Honeycutt, Kirk. 19 May 1997. "Lee Taking Over TriStar's Production." *The Hollywood Reporter*: 1, 22.

# David S. Lee

David S. Lee. Photo courtesy of Cidco Communications Corporation

**Full Name at Birth**: Sen-Lin Lee.

**Born**: 23 June 1937, Beijing, China.

**Education**: Montana State University, Bozeman, Montana, B.S. in mechanical engineering, 1960; North Dakota State University, Grand Forks, North Dakota, M.S. in mechanical engineering, 1962; honorary doctorate, Montana State University, Bozeman, Montana, 1993.

**Positions Held**: Manager of printer technology, Diablo Systems, Inc., Hayward, California, c. 1960s and 1970s; cofounder and executive vice president, Qume Corporation, 1973–78; executive vice president, ITT Qume, 1978–81; president, ITT Qume, 1981–83; vice president, ITT; group executive and chairman of ITT's Business Information Systems Group, 1983–85; president and chairman, Data Technology Corporation, Santa Clara, California, 1985–88; president (later chairman and chief executive officer), Qume Corporation (merged with Data Technology), 1988–90; founder and chairman, Cortelco Systems (later changed to eOn Communications Corp.), Atlanta, Georgia, 1991– ; chief officer, eOn and chief executive officer, Cidco Communications, Morgan Hill, California, 2000. Communications Corp., Atlanta, Georgia, 2001– .

**Awards, Honors**: President Bush's Asian/Pacific Heritage Award, 1992; Chinese Institute of Engineers—U.S.A. Achievement Award; Albert Einstein Technology Medal for Entrepreneurship (Israel), 1999.

**Summary**: Engineer and entrepreneur David S. Lee perfected the daisy-wheel printer in the early 1970s, which revolutionized the course of computer printer technology. Throughout his long career he has founded and led several leading-edge multimillion-dollar corporations, encour-aging other Chinese Americans to start high-tech companies in California's Silicon Valley.

## Early Years

Lee was born in Beijing, China, and lived there until age 13. His father was the head of Beijing's transportation systems and the family had to move 13 times to escape bombings and fires in the war-torn region. With the communist takeover of China, the family fled to Korea. They eventually relocated to Hong Kong and later to Taiwan, where Lee finished junior high school. The family's next destination in 1951 was Buenos Aires, Argentina, where Lee's father operated an import business and Chinese restaurant.

## Higher Education

After being educated in China, Hong Kong, Taiwan, and Argentina, Lee decided to pursue his university studies in the United States. With only $600 in his pocket he joined his sister in Montana and enrolled at Montana State University in 1956. His father had encouraged him to major in engineering; Lee decided upon mechanical engineering. He gained his bachelor's degree at Montana and a master's degree at North Dakota State University. He then pursued his doctorate at Ohio State University. Because his family remained in Argentina, Lee had to finance his education on his own, which he did through jobs with the Forest Service, a lumberyard, and college dormitories.

## Career Highlights

While living in Ohio, Lee obtained a position with nearby machinery giant, National Cash Register (NCR). Shortly thereafter, he relocated to California where he met his future wife, Cecilia, and worked briefly at Singer Company's calculator subsidiary. Joining a start-up computer printer company, Diablo Systems in Hayward, California, Lee would make his mark in the world of computer technology. As the manager of printer engineering at Diablo, his team would develop the first commercially successful daisy-wheel printer in 1972. Up to that time, IBM's standard 10 character-per-second ball-type printer had dominated the market. The Diablo printer, in contrast, was able to produce 30 characters per second.

Xerox Corporation subsequently purchased Diablo for $28 million, reaping Lee a $1 million profit. After being passed over for an executive post, Lee and a partner began their own independent company, Qume Corporation, in 1973. Qume specialized in creating daisy-wheel printers and within five years, it had become one of the largest printer companies in the world. In 1978, the company was sold to ITT for $164 million, personally netting Lee $10 million. Lee continued on at the international conglomerate in various high-level positions and traveled to Taiwan to secure computer manufacturing agreements. From 1983 to 1985, he was head of the ITT Business Information Systems Group, responsible for the conglomerate's personal computer peripherals businesses, including the Qume subsidiary. In the fall of 1985, ITT had merged the Business Information Systems Group with end-user telephone equipment operations into an umbrella organization, leading Lee to resign for other opportunities.

Lee organized 20 investors to purchase Data Technology Corporation, a struggling data storage subsystems vendor in Santa Clara, California, whose sales had dropped from $100 million to $2 million. In November 1985, he was named the company's president and chairman. By this time, the area's Silicon Valley was beginning to establish a reputation for technological innovation and enterprise. Both the Chinese Institute of Engineers and the Asian American Manufacturers Association (AAMA), groups established in the 1970s and early 1980s, helped to set a foundation for individuals to network and exchange ideas. Lee was a founding member and leader of such organizations, including the Monte Jade Science and Technology Association.

In June 1988, Lee made national news when he repurchased his original company, Qume, from French telecommunications giant Alcatel for $20 million. "It's like being reunited with my baby," Lee, then 51, said to *Business Week* (July 25, 1988).

Qume, however, was struggling. Its annual sales had plunged from a high of $273 million in 1984 to $70 million. Competition from dot-matrix and laser printers had severely affected the daisy-wheel printer manufacturer. Lee was convinced that liquid-crystal technology from Data Technology and Casio Computer Company of Japan would propel Qume back to the top. Cutting the combined companies' workforce and consolidating offices, Lee also embarked on reducing costs.

The company eventually went public but when the stock price began to falter, Lee organized a partnership with Wearne Brothers Ltd. of Singapore to acquire Qume again. Due to the downturn of the Taiwan stock market—one of the conditions of the buyout—the transaction failed. The same year Lee did, however, purchase Cortelco Systems, Inc., a communications solutions provider with a century-long history, based in Memphis, Tennessee.

In 1993, Cortelco split into separate companies: Cortelco International, Inc., Cortelco Kellogg, and CMC Manufacturing,

Inc., the latter two based in Corinth, Mississippi. In 1997, Cortelco International changed its name to Cortelco Systems.

Lee, now in his sixties, continued to expand his holdings. In 2000, he organized a group of investors to purchase the telephony equipment business of a Morgan Hill, California, company, CIDCO, Inc. Under Lee's leadership, CIDCO Communications is a separate company which focuses on the production of telephony hardware.

Also in 2000, Cortelco Systems announced that it would change its name to eOn Communications Corporation to signal a new strategic direction into both voice and Internet networks. An initial public offering was filed the same year. Months later Lee was named the new chief executive officer of the company.

In spite of Lee's multiple business pursuits, he has also made civic contributions to his region and community. He served as an advisor to both presidents George Bush and Bill Clinton through the Advisory Committee on Trade Policy and Negotiation, and additionally to Governor Pete Wilson through the California Economic Development Corporation (CalEDC). In 1994, he was appointed to the Regents of the University of California by Governor Wilson, a position that he holds to this day.

Lee's wife Cecilia, is also an entrepreneur in her own right. She is founder and president of hybridArts.com, a company based in San Jose which provides CD production. She is also chair of Asian Culture Teaching and founder and honorary chair of the Crystal Children's Choir. In addition to raising their three children, Cecilia Lee has also been a silent partner in many of her husband's business pursuits. They make their home in Los Altos Hills, California.

## Sources

Peterson, Jonathan. 6 August 1989. "Asian Entrepreneurs." *Los Angeles Times*: B1–B5.

Shao, Maria. 25 July 1988. "David Lee Is Back at Square One and He's Thrilled." *Business Week*: 62–63.

Wong, Gerrye. 23–29 March 2001. "Inventor of Daisywheel's Spin on Life." *AsianWeek*.

# Lilly V. Lee

**Full Name at Birth**: Lilly Mu Lee.

**Born**: 30 June 1930, Los Angeles, California.

**Death**: 19 August 2000, Los Angeles, California.

**Education**: City College, Los Angeles, c. 1948–49.

**Positions Held**: Real estate agent and then vice president of acquisitions, Lawrence Company, San Fernando Valley, California, c. 1970; Lilly Enterprises and Lilly Property Management Company, Los Angeles, 1973–2000.

**Summary**: Raised in a time in which girls could only aspire to become secretaries, Lilly Lee forged a successful real estate business in southern California while supporting two sons after the breakup of her marriage. A constant optimist, she maintained close ties to her ethnic community in Chinatown and became a philanthropic leader in cultural and charitable associations in both California and Asia.

## Early Years

Lee grew up amidst the tight-knit Chinese community in Los Angeles. Her father Mu Pin Sun, who came to the United States from China through Hawaii, operated an herbal shop in both the old and new Chinatowns. (The old Chinatown was relocated due to the building of a new train station in downtown Los Angeles.) The herbal shop was a gathering place for Chinese men who often stopped by to smoke water pipes, drink, and read newspapers.

Lee learned many lessons by watching her father dispense herbal medicine to the ill—even to people who could not afford to pay. Her father also was active in the community, and served as the president of the Chinese Consolidated Benevolent Association (CCBA). Lee, the youngest, with four older brothers, often sat quietly in the back of various banquets and association meetings. Whenever she had a question, she was told by family members: "A girl should not ask these questions."

Although she was sheltered within the confines of Chinatown on one hand, Lee also experienced the glamorous world of Hollywood. Through the referral of her father's friend, she worked in her first movie, *The Good Earth*, at the age of 3. Others followed, including *Too Hot to Handle* with the legendary Clark Gable. By the age of 12, however, Lee ceased her work with the Hollywood studios to make more time for her studies.

When Lee wasn't attending public school or Chinese-language school at the Chinese Catholic Center, she helped her family with the herbal shop. She also had her own flower stand in Chinatown where she sold gardenias on Saturday nights to tourists.

## Higher Education

Knowing that most young women in the 1950s either became clerks or secretaries before marriage and motherhood, Lee attended city college for two years with the intention of becoming a legal secretary. Soon after securing a position at a downtown law firm, she got married and eventually left the working world to raise two sons. During her marriage, however, her husband, who was

planning to retire at the age of 40, encouraged her to gain her real estate license. This license would prove to be the key to her financial independence and success.

## Career Highlights

Working with larger and larger real estate agencies, Lee graduated from selling single-occupancy residences to selling apartment buildings. She became well-versed in real estate syndication—in which multiple investors are secured for a large project—while at the Lawrence Company in San Fernando Valley, and became vice president in charge of acquisitions. After two years, she left to begin her own company in Beverly Hills in 1973.

She appealed to Chinese investors, and by the late 1970s, was brokering Los Angeles property deals with Hong Kong millionaires. In the 1980s, she had a personal net worth of more than $1 million, which was growing more than $500,000 annually with her real estate companies Lilly Enterprises, Inc. and Lilly Property Management Company. Both her sons, Randal Lee and Craig Lee, joined her business enterprises.

Seeing the future of U.S.–China relations and need for more cultural understanding, she helped to fund a "Pacific Rim Profiles and Technical Report" to provide information for business, government, and human services organizations about the changing demographics of Asian Pacific communities. A director of the Los Angeles Chamber of Commerce and president of its Women's Council, she served on the executive board of the Greater Los Angeles World Trade Association.

She was also on the board of the American Red Cross and United Way, Inc. Using her connections with diverse Asian Pacific American groups, she helped assemble a 40-member board of corporate and professional leaders to support the Asian Pacific

American Legal Center of Southern California. Her civic service garnered her an honorary "doctor of philanthropy" degree from Golden Gate University.

"The greatest deterrent to your success is yourself," stated Lee at the first West Coast Chinese American Women's Conference meeting in Los Angeles (*Los Angeles Times*, 23 August 2000).

She died on August 19, 2000 at the age of 70.

## Sources

Allen, John. 24 February 1986. "You Better Do Your Homework: Doing Business with L.A.'s Asians." *Downtown News*: 6.

Oliver, Myrna. 23 August 2000. "Businesswoman, Cultural Leader Lilly Lee Dies at 70." *Los Angeles Times*: B1, B6.

Suellen Cheng's interview with Lilly Mu Lee, 24 July 1982, 30 July 1982, Southern California Chinese American Oral History Project, UCLA Asian American Studies/Special Collections.

# Noel Lee

Noel Lee. Photo courtesy of Billy Douglas

**Born**: 25 December 1948, San Francisco, California.

**Education**: California Polytechnic State University, San Luis Obispo, B.S. in mechanical engineering.

**Positions Held**: Engineer, Lawrence Livermore Laboratory, Livermore, California, and Lawrence Berkeley National Laboratory, Berkeley, California, c. 1970s; drummer, Asian Wood, c. 1970s; founder and "Head Monster" (chief executive officer and president), Monster Cable Products, Inc., 1978– .

**Awards, Honors**: Dealerscope Hall of Fame, Dealerscope Consumer Electronics Marketplace magazine, 1999; Humanitarian Award, Los Angeles Unified School District, 1999; Ernst & Young Northern California Entrepreneur of the Year Award, Ernst & Young, 2000.

**Summary**: Noel Lee has combined his love for music with technology and business in launching Monster Cable Products, Inc., which produces high-quality audio, video, and computer cables and related accessories. Through specialized incentive and training programs for retailers, Lee has created an effective sales and marketing network.

### Early Years and Higher Education

Lee's parents, Chein-San and Sarah Lee, resided in China and South Korea before settling in San Francisco, California. His father had served as a correspondent for the Central News Agency of China for many years; he later worked as a language officer for the United Nations Military Armistice Commission in Seoul, South Korea.

Lee and his four sisters were all born and raised in San Francisco. "During my childhood through high school it was tough because discrimination against Asians was quite strong," he stated in an interview with ABCFlash.

Lee gained his mechanical engineering degree from California Polytechnic University in San Luis Obispo on California's central coast.

### Career Highlights

After graduating from college, Lee became a laser-fusion design engineer at University of California at Berkeley-managed Lawrence Livermore Laboratories in northern California. However, his passion remained music. While working as a scientist during the day, he devoted his evenings and weekends to playing drums in a band called Asian Wood and tinkering with his home audio system. At this time most systems were wired with ordinary "zip cord," the same cable used for electrical household and lamp wire. Lee discovered that larger cables constructed of more copper and different constructions, including various methods of braiding, resulted in better audio performance.

Around this time, the Asian Wood band had achieved some success and was offered a world tour. Lee quit his job at the Lawrence Livermore Laboratory, packed up his family, and went on the road. Unfortunately, only after two weeks, the tour was canceled. Lee and his family were stranded in Hawaii, and had to work their way back home.

After returning to San Francisco, Lee worked as an independent representative for some small speaker companies, but saw a future in his new cable product. Working out of his apartment and later, his in-laws' garage, he packaged a 12-gauge speaker cable in a clear plastic jacket. He called his new product, "Monster Cable," because of its monstrous size and powerful audio performance. His introduction of Monster

Cable at the 1978 Consumer Electronics Show in Chicago was met with a phenomenal response. Borrowing $250,000 from a bank, he officially launched Monster Cable Products, Inc.

In 1979, Monster Cable moved to a factory in San Francisco. From the beginning, Lee realized he had to create a dynamic marketing system to get his cables into the consumer's hands. While some audio product manufacturers only sold their product in a few specialized stores, Lee embarked on getting Monster Cable wares into diverse outlets—from high-end boutiques and mid-level chains to discount superstores, according to journalist Larry Alan Kay. Name recognition was crucial, and soon, due to displays and attractive packaging, Monster Cable became the top brand name among cable manufacturers. In keeping with Lee's interest in music, Monster Music, an independent record label and division of Monster Cable, was launched in 1989. A year later, the company moved its headquarters to south San Francisco, and within six years, it was doing $50 million in business with 400 employees in California and Israel.

Lee's successful strategy in working with retailers and their sales staff has also been well-documented. He adopted a sales method implemented by McDonald's fast food restaurants—workers are trained to increase sales by mentioning french fries with every hamburger sold. In the case of Lee's company, it was a matter of getting salespeople to mention Monster Cable whenever stereo systems were being purchased.

In 1998, Monster Cable invested 15 percent of its sales, or $13 million a year, into training and incentive packages, specifically the M4 Dealer Success Program, which trains salespeople on how to sell add-on products, and the M4 Manager's

Workshop, which trains mid-managers to motivate their salespeople. As part of the M4 program, salespeople who are able to get the largest percentage of customers to purchase Monster Cable products were rewarded with trips to Napa Valley, Hawaii, and even Germany.

Sales of Monster Cable products are inevitably in the retailer's interest. According to *Forbes* magazine (28 December 1998), Monster cables average a 45 percent gross profit margin, whereas other audio and video products yield about 30 percent. As a result, even though audio and video cables usually form a small percentage of a retailer's total sales, they make up a significant portion of gross profit.

To handle increased demand, Monster Cable unveiled a new facility and distribution center in 1998 in Brisbane, California, where its headquarters is currently located. Its diversification efforts have led to the creation of more than 1,000 products. A new division, Monster Power, was introduced to develop audio components and AC power conditioning products. In 1998, the company launched a new line, Home Theater Power Centers, high-end surge protectors that are color coded, flexible, and feature longer cords than those made by competitors. In 2000, Monster Cable announced the formation of Monster Game, a new division for the release of premium gaming accessories customized specifically for the PlayStation 2 Computer Entertainment System.

Lee, a member of the Asian Business League of San Francisco, has been honored by various organizations. In 1999, Lee was inducted into the Dealerscope Hall of Fame, along with such industry leaders as Dr. Sidney Harman of Harman International. The same year Los Angeles Unified School District recognized Lee with a Humanitarian Award for his contribution to

the Mobile Electronics Program, in which he donated $75,000 worth of cable.

## Sources

Eljera, Bert. 11–17 December 1997. "Making a Monster." *Asian Week*.

La Franco, Robert. 28 December 1998. "Selling Sizzle with Sizzle." *Forbes*: 66+ .

Lieber, Ed. 9 November 1998. "Monster Cable Ready to Pounce." *HFN: The Weekly Newspaper for the Home Furnishing Network*: 48.

Maren, Michael. June 1992. "The Monster Method." *Success*: 42+ .

Monster Cable Web site. www.monstercable.com [accessed *February 19, 2001*].

Warshaw, Michael. May 1996. "The Golden Key to Selling." *Success*: 44+ .

# Loida Nicolas Lewis

Loida Nicholas Lewis. Photo courtesy of Loida Nicholas Lewis

**Full Name at Birth**: Loida Nicolas.

**Born**: c. 1943, Sorsogon, Philippines.

**Education**: St. Theresa's College, Quezon City, Philippines; University of the Philippines, College of Law, Quezon City, Philippines, graduate, c. 1960s.

**Positions Held**: Administrative assistant, Law Students Civil Rights Research Council, New York City, New York, 1969; attorney, Manhattan Legal Services, New York City, New York, 1970–73; publisher of monthly magazine for Filipino American community, New York City, New York, 1971–79; lawyer, Law Offices of Antonio Martinez, New York City, New York, 1970s; general attorney, Immigration and Naturalization Services (INS), 1979–90; chairman and chief executive officer, TLC Beatrice International, New York City, New York, 1994–99.

**Awards and Honors**: Presidential Award for Filipino Individuals and Organizations Overseas.

**Summary**: After her charismatic husband, Reginald F. Lewis, died suddenly from brain cancer in 1993, his Filipino widow Loida Lewis eventually took the reins of his billion-dollar food company, TLC Beatrice International, as chairman of the board and chief executive officer. Through her leadership, the company—which was heralded as the world's largest African American-owned business when it was acquired through a highly publicized leveraged buyout in 1987—pared down its expenses, repaid its debt, and eventually was liquidated to optimize returns for shareholders.

### Early Years

Lewis was raised in a large, tight-knit Catholic family in the province of Sorsogon, Philippines. Her father, Francisco J. Nicolas, abandoned his dream of becoming a lawyer at the age of 21 after his fledgling lumber business began to expand and become profitable. It eventually became

NICFUR, one of the Philippines' largest and best-known furniture manufacturers. Nicolas infused some of his unfulfilled dreams into his five children.

### Education

After graduating cum laude with a bachelor's degree from St. Theresa's College, Lewis entered the University of the Philippines' College of Law, where she was involved with the university's student council and National Union of Students. She excelled in her studies and ranked seventh in her law school class. After graduation, she passed the Philippine Bar exam in 1968. Before she began work as a lawyer, her father rewarded her with a round-the-world trip. Her stop in New York City would eventually change the course of her life.

### Career Highlights

In New York City, Lewis lived with her sister Imelda, who was completing her master's degree in art history at Columbia University, at the Aberdeen Hotel. During this time, Lewis took a job as an administrative assistant with the Law Students Civil Rights Research Council, headed by Harvard Law School graduate Reynaldo Glover. Glover introduced Lewis to one of his Harvard classmates, Reginald F. Lewis, then 26, who was working at a Manhattan law firm: Paul, Weiss, Rifkind, Wharton, and Garrison in 1969. After only a few months of dating, the couple got married on August 16, 1969, in a lavish ceremony at the Paco Roman Catholic Church in Manila, Philippines. (Philippines vice president at the time, Fernando Lopez, served as godfather to the newlyweds.) When they entered Hawaii after a honeymoon in Japan, Lewis was detained by U.S. customs officials for 45 minutes after she informed the authorities that she planned to live permanently in the United States. Her difficulties with customs officials strengthened her resolve to someday practice immigration law in New York.

While her husband was launching his own law practice, Lewis worked at Manhattan Legal Services, a publicly funded law firm catering to low-income clients, for two years. During that time, she became pregnant with her first daughter, Leslie, who was born in 1973. She then left Legal Services and continued her work as publisher of a monthly magazine targeted for Filipino Americans. In 1974 she passed the New York bar examination, the first Asian woman to do so without attending a law school in the United States.

Lewis applied for a legal position at the U.S. Immigration and Naturalization Service, her ultimate goal after her treatment by customs officials in Hawaii. But she was eventually rejected by the federal agency. Disappointed yet undeterred, she began working for a law office specializing in Latino immigration, while also filing a lawsuit against the INS alleging discriminatory hiring practices. She was represented by her husband's law firm in the lawsuit; in the end, she won three years in back wages. In 1979, Lewis officially joined the INS as a general attorney.

As she worked as an INS attorney for the next 11 years, Lewis' husband left law to enter the world of high finance and acquisitions. When McCall Pattern Company, previously owned by Norton Simon Industries, was being auctioned by its new owner in 1983, he established TLC (The Lewis Company) Pattern Inc. in preparation for a corporate takeover. On January 29, 1984, his holding company, TLC Group, Inc. purchased the home sewing products and publishing operation for $20 million in cash and $2.4 million in notes. He then sold the company in June 1987 to a British textile

manufacturer for $65 million. In the same year Lewis' husband made international headlines when he used high-yield debt, or "junk bonds," to acquire the food giant, Beatrice International, for $985 million. The new company, TLC Beatrice International, with $1.8 billion in sales, was the first African American-owned firm to crack the billion-dollar ceiling.

Most of TLC Beatrice International's operations were located overseas; its 64 food-processing and distribution companies operated in 31 countries, predominantly within Europe. It was the largest wholesale distributor of food and grocery products to supermarkets in the Paris metropolitan area; it also consisted of franchises and stores under various names. In addition to being a major marketer and manufacturer of ice cream in Europe, companies under TLC Beatrice included the top maker of potato chips and snacks in Ireland.

The Lewis family eventually relocated to Paris in 1990. Two years later, Lewis' husband was diagnosed with brain cancer. On January 1993, he died of a brain hemmorhage at the age of 50.

After half-brother Jean S. Fuggett, an attorney and former professional football player, served at the helm of TLC Beatrice for a year, Lewis stepped in. Most observers were at first skeptical of Lewis' ability to run a billion-dollar company. "Reg and Loida had different styles," stated Reynaldo Glover, who eventually became part of the management team under Lewis' watch (*Black Enterprise*, September 1999). "Reg was more direct and in-your-face while Loida was more spiritual. In fact, she would open each meeting with a prayer. But they were similar in terms of challenging management to study every nuance, every nook and cranny of a corporate plan or proposal."

Lewis quickly acted to tighten expenses and optimize efficiency. She sold the company plane and moved the company to a less glamorous and expensive midtown Manhattan location. The staff was downsized and some smaller companies were sold to repay debt. Within three years, profits grew from $1 million to $19 million.

Knowing that her husband had wanted to take the company public, she investigated the possibility of an IPO as a device to expand TLC Beatrice. She discovered, however, that the international company, with most of its holdings in Europe, would be undervalued in the American stock market. Instead of pursuing an IPO, Lewis and her management team determined that it would benefit their stockholders the most if the conglomerate was liquidated in pieces. In 1997, TLC Beatrice sold its French food distribution business to Casino SA for $576 million. By 1999, most of the Beatrice empire had been dismantled.

In addition to supporting some of her husband's philanthropic causes, Lewis also invested in her home town of Sorsogon in the Philippines. She opened the town's first minimall and established a college, Lewis College, in her birthplace.

### Source

Cruz, Angie. May 1995. "The TLC Touch." *Working Woman*: 39.

Dumiao, Doris C. 30 October 2000. "Loida Nicolas Says She's Not Ready." *Philippine Daily Inquirer*.

Edmond, Alfred, Jr. March 1994. "Another Lewis Leads TLC." *Black Enterprise*: 13.

Fairclough, Gordon. 27 May 1999. "TLC Beatrice Prepares to Sell Last of Its Holdings." *The Wall Street Journal*: B5.

"Final Act." September 1999. *Black Enterprise*: 117–126.

Johnson, Roy. 5 July 1999. "Why TLC Beatrice Mattered." *Fortune*.

Lewis, Reginald F., and Blair S. Walker. 1995. *Why Should White Guys Have All the Fun?: How Reginald Lewis Created a Billion-Dollar Business Empire*. New York: John Wiley & Sons, Inc.

McCarroll, Thomas. 28 October 1996. "A Woman's Touch." *Time*: 60–62.

Solomon, Jolie. May 1996. "Operation Rescue." *Working Woman*: 55–59.

Stodghill II, Ron. 24 January 1994. "TLC Beatrice Could Use More Than TLC." *Business Week*: 35.

# Christine Liang

**Full Name at Birth**: Christine Chu.

**Born**: 1959, Taiwan.

**Education**: National Yang Ming University, Taiwan, graduate, 1979.

**Positions Held**: Founder, Asian Source, Inc. (ASI), Sunnyvale, California (later Fremont, California), 1987– .

**Awards, Honors**: Largest Woman-Owned Business in the Greater Bay Area, *San Francisco Business Times*, 1999; Twenty-fourth Largest Woman-Owned Business in the U.S., *Working Woman* magazine, 2000.

**Summary**: Christine Liang, the sister of the computer magnate James Chu, is the founder of one of the largest woman-owned technology-based corporations in the nation. Asian Source, Inc. (ASI), a Fremont, California-based wholesale distributor of personal computer components, did $820 million in business in 2000.

### Early Years and Higher Education

Liang was the youngest of six children born to Chu Chin-Tsu, a soldier in the Nationalist Air Force in Taiwan. Her parents had fled mainland China in 1949 and had settled in a small village, Pintong, in Southern Taiwan. Liang graduated from National Yang Ming University in 1979, and later became involved in the jewelry business in Taiwan.

## Career Highlights

After immigrating to the United States in the 1980s, Liang founded Asian Source, Inc. (ASI) in 1987 in a 15,000-square-foot building in Sunnyvale, California, with an initial investment of $16,500. Her older brother, James Chu, who was starting his own technological empire, ViewSonic, about the same time, helped Liang during the early years of her business, selling computer monitors and related products at cost. While Chu was attempting to create a strong brand name for his computer monitors, Liang focused on importing generic components from Taiwan and other parts of Asia and selling custom-built "white-box" systems to U.S. vendors.

ASI, quickly expanded into new markets while strengthening its management team. In 1989, Liang's husband, Marcel Liang, joined the company and eventually became chief executive officer chairman, but Liang retained 51 percent ownership of ASI. The Liangs understood that quick delivery to their customers, which included system integrators and value-added resellers (VARs), was crucial. As part of their sales strategy, they began opening regional branches, beginning in Dallas and Atlanta in 1991. Other locations followed in Kansas, Houston, New Jersey, Chicago, Los Angeles, Tampa, Denver, Miami, Toronto, and Portland. These facilities included warehouse space for products as well as a local sales staff.

In 1992, *Inc.* magazine named ASI one of the 500 fastest-growing companies in the nation. Knowing that the wholesale business can be somewhat erratic, ASI began to produce its own line of computers under its Nspire brand name. Three basic lines—home personal computers, business personal computers, and server systems—were created. In 1994, the company purchased three acres in Fremont to establish a new headquarters. That same year, it reached $300 million in sales.

Revenues exceeded $325 million in 1995 with 350 employees nationally. ASI guaranteed resellers deliveries within 24 hours, and consistently registered a 99 percent accuracy rate in shipment orders. In the mid-1990s, keyboards formed 16 percent of all sales, and only one-third of customers purchased between $100,000 and $500,000 a year. In time, however, ASI began to establish relationships with large vendors, including Microsoft, Samsung, Toshiba, and, of course, ViewSonic, operated by Liang's brother. In 1998, ASI had been designated Microsoft's Delivery Service Partner (DSP), which enables the company to distribute Microsoft's operating systems and applications. By 2001, ASI was offering 4,000 products to more than 10,000 customers, with a goal to be a leading distributor of motherboards in North America.

ASI has not been immune to the reorganization trends within the computer industry. For example, in 1999, 3Com Corporation cut ASI and six other distributors. ASI's Nspire personal computer, meanwhile, has been gaining good reviews.

The Liangs have a daughter and son.

## Sources

ASI Corporate Backgrounder, ASI.

ASI Web site. www.asipartner.com [accessed November 20, 2001].

Bole, Kristen. 24 May 1996. "Sign of Times: Tech Firm Now Top Women-Owned Business." *San Francisco Business Times*: 5B.

O'Heir, Jeff. 20 October 1997. "ASI Builds Business on Regional Model." *Computer Reseller News*: 198.

Rivera, Eddie. March–April 1996. "Christine Liang: Going for Broker." *Transpacific*: 78+ .

# Chin Lung

**Full Name at Birth**: Chen Kangda, also known as Chen Long (surname Chen).

**Born**: 12 December 1864, Nanshen village in Guangdong Province, China.

**Death**: 25 February 1942, China.

**Education**: Chinese Baptist Church, San Francisco, English Studies, c. 1870s.

**Positions Held**: Store clerk, San Francisco, c. 1882; tenant farmer, Sacramento-San Joaquin Delta, California (later including Oregon), c. 1898–1930s; investor in Sing Kee Tract farmland, California, 1912; operator of Sing Kee firm, Sacramento, California; operator of Shanghai Trunk Company, San Francisco, California.

**Summary**: Known as the "Chinese Potato King" in the Sacramento delta from 1890s and 1920s, Chin Lung represents a larger group of Chinese tenant farmers along the Pacific Coast. Eventually buying land in both California and Oregon before both states enacted their respective alien land laws, Lung also diversified into international trade and other related enterprises.

## Early Life and Education

Chin Lung was the fourth son of a middle-class peasant family in a village in China. Money was limited, so he wore the short pants of a boy even as a young adult. Weakened by hunger, he did not have the strength to even carry a bucket of fertilizer on his own. When he was about 18 years old, he joined his brother, who was working in a rice-importing company in San Francisco. There, by day, he sacked rice. At night, he attended English-language classes at the nearby Chinese Baptist Church. That experience in the 1880s would greatly benefit Chin Lung later as he expanded his agricultural empire.

## Career Highlights

From San Francisco, Chin Lung and other men from his Chinese village resettled in the Sacramento–San Joaquin Delta. Subject to frequent flooding, the area nonetheless had fertile soil that was made even more productive by Chinese and other immigrant tenant farmers. Tenant farmers leased acreage from landowners. Many times these tenant farmers were the ones to reclaim the land—that is, drain, till the soil, and build levees to prepare for planting.

Chin Lung began farming in this area in the 1880s, but he did not officially sign a lease for land until 1898, when he sharecropped 200 acres on Andrus Island in Sacramento County. He first grew asparagus but was barred from growing potatoes, a crop that was believed to stunt the production of asparagus. (Later it was the potato that would be at the center of this agricultural empire.) Working until his hands and feet became bloody, Chin Lung lived frugally, spending only one dollar a month for expenses beyond food and shelter. As a result, he was able to save enough money to go to China, marry, and bring his new bride—Leung Kum Kew—to California.

According to Sucheng Chan's "Chinese American Entrepreneur: The California Career of Chin Lung" (*Chinese America: History and Perspective*, 1987), Chin Lung's agricultural operation in northern California quickly grew. In 1900, he leased 1,125 acres in the Stockton area for $7,000 a year; he paid his lease through the mortgaging of his crops. Like other Chinese American tenant farmers, he received loans from European Americans and leased land from various landlords. Soon his farms were located in multiple counties, requiring Chin Lung to travel by boat and horseback to supervise his vast agricultural holdings, which profited $90,000 during its best year. He hired more than 500 farm laborers, all exclusively Chinese, to cultivate, harvest, and pack crops of potatoes, beans, onions, and asparagus. He also owned dozens of horses and two barges that transported supplies for purchase and crops for sale. Open to new technologies, he became the first Chinese to buy a Holt Caterpillar tractor and also invested in a potato-washing machine.

More than a hands-on farmer, Chin Lung was a master manager. He understood how to manage his labor force, as well as finance and distribute his products. This know-how led him to diversify into labor contracting for Alaska salmon canneries, retail store business, export-import trade, and even baggage manufacturing. When the California Alien Land Laws barred Chinese and Japanese immigrants from purchasing and even leasing land, Chin Lung acquired acreage in Oregon. In 1923, Oregon passed its own Alien Land Law, and Chin Lung began to buy land near his home village in China.

His wife, meanwhile, disliked living in California, and had relocated to Macau, a Portuguese colony in China. The couple maintained a long-distance marriage and had a total of five sons and two daughters. In 1933 Chin Lung retired and returned to China, leaving his businesses to his sons. He died at the age of 78 on February 25, 1942.

## Sources

Chan, Sucheng. 1987. "Chinese American Entrepreneur: The California Career of Chin Lung." *Chinese America: History and Perspective:* 73–86.

Chan, Sucheng. 1986. *This Bittersweet Soil: The Chinese in California Agriculture, 1860–1910.* Berkeley and Los Angeles, CA: University of California Press.

McCunn, Ruthanne Lum. 1988. *Chinese American Portraits: Personal Histories, 1827–1988.* San Francisco: Chronicle Books.

Ng, Franklin. 1999. "Chin Lung." In Hyungchan Kim, ed. *Distinguished Asian Americans: A Biographical Distionary.* Westport, CT: Greenwood Press.

# M

## Sonny Mehta

Sonny Mehta. Photo by Mark Gerson

**Full Name at Birth**: Ajai Singh Mehta.

**Born**: c. 1943, India.

**Education**: Cambridge University, Cambridge, England, c. 1960s.

**Positions Held**: Editor, Pan, London, England, c. 1970s; editor, Picador, London, c. 1970s; president, Alfred A. Knopf division of Random House, New York City, New York, 1987–98; president and editor in chief of Knopf Publishing Group, New York City, New York, 1998– .

**Summary**: As the president of the prestigious Knopf Publishing Group, Sonny Mehta has affected American publishing and books since coming to New York from London in the late 1980s. He has combined a strong literary sense with marketing skills to get his imprints' books on the bestseller list.

### Early Years

Mehta, the son of an Indian diplomat, was educated in New Delhi boarding schools. He also traveled frequently around the world with his father, thereby acquiring a broad view of the world. It was in New Delhi, however, when he purchased his first copy of J.D. Salinger's *Catcher in the Rye* from a sidewalk vendor. His exposure to this Western classic and his love for American contemporary culture shaped his intellectual and literary sensibilities.

## Higher Education

Mehta studied at the renowned Cambridge University in Cambridge, England. There he met another Indian intellectual, Gita Patnaik, the daughter of a prominent political leader. Among their classmates was feminist writer Germaine Greer who described Mehta and Gita as attracting the "most interesting—the only interesting— members" of cliques on campus and drawing "them into their circle." Mehta and Gita, who would become a critically acclaimed writer, eventually married.

## Career Highlights

After attending Cambridge, Mehta worked at a series of London paperback publishing houses, including Pan and Picador, now both connected to Pan Macmillan. He encouraged former classmate Greer to write *The Female Eunuch*, considered a *classic* feminist work, which was originally published by Paladin in 1970. While at Picador, Mehta published American writer Michael Herr's account of the Vietnam War called *Dispatches* in 1978; the book eventually became a British bestseller. He also helped to promote the works of Salman Rushdie and Gabriel García Márquez.

Mehta's work in London did not go unnoticed in New York, the heart of American publishing. As a result, when the beloved president and editor-in-chief of Alfred A. Knopf of Random House, Robert Gottlieb, announced that he was leaving his post to serve as the editor of the *The New Yorker* in 1987, Mehta was widely handpicked to take his place. The styles of the two leaders—past and present—were divergent: while Gottlieb was warm and fatherly, Mehta was viewed as taciturn and aloof with a predilection for late-night literary parties. Yet Mehta's marketing skills were sorely needed in an industry marked by consolidation and increasing competition from other entertainment sources.

Alfred A. Knopf, a prestigious publishing house, had been founded in 1915. In 1960, Random House, Inc. acquired Knopf, which was known for publishing critically acclaimed quality fiction that had won their writers Pulitzer Prizes. While comprising $100 million of Random House's $1 billion in annual revenue, Knopf was also a moneymaker.

Its cachet further rose in 1989, when the Vintage paperback line was moved from the Random House division to the Knopf division. Mehta, experienced in the paperback book business in London, hired Vintage's first editorial and marketing staff. He raised book prices by one and two dollars each, redesigned covers, and reintroduced paperback editions to bestsellers like new books. Under Mehta's leadership, Vintage flourished.

Mehta, whose taste gravitated toward dark fiction, continued to demonstrate a knack for creative marketing ideas. In 1990, he decided to publish an expensive companion book to the PBS series, *The Civil War*. The book, sold for $50, became a bestseller. That same year, Mehta courted controversy when he published Bret Easton Ellis' thriller, *American Psycho*. Viewed as misogynistic, the book was railed against by feminists, yet Mehta managed to sell $250,000 in copies. To protect Knopf's reputation, he published the book under the Vintage imprint.

"I think publishing as an activity should really be seeking danger, not running from it," he told *Esquire* (April 1993). "It should be provocative, not just for the sake of being provocative but because it has to keep asking questions."

To promote Josephine Hart's erotic novel *Damage*, Mehta sent 5,000 advance copies of the book—wrapped in red, white, black, and blue paper—to booksellers with a personal letter of endorsement as a Christmas gift. The book sold one million copies worldwide. He also had success with Donna Tartt's literary thriller, *The Secret History*, as well as Kazuo Ishiguro's *Remains of the Day*, Michael Ondaatje's *The English Patient*, and Cormac McCarthy's *All the Pretty Horses*.

In addition to gaining Vintage, Mehta has further expanded the Knopf Publishing Group. He added the Pantheon division and purchased the Everyman's Library classics. When Random House was purchased by the German media conglomerate Bertesmann AG in 1998, Anchor, a paperback imprint, was added to Mehta's responsibilities. As various imprints within the Random House company compete to acquire book properties, Mehta is often at odds with rival Bertesmann executives. (In 1999, Mehta underwent a triple bypass heart surgery, but in time, returned to work.) However, this internal competition is viewed as beneficial to the company's overall success. In 2000, Knopf published 11 hardcover bestsellers, while the other Random House division, led by Ann Godoff, produced 19.

In 2001, Mehta was again in the news when he signed a $10 million deal with former President Bill Clinton for the publishing of his memoirs.

Mehta and his wife, Gita, have a son, Aditya. The couple maintain residences in New York, London, and Delhi.

## Sources

Conant, Janet. April 1993. "The Very Furry Feet of Sonny Mehta." *Esquire*: 106+ .

Kirkpatrick, David D. 15 January 2001. "Literary Family Feud." *New York Times*: C1, C9.

Kirkpartrick, David D. 7 August 2001. "Publisher Will Pay Clinton over $10 Million for Book." *New York Times*: A1.

Random House Web site. www.randomhouse. com [Accessed December 24, 2001].

# Ismail Merchant

Ismail Merchant. Photo by Evan Agostini/Liason

**Full Name at Birth**: Ismail Noormohamed Abdul Rehman.

**Born**: 25 December 1936, Bombay, India.

**Education**: St. Xavier's College, Bombay, India, 1958; New York University, New York, New York, M.B.A.

**Positions Held**: Messenger for the Indian delegations to the United Nations, New York City, New York; account executive trainee, McCann-Erickson, New York City, New York; part-time night job, classified advertising department, *Los Angeles Times*, Los Angeles, California; founding partner and producer, Merchant Ivory Productions, 1961– .

**Honors and Awards**: Alumnus of the Year, New York University, 1990; Filmmaker of the Year Award, Motion Picture Bookers Club, 1992.

**Summary**: With financial creativity and persistent salesmanship, independent filmmaker Ismail Merchant has produced an unrivaled number of top films, including Academy Award winners *Howards End* and *A Room with a View*.

## Early Years

Born Ismail Noormohamed Abdul Rehman in Bombay, India, Merchant was the only son among the seven children of Noormohamed Haji Abdul Rehman and Hazra Memon. Merchant's father was involved in local politics during the turbulent period when India gained independence from England in 1947.

The uprisings following the partition of British India into separate Hindu and Muslim states had a telling effect on Merchant. At age nine, he gave a speech at a political rally in front of 10,000 people. He spoke about partition, a subject he hardly knew, and yet managed to inspire the crowd. Hoping that their son would become a professional, his parents enrolled him in both Muslim and Jesuit schools.

But it was through his relatives' network of friends that he met his first mentor in 1949. Her name was Nimmi, an Indian film actress in her twenties. Though he was only 13, the two became close friends. Nimmi often took young Ismail to the studios in Bombay, which was the hub of the country's film industry. She told him to become a star, and Merchant took those words to heart, setting a goal of producing movies in the United States for an Indian audience with a mix of Indian and American cast members.

## Higher Education

Merchant attended St. Xavier's College in Bombay, where he studied political science and English literature, among other subjects. It was during this time that he changed his surname to Merchant.

Though he was a good student, Merchant spent most of his time planning variety shows to raise money for the college. He graduated in 1958, and used the money from his final production to pay for his travel expenses and tuition for a master's degree in business administration from New York University.

Moving to New York opened a whole new world of art and culture for Merchant. He was particularly drawn to concerts and films, and it was here that he discovered the films of legendary Bengali director Satyajit Ray, as well as those by European artists such as Ingmar Bergman, Vittorio De Sica, and Federico Fellini. As a student, Merchant worked several months as a messenger for the Indian delegation to the United Nations and then got a job as an account executive at the advertising firm McCann-Erickson.

Through contacts from those two jobs, he pooled enough money to make his first film in 1960. Finished in one weekend, the 14-minute film *The Creation of Woman* was well-received. Bolstered by the reviews, Merchant set off for Hollywood once he had earned his M.B.A.

## Career Highlights

With little cash in his wallet, an undaunted Merchant wrote a fake press release before leaving for California, announcing that a famous Indian producer would soon be arriving in Hollywood, namely himself. None of the media responded to Merchant's press release. But he kept pushing forward. To make ends meet,

Merchant took two part-time jobs, one in the classified department of the *Los Angeles Times* and the other at a clothing store.

To be eligible for Academy Award consideration, a film had to play at a commercial movie theater for three days. Once Merchant discovered this, he asked the owner of a fine arts cinema in Los Angeles to show *The Creation of Woman* along with Bergman's popular film *The Devil's Eye*. The owner agreed, and Merchant's short was seen by enough academy members to earn an Oscar nomination. "I never take no for an answer," Merchant said in a 1987 *Time* interview. "It simply does not exist as an option."

On his way to Europe to attend the Cannes Film Festival, where *The Creation of Woman* was an official entry from the U.S., Merchant stopped in New York to attend the screening of a documentary *The Sword and the Flute*. He met the director, James Ivory, who had studied film at the University of Southern California. In May 1961, the two became partners, forming Merchant Ivory Productions, with the goal of making English-language theatrical features in India for the international market.

It started one of the most enduring partnerships in film history as the two set about producing the first of their more than 40 films together. Merchant's financial and marketing expertise contributed mightily to the team's success and enhanced their international profile. *The Householder* (1963) became the first film made in India to be distributed worldwide by a major American company (Columbia Pictures).

It was also during this time that the pair met Ruth Prawer Jhabvala, a Polish woman born in Germany who was raised in England and married to an Indian architect. They persuaded her to write a screenplay based on her comic novel, *The Householder*, the story of a young man's coming of age. It began a decades-long collaboration with Merchant-Ivory during which time she wrote almost all of their films. As the partnership developed, Merchant and Ivory drifted away from Indian subjects and staked a reputation for intelligent, tasteful adaptations of modern literary classics, especially those of E.M. Forster and Henry James.

The film version of James' satiric *The Bostonians* in 1984 earned Oscar nominations for best actress (Vanessa Redgrave) and best costume design. The best reviews of the team's career came in 1986 with *A Room with a View*, a romantic and lively adaptation of the Forster novel. Produced on a budget of $3 million, the film grossed $60 million worldwide. It received eight Oscar nominations and won three: best screenplay, best art direction, and best costume design. With their blockbuster hit, they were urged by Hollywood executives and Wall Street to go public, but they decided firmly against it. Merchant felt that Hollywood studio scripts were "shallow" and guarded against becoming "the flavor of the month."

Later successes include *Howards End* (1992), based on a Forster novel of class conflict. It won three Oscars: best actress (Emma Thompson), best screenplay, and best art direction. It also received best picture and best director nominations. A year later, they teamed Thompson and Anthony Hopkins again in *The Remains of the Day*, which received Oscar nominations across the board.

Merchant, who has also tried his hand at directing, is a devout Muslim, waking up at dawn every day for prayer. He has written a book about producing movies in India and is the author of four cookbooks. He divides his time between Bombay, London, and New York, where he has an apartment in Manhattan and a home upstate.

—*By John Saito Jr.*

## Sources

Asian Cinevision Web site. "Ismail Merchant." www.asiancinevision.org [Accessed November 18, 2001].

"Ismail Merchant." 1993. *Current Biography Yearbook 1993*. New York: Current Biography: 402–05.

Monaco, James and the editors of Baseline. 1991. *The Encyclopedia of Film*. New York: Perigee Books.

Pais, Arthur J. "Ismail Merchant—Cooking Up Movies." 10 March 1994. *Far Eastern Economic Review*: 66.

# William Mow

**Full Name at Birth**: Mow Chao Wei.

**Born**: 1936, Hangchow, China.

**Education**: Rennselaer Polytechnic Institute, New York, B.S. in electrical engineering, 1963; Purdue University, Ph.D. in electrical engineering, 1967.

**Positions Held**: Program manager, Litton Industries, Los Angeles, California, 1967–69; founder and president of Macrodata, Woodland Hills, California, 1969–76; founder and chief executive officer of Bugle Boy Industries, Inc. (formerly Buckaroo International), Chatsworth and Simi Valley, California, 1980–2000.

**Honors and Awards**: Juvenile Diabetes Foundation's Father of the Year Award; World Trade Hall of Fame inductee; Outstanding Electrical Engineer, Purdue University, 1995.

**Summary**: High-tech entrepreneur William Mow, educated as an engineer, built a successful apparel company, Bugle Boy, in the 1980s and 1990s. At its height, the California-based company boasted sales of more than $500 million and 317 outlet stores.

## Early Years

Born in Hangchow, China, Mow was one of five sons. His father was chief of the military committee for Chiang Kai-shek's Nationalist government who was later assigned to the United Nations in New York City. When Mow was 13, he traveled to the United States on the last plane to leave Shanghai before the city fell to the communists. The family eventually resettled in Great Neck, New York, where they opened a restaurant, the Yangtse River Café. Mow attended boarding school but returned home on the weekends to work at the restaurant. Paid in egg rolls rather than money, Mow sold the appetizers to his classmates.

## Higher Education

Mow worked his way through college—first at Rennselaer Polytechnic Institute in New York for his undergraduate degree in electrical engineering, and later at Purdue University, where he gained his doctorate in the same field in 1967.

## Career Highlights

Mow worked at Honeywell in Boston before following his older brother Harry, who worked at the RAND Corporation in Los Angeles, to southern California. After he worked two years at Litton Industries in Los Angeles, he saw a market for the testing of large-scale integrated semiconductor chips, and launched his own enterprise—Macrodata—in 1969 with $1.75 million in venture capital funding. Macrodata's cutting-edge testing procedure soon became a prototype in the high-tech field; most of the major semiconductor manufacturers were using the services of the Woodland Hills-based company by the early 1970s. Macrodata went public in 1973, and within a year it had grown to $12 million in sales.

A Milwaukee conglomerate, meanwhile, had bought control of Macrodata in the mid-1970s. A bitter conflict over understated losses and alleged fraud then ensued in 1976, resulting in Mow's forced resignation as president. Lawsuits were filed, and later Mow was vindicated when a California appeals court ruled that the conglomerate had intentionally understated Macrodata's loss to inflate the earnings of the parent company. Mow eventually received an $820,000 out-of-court settlement.

Although scarred from his experience in the high-tech field, Mow did not give up on his entrepreneurial dreams. He turned to the garment industry and started an import company called Dragon International. In 1977, with $200,000 in financing from a Taiwan investor and a loan after mortgaging his home, he launched Buckaroo International to sell his own line of young men's clothing.

Mow's early forays into the apparel business were difficult. His products were virtually ignored at trade shows, and in Buckaroo's inaugural year, the company lost $300,000. In 1981, Buckaroo had $4.1 million in sales, but $750,000 in losses.

At this point, Mow knew that he had to take some drastic measures. He changed the company's name to Bugle Boy, after youths who played the bugle during the Civil War, and placed an experienced retail man, Vincent Nesi, in charge of sales. Bugle Boy's fortune would turn within several years. Now focusing on moderately priced pants and shirts for the young men's and boy's market, the company capitalized on the parachute pants craze of the 1980s and put all its resources in producing these baggy pants made of nylon. Ten million pairs of parachute pants were sold in 1984. "I cornered the nylon twill market in Tai-

wan," Mow explained to the *Los Angeles Times* (August 8, 1989). "I virtually put the umbrella people out of business that year."

As the apparel industry, especially for young people, is based on trends, the demand for parachute pants did not last long. Soon returns were piling up and Bugle Boy now faced a negative worth of $5 million. However, Mow and Nesi, who later became president, took advantage of Bugle Boy's name recognition and quickly began producing a new line of clothing. Department stores were now only too willing to carry the Bugle Boy label.

Also instrumental to Bugle Boy's success at this time was its innovative advertising campaign. As part of its introduction of its jeans line, the company launched television ads which popularized the slogan, "Are those Bugle Boy jeans you're wearing?" By 1990, sales exceeded the $500 million mark.

Mow publicly discussed his target to reach a billion dollar in sales—but this goal would not be realized. He attempted to branch out into the older men's market and then opened 109 nationwide outlets—an effort which grew to 317 stores at its peak. In 2000, Bugle Boy began turning its attention to the women's market, especially girls and teens. These diversification efforts, however, did not succeed. The boys market had been alienated, and the outlets competed against retail stores, who were less enthusiastic about carrying Bugle Boy clothing.

In February 2001, the company could not withstand its heavy debt load and liquidity problems and filed for Chapter 11 bankruptcy protection. Mow was replaced by an interim chief executive. Bugle Boy abandoned its headquarters building in Simi Valley in California's San Fernando Valley and began laying off its 3,796 workers. Its 216 retail and factory outlet stores were also closed and liquidated.

The Bugle Boy label will continue, however. Perry Ellis International, as well as other apparel companies, have bid to acquire the Bugle Boy trademark and other assets. As Perry Ellis chairman and chief executive officer George Feldenkreis described in a statement to *Business Wire* (7 February 2001): "The Bugle Boy name has a long history with brand awareness ratings among consumers that have consistently ranked among the highest in the country."

## Sources

Chepesiuk, Ron. June 15–21, 2001. "Were Those Bugle Boys You Were Wearing?: Taps for an Apparel Company Legend." *Asian-Week*.

Ellis, Kristi. February 5, 2001. "Bugle Boy Debt Surpasses $100 Million." *WWD*: 18.

Starvo, Barry. August 8, 1990. "Bugle Boy to Battle on New Fronts." *Los Angeles Times*: B1, B10.

# N

## Shoji Nagumo

**Born**: 29 October, 1890, Niigata, Japan.

**Died**: 22 February 1976, Alameda, California.

**Education**: Tokyo Koto Shihan Gakko, Tokyo, Japan, graduate, 1917.

**Positions Held**: Farm laborer, 1918–20; Japanese-language magazine publisher, 1921–23; gardener, 1923–73; organizer of the League of Southern California Japanese Gardeners Association, 1937–41.

**Awards, Honors**: Medal, Japanese government, 1970.

**Summary**: Shoji Nagumo was a key leader in the maintenance gardening field in North America. Maintenance gardening, the tending of primarily residential lawns, served as a key industry among those of Japanese ancestry in California, Washington, and Canada from the 1930s to the 1970s.

### Early Years and Higher Education

Born in the mountainous Niigata region in Japan, Nagumo graduated from high school in 1911. He then traveled to Tokyo to pursue higher education. Nagumo graduated from Tokyo Koto Shihan Gakko, a highly regarded teaching college in Japan. With his degree in 1917, he could easily have secured a comfortable living in his homeland with his wife Umeo, but Nagumo opted to come to America on what was supposed to be a special study abroad program.

"In Europe, countries previously annexed to Germany were undergoing chaos one by one; America alone stood invincible," he wrote in his autobiography, *A Pioneer in America*. "I desperately wanted to go to America no matter how hard I would have to work; I was eager to experience first-hand what life was really like there." While his wife Umeo stayed back in suburban Tokyo to teach grade school, Nagumo traveled on the *Siberia Maru* to San Francisco in 1918.

### Career Highlights

After arriving in San Francisco, Nagumo worked as a farm laborer on a grape farm within the Yamato Colony in Livingston, California. This Christian Community, begun by *Nichi Bei Times* newspaper publisher Kyutaro Abiko, was located in an arid region north of Fresno, California. From there, Nagumo traveled through and worked in many agricultural labor camps in such towns as Stockton and San Jose.

Always curious about different cultures, Nagumo, who had studied classical Chinese literature and had converted to Christianity in Japan, befriended a Catholic priest at a Spanish-speaking church in Oxnard, a farming community just north of Los Angeles. A believer in land ownership as key to self-sufficiency, Nagumo debated an eventual move to Mexico because of U.S. alien land laws that barred Japanese immigrants from buying property. "When I thought about my past and future, I knew I could never rise above being a laborer, even if I continued this kind of work for many years," wrote Nagumo.

Before Nagumo could follow up on his plans to move to Mexico, he was struck down with influenza during an epidemic. As he recovered, his wife finally arrived from Japan in 1920. Nagumo then decided to develop Japanese-language teaching materials while in the United States. Investing his own money, he signed a contract with a Japanese printer to produce a magazine and began to secure subscribers in Los Angeles. However, due to the great Tokyo earthquake of 1923, the print house was destroyed, and his fortune lost. As a result, he had to turn to another occupation to support his growing family: gardening.

By 1918, 10 percent of Japanese American men in Los Angeles worked as gardeners. First entering the field as domestics of large estates, immigrant Japanese found that they could sustain a good living by working for multiple customers. Many involved in farming learned to transfer their agricultural skills into tending lawns and gardens in the cities. Boardinghouses were considered a training ground for beginners, who often worked as helpers for more established gardeners.

Hollywood, with its image-conscious movie stars, and Beverly Hills were ideal locations to start a gardening business. Nagumo, through an acquaintance, found a modest home for his family in Hollywood, where he started gardening at only five dollars a day. After some time, Nagumo found work with the Bowman Brothers, a small building developer. Able to speak Spanish, he hired Mexican helpers. Business was good, and Nagumo, whose children at one time had only one set of clothing, was able to survive the Depression. The Bowman Brothers, on the other hand, eventually went bankrupt.

By the spring of 1933, Nagumo sensed the need for an umbrella organization for Japanese American gardeners, who, by his personal survey, numbered 7,000 to 8,000. (Other sources place that number to be 3,000.) Due to the lack of employment opportunities, more European Americans entered gardening, and posh communities like Beverly Hills began a campaign to get rid of Japanese gardeners and send them "back to Manchuria." To address such movements, Nagumo helped establish regional gardening associations, which led to the formation of the League of Southern California Japanese Gardeners Association in 1937.

By 1940, the League had 900 members. On April 1, 1940, Nagumo was able to use his publishing expertise to launch the inaugural issue of *The Gardener's Monthly*, or *Gadena no Tomo*. The last issue of the prewar trade magazine was dated December 1941, the month in which Pearl Harbor was bombed.

While many Japanese leaders, especially Buddhist priests and Japanese-language teachers were arrested shortly after the bombing of Pearl Harbor, Nagumo was not similarly chosen. The membership list and minutes of the League were confiscated by the FBI, however. Nagumo and his family were sent to Pomona Assembly Center and then later moved to Heart Mountain internment camp, where Nagumo served as block manager, council leader, and organizer of the camp's Victory Garden or (vegetable garden). Japanese nurserymen and others related to gardening and agriculture also created gardens of beauty behind barbed wire.

After the war, Nagumo and his family returned to Hollywood. An even greater number of Japanese American men—even those with college degrees—turned to gardening as they discovered other jobs closed to them. With a small amount of capital, they could acquire used pickup trucks and lawnmowers to fulfill a demand for attractive lawns and gardens during the postwar housing boom. Again, Nagumo and other younger leaders saw a need to organize to ward off outside unionization attempts and fight against a state licensing proposal—which was viewed as a tool to limit non-English-speaking gardeners. In 1956, the Southern California Gardeners' Federation was formally incorporated. At its height, 4,000 individuals were members of this trade organization, which offered medical insurance and other work-related benefits.

While also caring for his wife, who suffered a debilitating stroke in 1956, Nagumo continued to lend his skills to the Southern California Gardeners' Federation. He was a regular contributor to the postwar trade magazine; also his book *Gadena Goroku: A Gardener's Essays* was published by the organization in 1960. He received a medal from the Japanese government in October 1970 for his contributions to the community and the development of the gardening industry.

He continued to garden until his early eighties. He passed away on February 22, 1976, at the age of 85. Although very few Japanese Americans have continued in the maintenance gardening profession, this industry helped this ethnic group to establish its economic foundation—thereby enabling future generations to pursue a variety of professions.

### Sources

Hirahara, Naomi, ed. 2000. *Green Makers: Japanese American Gardeners in Southern California.* Los Angeles: Southern California Gardeners' Federation.

Nagumo, Shoji. 1982. *A Japanese Pioneer in America: An Autobiography of Shoji Nagumo.* Reiko Nagumo, ed., Misue Sautter, trans. Unpublished.

Tsuchida, Nobuya. 1984. "Japanese Gardeners in Southern California, 1900–1941," *Labor Immigration under Capitalism.* Lucie Cheng and Edna Bonacich, eds. (Berkeley: University of California Press): 435–69.

# Robert C. Nakasone

**Full Name at Birth:** Robert Carey Nakasone.

**Born:** 1947, Chicago, Illinois.

**Education:** Verdugo Hills High School, Verdugo Hills, California, graduate, 1966; Claremont McKenna College, Claremont, California, B.A. cum laude in economics, 1969; University of Chicago Graduate School of Business, Chicago, Illinois, M.B.A. with honors, 1971.

**Positions Held:** Executive, Osco Drug Store, division of Jewel Companies (acquired by American Stores, Inc. and now part of Albertson's Inc.), Chicago, Illinois, 1971– ; vice president, real estate and growth and development, Osco Drug Store, Chicago, Illinois, circa 1973–79; president, Brighams Ice Cream and Restaurant, division of Jewel Companies, Boston, Massachusetts, 1979–83; president, Midwest division of Jewel Food Stores, Chicago, Illinois, 1983–85; president, USA Toy

Stores/Toys "R" Us, Paramus, New Jersey, 1985–89; president, Worldwide Toy Stores/Toys "R" Us, Paramus, New Jersey, 1989–94; president and chief operating officer, Toys "R" Us, Paramus, New Jersey, 1994–98; chief executive officer, Toys "R" Us, Paramus, New Jersey, 1998–99.

**Summary:** Robert C. Nakasone became the highest ranking Asian American executive at a Fortune 100 retail company when he was named chief executive officer of New Jersey-based retailer Toys "R" Us in 1998.

## Early Years

Nakasone was born in Chicago to Seattle-born parents who resettled in Illinois after being incarcerated in an internment camp for Japanese Americans at Minidoka, Idaho, during World War II. The family moved to San Fernando Valley in southern California, where Nakasone excelled at Verdugo Hills High School. He was on the varsity baseball, football, and track teams, and in 1966 served as student body president.

## Higher Education

Nakasone attended Claremont McKenna College in Claremont, east of Los Angeles, and majored in economics. After graduating cum laude in 1969, he continued his studies at the University of Chicago Graduate School of Business. He received his M.B.A. degree with honors in 1971.

## Career Highlights

Nakasone's first job after business school was with the Jewel Companies of Chicago, which is now part of Albertson's, Inc. At that time, Jewel Companies, a diversified retailer, consisted of various divisions, and Nakasone was assigned to work in its Osco Drugs/Savon Drug division, then the second largest drugstore chain in the United States, for several years. At the age of 26,

he was named the youngest vice president in the history of Osco Drugs. In this capacity, he was responsible for real estate and growth and development for Osco.

In five years, Nakasone was promoted again: this time he would become the youngest president of Brighams Ice Cream and Restaurant, another division of Jewel Stores located in Boston, at the age of 31. He remained president until 1983, when he returned to Chicago as the head of Jewel Food Stores' Midwest division.

Nakasone's skill in merchandising did not go unnoticed. When Jewel Stores was undergoing a merger with American Stores, Inc. in 1985, Toys "R" Us, the giant toy retailer, approached him to serve as president of the U.S. toy store division. At the time, the New Jersey-based company had 164 stores in the United States; sales were approximately $1 billion. Nakasone described the opportunity as an "offer of a lifetime" in an article in *The Rafu Shimpo* (22 March 1995). Thus began Nakasone's career with which was then the largest, fastest-growing, and profitable toy retailer in the world.

In 1989, Nakasone became president of worldwide toy stores for Toys "R" Us, a position that included the company's international and domestic divisions. During his tenure in this position, Nakasone made significant inroads into the Far East. In 1993, Toys "R" Us became the first major large-scale retailer to enter Japan. In two years, there would be at least 30 stores in this foreign market.

Nakasone was named president and chief operating officer for Toys "R" Us in 1994, and Michael Goldstein, the former chief financial officer, became chief executive officer. In 1995, Nakasone told *The Rafu Shimpo*: "I definitely would encourage other Asian Americans and Japanese Americans to go into retailing. If you're action-oriented and enjoy a fast pace, I think retailing is a great occupation to be in."

Nakasone went on to make history when he was called to the top spot—chief executive officer—in February 1998. However, with the title came a heavy responsibility: how to stimulate growth with weak sales and $2.28 billion in inventory. Toys "R" Us, which had invested little into Web site development, was also ill prepared to compete with Internet retailers of the late 1990s.

It was actually another traditional "bricks and mortar" retailer, Wal-Mart, that proved to be a real threat. In 1998, Wal-Mart surpassed Toys "R" Us as the top toy retailer in the nation. Toys "R" Us, meanwhile, lost $442 million during the first nine months of the same year, mostly due to a major restructuring in which 59 Toys "R" Us stores, mostly in Germany and France and 31 Kids "R" Us stores were closed. Three thousand jobs were also cut.

Nakasone attempted to reenergize the toy company during these lackluster years. According to *Business Week* (4 December 2000), he invested $100 million to redesign at least 170 stores—complete with a new Under a Dollar section, a Learning Center, and hands-on video stations. The company's inventory was slashed by $500 million, a move that unfortunately angered suppliers. Disney's Magic Institute was contracted to advise the staff on how to deal with customer service problems. In August 1999, the Imaginarium, a retailer of educational toys, was acquired to capture the high-end market, while more than $30 million was earmarked to develop the company's Web site toysrus.com.

In spite of such efforts, Nakasone abruptly resigned in August 1999. Most media reports cited his resignation was due to "differing views regarding the direction of the company." In an article in *Fortune* magazine (27 September 1999), Nakasone's relationship with the company's board of directors is described as one possible reason for his withdrawal from Toys "R" Us. At the time of his resignation, the company had 1,500 stores.

Nakasone has been involved in some philanthropic activities, including serving on the board of directors of the Congressional Asian-Pacific American Caucus Institute. He was also honorary chairman of the Japanese American National Museum Leadership Campaign. He remains a trustee of Claremont McKenna College and a member of the board of directors of Staples, Inc.

He is married to his high school classmate, Lynn Weaks. They have four children: Anna, Robert, Sarah, and Tom.

### Sources

de Llosa, Patty. 27 September 1999. "Toys Were Us." *Fortune*: 145 + .

Goldman, Abigail, and Greg Johnson. 27 August 1999. "Toys R Us CEO Resigns; 'Differing Views' Cited." *Los Angeles Times*: C1.

Nakayama, Takeshi. 22 March 1995. "Sky's the Limit." *The Rafu Shimpo*: 1.

# Josie Natori

Josie Natori. Photo courtesy of the Natori Company

**Full Name at Birth**: Josefina Almeda Cruz.

**Born**: 9 May 1947, Manila, Philippines.

**Education**: Manhattanville College, Purchase, New York, B.A. in economics, 1968.

**Positions Held**: Associate in corporate finance, Bache Securities, New York City, New York, (later in Manila, Philippines), 1968–71; investment banker, Merrill Lynch Pierce Fenner & Smith, New York City, New York, 1971–75; vice president of investment banking, Merrill Lynch Pierce Fenner & Smith, New York City, New York, 1975–77; founder, chief executive officer, The Natori Company, New York City, New York, 1976– .

**Awards, Honors**: Galleon Award, Philippines President Corazon Aquino, 1988; Business Woman of the Year, New York Partnership, 1998; Women of Heart Award, The American Heart Association and *Woman's Day* magazine, 2000

**Summary**: Josie Natori successfully segued from the world of securities to launching her own New York-based apparel corporation, Natori Company. A native of Manila, Philippines, she is a pioneering female entrepreneur in the United States.

## Early Years and Higher Education

Natori was the oldest of six children in Manila, Philippines. Her father, Felipe F. Cruz, had established a thriving construction firm, F.F. Cruz & Company, and her mother, Angelita, worked as a pharmacist. Natori was encouraged to pursue the arts, and at the age of nine, was already performing classical piano as a soloist with the Manila Philharmonic Orchestra.

When it came time for Natori to go to college, she moved to the United States at the age of 17 and enrolled in Manhattanville College in Purchase, New York. There she studied economics and finance.

## Career Highlights

After graduating with her bachelor's degree in 1968, Natori was able to secure a position as an associate in corporate finance with Bache Securities in New York City. After only six months, she was sent to the Philippines to help establish the Manila office, where she was the site's only broker. In 1971, she moved to Merrill Lynch Pierce Fenner & Smith, becoming the first woman to become an investment banker in the firm. In four years, she broke through the glass ceiling again when she was named vice president of investment banking. During this time, she would also experience a personal milestone; marrying another investment banker, Kenneth Natori.

In spite of her success in the financial world, Natori wanted to expand her horizons and officially founded her own enterprise, J.A.C. Natori, later known as The Natori Company in 1976, the same year she gave birth to her son. "After that achievement at Merrill Lynch, I felt I wanted a challenge in a different direction," she said in an interview with *WWD* (2 May 1985). "I wanted to do something with the Philippines. I felt it hadn't gotten recognition for its capabilities. It was only associated with cheap, mass-market merchandise."

The answer came in the form of an embroidered tablecloth made in the Philippines, which inspired the creation of multicolored blouses. In the beginning of 1977, Natori then called Bloomingdale's to see if the retailer would be interested in carrying her product, but a buyer for the chain suggested the blouse be redesigned as a nightshirt. Natori complied, lengthening the garment so that it could be worn as either a blouse or a nightshirt, and by April 1977, she received her first order of 1,000 nightshirts to be sold in lingerie departments. Quitting her job at Merrill Lynch,

Natori entered the garment trade full-time with an initial $200,000 investment. She first worked out of her and her husband's apartment and flew to the Philippines to oversee production. Having no formal design training, Natori worked with a freelancer to execute her ideas. According to *Nation's Business* (February 1995), friends and family members were key in the early years of the Natori Company. Relatives helped to cut scalloped edges for 1,000 blouses, and an uncle, a former surgeon, sewed on labels.

By August 1977, Natori had designed a line of sleepwear using Philippines fabrics and embroidery. Saks Fifth Avenue launched the line with a full-page advertisement in the *New York Times*, and Natori could now move her showroom from her East Side living room to a larger space within New York City. She contracted with two factories in the Philippines for the manufacturing of her product until she established her own factory in Manila, which was constructed and operated by her father, Felipe. Political turmoil in the Philippines in 1983 did reduce deliveries during the holidays, but the situation stabilized enough that production facilities were further expanded.

Over the years, The Natori Company has also increased its product offerings. In terms of its core business, sleepwear and lingerie, Natori established three distinctive lines: elegant Natori collection for women in their 30s through 50s; the less-formal Natori II; and Josie, designed for women in their 20s and 30s. Daywear apparel was added early, then at-homewear debuted in the fall of 1983. In 1984, adopting the theme of "The Natorious Woman," Natori launched a collection of boudoir accessories, including travel bags and sachets. During the same year, it moved into a new full-floor showroom at 40 East 34 Street in Manhattan, New York City. By this time, 70 employees worked in New York, while more than 550 individuals were employed in the Manila factory.

In 1985, another family member officially joined the Natori team: Natori's husband, Kenneth, a Japanese American who also had an illustrious career in the finance world. He left his position director and senior executive vice president of Shearson Lehman American Express to become chairman of The Natori Company. Kenneth, co-owner of the company, had been involved behind-the-scenes from its inception.

A constant challenge for the company has been to cultivate other product lines, while also supporting its core business in lingerie. In 1989, Eve Stillman lingerie company was purchased by Kefco Apparel, Inc., a Natori-owned company. In 1990, Natori reached revenues of $25 million, including direct sales and licensing royalties. Two years later, revenues had grown to $33 million with the introduction of Josie Natori Couture, a ready-to-wear line consisting of eveningwear, including dresses and separates. Still, 86 percent of the revenues originated from sleepwear. To expand her market, Natori adopted creative marketing strategies, such as opening a costume show at New York's Metropolitan Museum of Art. New product offerings included costume jewelry, home furnishings through a licensing agreement with Revman Industries, and two fragrances—Natori and Josie—with Avon. International distribution was also expanded, particularly in Europe and Japan.

"I don't think I could have survived the rag trade if I did not have the background on Wall Street," Natori was quoted in article in *WWD* (10 April 1987). "I learned to work with companies and raise money. I don't consider myself a designer. I work with concepts. I'm very pragmatic."

Natori serves on the boards of Manhattanville College, Educational Foundation of Fashion Industries, Alltel Corporation, and Philippine American Foundation. She is also a trustee of the Asia Society and Asian Cultural Council. She is on the advisory board of The Keep Walking Fund, which encourages young entrepreneurs and social pioneers.

She and her husband have a son, Kenneth Natori Jr.

## Sources

Haynes, Kevin. 10 April 1987. "Three SA Women: How They Built Their Business Niches." *WWD*: 2.

Monget, Karyn. 11 July 1991. "Breaking Out of the Boudoir." *WWD*: 4+ .

Santamaria, Sam. 4–10 July 2001. "Fund Lauds Fashionable FilAm." *Philippine News*.

Willen, Janet L. February 1995. "Fashioning a Business." *Nation's Business*: 14.

Wilson, Joyce. 2 May 1995. "Josie Natori: Intimate Apparel's Fast Learner." *WWD*: 26.

"Working Woman 500: The Women Behind the Numbers." May 1998. *Working Woman*: 50.

# Kim Ng

**Born**: 1968, New York.

**Education**: University of Chicago, B.A. in public policy, 1990.

**Positions Held**: Special projects analyst, Chicago White Sox, Chicago, Illinois, 1990–95; assistant director of baseball operations, Chicago White Sox, Chicago, Illinois, 1995–96; director of waivers and player records, American League, 1997–98; assistant general manager, New York Yankees, New York City, New York, 1998–2001; vice president/assistant general manager, New York Yankees, New York City, New York, 2001; assistant general manager, Los Angeles Dodgers, Los Angeles, California, 2001– .

**Summary**: Kim Ng is the highest ranking Asian American female baseball executive in the history of the sport. A native of the New Jersey area, she has worked in management positions with the Chicago White Sox, American League, New York Yankees, and the Los Angeles Dodgers.

## Early Years

Ng, the oldest of five daughters, spent her childhood in Fresh Meadows, located in Queens, New York, and Ridgewood, New Jersey. Both her father, Jim Ng, a native of China, and her mother worked in banking. They also were avid athletes and sports spectators: "We'd go skiing almost every other weekend in winter. My dad played tennis and softball. He loved to watch football. My mom played tennis, she was really good. Sports was just part of our life every day," she said to the *Los Angeles Times* (11 December 2001).

Her father Jim, who died when Ng was in grade school, also loved baseball. Ng herself was a New York Yankees fan. She also played tennis and softball at Ridgewood High School.

## Higher Education

At the University of Chicago, Ng studied public policy while also playing on the college softball team as an infielder. She intended on eventually becoming a banker like her parents, but did not receive any offers from financial institutions after graduation. She was working on campus when her former softball coach told her about an internship with the Chicago White Sox major league baseball team. "I printed out my resume, raced down there, had two interviews and landed the internship," she told the *Los Angeles Times*. "And I realized I didn't want to work for a bank. I'd much rather work in sports."

## Career Highlights

The Chicago White Sox internship encompassed a wide range of responsibilities. In addition to working on computers for the monitoring of statistics, performances, and salaries, Ng sat in on contract negotiations and arbitration hearings. "She had a tremendous aptitude for computers and that's what got her foot in the door," former assistant general manager Danny Evans told the *Daily News* in New York (4 March 2001). "Within the first month of her working with us, it was obvious she needed to be full-time."

As a result, Ng was offered a position as a special projects analyst. She further developed a new computer system and helped scout potential players. "I even held the radar gun at our home games," Ng said to *Asian Week* (1 April 1998). "I did anything anyone asked me to do."

Most importantly, Ng got more experience in arbitration and contract negotiations with high-level agents. In arbitration hearings, Ng had to argue against her club's own players in determining their new salaries. In 1994, she was able to convince the arbitration panel to give White Sox pitcher Jack McDowell, a recent Cy Young award winner, $5.3 million instead of the $6.5 million he was asking for.

"You go in and hopefully the player understands that you are just doing your job," she told *Asian Week*. "But sometimes things are said. After it's over you say, 'good luck, now go out there, and do your best,' but you've just told the arbitrator that this person doesn't deserve the money they want. So it's inherent in the system that there will be bad feeling afterwards."

In 1995, the White Sox promoted Ng to assistant director of baseball operations.

She stayed with the club until 1997, when she was named the director of waivers and records for the American League. In this position, she helped general managers of all American League teams to decipher Major League baseball regulations. She also approved player transactions and contracts.

Through her involvement with high-level Major League executives, Ng worked closely with Brian Cashman, the New York Yankees assistant general manager. When Cashman was elevated to general manager, he recruited Ng to be assistant general manager in 1998.

At 29 years of age, Ng became the youngest and second woman assistant general manager in the Major Leagues—and with her favorite childhood team, the Yankees, no less. "At first, she couldn't quite believe it," commented her husband, Tony Markward to the *Daily News*. "It was a few days before she came down from the shock."

In this new position, Ng worked together with Cashman in putting together the best team possible. During Ng's tenure as assistant general manager, the Yankees won four World Series championships. "Naturally, in a sport as old and big as baseball and with a team like the Yankees, she's had to prove herself, probably more than a man. But she's been put through the test and she passed with flying colors," commented legendary Yankees owner George Steinbrenner to the *Daily News*.

At the end of the 2001 season, Ng announced that she would resign from the Yankees. It was later revealed that Ng would follow her original mentor formerly connected with the Chicago White Sox, Danny Evans, to the West Coast. In her new assignment, Ng would be assistant general manager of the Los Angeles Dodgers under general manager Evans.

Regarding the possibility that Ng could be professional baseball's first general manager, Evans said in March 2001: "She would run a team like a business and do a great job. I think she'll be the first woman GM in baseball if she decides that she wants that."

### Sources

"A Breakthrough in the Bronx." 16 March 1998. *Sporting News*: 21.

Harlan, Heather. 1 April 1998. "A League of Her Own." *Asian Week*: 9.

McCarron, Anthony. 4 March 2001. "Power of a Woman." *Daily News* (New York): 90.

Pucin, Diane. 11 December 2001. "Dodger Executive Adds a New Ring." *Los Angeles Times*: D1.

# Win Chuai Ngan

Win Chuai Ngan. Photo courtesy of Wichai Chuai Ngan

**Born**: 10 November 1956, Thailand.

**Positions Held**: Garment worker, S.K. Fashion, El Monte, California, 1988–92; co-owner, Win's Thai Cuisine, Van Nuys, California, 2000– .

**Awards, Honors**: Small Business of the Year, Asian Pacific Islander Small Business Program, 2001.

**Summary**: Win Chuai Ngan and his partner Sukanya Sutthiprapha successfully launched a restaurant in southern California after being held captive in a garment sweatshop in El Monte for years. They are among the first of the Thai garment workers to become entrepreneurs.

### Career Highlights

Ngan was the oldest of six children in an agricultural family in northeastern Thailand. As were dozens of other immigrants from rural Thailand and Latin America, Ngan was lured from his homeland to work for a garment manufacturer in southern California. Instead of experiencing the American dream, he found himself in slave-labor-like conditions, in some cases held under armed guard in apartment buildings, and forced to sew garments, iron, and package. According to attorney and civil rights activist Julie Su (interview with Corporate Watch), the workers were being paid less than 60 cents an hour. Eight to ten men and women worked in one room of an apartment and slept in the other room. A seven-foot wall surrounded the two-story apartment complex in El Monte; later a ring of razor wire and iron guardrails with sharp ends pointing inward were added to keep the workers captive.

"I worked nonstop, 16 to 18 hours a day, making seams," Ngan was quoted in an article in the *Los Angeles Times* (25 October 2001). "After the work, we'd just move around the house, not outside. They threatened us if we tried to go outside, if we tried to run away. I was afraid."

After living under these conditions for four years, Ngan was able to escape in 1992 with only $300 in his pocket. He scaled the wall at night; at this time, the company had not yet instituted armed guards or installed the barbed wire. Yet the fear of reprisal was still deeply felt by Ngan and his younger brother, Suwichai Chuai Ngan, who was also able to gain his freedom. Most of the workers, more than 70, however, remained in the El Monte sweatshop until August 1995, when the compound was raided by authorities. The workers were then detained by the Immigration and Naturalization Service (INS), but eventually released due to the public outcry and work by various community organizations, including the Asian Pacific American Legal Center. Eventually, the operators of the sweatshop pled guilty to criminal counts of involuntary servitude and other charges and were sent to prison. A lawsuit against the manufacturers and retailers connected with the sweatshop resulted in monetary awards for most of the workers.

Meanwhile, other social service agencies, including the Thai Community Development Center and Sweatshop Watch assisted the workers to find garment jobs with reputable companies in southern California. Ngan continued to work in the sewing trade, while his brother launched a garment factory cooperative.

Befriending another former sweatshop worker, Sokanya Sutthiprapha, Ngan began to contemplate starting an independent enterprise. Through the help of the Thai Community Development Center in Los Angeles, the couple learned the methods of launching a business. Sutthiprapha, who worked as an assistant cook at a Thai restaurant in Eagle Rock for five months, realized the market for food from her homeland in America. Ngan and Sutthiprapha then began investigating a location for a restaurant, and identified a Thai eatery that was for sale for $10,000. With an additional startup investment of $10,000, the couple paid for equipment, food, and other expenses. They

also successfully negotiated the municipal permit and leasing process—in spite of their limited English-language ability.

Win's Thai Cuisine officially opened its doors on November 4, 2000, with only $150 in receipts during the first day, due to the complimentary food and beverages provided to relatives and guests. The restaurant soon gained a following with a multiethnic clientele and profits have since multiplied.

In recognition of the achievements of these two former sweatshop workers, the Asian Pacific Islander Small Business Program recognized both Ngan and Sutthiprapha with its Small Business of the Year Award in 2001. The couple were married on November 9, 2001.

### Sources

"Interview with Julie Su, Asian Pacific American Legal Center." Corporate Watch Web site. www.corpwatch.org/feature/sweatshops/elmonte.html [accessed October 28, 2001].

Robinson-Jacobs, Karen. 25 October 2001. "From Virtual Slavery to Being Boss." *Los Angeles Times*: C1, C6.

# Ted Ngoy

**Born**: Cambodia.

**Positions Held**: Salesperson and general manager, Winchell's Donuts, c. 1975; founder, Christy's Donuts, La Habra, c. 1976 to 1997; leader of Free Development Republican Party, Cambodia, 1998; special representative of the Phnom Penh Chamber of Commerce, 1999; founder of Federation for Advanced Agriculture Development of Cambodia, c. 2000.

**Summary**: Ted Ngoy, referred to as the "Doughnut King," is recognized for opening the door for Cambodian American entrepreneurs to dominate the doughnut shop industry in California in the 1980s and 1990s. According to the *San Jose Mer-*

*cury*, Cambodian Americans owned and operated as much as 90 percent of the 5,000 independent shops in the state as of the year 2000. Although Ngoy eventually returned to his native Cambodia, he leaves a legacy in the United States: some of those Chinese Cambodians he trained and hired have gone on to launch large doughnut supply businesses.

### Early Years

Ngoy, like many tens of thousands of his countrymen and women, fled Cambodia during the Vietnam War in the 1970s for a better life in the United States. Many of these refugees arrived penniless, but they soon devised ways to make a living. Chinese Cambodians in particular had been involved in business, rather than agriculture, so entrepreneurship was an attractive option.

Ngoy himself came to America in 1975, and settled in Orange County, California, near the flourishing Cambodian community in the city of Long Beach. After working two jobs simultaneously—as a custodian and gas station attendant—Ngoy then began work at a Winchell's Donut franchise, where he discovered that making doughnuts wasn't "too high tech," according to *Asian Week* magazine. Sensing a good business opportunity, he borrowed some money and purchased his first doughnut shop around 1977.

### Career Highlights

Key to Ngoy's success were networks developed within his ethnic community. Borrowing money from a Chinese Cambodian credit rotation association referred to as a *hui*, he employed family members and friends.

"Ngoy is the one who found a way for Cambodian immigrants to become part of the American dream of owning their own business," said Dennis Wong of the Asian Business Association (ABA) to *Asian Week* (5 March 1993). "Taking a loan from an Asian loaning society, Ngoy was able to buy two stores, operate them for awhile and then sell to someone in the community or a family member who wanted to buy them. That's how they go into it."

Ngoy explained his business strategy to the *Los Angeles Times* in 1987: buying the stores, he would enter into partnerships with his managers and share the profits with them. In this way, he was able to expand his Christy's Donut chain into 32 shops from San Diego to the San Francisco Bay area. When asked about his business philosophy, he stated, "No. 1 is determination. Working hard is important. No. 2 is courage. No. 3 is starting carefully. Don't just jump into something you don't know."

The doughnut business fit the needs of the immigrant community; it required relatively low startup capital ($30,000–$60,000), few baking skills, and minimal English-language abilities. Although the work and hours were demanding, family members, from teenage children to adults, often lent a hand to ensure the financial success of the business.

In 2000, 90 percent of the 5,000 independent doughnut shops in California were owned by Cambodians. Large companies such as B & H Distributors, a doughnut and restaurant supply business with headquarters in Hayward and Santa Ana, both in California, can be linked back to a store owned by Ngoy.

Ngoy's financial success in the United States, however, was limited. After incurring some heavy debts, he eventually returned to his native Cambodia. His passion for entrepreneurship and personal charisma continues as he attempts to make a political and economic impact on his homeland. In 1998, he ran unsuccessfully for the National Assembly as the leader of his own Free Development Republican Party. "Elections first, then doughnuts," he joked in a report by the Associated Press. "Hard work, determination, integrity, and know-how, those things are not enough. You need a good system, a free-enterprise system."

After serving as a special representative of the Phnom Penh Chamber of Commerce, Ngoy is now involved in promoting hybrid seeds through his organization, the Federation for Advanced Agriculture Development of Cambodia.

### SouFrces

Ariya, Hout Sry. 15 November 2000. "National Seed Agency in the Cards," *Phnom Penh Daily.*

Do, Julian. 5 March 1993. "California's New Donut Kings—Cambodian Refugees." *Asian Week*: 10.

Gardiner, Debbi. 22–28 June 2000. "Donuts Anyone?" *Asian Week.*

Lee, Gen Leigh. 1996. "Chinese-Cambodian Donut Makers in Orange County: Case Studies of Family Labor and Socioeconomic Adaptations." In Bill Ong Hing and Ronald Lee, eds. *Reframing the Immigration Debate.* Los Angeles: LEAP Asian Pacific American Public Policy Institute and UCLA Asian American Studies Center: 205–19.

"Malaysian Investors Explore Business in Cambodia." 8 August 1999. *Kyodo News International.*

May, Lee. 2 February 1987. "Asians Looking to Broaden Horizons." *Los Angeles Times.*

McDowell, Robin. 21 July 1998. "Election Lures Hopefuls Home." *Associated Press.*

"Miracle, Mirage View over Rice Seeds." 21 September 2000. *Phnom Penh Daily.*

# Sean Nguyen

**Full Name at Birth**: Son Van Nguyen.

**Born**: 20 December 1963, South Vietnam.

**Education**: Northwestern Electronics Institute, Minneapolis, Minnesota, 1987.

**Positions Held**: Technician, Multi-Tech Systems, Mounds View, Minnesota, 1981–90; founder, president, Nguyen Electronics Inc. (NEI), Blaine, Minnesota, (later moved to Minneapolis), 1986–97; founder, VidTech Microsystems, Minneapolis, Minnesota, 1992–97; founder, Tertronics, Milpitas, California, circa 1994; founder, Texatronics Distribution, Dallas, Texas, 1997–2000; president, chief executive officer, Texatronics Inc., Richardson, Texas, 2000– .

**Awards, Honors**: Young Entrepreneur of the Year, U.S. Small Business Administration, 1993

**Summary**: Sean Nguyen moved from assembling circuit boards in a factory in Minnesota to founding and leading multimillion-dollar high-tech manufacturing companies in Minneapolis, California's Silicon Valley, and Richardson, Texas. Nguyen's family members, also refugees from Vietnam, have played a large role in Nguyen's enterprises: his brother Tung helped establish the Texas company, Texatronics.

### Early Years

Nguyen, his two brothers, and three sisters were raised in South Vietnam. His father Tam was a rice farmer, and as a child, Nguyen helped harvest rice and raise ducks. He also sold ice cream on the side, exhibiting an early sign of an entrepreneurial spirit.

When the communist government took over the village, they confiscated the Nguyen family farm, and Nguyen's parents formulated a plan for escape. Seventeen-year-old Nguyen, his older brother Dung, and their father fashioned a crude sailboat in the jungle with three dozen other Vietnamese. In 1980, the group departed for Thailand on their makeshift vessel. It was decided that only the three oldest male members of the Nguyen family would make this trip, as they had heard stories of refugee women being raped at sea by pirates.

The sailboat, in fact, was raided seven times during their four-day voyage. The women passengers were assaulted and everything was stolen, even Nguyen's jacket and the motor. However, winds blew the boat safely to Thailand, where the Nguyens stayed in refugee camps for several months before a cousin who had previously emigrated to Minneapolis, Minnesota, made arrangements for a Lutheran church to sponsor them.

### Career Highlights

When the Nguyens arrived in a suburb near Minneapolis, they lived with about a dozen other refugees in a two-room apartment. Although Nguyen could not speak English and knew nothing about electronics, he was able to secure a job as a technician at modem manufacturer, Multi-Tech Systems, in a town called Mounds View. For minimum wage—four dollars an hour—Nguyen assembled circuit boards. He worked double shifts, and in time was promoted to engineer and then production manager. Because supervisors were required to hold college degrees, Nguyen attended Northwestern Electronics Institute in Minneapolis.

In 1986, he was able to convince his supervisor to allow him to take modem parts home for assembly and testing. In return, he didn't want overtime, but payment per unit as an independent business entity. Therefore, after putting a full day in at Micro-Tech, he worked in the basement of his home at night, along with his father, brothers, and relatives. Nguyen called his nascent operation Nguyen Electronics, Inc. (NEI).

In its first year, NEI made $50,000, just from work provided by Micro-Tech. In 1987, sales quadrupled to more than $200,000. In 1988, NEI moved from Nguyen's basement to a larger space in the

Minneapolis area. Nguyen invested his life savings in a down payment on a $150,000 assembly machine, which would allow for the assembly of 3,500 circuit boards per hour. Although he didn't make enough profit to cover the monthly payments for the machine at that time, NEI's increased production capacity eventually attracted more customers within Minnesota.

Throughout this time, Nguyen maintained his day job at Micro-Tech, but realized that he needs to commit to his company full-time to ensure its success. In 1990, when sales had surpassed $400,000, he finally left Micro-Tech to serve solely as president of NEI. By 1992, NEI had revenues of $4 million. Some of that profit went into the launch of a subsidiary, VidTech Microsystems, which produced graphic accelerator boards that speed up a computer's visual display.

Shortly thereafter, Nguyen created another company, Tertronics, named after his wife, Terri, also a former refugee. Tertronics, which programs memory chips and floppy disks, was based in Milpitas, California.

During this time, Nguyen's younger brother Tung had been reunited with the family. He learned about the computer manufacturing process in Minnesota and took his know-how and five workers down to Texas. "I didn't want to compete with my brother up there," Tung said in an interview with the *Dallas Morning News* (30 November 2001). "And I saw a big opportunity for the electronics business compared to Minnesota."

In 1995, Tung set up his business, Texatronics, with five staff members in his apartment in Arlington, Texas. They began with repairing motherboards overnight for AST Computers in Fort Worth. As they expanded, Texatronics moved into an office space in the city of Richardson.

Meanwhile, Nguyen was receiving nationwide recognition for his business skills.

In 1993, he was named Young Entrepreneur of the Year by the U.S. Small Business Administration, entitling him to a visit at the White House with President Bill Clinton. His companies were also attracting equity investors. In 1995, NEI received $750,000 from four private investors, two of them Vietnamese restaurateurs, and two local venture capital firms. In 1997, Plexus Corporation, a contract electronics manufacturer in Neenah, Wisconsin, acquired both NEI and Tertronics in a private transaction. Nguyen, the two companies' majority owner, continued to manage the operations of the factory in Milpitas, California, for a year. Then, in 1998, Tung called Nguyen for help: Texatronics needed to take the next step to become a full-fledged electronic contract manufacturer.

"Everything I know I learned from him, and I knew he could do it," Tung said to the *Dallas Morning News*.

So Nguyen made another move, this time from California's Silicon Valley to Richardson, Texas. The two brothers launched a new company, Texatronics Distribution, in Dallas to manage production materials. In 2000, Texatronics, Inc. and Texatronics Distribution merged, with Nguyen becoming president and chief executive officer. Tung was named chief operating officer.

In spite of their fast growth—their revenues were expected to reach $24 million in 2001—Texatronics is still in the shadow of giant contract electronics manufacturers. However, Nguyen's strategy is niche marketing. Texatronics specializes in low-volume projects that require complex work and fast turnaround, according to the *Dallas Morning News*. Nguyen's experience in building prototypes has enabled Texatronics to build relationships with high-tech corporations, many that are based in Texas' Telecom Corridor.

Crucial has been management of the company's personnel. Like in Minnesota corporations, most of Texatronics employees are Asian immigrants. "We don't have a patent. We don't have a product," Nguyen said to the *Dallas Morning News*. "We have people who give this company really strong growth."

Texatronics, which has expanded into Austin and Houston, has approximately 100 customers, including Texas Instruments and Raytheon. Increased demand for quick-turn prototype services led to the opening of a fourth plant in Phoenix, Arizona, in January 2002.

## Sources

Gruner, Stephanie, Christopher Gibbons, and Vera B. Gibbons. December 1993. "The Entrepreneur of the Year Register." *Inc.*: 135+ .

Manners, John. 1994. "How Five Thrive by Striving to Serve." *Money*: 48+ .

"Plexus Buys Assets of Two—NEI, Tertronics Added in Accord with CEM's Expansion Strategy." 24 November 1997. *Electronic Buyers' News*: 102.

Reddy, Sudeep. 30 November 2001. "Desire to Help Family Fuels Business Success." *Dallas Morning News*.

Serant, Claire. 19 November 2001. "Texatronics Pushes Prototype Services—To open Fourth Plant to Tap Further into Texas; Growing Telecom Market." *Ebn*: 46.

Texatronics Web site. www.texatronics.com [accessed November 29, 2001].

"Vietnam: Business Rushes to Get In." 5 April 1993. *Fortune*: 98+ .

# Ko Nishimura

Ko Nishimura. Photo courtesy of Solectron Corporation

**Full Name at Birth**: Koichi Nishimura.

**Born**: 1938, Pasadena, California.

**Education**: Pasadena Junior College, Pasadena, California, A.A. in physical education; San Jose State University, San Jose, California, B.S. in electrical engineering; San Jose State University, M.S. in electrical engineering; Stanford University, Stanford, California, Ph.D. in applied materials science.

**Positions Held**: Associate engineer, Lockheed Missiles & Space Company; test engineer, International Business Machines Corporation (IBM), 1965; chief operating officer, Solectron Corporation, Milpitas, California, 1988; president, Solectron Corporation, Milpitas, California, 1990; chief executive officer, Solectron Corporation, Milpitas, California, 1992; chairman of the board, Solectron Corporation, Milipitas, California, 1996– .

**Honors and Awards**: *Electronic Business'* 1999 CEO of the Year; Silicon Valley Engineering Hall of Fame, 2000.

**Summary**: Since joining the company in 1988, Ko Nishimura has turned Milpitas, California-based Solectron Corporation into the world's top contract manufacturer of computer and electronic products. Solectron's success as a Fortune 500 firm is based on good management, clear vision, and Nishimura's highest commitment to customer service.

## Early Years

At age three, Nishimura and his family were forced to leave their home in Pasadena, California, for an internment camp in Manzanar, California, during World War II. The family returned to Pasadena after the war and moved into a house a few blocks from the Rose Bowl and in the same neighborhood where Jackie Robinson lived.

Nishimura didn't start learning English until he was in first grade. But he adapted quickly and excelled in sports, becoming a starting defensive back in football at Muir High School and Pasadena Junior College. On the weekends he also assisted his grandfather on a gardening route.

## Higher Education

A self-professed "mediocre" student, Nishimura was playing football at the junior college when he dislocated his shoulder that put an end to his career. He transferred to San Jose State University as a physical education major but switched to engineering after he grew fond of his work as a part-time technician at Lockheed Missiles & Space in nearby Sunnyvale.

Nishimura earned his bachelor's and master's degrees in engineering from San Jose State and would later receive his doctorate in materials science from Stanford University while working for IBM.

## Career Highlights

As a child, Nishimura saw his father go to the University of California at Berkeley to become an engineer. Due to discrimination, however, his father never got a chance to practice his profession and had to work instead at a fruit stand.

Circumstances were better for Nishimura. As an associate engineer at Lockheed, he worked on programs to simulate satellite orbit behavior. In 1965, he joined IBM as a test engineer, working on the company's System 360 disk drive units. To this day, Nishimura says that it remains his favorite job. For 23 years, he climbed the ladder at IBM, and driven by a desire never to be satisfied, he earned a reputation as being something of a maverick.

In 1988, Nishimura took an offer to become the chief operating officer of Solectron, an 11-year-old company started in Milpitas, just north of San Jose in Silicon Valley. The offer came from Solectron chief executive officer Winston Chen, who wanted to build a world-class manufacturing company. At IBM, Nishimura had been Chen's supervisor; now, they were partners.

Like other contract manufacturers, Solectron worked with high-volume original equipment manufacturers (OEMs) of computers and electronics. Until the early 1990s, OEMs sought out the services of contract manufacturers only when their own plants were too busy to complete the job. But due to falling prices, narrowing profit margins, and shrinking product lifecycles, OEMs began outsourcing manufacturing its products to experts like Solectron.

The name "Solectron" does not appear on any product. Still, what Solectron makes is very familiar: personal computers, cell phones, inkjet printers, and medical equipment for such giants as IBM, Hewlett-Packard, and Motorola.

At the time Nishimura joined Solectron, the entire contract manufacturing sector was deemed as being an unsophisticated collection of low-paying assemblers. "We used to be thought of as a sweatshop industry," Nishimura said in an interview with *Fast Company* (November 1999).

But that concept changed, due in large part to Nishimura's almost obsessive commitment to the highest standards in customer service. As a young adult, Nishimura's first job was pumping gas and fixing cars at a local Richfield gas station, where customers were willing to pay a penny more per gallon for friendly service and extra hustle. When he did a lube job, Nishimura washed the car, inside and out, resulting in regular return business.

At Solectron, Chen had established a system for assessing customer satisfaction not on a yearly or quarterly basis, but once a week. Customers rated Solectron on five criteria: quality, responsiveness, communication, service, and technical support.

But Nishimura searched for ways to improve Chen's "customer-first" model. He saw an ad in a trade publication seeking applicants for the Malcolm Baldrige National Quality Award. Congress had established the award in 1987 to help revive the nation's then-weakening manufacturing sector. He felt that the Baldrige's strict evaluation process could serve as a benchmark for continued improvement. Nishimura set about incorporating the Baldrige prescriptions, starting a "customer executive survey" on Solectron clients' long-term technology and production needs.

It took several years, but on its third application, Solectron won the Baldrige award in a White House ceremony in October 1991. It was the first and only time a company in the often-maligned outsourcing industry had earned the prize. In 1997, Solectron won the award again.

"We want to be the best at what we do," Nishimura told *Fast Company*. "Our internal process, which we administer every 18 months, keeps us focused on continuously improving things for our customers. That's the only way to be the best."

Even competitors respect Solectron. "They give the whole industry a good name," Michael Marks, CEO of San Jose-based Flextronics International Ltd., told *Electronic Business*.

By 1999, the Fortune 500 firm's revenues increased from just less than $300 million in 1989 to more than $8 billion, and its stock split four times since its initial public offering in 1989. It grew from a single site in Silicon Valley to 27 sites on four continents. It continued to expand its services to include design, fulfillment, and repair.

The man who had once taken over the newspaper route for two college-bound sons and bragged of being named *San Jose Mercury News'* "Paper Delivery Boy of the Week" continued to live in a modest tract home while driving to work in a Honda Accord—despite having a net worth of more than $50 million.

Despite the downturn in the economy, Solectron has continued to expand, largely by acquiring plants from brand-name companies. In 2000, Nishimura bought two Sony plants, paid $900 million to take over a portion of Nortel's networking equipment manufacturing operations and exchanged $2 billion in stock for Smart Modular Technologies, a maker of memory modules.

Then, Nishimura completed his biggest deal ever: the $2.4 billion takeover of Nat-Steel Electronics, the primary supplier of Apple Computer motherboards that is partly owned by the Singapore government.

Whatever the economic climate, Nishimura said that he continues to be bound by his job to expand Solectron for the sake of customers, shareholders, and employees. "If you can't make the customer successful, you won't be either," he said in a 1999 interview with *Electronic Business*.

He and his wife Holly live in San Jose and have three sons, Bobby, Greg, and Mark.

—By John Saito Jr.

## Sources

Einstein, David. 12 July 2000. "The Biggest Company You've Never Heard of." *Forbes*.

Landers, Peter. 14 June 2001. "Foreign Aid: Why Some Sony Gear Is Made in Japan—By Another Company—Solectron Succeeds in Selling an American Idea: Let a Specialist Take the Risk—A Whirlwind Trip to Hawaii." *Wall Street Journal*: 1.

Markels, Alex. November 1999. "The Wisdom of Chairman Ko." *Fast Company*.

Roberts, Bill. December 1999. "CEO of the Year: Koichi Nishimura, Contract Manufacturing Visionary." *Electronic Business*: 62.

Sheerin, Matthew. 12 July 2000. "The Hot 25: Ko Nishimura, Chairman, CEO." *Electronic Buyers' News*.

Smart, Tim. 12 May 1999. "The Factory of the Future; Little-Known Solectron makes High-Tech Industry's Products." *The Washington Post*: E01.

Williams, Elisa. 8 January 2001. "Solectron: Delivery Boys." *Forbes*: 118–119.

## Indra K. Nooyi

**Born**: 28 October 1955, Chennai, India.

**Education**: Madras Christian College, Madras, India, B.S. Indian Institute of Management, M.B.A., Calcutta, India;

Yale University, M.A. in public and private management, 1980.

**Positions Held**: Strategic consultant, Boston Consulting Group, 1980–86; vice president and director of corporate strategy and planning, Motorola, 1986–90; senior vice president of corporate strategy and planning, Asea Brown Boveri, 1990–94; senior vice president of corporate strategy and development, PepsiCo., Inc., 1994–99; chief financial officer, PepsiCo, Inc., 2000– ; and president, PepsiCo, Inc., 2000– .

**Honors and Awards**: 50 Most Powerful Women, *Fortune* magazine, October 2000; Human Capital Advantage Award, Hunt Scanlon Advisors, 2001.

**Summary**: As the president of PepsiCo, Inc., Indra Nooyi is one of the highest-ranking India-born women in corporate America. She has successfully blended her ethnic identity, unique personality, and management skills into leading a $20 billion company.

### Early Years

Nooyi was born in Chennai, India, to a mother who encouraged her daughters to pursue their dreams. Every night at dinner Nooyi and her sister would take turns pretending that they were the president of India. "If you were elected president of India and had to give an inauguration speech, what would you say?" Nooyi's mother would reportedly ask. This was merely a game but it confirmed to Nooyi that she could indeed be anything she wanted if she tried.

### Education

Nooyi gained her undergraduate degree from Madras Christian College, located near her hometown, and her master's degree in business administration from the top-ranked business school in India, Indian Institute of Management in Calcutta. During her college years, she played lead guitar in an all-girl rock band. (While in India, Nooyi also worked as a product manager with Johnson & Johnson and textile firm Mettur Beardsell.)

In 1978, Nooyi traveled to the United States to attend Yale University for more graduate studies. "For the first time in my life, I learned what it is to be an outsider," Nooyi stated in a commencement speech to the Convent of Sacred Heart Academy in Greenwich, Connecticut, in 2001. "Not just to be different, but to be excluded."

After one year of graduate school at Yale, Nooyi prepared for summer job interviews. At that time, she only owned Indian saris for formal occasions, so she purchased an interview outfit at K-Mart—a bright blue polyester suit and striped blouse—and wore that in addition to her snow boots. The interview did not go well. Her career counselor advised her to wear her sari next time. "If they can't accept you," the counselor said, "it's their loss, not yours."

### Career Highlights

After Nooyi graduated from Yale in 1980, she did get a job—at the esteemed Boston Consulting Group. She worked there for six years directing international corporate strategy projects for textile and consumer goods companies, retailers, and specialty chemicals producers. In 1986, she moved to Motorola as vice president and director of corporate strategy and planning. At the electronics company, she advised the chief executive officer; in 1990, she moved to the Swiss industrial, energy, and automation giant—Asea Brown Boveri (ABB)—which had established its U.S. headquarters in Connecticut. As part of the top management team responsible for both the U.S. market and the worldwide industrial market, she helped to generate about one-third of ABB's $30 billion in global sales.

Four years later, Nooyi had built a strong reputation as an effective strategist and was being courted by both General Electric and PepsiCo. Nooyi decided to make the move to PepsiCo, the multinational food and beverage company headquartered in Purchase, New York. As senior vice president of corporate strategy and development, Nooyi worked closely with then-chief executive officer of PepsiCo's fast-food division, Roger Enrico, who had just returned to the company after a 14-month sabbatical. Together, they examined their fast-food chains—the twenty-nine thousand Pizza Hut, Taco Bell, and Kentucky Fried Chicken restaurants. "Their conclusion: The industry was overbuilt, and success required a different culture than that of a packaged-goods company," reported *Business Week* (10 April 2000).

As a result, in 1997, a year after Enrico had been promoted to chief executive officer of the entire company, PepsiCo spun off its restaurant business into a new company, Tricon Global Restaurants, Inc. Shortly thereafter, Nooyi also determined that PepsiCo's bottling operations were devaluating its stock and lowering its profit margins—and, as a result, Pepsi Bottling Group became an independent publicly traded company in March 1999.

While focusing on building PepsiCo's packaged food and beverage ventures (Frito-Lay and Pepsi-Cola), Nooyi has also been instrumental in acquisitions and mergers. In a key move in 1998, she convinced PepsiCo to purchase Tropicana juice business from Seagram Co. for $3.3 billion, despite some reluctance by top executives. The decision further heightened PepsiCo's

penetration of the market: in 2000 Tropicana Pure Premium, the nation's top-selling orange juice, surpassed Campbell Soup as the third-largest grocery brand.

By this time, Nooyi, elevated to chief financial officer, had established a strong working relationship with Steven S. Reinemund, PepsiCo's president and chief operating officer at the time. Coined "the dynamic duo," they represent disparate styles and approaches: Reinemund, a former Marine, has been described as operational and hands-on, while Nooyi, often outfitted in saris and scarfs, is known for her personable, big-picture thinking.

In 2001, after PepsiCo acquired Quaker Oats Company in a $13.8-billion deal, Reinemund was elected chairman and chief executive officer of the company, while Nooyi was named president at the age of 45. She is expected to succeed Reinemund as chief executive officer someday.

Nooyi has been viewed as a role model for Indian American women. In 2000, she was named forty-third in *Fortune* magazine's 50 most successful women in America. "She has never distanced herself from her Indian identity," reported the Florida-based Indian magazine *Desh Videsh*. She holds close to her Hindu religion, and even paid a visit to her family deity at a Hindu temple in Pittsburgh after the Quaker Oats acquisition, according to the publication *World and I* (May 2001). The Greenwich, Connecticut, home that she shares with her husband, Raj, a management consultant, and her two daughters has a *puja*, or Hindu prayer room.

She continues to play electric guitar and is an avid reader. She also serves on the board of directors for Timberland and the PepsiCo Foundation. She is a member of the board of trustees for Convent of the Sacred Heart School and the advisory board of the Greenwich Breast Cancer Alliance. She also belongs to the advisory board of Yale University President's Council of International Activities.

## Sources

Byrne, John A. 10 April 2000. "A Potent Ingredient in Pepsi's Formula." *Business Week.*

Byrnes, Nanette. 29 January 2001. "The Power of Two at Pepsi." *Business Week*: 102–104.

"Indra Nooyi." *Yale School of Management Twenty-fifth Anniversary Celebration.* http://www.yalesomtwenthfifth.com/nooyi.htm. [accessed August 2, 2001]

Indra Nooyi's commencement speech, Convent of Sacred Heart, Greenwich, Connecticut, 2001.

Pandya, Meenal. May 2001. "No Going Back—Indian Immigrant Women Shape a New Identity." *World and I*: 204.

# O

## Scott D. Oki

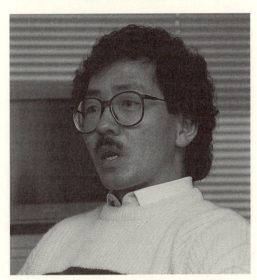

Scott D. Oki. Photo © Doug Wilson/CORBIS

**Born**: 5 October 1948, Seattle, Washington.

**Education**: University of Washington, 1968; University of Colorado, Colorado Springs, Colorado, B.A. magna cum laude in accounting and information systems, 1974; University of Colorado, Colorado Springs, Colorado, M.B.A., 1975.

**Positions Held**: Programmer, systems analyst, and project leader, Looart Press Inc., Colorado Springs, Colorado, 1975; marketing executive and product manager, small business computer systems, Hewlett-Packard Company, Palo Alto, California, 1976–80; cofounder and vice president, medical office management computer systems, Sequoia Group, Inc., Larkspur, California, 1980–82; head of international sales, Microsoft Corporation, Redmond, Washington, 1982–86; senior vice president, sales, marketing, and services, Microsoft Corporation, Redmond, Washington, 1986–92; chairman and chief executive officer, Oki Developments, Inc., Bellevue, Washington, 1992– ; cofounder and partner, Social Venture Partners, 1997– .

**Summary**: Third-generation Japanese American Scott Oki built up the then-fledgling Microsoft Corporation's international sales division in the 1980s; within four years, the division grew to more than 40 percent of the software company's revenues. Retiring as the senior vice president of sales, marketing, and services after 10 years of dedicated work for Microsoft, Oki has used his stock options to fund philanthropic and entrepreneurial endeavors.

## Early Years

Oki was raised in the working-class neighborhood of the Rainier Valley section of south Seattle. His parents, Bob and Kim Oki, had met and married while incarcerated in a Japanese American internment camp in Minidoka, Idaho. Making their new home in Seattle after World War II, Oki's father worked at the Post Office, while his mother took a job as a secretary for a governmental agency.

Other members of the household were Oki's younger brother and sister and their immigrant grandmother, who spoke only Japanese. To help ends meet, the family tied fishing flies at the kitchen table in the winter and worked the strawberry fields in nearby Auburn in the summer.

When Oki was in the Boy Scouts, his father founded the Imperial Drum & Bugle Corps that performed in parades and jamborees. Oki played the drums, while his parents handled the fund-raising aspects. Oki eventually became an Eagle Scout. Because Oki's father wanted his son to pursue electrical engineering, Oki took scientific-oriented classes in high school.

## Higher Education

Oki entered the University of Washington in Seattle, but did not take his studies seriously. Most young men in the late-1960s were preoccupied with the Vietnam War. Oki himself had received a low draft lottery number, thus increasing his chances of being on the front lines of combat. Instead of waiting to be drafted, Oki enlisted in the Air Force. While serving at the academy in Colorado Springs, Colorado, he was assigned to play the drum in the band. He was also able to attend classes at the University of Colorado. This time Oki applied himself and by the time his four years of military service was over, he was only six credits short of getting a bachelor's degree in accounting and information systems. He then went on to gain an M.B.A. in a year, graduating first in his class.

## Career Highlights

Oki first intended to be a certified public accountant, but a professor who had initially encouraged Oki to pursue computer science recommended that he work as a programmer for a local company called Looart Press. After a year he secured a new job with Hewlett-Packard, first as an accountant in Colorado Springs and then moving to the headquarters in Palo Alto, California, as a member of the marketing team for mini-computers, the leading-edge equipment before the age of personal computers. He also served as the product manager for the BASIC computer language, which was running on the Hewlett-Packard machines.

After four years, he, along with some graduates of Harvard Business School, formed their own startup, Sequoia Group, in nearby Larkspur in 1980. The Sequoia Group was designed to develop and sell turnkey computer systems to medical offices. The venture eventually collapsed and was acquired by Corning Glass.

Before the company filed for bankruptcy, Oki had already left the partnership and was doing consulting work for MicroPro, the maker of the WordStar word processing program. He had sent a letter inquiring about work possibilities to a relatively new company called Microsoft, which had opened in the Seattle suburb of Redmond. At the time, the software company had approximately 100 employees; a majority of them were engineers.

After interviews with multiple executives, including founder Bill Gates, Oki was hired as marketing manager of special accounts. These accounts included IBM and

ASII in Japan. After a month, Oki submitted a business plan and proposal asking for $1 million to open an international sales division. Gates approved the plan—which would involve the launching of at least three subsidiaries in Europe and management of accounts in Japan—and Oki was soon spending most of his time overseas, hiring and managing sales staff. Flying regularly to London, Paris, Munich, Milan, Tokyo, and Stockholm, Oki was working 100-hour weeks and rarely took a day off. By 1984, he logged more than 400,000 flying miles and became Pan Am's most frequent flier.

During this time, IBM had begun delivering shipments of its first personal computer, originally introduced in 1981. IBM had licensed MS-DOS (Microsoft Disk Operating System), a Microsoft product, as its operating system, but foreign companies, viewing IBM as a competitor, preferred to use alternative operating systems. Through Oki's work, these international companies were actually won over to adopt MS-DOS. Within four years, the international division was generating 40 percent of the company's total revenues, according to *Washington CEO* (May 1996).

"I looked at Microsoft as a vehicle where I felt I could make a significant contribution," Oki stated to *Washington CEO*. "And I think I did. The beauty of the job was the independence. It was a real meritocracy. But you had to deliver the bacon."

Oki's success with the overseas market led Microsoft to place Oki in charge of the domestic sales division in 1986. As the vice president of sales, marketing, and services, Oki faced a major restructuring of the U.S. sales operation, which included layoffs and closure of offices. Within five years, revenues had risen from $100 million to $1 billion. During this time, Oki also successfully lobbied for the promotion of Windows above other operating systems.

After six years, Oki, who had married and started a family by this time, wanted a reprieve from his 100-hour work weeks. In 1992, he submitted his resignation and left with a reported 500,000 shares of Microsoft stock. His personal wealth has been estimated by sources as ranging from $100 million to $750 million.

With his career with Microsoft over, Oki and his wife Laurie have now focused their time on their philanthropic efforts, mainly through the Oki Foundation, which had been initially designed as an estate planning measure in 1986. Now housed in a former church building in downtown Bellevue, the foundation invests profits and revenues from its company, Nanny & Webster, a manufacturer of baby blankets, and its professional soccer team, Seattle Sounders, to aid Puget Sound-area children's charities. Major gifts have come from the Okis' personal wealth, including a $1 million unrestricted gift to the Children's Hospital in 1993. Oki sits on more than 20 nonprofit boards, and he was named to the University of Washington Board of Regents in 1993.

In 1997, Oki and software magnate Paul Brainerd cofounded Social Venture Partners, a "venture philanthropy" group that solicits money as well as management expertise for nonprofit organizations. Starting with 36 founding partners, the group has grown to more than 250.

Regarding his philanthropic strategy, Oki told *Town and Country* (June 2000): "I get organizations to create an infrastructure to raise money far more effectively and efficiently."

An avid golfer, Oki also started Oki Development, which develops, owns, and manages golf facilities and country clubs. In 1990 Oki opened Seattle's first-class golf course, The Golf Club, at Newscastle; among his other enterprises is a Japanese restaurant, Nishino. He also supports the Seattle Chess Foundation.

He and his wife Laurie have three children: Alexander, Nicholas, and Callan.

### Sources

Gullo, Jim. June 2000. "Great Scott!" *Town and Country*: 166.

Kleiner, Adam. May 1996. "Scott Oki Inc." *Washington CEO*.

"Scott D. Oki, Multimillionaire Philanthropist." IMDiversity: Asian-American Village. http://www.imdiversity.com [accessed August 16, 2001].

# George Ow Jr.

**Born**: 3 January, 1943, Santa Cruz, California.

**Education**: Monterey Peninsula College, Monterey, California, A.A., 1963; San Francisco State College, San Francisco, California, B.A. in business, 1965; University of California, Los Angeles, Los Angeles, California, M.B.A., 1966.

**Positions Held**: Principal, Ow Properties, 1970– .

**Summary**: George Ow Jr. has made his mark as a real estate developer and investor in his native Santa Cruz, while also gaining a reputation as a philanthropist and supporter of artists and social causes.

### Early Years

Ow is the oldest of seven brothers and sisters of George Ow Sr., and Emily Ow of Santa Cruz. George Ow Sr., had settled in the Santa Cruz area in 1937 after immigrating from China at the age of 16. Starting out as a grocery store operator, George Sr. soon moved into real estate development and investment. Among his projects were the King's Plaza Shopping Center in Capitola and King's Village Shopping Center in Scotts Valley, both in the Santa Cruz area.

While his parents worked long hours to make their grocery store financially viable, Ow spent his early childhood in Santa Cruz's Chinatown, and was cared for by his extended family. Often, he was the only Asian child in his small elementary school. To avoid the taunts and harassment in the schoolyard from other children, he spent much of his recess time in the classroom reading books, and developed a love of reading.

### Higher Education

Ow attended nearby Monterey Peninsula College for his associate of arts degree, and then completed his bachelor's degree at San Francisco State College. He then moved to Los Angeles to gain his M.B.A. from the University of California, Los Angeles. After completing his higher education, George Ow Jr., married for the first time in December 1966. In January 1967, he went on active duty with the United States Army until 1970, and served one year in Vietnam.

### Career Highlights

Returning home in 1970, George Ow Jr. took over management of the family's real estate business and has expanded the operations into other retail businesses. He also became involved in the Erhard Seminars Training (EST) self-awareness movement in 1974 through his first wife, Lisa. And although they were divorced the next year, Ow attended every EST seminar the following three years.

Meanwhile, the Ow family enterprises grew to include—in addition to the King's Plaza Shopping Center in Capitola and the

King's Village Shopping Center in Scotts Valley—a chain of pizza parlors called The Pizza Company, a 1950s-style diner called the Pontiac Grill, the Capitola Book Café, a book publishing company called the Capitola Book Company, the Imperial Courts Tennis Club in Aptos, and a number of small developments throughout the Santa Cruz County area. In the spring of 2000, Ow Properties purchased the sprawling SCI Systems building property near the Watsonville Airport with plans to seek a tenant—preferably a high-tech firm—or to resell the 86,000-square-foot structure.

After suffering a heart attack in 1988, Ow relinquished a number of their operations, including The Pizza Company, Pontiac Grill, and Capitola Book Café. In 1994, Ow gave priority to his wife Gail Michaelis-Ow and their two sons, as well as to an older son from Ow's previous marriage. He started delegating much of the family business responsibility to his brothers and sisters and their children.

Ow has also built a reputation as a supporter of community activities, needy students and struggling artists. He helped finance *Forbidden City, USA*, a documentary directed by Arthur Dong about a famous Chinese nightclub in San Francisco that reached the height of its popularity in the 1930s and 1940s. Ow has also funded films by Steven Okazaki.

The Ow family established the Ow Family American Dream Scholarship program, which has funded hundreds of scholarships to students at local high schools, Cabrillo Community College, and the University of California at Santa Cruz. The program has been funding these $500 scholarships for the past 19 years. They also fund an NAACP scholarship program to help local African American high school and community college students.

In furthering the Chinese history and culture in the Santa Cruz and Monterey Bay area, Ow's Capitola Book Company has sponsored and published Sandy Lydon's *Chinese Gold* and *Growing Up on Grove Street*, which record the struggles and early life of Chinese immigrants and their children in the area. Another Capitola book is *The Japanese in the Monterey Bay Region: A Brief History*, also by Lydon.

Ow has commissioned giant murals and sent a young sculptor to Italy. The Ow Family Properties has donated money for a proposed museum to honor the generations of Pajaro Valley farmworkers—Successive waves of immigrants, from China, Japan, Portugal, Korea, Yugoslavia, the Philippines, and Mexico have come to the Pajaro Valley to work in its fields and orchards.

—By Takeshi Nakayama

### Sources

"Cultural Historian Awards." 1997. Chinese Historical and Cultural Project Press Release.

Holbrook, Stett. 1 October 1999. "City Library Eyed for Farmworker Museum." *Santa Cruz Sentinel*.

Kleist, Trina. 30 March 2000. "Developer Ow Buys Airport Site." *Santa Cruz Sentinel*.

Scheinin, Richard. 14 January 1990. "Developing Dreams: The Family Saga of George Ow Jr." *San Jose Mercury News*: 1L+ .

# P

## Cecilia Pagkalinawan

**Born**: c. 1967, Manila, Philippines.

**Education**: Hofstra University, B.A. in communications studies.

**Positions Held**: Media specialist, Young & Rubicam; vice president of client services, K2 Design New York, New York; executive producer and creative director of the Interactive Division, Messner Vetere Berger McNamee Schmatterer/Euro RSCG, project manager and president of U.S. division, Abilon Corporation, New York, New York 1997; founder, Boutique Y3K, New York, New York 1998–2001.

**Awards, Honors**: New York City Woman Business Owner of the Year, National Association of Woman Business Owners, 2000.

**Summary**: Cecilia Pagkalinawan was an Internet pioneer in New York's Silicon Alley during its heyday in the mid-1990s. An e-commerce entrepreneur who combined merged technological know-how with a sense of style, Pagkalinawan served as a role model for other young Asian American women interested in dot-com careers.

### Early Years

As a child in the Philippines, Cecilia Pagkalinawan dreamed of being the first woman president of her country. She had four siblings, and when her youngest brother Jovito was born with a hole in his heart, the family decided to move to the United States to gain access to better medical care.

The transition for then eight-year-old Pagkalinawan was not easy. "I got teased for a while because I looked different, I had an accent," she told a reporter at *Asiaweek*. "The worst thing was people assuming I was stupid because I had an accent or I didn't speak English appropriately."

Yet Pagkalinawan did not give up. She improved her English, joined sports teams, and became a cheerleader. Because funds were limited in her large family, she sewed her own clothes and shopped in second-hand stores. She also made time to participate in walkathons, food drives, and a fund-raiser to purchase the first computers for her grammar school.

### Career Highlights

After gaining her bachelor's degree in communications studies at Hofstra University, Pagkalinawan worked in a variety of media and marketing jobs. With the purchase of a laptop computer loaded with Internet capabilities, she was instantly connected to news from the Philippines and her friends in Europe and Asia. Sensing the World Wide Web's potential, she began work at K2 Design, an pioneering Web-development agency, and eventually became vice president of Creative Affairs and Client Services.

At K2, Pagkalinawan began to establish herself as a player in Silicon Alley, the high-tech district in Manhattan. She created one of the first online malls, "marketplaceMCI," and developed virtual stores for established retail companies. She also produced New York City's first live Webcast opening of a Broadway production, "Bring in da Noise, Bring in da Funk."

She later joined a European advertising firm, Messner Vetere Berger McNamee Schmatterer/Euro RSCG, where she oversaw successful online advertising and marketing campaigns for established companies, including Volvo, which tripled its online advertising budget to $3 million. While developing her career, Pagkalinawan also made time for philanthropy. In 1997, she cofounded MOUSE (Making Opportunities for Upgrading Schools and Education), a volunteer group of more than 100 Silicon Alley professionals dedicated to helping youth sharpen their technology skills.

It was a new job with the Canadian-based e-commerce company Abilon International that would present Pagkalinawan with perhaps her most defining career moment. Promoted to president of the Abilon Corporation, the company's U.S. division, Pagkalinawan was informed six months later that the company was closing operations due to a loss of funding.

Instead of accepting a $60,000 guaranteed severance package, she offered to buy the New York company and its clientele for one dollar. Abilon agreed. Pagkalinwan's first order of business as CEO was to change the agency's name to Boutique Y3K, with an emphasis on shopping and the future.

To keep her Boutique Y3K afloat and productive, Pagkalinawan needed venture capital. As described in an article by Cybergrrl.com founder Aliza Pilar Sherman, Pagkalinawan immersed herself in business books and periodicals. She also consulted with other chief executive officers, all men, to learn how to close venture-capital deals. Among those she approached was an executive she had met while working on the MOUSE project to wire a New York City high school.

She first raised $150,000 and by January 2000, Boutique Y3K had $15 million in venture capital. By 2001, Boutique Y3K was fully established as "an e-commerce solutions provider and e-tailing consultant" for the fashion, entertainment, media, and luxury goods and service industry.

"She chose a winning strategy," entrepreneur Bob Lessin, CEO of Wit Soundview, stated to Sherman. "Rather than chasing enticing dot-coms, she chose to focus on Web initiatives on established companies. It is these companies that will largely be the survivors of the Internet (economy)."

In spite of this sound business strategy, Boutique Y3K unfortunately fell victim to the same financial woes as other Internet companies. In April 2001, after laying off six of her 20 employees, Pagkalinawan was faced with dismissing eight more, including her brother, Ray. The unexpected death of her sister led Pagkalinawan to further reevaluate her priorities. "In every industry, whether it's finance or automotive or fashion, there are some people who can claim a piece of the business from the establishment. I think what's unique about the infancy of Silicon Alley is that it was a huge drove of us that forced this thing to happen, and created something out of nothing," Pagkalinawan stated in the book *Digital Hustlers.*

Pagkalinawan, who was featured in numerous business and Asian American publications, was named New York City Woman Business Owner of the Year by the National Association of Women Business Owners (NAWBO) in 2000.

### Sources

Ghahremani, Yasmin. 25 February 2000. "Redefining Geek Chick." *Asiaweek.*

Kait, Casey and Stephen Weiss. *Digital Hustlers: Living Large and Falling Hard in Silicon Alley.* New York, New York: HarperTrade, 2001.

Raymond, Joan. 2 April 2001. "Ready, Aim, Fire." *Business Week.*

Rewick, Jennifer. 15 November 2000. "Cecilia Pagkalinawan." *Wall Street Journal.*

# Doan Lien Phung

Doan Lien Phung. Photo courtesy of Doan Lien Phung

**Born**: 1 January 1940, Battrang, Hanoi, Vietnam.

**Education**: Florida State University, Tallahassee, Florida, B.S. in physics (Phi Beta Kappa), 1961; Massachusetts Institute of Technology, Cambridge, Massachusetts, M.S. in physics and nuclear engineering, 1967; Massachusetts Institute of Technology, Cambridge, Massachusetts, Ph.D. in nuclear engineering, 1972.

**Positions Held**: Chief scientist, Oak Ridge Associated Universities' Institute for Energy Analysis, Oak Ridge, Tennessee, 1975–83; cofounder, president, and chief executive officer, PAI Corporation, Oak Ridge, Tennessee, 1983– .

**Awards, Honors**: Entrepreneur of the Year, Small Business Administration Nashville District, 1993; administrator's Award of Excellence, Small Business Administration, 1997; Alumnus of the Year, Florida State University, 1997, Community Award of the Year, Oak Ridge, Tennessee, 1999.

**Summary**: Doan Lien Phung and his wife, Thu-Le Doan, lead PAI Corporation, an environmental service company headquartered in Oak Ridge, Tennessee, which was identified as one of the 500 fastest-growing companies in the nation in the 1990s. The Phungs, active philanthropists, have contributed funds to educational institutions within Tennessee and their native homeland of Vietnam.

### Early Years

Phung's father, Thanh Van Phung, was a fervent Vietnamese nationalist who had joined with leader Ho Chi Minh to force the Japanese and then the French out of Vietnam in the 1940s. Phung, his mother, and five brothers and sisters stayed behind in the village of Battrang. During a famine that left 2 million dead in 1944 and 1945, the family survived due only to the resourcefulness of Phung's mother, who had managed to save a stash of rice.

Instability continued when the French returned to occupy Vietnam after World

War II. To escape from incidents of violence, the Phungs hid in the mountains in the villages of Long Kham and then Cao Mi. In both cases, the family was fed and housed by strangers.

In spite of their nomadic existence, Phung was able to pursue an education. He learned to write using green paper partially made of bamboo. Instead of having an endless supply of paper, Phung, armed with a rubber eraser, had to use the same paper over and over again.

## Higher Education

Phung earned a scholarship from the South Vietnamese government to attend Florida State University in 1959. He studied physics under Professor Hans Plendl, and was chosen for the honor society, Phi Beta Kappa. He was able to graduate in two years.

From Florida, Phung traveled north to enter the master's program in physics and nuclear engineering at Massachusetts Institute of Technology. After earning his dual degrees in 1964, Phung returned to Vietnam to complete the terms of his scholarship by working for the government. He worked for three years at a research reactor north of Saigon, where he used radioisotopes for research in hydrology and in hospitals. By this time, the conflict between North and South Vietnam had intensified, so Phung decided to return to the United States. There, he was able to secure a positions at an engineering firm in Boston and began saving money to bring the rest of the family—which now included 10 brothers and sisters—to the United States. "One by one, I was able to bring them to this country for school, until I didn't have a mission anymore," he said, quoted on a Web site connected with the Oak Ridge National Laboratory. During this time, he also gained his doctorate in nuclear engineering

from the Massachusetts Institute of Technology in 1972. Three years later, he was able to send for his parents and three youngest siblings, who were airlifted out of Saigon one week before it fell to the communists in 1975.

That same year, Phung moved south and accepted a position as chief scientist at Oak Ridge Associated Universities' Institute for Energy Analysis in Oak Ridge, Tennessee, where a national laboratory and two production plants had been established in 1943 to study nuclear technologies and to manufacture enriched uranium for weapons and power plants. The Oak Ridge National Laboratory subsequently enlarged its focus from nuclear weapons to the production of radioisotopes for research and to a spectrum of scientific endeavors including the greenhouse effect of energy production and radioactive waste disposal.

After Phung's youngest sister graduated from the University of Tennessee in 1983, Phung and his wife Thu-Le began to plan a new future for themselves. Together they created PAI Corporation in the basement of their Oak Ridge home. The company was designed to be an engineering consulting firm specializing in safety and environmental compliance. Phung became the company's president and chief executive officer, while his wife was chairman and treasurer. One of their first contracts was with the Oak Ridge National Laboratory for research in nuclear plant safety.

For five years, the two continued to work out of their basement with fewer than 10 employees. In 1988, PAI secured a $1.5 million contract to conduct a safety analysis of three Martin Marietta sites in Oak Ridge. Rapid growth continued, and by 1991, PAI had 60 employees and annual revenues of $5.1 million. That year and two subsequent years, *Inc.* magazine named PAI Corporation as one of the 500 fastest-growing companies in the United States. Helping to fuel the growth was the campaign to clean up nuclear and hazardous material contamination from government sites, including the Oak Ridge area.

"We are so much more competitive than bigger companies doing the same thing," said Phung in an article in the *Knoxville News-Sentinel* (22 May 1994).

In 1993, the tenth anniversary of the company, PAI had expanded to support 300 full-time employees, $150 million in annual revenue, and eight branch offices throughout the United States. In commemoration of their tenth year of business, PAI announced the establishment of a $15,000 endowment to local public schools. That same year, Phung traveled to the Vietnamese village where he had learned to write on bamboo paper to establish Doan Phung Awards to exceptional students.

Phung and his wife Thu-Le Doan have also donated money to various educational institutions, including Pellissippi State and Roane State community colleges, Florida State University, Massachusetts Institute of Technology, the University of Nevada, and Georgetown University. The Phungs' Fund for the Encouragement of Self-Reliance provides low-interest loans to families and connective surgery for disabled children in Vietnam.

## Sources

Bridgeman, Ron. 28 November 1993. "PAI Celebrates 10 Years as Oak Ridge Company Firm Donates $15,000 to Oak Ridge Schools for Endowment." *Knoxville News-Sentinel*: AC2.

"Doan Phung." Oak Ridge National Library. http://www.ornl.gov/diversity/phung.html.

*PAI Corporation*. http://www.paicorp.com. [accessed September 20, 2001]

"Ridge Consulting Company Grows 70% a Year Since '83." 22 May 1994. *Knoxville News-Sentinel* (Special Section: Greater Knoxville First & Future 50): 16.

# Q

## Safi U. Qureshey

**Born**: 1951, Karachi, Pakistan.

**Education**: University of Karachi, B.S. in physics, 1970; University of Texas at Austin, B.S. in electrical engineering, 1975.

**Positions Held**: Founder (and also chief executive officer and chairman) of AST Research Inc. with Albert Wong and Tom Yuen, 1980–97; managing partner of IrvineVentures, 1997– ; Regent's professor at the Graduate School of Management, University of California at Irvine, 1998.

**Awards, Honors**: Distinguished Alumnus, University of Texas, Arlington, 1993; International Entrepreneur of the Year, University of Illinois, Carbondale, 1994; UCI Medal, distinguished service with University of California at Irvine, 1995.

**Summary**: Safi Qureshey, a cofounder of the former computer giant AST Research, has pioneered the way for Pakistani and East Indian entrepreneurs to launch new enterprises in the United States. Since selling his company, he has been active as a venture capitalist—mostly in southern California's Orange County region.

## Early Years

Qureshey was born in Karachi, a thriving port city in southwestern Pakistan. During his youth in the 1950s, Pakistan, which was newly created out of British India in 1947, was experiencing great political turmoil and international conflict.

## Higher Education

Qureshey attended college at the University of Karachi at a young age and graduated at the age of 19 with a bachelor's degree in physics. In 1971, the same year in which civil war broke out between East and West Pakistan, he traveled to the United States to pursue his advanced education. He studied at the University of Texas at Austin and worked at a 7-Eleven, sometimes from 11 a.m. to 7 p.m. In 1975, he graduated with a degree in electrical engineering.

## Career Highlights

After gaining his degree, Qureshey worked at various electronics and computer manufacturers. It was through a job as a test engineer at Computer Automation in Orange County, California, that he met Thomas Yuen, an immigrant from Hong

Kong. Together, with another friend, Albert Wong, also from Hong Kong, they discussed leaving their jobs to start their own computer hardware company in southern California.

With $2,000 in capital and a garage as their headquarters, the three engineers began their corporation, which they named AST for the first letters of their first names, in 1980. Straws were drawn, and Qureshey became AST's president, although the three, in reality, shared leadership duties. AST was first devoted to the production of computer boards that would give IBM's personal computers more power and memory. Called the Six Pack Plus, the add-on circuit board had the ability to upgrade a computer with 64K memory to 256K. Within three years, AST Research, through products like the Six Pack, earned more than $100 million in annual revenues.

1984 was a landmark year for Qureshey, both professionally and personally. Qureshey became naturalized that year; in December, Irvine, California-based AST went public.

The company had to change focus when IBM began to address its upgradeability needs. As a result, AST began producing IBM-compatible PCs that quickly gained a reputation for being well made, state of the art, and innovative. By 1989, eight models were being offered to mostly corporate customers, resulting in a 44 percent rise in sales within the past three years. The company was the first big PC maker to offer different product lines to specific market segments—yet it was also known for its low-profile marketing tactics.

Difficulties lay ahead. One of the founders, Wong, resigned in 1988, around the time AST posted its first-ever loss—$8.9 million—in the 1989 fiscal year, and 6 percent of its workforce was cut back. A corporate restructuring followed, along with the creation of a five-member executive committee.

The 1990s were marked by great milestones, setbacks, and changes. To celebrate the production of its one millionth computer in 1991, AST made a special presentation to President George Bush. A year later, the company would lose another cofounder, Yuen, leaving Qureshey as the only remaining person of the original trio at the company.

Convinced that only big computer makers would survive, Qureshey embarked on a plan to acquire Tandy Computer in 1993 for $105 million. The acquisition expanded the company's manufacturing capacity, making AST the fourth largest microcomputer manufacturer in the United States. This acquisition, however, would have its cost. In fiscal year 1995, AST announced that it was projected to lose $39 million. In spite of Qureshey's efforts to stimulate business in China on a U.S. trade mission with Commerce Secretary Ron Brown, more layoffs and the closing of its Fountain Valley, California, plant followed. AST found needed help from South Korean manufacturer Samsung Electronic Company, which invested $378 million for a 40 percent interest in the company in 1995. In 1997, Samsung entered an agreement to acquire AST for $475 million. Soon-Taek Kim, would be the new chief executive officer.

Since Samsung's takeover of AST (the company no longer produces any equipment), Qureshey has devoted his time as a venture capitalist. He has spent more than $7 million in a dozen southern California startup companies, and even launched a $50-million business incubator, Irvine-Ventures. He was the founding president of the IndUS Entrepreneurs, or TiE, a networking organization that nurtures enterpreneurship among South Asians, specifically those from India, Pakistan, Bangladesh, Nepal, and Sri Lanka. A Republican, he formerly served on the President Bill Clinton's Export Council. He also was a founding member of the California Business-Higher Education Forum and was a Regent's Professor at the Graduate School of Management, University of California at Irvine.

"I didn't go to a prestigious university. I had no special training. I started so late, even my mother is surprised," Qureshey spoke of his success at a news conference in Sweden in 1994.

Since making a hajj to Mecca in 1987, Qureshey has been a devout Muslim and committed to the Islamic ritual of praying six times a day whenever possible. He and his wife Anita have actively supported University of California at Irvine, contributing to the UCI Farm School and providing the lead expansion gift of $1 million to the Bonney Center for the Neurobiology of Learning and Memory.

Qureshey is also devoted to his two sons and a daughter who was tragically left in a coma after a swimming accident in 1989. "It brought a new dimension to my life," he reported to a *Forbes* reporter in 1994. "You see the loss and wonder how are you going to deal with it. It never gets easy. You realize the extreme ends of the human experience. I hope I am better because of it."

## Sources

Jacobs, April. 5 May 1997. "Struggling AST Gets New Chief." *Computerworld*: 33.

Nulty, Peter. 24 April 1989. "Growing Fast on the 500's Fringe." *Fortune*: 69.

Rapaport, Richard. 5 December 1994. "Mission Imperative: AST Research CEO Safi Qureshey Stumps for Greater International Presence." *Forbes*: 76–77.

Reese, Jennifer. 13 December 1993. "AST Research: The Payoff from a Good Name." *Fortune: 163*.

# S

## Scott M. Sassa

**Full Name at Birth**: Scott Michael Sassa.

**Born**: 1959, Los Angeles, California.

**Education**: University of Southern California, Los Angeles, California.

**Positions Held**: Assistant, Rogers & Cowan Public Relations Agency, Los Angeles, California, 1981; director of sales promotion, Turner Broadcasting Systems, Atlanta, Georgia, 1982; vice president/general manager, Turner Broadcasting Systems' Cable Music Channel, Atlanta, Georgia, 1983; vice president, programming, Playboy Channel, Los Angeles, California, c. 1984; vice president of network management, Fox Broadcasting Company, Los Angeles, California, 1986; vice president of new business development, Ohlmeyer Communications Company, Los Angeles, California, c. 1987; executive vice president, Turner Network Television, Atlanta, Georgia, 1988; chairman and chief executive officer, Marvel Entertainment Group, New York City, New York, 1996; president, NBC Television Stations, New York City, New York, 1997; president, NBC Entertainment Division, Burbank, California, 1998; president, NBC West Coast Operations, Burbank, California, 1999– .

**Summary**: Scott Sassa, a talented and well-traveled television executive who helped launch the Fox, TNT, and Cartoon networks, has risen to one of the highest positions at NBC as its president of West Coast operations.

### Early Years

A third-generation Japanese American, Sassa was born in Los Angeles, California, and lived in the nearby middle-class suburb of Torrance from the age of five. His high school years were uneventful, other than he was once caught smoking marijuana, according to *Current Biography*.

### Higher Education

Sassa went on to study business and finance at the University of Southern California (USC), where he was a yell leader on the cheerleading squad. Leaning toward becoming a banker, Sassa interned at Smith Barney during his last semester at USC. The job bored him so much, he dropped out of school, even though he was only a few credits from graduating. He became inspired by an article he read about Hollywood executives who had achieved success at an early age. The article also noted that one of the best fields for rapid growth was the entertainment business.

### Career Highlights

After working less than a year at a top Hollywood public relations firm, Sassa used his USC connections to land a job at Turner Broadcasting Systems (TBS) in Atlanta, Georgia—first as an assistant and later as its director of sales promotion. At Turner, he was able to delve into many projects, creating the music-video show *Night Tracks* while assisting in Ted Turner's attempts to buy CBS and MGM.

Sassa was then asked to create a music video network to rival MTV. The Cable Music Channel went on the air in three months and was gone 45 days later when MTV bought it out. Following that failure, Sassa left TBS to become vice president of programming at the Playboy Channel in Los Angeles before being hired as a vice president by Fox Broadcasting, which was trying to launch a fourth television network. He developed Fox's initial business plan and ran its advertising, promotions, operations, and administration departments. Within two years, Sassa was fired. His boss, Barry Diller, said that Sassa was in over his head. Diller would later admit that letting Sassa go was one of his most "supreme mistakes."

The news was devastating to Sassa, but didn't keep him from moving forward. He took a job with Don Ohlmeyer, who at the time ran his own business called Ohlmeyer Communications, an independent television production company in Los Angeles. Sassa then returned to Turner Broadcasting to help build Turner's cable empire. The anchor station was Turner Network Television (TNT), launched in October 1988. At the time, cable television was a young business. Only about 50 million of the 93 million television homes nationwide were hooked up to cable. The trick was to continue making cable channels attractive in order to keep current subscribers and to lure new ones. But to nonsubscribers, cable was perceived as little more than stations running old and tired network reruns. To rise above the 50-million subscriber level, cable needed to offer something new.

TNT used Turner's library of MGM films as its base and then slowly began adding original movies and major sporting events. "But we couldn't do it on the cheap," Sassa said in an interview with the *Los Angeles Times* (1 July 1991). "Cable has always been guilty of spending a buck and a half on its shows. But the viewer doesn't care that we don't have the money to compete with network programming. So we had to spend the money and we had to do it big. The goal was to get our movie on the cover of *TV Guide*. Now, I'm not living in a fantasy world that someone will walk through the checkout line at the market and see Farrah Fawcett on the cover of *TV Guide* talking about (her cable movie) and say, 'Oh, my God, I have to subscribe.' But it serves as a trigger for them to rethink cable. They might go, 'Well, my friends are always talking about CNN and the kids are always bugging me about MTV.' And now we (at TNT) have the NBA and the NFL, and the cumulative effect makes cable sexier and more exciting."

Sassa is credited with launching seven networks over a seven-year period. From 1992 to 1996, he was responsible for all operations and programming for TBS, TNT, Cartoon Network, Turner Classic Movies, and Turner's international entertainment networks in Europe, Asia, and Latin America. As a major decision-maker, Sassa answered only to Turner, who described Sassa as "brilliant."

In 1996, when Turner agreed to merge TBS with Time Warner, Sassa boldly campaigned to be named Turner's second-in-command. But Turner chose someone else, and Sassa left Turner. The year before, he had made about $1.5 million in salary and bonuses. He was also one of eight TBS officers entitled to a share of the $19.5 million in stock available for payments once they left Time Warner. He joined comic book giant Marvel Entertainment Group as its CEO. But his stay lasted only several weeks after the company went bankrupt. (Marvel Entertainment Group was eventually purchased by Toy Biz, now called Marvel Enterprises.)

In September 1997, though he had no experience in operating a television station, General Electric, which owns NBC, hired Sassa as president of its television stations division. It made him responsible for overseeing the operation of the network's 11 owned and operated TV stations. The stations accounted for $500 million in annual revenue, and after Sassa took over, two more stations were added. Little more than a year later, Sassa was promoted to president of NBC Entertainment. The job left Sassa with the daunting task of rallying the network from falling ratings and earnings due in part to the end of popular sitcom *Seinfeld* and the loss of broadcasting rights for National Football League (NFL) games.

But Sassa oversaw the development and production of NBC's new prime-time series for the 1999–2000 season, including such popular shows as *The West Wing, Law and Order: Special Victims Unit,* and *Third Watch.* He took over as head of West Coast operations from Ohlmeyer in May 1999, overseeing all of NBC's entertainment-related business.

The high-profile position has thrust Sassa into the national spotlight. On many occa-

sions, he has had to address media and public concerns on issues of quality programming and ethnic diversity. He made headlines early in 1999 when he told reporters that NBC would have more family shows and less sexual content. "We have obviously gotten the word out to producers that sex for sex's sake is not going to be a good thing," he said during an annual Television Critics Association (TCA) meeting in Los Angeles in July 1999. "Because we deal with adult-themed programming, there will be sexual content (on NBC), but it's going to have to be germane to the story line and not gratuitous."

He also admitted that NBC could do a better job when it comes to diversity. "I don't know that I'm qualified to tell you how African Americans feel about how they're portrayed or what they see on television, and I don't think I'm capable of telling you how Latinos feel about how they're portrayed or what they see on television," Sassa said before the TCA group. "But I can tell you how I feel about seeing Asian Americans portrayed on television. And I've got to tell you, growing up, seeing David Carradine as a Chinese guy pissed you off."

As one of the bright and young television executives, Sassa has continued to fascinate many in the industry for his ability to align himself with legendary bosses and thrust his career upward. "If you're in the right place and do bad work, you get more attention than if you're in the wrong place and do good work," Sassa once said in a *Fortune* interview (1 February 1999). "The karma at the hot place is powerful."

—*By John Saito Jr.*

## Sources

Hiraga, Alissa. 7 July 2000. "The Man Behind Must See TV." *The Rafu Shimpo.*

Katz, Richard, and Freeman, Michael. 8 September 1997. "Sassa's First Task: Access." *Mediaweek:* 5.

Lieberman, David. 17 September 1996. "Executive to Resign from TBS." *USA Today*: 1.B.

"NBC Corporate Executives: Scott Sassa." NBC Web Site. www.nbc/nbc/header/Executive;_Bios/sassa_scott.shtml. [accessed November 15, 2001]

Pope, Kyle. 27 October 1998. "Sassa Takes Unusual Path to NBC Post." *The Wall Street Journal*: B1.

"Sassa, Scott." 2000. Bronx, New York: *Current Biography Yearbook 2000*: 490–93.

Schlosser, Joe. 2 August 1999. "Sassa Seeks Role Models." *Broadcasting & Cable*: 10.

Sellers, Patricia. 1 February 1999. "Can Scott Sassa Revive NBC? Can Anyone?" Fortune: 30–34.

Weinstein, Steve. 1 July 1991. "Missionary for Turner TV Scott Sassa Sees Cable as the Future of Television." *Los Angeles Times*: 1.

# Leslie Tang Schilling

**Born**: c. 1955, Hong Kong.

**Education**: University of California, Berkeley, Berkeley, California, B.A. in economics and political science, 1976; American Graduate School of International Management, Glendale, Arizona, M.B.A. in international management, 1979.

**Positions Held**: Trust portfolio manager, Wells Fargo Investment Advisors, San Francisco, California, 1976–68; Chartered Bank of London, San Francisco, California, 1979–80; founder, president, LTDD, Inc., San Francisco, California, 1980– ; founder, president, Golden Bay Investments, San Francisco, California, 1980– .

**Summary**: Leslie Tang Schilling, a member of a leading Hong Kong industrialist family, has been active in San Francisco as both a real estate developer and philanthropist.

## Early Years and Higher Education

Schilling, a scion of the influential and well-educated Tang family, was born in Hong Kong. Her grandfather, Ping Yuan Tang, was from Shanghai, China, and had received his bachelor's degree in business management from Massachusetts Institute of Technology (MIT) in Cambridge in 1923. He returned to Shanghai and built up a conglomerate in textiles, cement, and flour. Fleeing the Chinese communist government in 1949, Ping Yuan resettled in Hong Kong, where he established South Sea Textiles. The manufacturing company grew to dominate Hong Kong's textile industry for decades.

Schilling's father, Jack C. Tang, was also educated in the United States: he received his bachelor's degree in chemical engineering at MIT and his master's of business administration at Harvard. He assumed the chairmanship of South Sea Textile at Ping Yuan's death in 1971 and later became the chairman of Tristate Holdings Ltd. in Hong Kong.

Schilling, the second of three children, spent her formative years in Hong Kong. However, like her other family members, she went to the United States for her college education. She studied both economics and political science at the University of California, Berkeley. She later received her M.B.A. from the American Graduate School of International Management.

## Career Highlights

After gaining her bachelor's degree in 1976, Schilling secured a job at Wells Fargo Investment Advisors in San Francisco as trust portfolio manager. According to *Business Week*, she observed that many of her colleagues were selling off their clients' real estate holdings—rather than stocks and bonds—because returns were difficult to measure. In contrast, Schilling felt that high profits could be made from real estate. She then joined the San Francisco office of Chartered Bank of London and worked under Sid Wolkoff, a 40-year veteran of the real estate industry. After a year, she left Chartered Bank to launch her own real estate company, LTDD, Inc., in 1980 with seed money from her parents.

From its inception, LTDD was designed as both a property manager and a general partner for California limited partnerships that invest in office and retail buildings in the San Francisco area. In 1986, Schilling and her investing partners purchased an empty lot at 212 Stockton Street for $10.2 million. The lot, which had been owned by former President Ferdinand Marcos, was developed into a six-story office building amidst its Union Square neighborhood, home to various high-end department stores and boutiques. LTDD also purchased and renovated a building at 944 Market Street, where the company established its headquarters. By 1988, Schilling had purchased six San Francisco office buildings for $35 million and was managing 250,000 square feet of commercial space. Among its subsequent holdings were included an 80,000-square-foot office building at 149 New Montgomery Street in San Francisco, which was sold by LTDD for $11 million in 1998.

Schilling also founded Golden Bay Investments, Inc. to manage and invest a portfolio in bonds, currency hedges, Asian stocks, U.S. equities, venture capital, and small businesses. In the 1980s, she invested $500,000 for the rights to an intelligent software system for controlling manufacturing equipment.

Probably most notable about Schilling and the extended Tang family is their high level of giving and philanthropy. As of the mid-1990s, the Tang family donated approximately $10 million to MIT for the Tang Scholarship Fund and the construction of the Jack C. Tang Center of Management Education. Five million dollars was given to Schilling's alma mater, the Uni-

versity of California, Berkeley. Schilling also lends her support to the Asia Foundation's Give2Asia philanthropic project and Asia Pacific Fund. In the past, she was active in the Concerned Business Persons of the Tenderloin, a nonprofit organization committed to helping low-income elderly and families in the Tenderloin area of San Francisco.

Schilling, who was elected to the MIT Corporation board in 1998, also is a trustee of the University of California at San Francisco Foundation and the San Francisco Zoological Society. She was the first woman president of the Asian Business League of San Francisco. At that time, she stated to *Business Week* (31 October 1988): "We're after real empowerment of Asians who aren't afraid to say what they think."

She has also sat on boards of the Golden West Financial Corporation, KQED, Pacific Bank, and San Francisco Economic Corporation.

Schilling is married to Alexander Schilling, who is also involved in the management of the businesses.

### Sources

"14 New Members Are Elected to MIT Corporation." 10 June 1998. MIT press release.

Iwata, Edward. 14 July 1996. "Some Seasoned Taipans Unfazed by Change." *San Francisco Examiner*: B1+ .

Levine, Jonathan B. 31 October 1988. "Leslie Schilling: Who Says a Developer Can't Be a Do-Gooder." *Business Week*: 65.

Nicklin, Julie L. 15 December 1995. "Courting Foreign Donors." *Chronicle of Higher Education*: A31+ .

Shaw, Jan. 4 April 1988. "Leslie Tang Is Tired of Hearing Bellyaching about San Francisco." *San Francisco Business Times*: 12+ .

"Tang Family Gives $4.7 M to MIT." 27 January 1993. MIT press release.

# Charley Shin

**Born**: 1964, Seoul, South Korea.

**Education**: Ohio State University, Columbus, Ohio, B.A. in business administration.

**Positions Held**: Founder, president, chief executive officer, Charley's Steakery, Inc., Columbus, Ohio, 1986– ; founder, president, chief executive officer, Gosh Enterprises, Columbus, Ohio, 1991– .

**Awards, Honors**: Entrepreneur of the Year, Ernst & Young, 1999; Blue Chip Enterprise Initiative, State of Ohio, 1999.

**Summary**: Charley Shin was able to integrate the popular Philadelphia cheesesteak sandwich into a successful quick-serve franchise, Charley's Steakery, which has expanded well beyond its flagship location in Columbus, Ohio, into dozens of states and even foreign countries.

## Early Years and Education

Shin resided in South Korea until age 13. In 1977, he, his mother Young Pak, and his sister Chung Choe immigrated to the United States and settled in Ohio. Shin's mother opened a small Japanese restaurant to financially support the family. Shin helped at the restaurant; his first job was washing dishes. "I loved the energy of a busy restaurant," Shin wrote in *The Columbus Dispatch* (17 August 1998). "Most importantly, I learned that, no matter what I do, I have to give it my all and be proud. I'll tell you, those dishes sparkled."

At a young age, Shin, also a devout Christian, knew that he wanted to build a Fortune 500 company. "I was that weird kid reading *Fortune* magazine and *Forbes* in high school," he said to *The Columbus Dispatch* (31 July 1995). "I wanted to be a big man. I wanted to be a millionaire."

Shin majored in finance and real estate at Ohio State University in Columbus,

Ohio. "I was always carrying around a business plan for some idea of mine right along with the ones I was doing for class," he stated in *The Columbus Dispatch* article.

## Career Highlights

The right idea came when Shin was on a trip with his family one summer. They were on their way to see some relatives near Philadelphia, when they spied a long line stretching from a rundown eatery. Curious, Shin joined the line and had his first cheesesteak, a sandwich that originated in south Philadelphia in the late 1920s. The sandwich made a lasting impression because when Shin's mother sold her Japanese restaurant after suffering a back injury in 1984, Shin refined the cheesesteak concept.

Two years later, Shin, now a junior in college and 22 years old, identified a prime location—a corner storefront near campus—for his restaurant venture. With his mother's lifetime savings of $55,000, Shin opened Charley's specialty sandwich shop in the 450-square-foot location that could only hold 14 seats. "Our second week of opening, we had a line out the door, and that line never stopped," Shin said to *Business First–Columbus*. "I knew we had something wonderful people wanted." During its first year of operation, Charley's grossed more than $220,000 in sales.

Shin's emphasis was on fresh ingredients, including grilled steak, hand-cut gourmet fries with toppings, and fresh-squeezed lemonade. A local entrepreneur, Barry Zacks, who was also experimenting with a new quick-serve concept in a former pizzeria down the street from Charley's, which was eventually renamed Charley's Steakery, met with Shin and encouraged him to move into malls. Ironically, Zacks' venture failed, and before he officially closed his doors, he offered his space to

Shin. That restaurant became Shin's flagship, which still exists today.

For his next location, Shin worked with Bank One for his financing, using a loan from a friend as collateral. Profits from the restaurant paid for his loans and also provided cash for his third location. He established a partnership for his fourth and fifth units. In 1991, Shin faced a crossroads: should he continue expanding at a pace of two stores a year or begin franchising? He opted for the latter and established Gosh Enterprises, Inc., as the franchising company. Among those to become franchisers were Shin's two top managers, who joined to open a Charley's Steakery in a mall location passed up by the company. Soon after, trade magazines such as *Restaurant & Institutions*, *Success*, and *Entrepreneur* were naming Charley's Steakery as one of the fastest growing franchise chains. Shin expanded his menu to include other sandwich varieties, as well as salads.

By 1998, Charley's Steakery had 47 U.S. franchises, seven Canadian franchises, and 12 company-owned stores; moreover, sales reached $25 million. While most of the franchises were located in mall food courts, new opportunities were found within airports, athletic stadiums, military bases, convention centers, gasoline station convenience stores, and even a zoo. By 2001, the number of units had grown to 113 U.S. franchises in more than 25 states and five overseas franchisees in Japan, Puerto Rico, and Korea. Franchisers are required to have at least $150,000 in financing and are encouraged to participate in developmental workshops held throughout the year.

While Shin fulfilled his childhood dream to become "a millionaire," he also stays close to his religious beliefs. One of his policies is to close the company stores on Sundays so that employees have time with their families. He supplies The Faith Mission, a Columbus-area shelter, with fresh sandwiches; employees also donate funds to Hunger Task Force, a nonprofit group in Ohio.

After being chosen as Entrepreneur of the Year in 1999, Shin gave this advice for beginning entrepreneurs: "Always do the right thing, reach for excellence every single time whatever you do, and don't be afraid."

Shin, his wife Sungae, and family reside in the Columbus area.

### Sources

"Franchise Features: Charley's Steakery." Franchise Direct. www.franchise-direct.com. [accessed November 6, 2001]

"Franchise Zone." Entrepreneur.com. www.entrepreneur.com/Franchise_Zone [accessed October 1, 2001].

Shin, Charley. 17 August 1998. "Charley Shin." *The Columbus Dispatch*: Business Today, 2.

Walkup, Carolyn. 2 December 1996. "Midwestern Chains Dish Up Regional Favorites to Lure Growth-Market Guests." *Nation's Restaurant News*: 39–44.

Woodard, Kathy L. 2 July 1999. "Entrepreneur of the Year: Retail/Food Service Award Recipient Charley Shin." *Business First–Columbus*: A11.

# Joe Shoong

**Born:** 1879, China.

**Died:** 13 April 1961, San Francisco, California.

**Positions Held:** Clerk, dry goods store, Vallejo, California, c. 1900s; proprietor and owner, Sing Lee Company, Vallejo, California, 1903–05; founder, president, chairman, Joe Shoong & Co. (later changed to National Dollar Stores Ltd.), San Francisco, California, 1905–59.

**Summary:** Joe Shoong, the founder of the National Dollar Stores, was one of the earliest Chinese American millionaires. Building a chain of 55 departments stores throughout seven western states, he was active in both civic and philanthropic affairs. While Shoong made it possible for those of Chinese ancestry to work in managerial positions, he was also involved in a highly publicized labor struggle in San Francisco's Chinatown.

### Early Years

Shoong, the son of Joe Gon Lim and Wong Shee Shoong, spent his childhood years in his native China, in the Chungshan district in the southern part of the country. He eventually immigrated to the United States around the turn of the twentieth century.

### Career Highlights

Shoong eventually settled in Vallejo, California, a town just north of San Francisco. There, he worked as a clerk in a dry goods store before opening his own women's apparel shop, Sing Lee Company in 1903. Two years later, he moved the business to the Fillmore district of San Francisco. The partnership, called Joe Shoong & Company, operated the Chinese Toggery, also known as Chung Hing or Zhongxing. By 1907, the business' main store and office headquarters had been moved to Market Street in downtown San Francisco.

The Chinese Toggery and Joe Shoong Company sold household goods, as well as men's, women's, and children's apparel. Over the next 60 years, the company saw tremendous growth. First capitalized at $20,000, the Chinese Toggery opened its first Sacramento branch in 1916. A second branch followed in San Jose in 1918. In 1920, the business had eight branches and was incorporated in California with Shoong as president and chairman. During the next eight years, Shoong continued expansion efforts, not only in California but also in the Northwest, including cities like Seattle, Portland, and Tacoma. In 1928,

the store chain, which had one million dollars in capital, was renamed National Dollar Stores Ltd., with Shoong continuing as president and chairman of the corporation. Shoong and his family owned 51 percent of National Dollar Stores; the rest of the shares were held by other Chinese Americans. Shoong also organized and operated a subsidiary, National Shoe Company, and invested in real estate.

According to Thomas W. Chinn, author of *Bridging the Pacific: San Francisco Chinatown and Its People*, Shoong's "formula for success was simple: to provide the same quality merchandise and services at the same low prices that he would appreciate if shopping for himself."

He was also one of the first large employers to offer Chinese Americans high-level white-collar jobs. While each store was usually managed by a Chinese manager, the clerks, in contrast, were predominantly European American.

By 1937, National Dollar Stores had sales of $7 million and $170,000 in profits with 37 branches in California, Washington, Oregon, Utah, Nevada, Hawaii, and even Missouri. Shoong himself was making $141,000 a year in salary and $40,000 in stock dividends. *Time* magazine reported that he lived in a large stucco house in Oakland, owned five cars, and was a member of the Shriners and the Masons. He had funded a school for 350 children in the Chungshan District of China, eventually donating a total of $200,000, in addition to establishing a one-room Joe Shoong School in the Chinese community of Locke, located south of Sacramento, for the promotion of Chinese-language and cultural education. Shoong also provided $24,000 toward the construction costs of the Chinese Hospital in San Francisco and $70,000 to the University of California for scholarships.

In spite of his prominence and philanthropic activity, Shoong was not immune to criticism within the Chinatown community. To supply the chain with women's dresses, a factory had been created in Chinatown. Reportedly the cleanest, most modern, and best paying ($13.33 a week) within Chinatown, the National Dollar Store factory was nonetheless on its way to becoming a closed-union shop after a vote among factory workers endorsed the International Ladies' Garment Workers' Union (ILGWU) in January 1938. However, two weeks later, National Dollar Stores announced that the Chinatown factory was being sold to Golden Gate Manufacturing, a new company operated by former National Dollar Store employees. A 105-day strike by factory workers followed, the longest strike in the history of Chinatown at the time. Lawsuits were filed by both parties until a settlement was finally reached in June 1938. Golden Gate Company became a closed-union shop but only stayed in business for a year.

National Dollar Stores continued to expand for the next 20 years at a rate of one or two branches a year. While growing his business, Shoong served as vice president and director of the Columbus Savings and Loan Association in San Francisco. In 1941, he launched the Joe Shoong Foundation with an initial endowment of $1 million. The foundation, which was later administered by Shoong's son Milton, went on to support a variety of organizations, including the Chinese Community Center in Oakland, the Chinese Historical Society of America, and an endowed chair at the Walter A. Haas School of Business at the University of California, Berkeley.

After Shoong retired in 1959, his son Milton, educated at the University of California, Berkeley, became president and chairman of National Dollar Stores, Inc. When Shoong died in 1961, the National Dollar Stores had 55 stores and 700 employees with $12 million in sales. National

Dollar Stores continued operation until 1996, when 21 remaining stores were finally liquidated in San Francisco, Los Angeles, San Diego, and Hawaii.

### Sources

Chen, Yong. 2000. *Chinese San Francisco, 1850–1943*. Stanford, CA: Stanford University Press.

Chinn, Thomas W. 1989. *Bridging the Pacific: San Francisco Chinatown and Its People*. San Francisco, CA: Chinese Historical Society of America.

Krich, John. 9 November 1997. "A Frontier Chinatown." *The New York Times*: 12, 14.

*National Cyclopaedia of American Biography*. Volume 51. 1969. New York: James T. White & Co.

"National Dollar Stores Begins Liquidation Sale, Concluding a Family Retail Tradition That Began in 1903." 15 February 1996. *PR Newswire* [Financial News].

"Toggery Trouble." 28 March 1938. *Time*: 55–56.

Yung, Judy. 1995. *Unbound Feet: A Social History of Chinese Women in San Francisco*. Berkeley, CA: University of California Press.

# John J. Sie

John J. Sie. Photo courtesy of Starz Encore Group

**Born**: 1936, China.

**Education**: Manhattan College, New York City, New York, B.S. in electrical engineering, 1957; Polytechnic Institute of Brooklyn, Brooklyn, New York, M.A. in electrophysics.

**Positions Held**: Engineer, RCA's Defense Electronics Division, 1958; cofounder and president of Micro State Electronics Corp. (now a subsidiary of Raytheon Co.); head of interactive services division, General Instrument's Jerrold Electronics Corporation, 1972; senior vice president of sales and planning, Viacom International's Showtime, New York City, New York; senior vice president of strategic planning, Tele-Communications International Inc., Greenwood, Colorado, (later moved to Englewood, Colorado), 1984–91; founder, chairman and chief executive officer, Encore Media Group (later changed to Starz Encore Group), Englewood, Colorado, 1991– ; chairman and chief executive officer of International Channel Networks, Englewood, Colorado, 1995– ; founder and chairman of Encore International, Englewood, California, 1995– ; principal, JJS Communications, Inc.

**Awards, Honors**: Vanguard Award, National Cable and Telecommunications Association, 1982; Grand Tam Award, Cable Television Association for Marketing, 1986; Bill Daniels Denver Business Leader of the Year Award, *Denver Business Journal*, 2001; Lifetime Achievement Award, National Association of Minorities, 2001; Bridge Builder Asian American Leadership Award, 2001.

**Summary**: John J. Sie built a reputation as a media-distribution mogul who backed pay-television-movie channels. In a span of 10 years, Sie took his company, Starz Encore Group, from a startup to the nation's leading provider of premium movie chan-

nels for cable and satellite distribution. Working with his daughter, Michelle Sie Whitten, he has reestablished connections with his birthplace, mainland China, to become the first American cable executive to enter the Chinese market, the largest untapped viewing audience in the world.

### Early Years and Higher Education

At the age of one, Sie was taken from his hometown in Nanjing, China, by his family as they fled the encroachment of the Japanese military. They escaped to Shanghai and in 1949, they faced another watershed event—mainland China's Cultural Revolution. Sie, then 13, huddled in a cargo ship with the members of his family on a voyage to Taiwan. The family lived in Taiwan for a year before immigrating to the United States in 1950.

Sie studied electrical engineering at Manhattan College in New York and went on to gain his master's degree in electrophysics from Polytechnic Institute of Brooklyn.

### Career Highlights

Sie began his career in the defense industry as an aerospace electronics engineer. His first job was with RCA's Defense Electronics Division before he eventually cofounded Micro State Electronics Corporation, which was eventually acquired by the defense contractor, Raytheon Company. In 1972, Sie would make a defining move when he interviewed for a job as the head of the interactive services division of General Instrument's Jerrold Electronics Corporation. The interviewer was the corporation's President, John Malone, considered to be the architect of the cable television industry. Not only did Sie get the job, he also began a strong working friendship with Malone that would lead to other opportunities in the future.

After a stint with Jerrold, Sie went to work at Viacom International's Showtime cable channel, based in New York City. He later joined Malone at his company, Tele-Communications International, Inc., headquartered in Colorado. As senior vice president of strategic planning, Sie led the nation's largest cable company in securing deals with satellite companies and marketing a direct broadcast package of program services to cable operators. At this time, he also began to consider the implications of high-definition television (HDTV) fiber optics, telecommunication, and cable integration issues.

In 1991, Sie founded his own pay-service cable company, Encore Media Group, through support of Liberty Media Corporation, also owned by Malone. Liberty provided startup capital for a majority stake in Encore; Sie began with less than a third of the company. Encore launched its programming—hit movies from the 1960s, '70s, and '80s—in 6.3 million homes served by TCI or its affiliate, United Artists Entertainment. At the time, fewer than 40 percent of cable subscribers took pay services, presenting a challenge for Encore and its chairman and chief executive officer, Sie.

Within four years, Encore Media Corporation was making a profit. In 1994, Sie established a first-run movie channel, Starz!, with rights to 40 percent of Hollywood's studio output. The company committed $4 billion to its library and Hollywood studio output product over 10 years, an average of $400 million a year, with final payments tied to box office receipts, according to *Broadcasting and Cable* (24 November 1997). Sie saw the video-rental chains, not the other movie channels, as competition. Eventually Starz Encore backed a pay-TV idea called "subscription video on demand" (SVOD),

which allowed a subscriber to pick from a monthly movie menu for a flat fee. The home viewer could access a DVD-like capability and watch movies selected with the ability to rewind, pause, or fast forward.

Sie's interest went beyond the domestic market. In 1995, he launched the International Channel to provide international foreign-language programming to cable subscribers in the United States, and Encore International to export programing to China. Sie's daughter, Michelle Sie Whitten, was instrumental in Sie's foray into the land of his birth. Michelle entered Peking University in 1987 to study the Chinese language. However, after he made a visit to see what she was doing, he quickly became impressed with China's free-market revolution, and eventually persuaded his daughter to work for him after she completed a master's degree in East Asian Studies and a graduate certificate in business administration from Harvard University.

As a result, Encore International became the first American cable television programmer to officially enter the Chinese market, the largest untapped viewing audience in the world, at an estimated one billion individual viewer potential. Encore International worked closely with Chinese censors to introduce Western dramas in a block of nightly programming through China's state-run China Central Television (CCTV) and made the broadcast of state funeral services of China's late premier Deng Xiaoping available to C-SPAN for viewers in the United States.

In 1999, Encore Media Group changed its name to Starz Encore Group. By 2000, Starz Encore, a wholly owned subsidiary of Liberty Media Group, was earning $235 million on revenues of $733 million. With 107 million paid subscribers, the company now has 15 domestic channels; two more channels were introduced in 2002. On the other hand, Encore International, with daughter Michelle as president, has become the largest provider of western television to China.

Sie and his wife Anna have four other children in addition to Michelle.

—*By Joyce Nako*

### Sources

Bryer, Amy. 21 September 2001. "Cable CEO Offers Views about Life, Business." *Denver Business Journal*: 23A+ .

Cantwell, Rebecca. 20 December 1998. "Business Person of the Year: Tele-Visionary TCI's John Malone Shaping the Future of Communications." *Rocky Mountain News*: 1G.

Coleman, Price. 24 November 1997. "John Sie: All the Right Movies." *Broadcasting & Cable*: 28–31.

Dubroff, Henry. 28 August 1998. "A Visionary Tries to Topple HDTV's Tower." *Denver Business Journal*.

Harris, Kathryn. 24 June 1991. "It's Scary." *Forbes*: 133.

Iritani, Evelyn. 14 October 2001. "Tuned In to China's TV Future." *Los Angeles Times*: C1, C4.

Lewis, Al. 9 April 1999. "China Dollar in Deals with the East, Encore Media's Sie Means Business." *Rocky Mountain News*: 1B.

"Profiles of Outstanding CEOs." 1 October 2001. *ColoradoBiz*: C49+ .

"Sie's International Outlook." 24 November 1997. *Broadcasting & Cable*: 31.

Starz Encore Web site www.starzencore.com [accessed December 30, 2001].

# Kay Sugahara

**Full Name at Birth**: Keiichi Sugahara.

**Born**: 18 March 1909, Seattle, Washington.

**Died**: 25 September 1988, New York.

**Education**: University of California, Los Angeles, B.A., 1932.

**Positions Held**: Fruit stand worker, c. 1930; founder of Universal Foreign Service Company, 1932; Office of Strategic Services (OSS), c. 1940s; chairman, Fairfield-Maxwell Ltd., c. 1950–88; chairman, U.S.–Asia Institute, 1982–87.

**Summary**: Kay Sugahara, referred to as the "Nisei [second-generation Japanese American] Onassis," was an international shipping magnate who gained fame when he proposed that Japan offer a $10-billion aid package to the United States to improve relations between the two countries in the 1980s.

### Early Years and Education

Born in Seattle, Sugahara and his family moved to Los Angeles when he was just an infant. His childhood was traumatic: his mother died when he was six; seven years later, his father passed away. "When my father died, I wept alone because my sisters were put in an orphanage for girls and my brother was given for adoption," he told writer Kango Kunitsugu in a 1983 interview.

Sugahara, now an orphan, had to fend for himself while only a teenager. He lived in a Methodist church dormitory. When he wasn't attending junior high school, he worked at a fruit stand for two dollars a week. Helping to sustain him emotionally was a university student from Japan, who told Sugahara to read classic Russian writers such as Leo Tolstoy and Fyodor Dostoevsky.

Looking forward to his junior high school graduation, Sugahara purchased a new suit. On the day of the ceremony, the dormitory burned down, destroying all of Sugahara's possessions, including his graduation outfit. Sugahara had to borrow a friend's suit that did not fit well, but participated in the graduation nonetheless. He continued to excel in high school, even winning an oratorical contest, and went on to the University of California, Los Angeles.

## Career Highlights

After graduating from college in 1932, Sugahara became the first Nisei customs broker in the mainland United States. He worked with two men to launch the University Foreign Service Company—customs brokers and foreign-freight forwarders. While the rest of the nation was recovering from the Great Depression, Sugahara was finding great success in the international trade arena, and represented most of the Japanese importers in southern California. By the age of 29, he had become a millionaire.

He married Yone Kuwahara and had three sons, Kaytaro, Bryan, and Byron. Also in the late 1930s, he became involved in Japanese American community groups and events such as the Nisei Week Japanese Festival in Little Tokyo. His success was suddenly cut short with the United States' entry into World War II and the loss of his ships in the Pacific. He and his family were forcibly removed to an internment camp in Colorado. Several months later, he was recruited by the Office of Strategic Services (OSS), the forerunner of the Central Intelligence Agency, to do propaganda work. He served in India during the war while his family remained in the desert camp in Colorado.

Sugahara's years with the OSS spurred on his involvement with U.S.–Japan relations. Before the end of the Pacific war, Sugahara worked with officials of the State Department concerning the U.S. Occupation's policy. He and his colleagues recommended that Japan's emperor system should still remain at least symbolically, a stand eventually adopted by President Harry Truman.

After the war, Sugahara rebuilt his shipping empire, which was now based in New York. He eventually became the chairman of a conglomerate, which he named Fairfield-Maxwell Ltd. (Fairfield, the English translation of his surname, was combined with Maxwell, the name of a U.S. intelligence officer who trusted Sugahara with sensitive information on the Japanese Army.) Through a network of 40 U.S. subsidiaries, Fairfield-Maxwell owned or managed oil tankers and refrigerated vessels while engaged in oil exploration in Texas. Sugahara at one time had offices in London, Tokyo, Australia, and Bermuda.

In 1982, Sugahara became chairman of the U.S.–Asia Institute, a nonprofit organization founded in 1979. That same year in March, he proposed a program, "Partnership for Prosperity," in which low-interest loans would be offered by Japanese banks to fund ventures to stimulate growth in America. This plan, unveiled at the National Governors' Association meeting in Washington, D.C., was intended to stall the deterioration of U.S.–Japan relations in light of a $25 billion trade imbalance. Under this "partnership," the U.S.–Asia Institute would handle all loan applications and transfer the funds from Japan to the United States. Shortly after the announcement, the Institute was flooded with thousands of telephone calls and hundreds of proposals.

Sugahara remained the head of the Institute until 1988, a year before his death. He died of liver cancer at his home in Pelham Manor, New York, and is interred in Arlington National Cemetery.

## Sources

Buckley, Jerry. 1 March 1982. "A Japanese Marshall Plan," *Newsweek*: 58.

Kanazawa, Teru. August 1985. "Kay Sugahara—'Nisei Onassis.'" *Tozai Times*: 1, 10–11, 20.

"Kay Sugahara Is Dead: Ship Executive Was 79." 27 September 1988. *The New York Times*.

Kunitsugu, Kango. 1983. "Grand Marshal Kay Sugahara." *1983 Nisei Week Japanese Festival* (Los Angeles): 56–57, 103.

# T

## George Tanimura

**Born**: c. 1925, Hollister, California.

**Positions Held**: Independent farmer, Aromas, California (expanded into Salinas, California), 1948–82; cofounder and chairman of the board, Tanimura & Antle, Salinas, California, 1982– .

**Awards, Honors**: National Asian Pacific American Heritage Month Honor (Tanimura Family), U.S. Department of Agriculture, 2001.

**Summary**: George Tanimura and his siblings reestablished their lives after World War II with only 20 acres in the Salinas Valley, also referred to as "The Salad Bowl of the World." Forming a partnership, Tanimura & Antle, in 1982, Tanimura is the chairman of the largest independent grower and shipper of lettuce in the nation.

### Early Years

The son of Japanese immigrants, Tanimura was the eldest of 13 children. The family worked together on a small vegetable farm in Hollister, California, an agricultural community in the Salinas Valley during the Great Depression and before World War II. The bombing of Pearl Harbor occurred when Tanimura was 16 years old. The family members, like other persons of Japanese ancestry in the region, eventually were forcibly removed to an internment camp in Poston, Arizona. While in Poston, Tanimura grew lettuce in camp to supplement his family's food rations.

### Career Highlights

After World War II, Tanimura and his siblings returned to California, where, because of racial hostility opportunities were still limited for Japanese Americans. Tanimura worked as a farm laborer and sugar beet hauler for a few years. In 1948, he and his brothers purchased a 20-acre farm in Aromas, California. Additional agricultural acreage in nearby Salinas, where Tanimura and his wife Masaye resided, would come from a family friend, who also offered the use of farm equipment.

Tanimura and his brothers first grew green onions and lettuce; all iceberg lettuce was sold exclusively to a Salinas grower and shipper called Bud Antle. During World War II, the demand for iceberg lettuce had skyrocketed; fresh lettuce from

California had been shipped to military troops. The market for iceberg lettuce continued to be strong after the war, and lettuce specialists like Bud Antle thrived.

Bud Antle, like the Tanimura farm operation, was a family business involving successive generations. Lester Antle had cofounded the company with his son, Bud, in 1942. In 1949, Bud's son Bob worked in the fields as a youngster and befriended the Tanimura family. The Tanimuras expanded their operation to include celery, romaine, sweet anise, and endive crops, while the Antles diversified into celery, carrots, and cantaloupes. They continued an informal business relationship by splitting all costs and returns on any joint projects.

In 1982, the two agricultural farms formalized their relationship by forming a partnership, Tanimura & Antle. George Tanimura was named chairman of the board, while Rick Antle, representing the fourth generation of the Antle family, became president. "If you work hard and try hard, you've got just as much chance as anyone else. When you get a good producer with a good marketer, it's pretty hard to beat," stated Tanimura in the Tanimura & Antle Web site.

The partnership pioneered new trends of growing and selling vegetables for the next 20 years. In terms of agricultural practices, Tanimura & Antle, also known as T&A, was one of the first companies to invest heavily in drip irrigation, according to an article in *American Vegetable Grower* magazine (October 1999). They also converted much of their acreage to 80-inch beds to facilitate easier planting and harvesting. In 1999, T&A joined organic grower Natural Selection Foods as a one-third partner under the Earthbound Farms brand. Under the agreement, T&A transitioned 1,500 of its prime agricultural land to organic practices. As one alternative to the use of pesticides, the company manufactured the "Salad Vac," a device that vacuums pests off produce.

T&A also grows much more than lettuce; its crops include a wide variety of vegetables, melons, cotton, and even compost. One of the largest producers of compost at 50,000 tons per year, the company uses lettuce culls, in additional to other organic material, to create a rich additive to create good, productive soil.

Their farm properties—35,000 acres in production—now stretch from the Salinas Valley to Yuma, Arizona, and even into Mexico. In 1998, a 78,000-square-foot processing and distribution plant was built by the company in Montreal, Canada, to serve Eastern Canadian and American supermarket and food service customers. In June 2001, T&A opened a 98,000-square-foot salad plant in Jackson, Georgia, to produce 750,000 pounds of packed produce per week for Southeast retailers.

In terms of the product marketing, packaging has been key. T&A has found great success in prepackaged salads and greens sold under the labels of SaladTime and Cool Cuts (precut carrots, celery, and apples with a variety of dips). In 1997, the company teamed with ConAgra Brands, Inc. to introduce "Health Choice Salad Bar Select" in which consumers are able to mix and match prepared salads and toppings.

Farming in the twenty-first century also has its unique set of challenges. In addition to facing certain unpredictable factors such as weather conditions, Tanimura must also contend with increased competition from overseas operations. China, for example, has been taking away the Japanese market from U.S. growers like T&A. He is exploring the possibility of producing new crops such as asparagus, popular in Asia. "We've got to find a new business because of China," he said to the *Los Angeles Times* (8 August 2001).

In his mid-seventies, Tanimura continues to work, and visits his various ranches throughout the United States and Mexico on a regular basis. His two sons, Gary and Keith, are also part of the T&A operation.

### Sources

Brazil, Eric. 22 April 2001. "Organic Farming Sprouts Businesses." *San Francisco Chronicle*: A25.

Iritani, Evelyn. 8 August 2001. "Farmers' Fears Take Root." *Los Angeles Times*: A1, A6.

Melnick, Rick. October 1999. "Producing a Partnership." *American Vegetable Grower*: 26+.

Tanimura & Antle Web site. http://www. taproduce.com [accessed August 8, 2001].

## Cora M. Tellez

Cora M. Tellez. Photo courtesy of Ron Sorensen

**Full Name at Birth**: Corazon Reyes Manese.

**Born**: 29 June 1949.

**Education**: Mills College, Oakland, California, B.A., 1972; California State University, Hayward, California, M.A. in public administration, 1979.

**Positions Held**: Program planner, City of Oakland, Office of Economic Development and Employment, 1972–77; assistant executive director, City of Oakland, Office of Economic Development and Employment, 1978; manager, membership accounting and claims, Kaiser Foundation Health Plan, Inc., San Francisco, California, 1978; director, health plan and hospitals/outside services, Kaiser Foundation Health Plan, Northern California Region, San Francisco, California, c. 1980s; associate regional manager Kaiser Foundation Health Plan, Hawaii Region, Honolulu, Hawaii, c. 1990; vice president and regional manger, Kaiser Foundation Health Plan, Hawaii Region, Honolulu, Hawaii, c. 1994; senior vice president and regional chief executive officer, Blue Shield of California, 1994–97; president and chair, Prudential Health Care Plan of California, Inc., San Francisco, California, 1997–98; president and CEO, Health Net of California, Woodland Hills, California, 1998–2001; head, Western Division of Foundation Health Systems Inc. (later renamed Health Net, Inc.), Woodland Hills, California, 2000–01; president, Health Plans Division of Health Net, Inc., 2001– .

**Awards, Honors**: Corporate Leadership Award, *Filipinas* Magazine, 1999; Deborah Award, Anti-Defamation League, 2000; Leadership Award, Leadership Education for Asian Pacific Americans (LEAP), 2000; Woman of the Year, Women Health Care Executives, 2001.

**Summary**: With her wide range of experience in managed health care, Cora M. Tellez has led turnarounds in struggling health-maintenance organizations (HMOs) in California. Under her leadership, Health Net of California, a subsidiary of Health Net, Inc. (formerly known as Foundation Health Systems, Inc.), has become one of the state's largest HMOs with 2.5-million members.

## Higher Education

Tellez attended Mills College, an all-women's school in Oakland, where she excelled, entering the Phi Beta Kappa society in 1970. After graduating in 1972, she stayed in the Oakland area and worked for the city for six years while gaining her master's degree in public administration from California State University, Hayward.

## Career Highlights

After six years working for the city of Oakland, Tellez entered the managed health care industry, where she would eventually make her mark as a strong administrator and influential leader. At Kaiser Permanente, she oversaw plans to monitor and contain costs incurred outside of Kaiser services in northern California, estimated at $232 million in 1989. With her next promotion as chief operations officer for Kaiser's Hawaii region, Tellez commuted from Honolulu to San Francisco so that her family would not be uprooted from the mainland.

Hawaii, described as the "healthiest state" in the nation in 1992, was viewed as a model for national health reform. At that time, approximately 93 to 98 percent of its residents had some form of health insurance; long-term health care, however, was sorely lacking to serve the needs of the Islands' growing elderly population. Moreover, small businesses felt overburdened by laws requiring them to provide health insurance for employees. In fact, Small Business Administration head Patsy Saiki, a former Hawaii congresswoman, argued against the viability of the federal government's adoption of the Hawaii-style health care plan.

Tellez eventually became regional manager of the Hawaii Region, which encompassed 13 clinics located on the islands of Oahu, Maui, and Kona and a 200-bed hospital in Moanalua. She turned around the financial and operational performance of the plan (net income tripled in her first year). The operation involved 3,400 employees with annual revenues of $300 million. While on the Islands, Tellez also participated in civic affairs: she served as a director of the Bank of Hawaii, vice chair of the Hawaii Roundtable, and a director of University of Hawaii Foundation and served on the boards of several nonprofit community organizations.

In 1994, Tellez returned to California as a senior vice president of Blue Shield of California. Head of the Large Group & National Accounts Business Unit, Tellez was in charge of product development, financial affairs, marketing, and claims. Revenues for the previous year hit $912.6 million; operations included four sales offices and eight service centers.

In time, Tellez was elevated to chief executive officer of Blue Shield's Bay Area Region. She was now responsible for all sales, marketing, provider relations, underwriting, medical management, and finance for this 285,000-member region.

Tellez's high profile in the health care field led to more career moves and more challenges. When Prudential Insurance Company of America's California health care plan suffered its fourth consecutive year of losses, it turned to Tellez for help. In 1997, she was named president and chair of Prudential Health Care Plan of California, Inc. in San Francisco.

Within a year and a half, the Prudential subsidiary was operating profitably, generating $1 billion in revenues in California, Colorado, Utah, and Arizona. That performance led to an announcement by publicly traded Foundation Health Systems, Inc. at the end of 1998: Tellez would be serving at the helm of its troubled California HMO based in Woodland Hills, California. As the new president and chief executive officer of Health Net of California, the state's fourth-largest health care provider with 2.2 million members, Tellez was expected to lead a financial rebound.

"She's impressive and focused and has a track record of leading organizations in a very successful fashion," Jay Gellert, CEO of Foundation Health Systems, stated in *Modern Healthcare* (16 November 1998). Health Net, which had absorbed a Sacramento HMO in 1997, had apparently contributed to the parent company's dismal performance. Foundation Health Systems had posted a net loss of $88.6 million, compared with a net income of $60 million a year earlier.

Placing her own executive team in the Woodland Hills headquarters, Tellez faced a number of challenges during the next three years. Because Health Net had been previously underpricing its medical services, premiums for business groups were raised seven percent in 1999. This rate increase was met with predictable disenrollments—some 50,000 members left Health Net for other plans. Pricing discipline along with tight focus on overhead cost enabled Health Net of California to increase its operating margin by more than 80 percent in 1999.

At this time, California's public employees pension fund, citing fiscal issues, also pushed its one million members to select another health care provider other than Health Net or Kaiser Permanente. However, this effort was not effective, as both plans ranked high in consumer satisfaction surveys.

To maintain its enrollment levels, Health Net implemented innovative plans, such as a special agreement to provide medical services for non-California employees of California-based employers. In

July 2000, it was the first health plan approved to provide coverage for acupuncture and herbal supplements in both northern and southern California through HMO benefits.

The changes in the health care system continued to place pressure on Health Net and other HMOs. With the failure and closure of physician groups like Family Health Care of Ventura County, Health Net had to ensure that their members would continue to receive quality care. In 2000, Health Net's parent company, which had been renamed Health Net, Inc., consolidated its commercial operations into two divisions and expanded Tellez's duties to oversee the Western division, comprising Health Net, QualMed of Oregon, Intergroup of Arizona, and FHS Life & Health. A new Health Net of California president, Hugh A. Jones, was subsequently named, leaving Tellez to focus her attention on responsibilities as chief executive officer and head of the Western Division.

In 2001, Tellez was named president of Health Net, Inc.'s new national Health Plans Division, overseeing the company's health plans in Arizona, California, Connecticut, New Jersey, New York, Oregon and Pennsylvania, the medical management function, and life insurance and pharmacy benefit management subsidiaries. In adition, Tellez is responsible for Health Net, Inc.'s national marketing and product development efforts. That same year, Health Net, Inc. sold its Florida Health Plan business—heralded as a good move because of its low market share in the Florida insurance market. Commercial enrollment in California, on the other hand, continued to grow. Health Net, Inc. also prepared to move into a new two-building complex within Woodland Hills.

Tellez, who has been a guest lecturer at several universities in California, is viewed as a leader in her field. In 2001, Health

Care Executives of Northern California awarded her with its Woman of the Year Award. She also serves on the boards of the Institute for the Future, S.H. Cowell Foundation, Mills College, California Business Roundtable, Philippine International Aid, Golden State Bancorp, and Catellus Development Corporation.

## Sources

"Cora Tellez Is Named President and CEO of Health Net HMO." 16 November 1998. *Wall Street Journal*: B5.

"The Doctor Is In (Again): A Roundtable Discussion on Who's Really Making the Managed Care Decisions." *Sacramento Bee*. 8 August 1999.

Health Net News. http://wwwz.healthnet.com/general/news/releases [accessed August 21, 2001].

Health Net of California, Office of Public Affairs, 2002.

Rauber, Chris. 16 November 1998. "Tellez Named New Health Net CEO." *Modern Healthcare*: 14.

## Masayuki Tokioka

Masayuki Tokioka. Photo courtesy of Island Insurance Companies

**Born**: 22 May 1897, Okayama, Japan.

**Died**: 2 August 1998, Honolulu, Hawaii.

**Education**: University of Hawaii, Honolulu, Hawaii, B.A., c. 1920s; Harvard College, Cambridge, Massachusetts, M.B.A., 1925.

**Positions Held**: Cofounder and chairman, Island Insurance Company, Honolulu, Hawaii, 1939–97; founder, National Mortgage and Finance Co./International Savings & Loan Association (now City Bank), Honolulu, Hawaii, c. 1940s.

**Summary**: Masayuki Tokioka, the first person of Japanese ancestry to gain his M.B.A. from Harvard, founded a number of businesses—including an insurance company, mortgage enterprise, and savings and loan—which has aided ethnic minorities and newcomers to Hawaii to establish their homes and careers.

### Early Years

At the age of 12, Tokioka journeyed to Hawaii with his mother in 1909 on the *Chiyu Maru* from the southern farming prefecture of Okayama, Japan. Already in Hawaii were Tokioka's father and brother, Bunji. A number of Japanese immigrants had settled on the islands by that time; 70 percent of those working on sugar plantations were of Japanese ancestry.

### Higher Education

After graduating from McKinley High School in Honolulu, Tokioka gained his bachelor's degree from the University of Hawaii. He then went on to Harvard Business School—he became the first person of Japanese ancestry to receive his M.B.A. from the institution. He returned to Hawaii to work at International Trust before launching his own enterprises.

### Career Highlights

One of Tokioka's early businesses was Newfair Diary in the Kapahulu district of Honolulu. In 1939, he cofounded Island

Insurance and later National Mortgage and Finance Company Ltd. and International Savings and Loan. His partners were members of the powerful plantation oligarchy and financial leaders in the Japanese American community. Many immigrants and aspiring entrepreneurs were given loans or financial aid from Tokioka's enterprises, when no other company would, according to George Engebretson's biography of Tokioka, *A Century of Trust.*

"He was generous in the criteria he used to make loans," stated former Islander Insurance president Wayne Arakaki, who worked with Tokioka from 1974 until the 1990s (*Honolulu Star-Bulletin*, 13 August 1998). "He used to make loans primarily based on character and ideas."

Joe Pacific was one such individual who benefited from Tokioka's generosity. Moving to the Islands after losing his shoe repair business in New York City during the Great Depression, Pacific worked for a while as a welder. He then attempted to restart a shoe repair business in Hawaii, but was turned down by every financial lender—until he approached Tokioka's National Mortagage and Finance. When asked about collateral, Pacific merely raised his hands and stated, "only these." He was given a business loan; Pacific enterprises expanded to include eight locations.

Tokioka loaned millions of dollars to thousands of young entrepreneurs, according to the *Honolulu Star-Bulletin*. He revived the Japanese Chamber of Commerce after World War II, and was key in the building of Makiki Christian Church. He also contributed to the establishment of the Japanese Cultural and Trade Center in San Francisco and the Japanese Cultural Center in Honolulu. He was also involved with the Kuakini Medical Center, Honolulu Lions Club, State Employees Retirement System, and Oahu Development Conference.

Over time, Tokioka's thrift, International Savings and Loan, established a strong presence among Filipino Americans on Oahu, Hawaii's most populous island. Recognizing this important market, CB Bancshares, Inc., the owner of City Bank, acquired International Savings for $51.7 million in cash and stock in 1994. Three years later, the thrift and bank were merged together and currently operated under the name City Bank, with $1.7 billion in assets with 21 branches. Tokioka's son Lionel serves as chairman of the board of CB Bancshares.

Tokioka's other son Franklin is also involved in the financial world in Hawaii. He is the president of the venture-capital firm, Pacific Venture Capital. He is also the chief investment officer for Honolulu-based Island Insurance, which remains the only locally owned and underwritten insurance company in Hawaii. In 1998, the year of Tokioka's death, Island's assets were at $275 million. The company, which employs more than 200 people, is currently undergoing attempts to modernize.

Tokioka continued to go in to work until age 100. He died at the age of 101 in his home in the community of Kaimuki. He was survived by his wife Harue, two sons, and many grandchildren and great-grandchildren.

"In spite of his traditional Japanese style, that stern adherence to discipline, inside he had a real soft spot for people," stated Tsuneo Tanaka, an Island Insurance employee for 42 years who retired on company profit shares. "The discipline he gave us was really Japanese style, but his fairness was American style."

## Sources

Cournoyer, Michelle. 13 August 1998. "Masayuki Tokioka Dies at Age 101." *Honolulu-Star Bulletin*.

Engebretson, George. 1 December 1993. *A Century of Trust*. Honolulu, HI: Island Insurance Company, Ltd.

Gillingham, Paula. 14 August 1998. "Tokioka Opened Doors in Hawaii for Immigrants." *Pacific Business News*.

# David Tran

**Born**: circa 1949, Vietnam.

**Positions Held**: founder, Huy Fong Foods Inc., Rosemead, California (originally in Los Angeles), 1980– .

**Summary**: David Tran perfected a popular line of chili sauces in his new home of the United States after escaping from his native country of Vietnam in 1978. Named after the Taiwanese vessel that transported Tran safely to California, Huy Fong Foods, Inc., identifiable by its rooster logo, is headquartered in Rosemead, California, where the hot sauce is exclusively manufactured.

## Early Years

Tran's family immigrated to Vietnam fron Teochlu, China, and prospered as entrepreneurs. In addition to a market and a vacuum tube factory, the Tran family also farmed chiles. Tran, however, did not make much money on his chile crop, and began producing a red serrano hot sauce called *sriracha*, a traditional Southeast Asian sauce named after a town in Thailand.

## Career Highlights

Tran later served as a major in the South Vietnamese army during the Vietnam War. He, his wife, and two children fled the country in 1978, traveling to America after a short time in Hong Kong. After living in Boston for a few months, Tran moved to Los Angeles, seeking an Asian market for his hot sauce. Tran financed his venture through some savings and, with the help of relatives, launched Huy Fong Foods, Inc. in a $700-a-month factory space in Los Angeles' Chinatown. *Huy Fong* was the name of the Taiwanese freighter that carried the Trans out of Vietnam.

"I thought I might make a thousand dollars a month, and I wouldn't have to work for somebody else," Tran stated in an article in the *Los Angeles Times* (17 January 1997).

Tran's early capital investments included a used 50-gallon electric mixer and a van, which was used to transport the chile sauce to Asian supermarkets and Vietnamese restaurants throughout California. Huy Fong's first chili sauce was called Pepper Sate Sauce, identifiable by the company's rooster logo. (According to the Chinese astrological calendar, Tran was born in the Year of the Rooster.) The sauce, which Tran says originates from the Ming Dynasty in China, consisted of chili paste, garlic, spices, and soybean oil. Fresh chiles were purchased from the local Los Angeles produce market every day.

From the very beginning, Tran did not advertise his products, but included the company's phone number on each container. After the introduction of its *sriracha* sauce in 1983, Huy Fong was soon deluged with orders. What made the sauce distinctive was not only its spicy taste but also its packaging. Tran sold his *sriracha* sauce in 17-ounce and 28-ounce clear plastic squeeze bottles with bright green caps in stores for $1.50 to $3.

Soon not only Asian restaurants in California but hot dog stands in Ohio, taverns in Mississippi, and sushi bars in Hawaii were using the product. To accommodate the demand, Huy Fong moved into a 68,000-square-foot building in Rosemead, California, east of Los Angeles in 1986. A year later, Tran was selling $7 million of hot sauces.

Huy Fong offers other sauces, such as *sambal oelek* and chili garlic, but *sriracha* remains its bestseller.

## Sources

Hong, Peter Y. 17 January 1997. "Refugee's Concoction a Sizzling Success." *Los Angeles Times*: A1+.

Huy Fong Foods. http://www.huyfong.com. [accessed October 2, 2001].

# David Du Tran

**Name at Birth**: Du Tran.

**Born**: 1941, Van Co, South Vietnam.

**Positions Held**: Owner, bicycle factory, South Vietnam, c. 1970s; founder, Delta Food Company, Westminster, California, 1982; founder, Little Saigon Supermarket, Westminster, California, 1982– ; president, Vanco Trading, Inc., Westminster, California, 1984– .

**Awards, Honors**: Business Person of the Year Award, United States Congress, 1990.

**Summary**: David Du Tran has built a diversified group of businesses in southern California under his parent company, Vanco Trading, Inc., named after his home town in Vietnam. His $20 million empire had humble beginnings: Tran sold produce from his car shortly after fleeing to the United States in 1975.

## Early Years

Tran was born in Van Co, a village in South Vietnam, during World War II. He was raised in a thatch-roofed hut with thin bamboo walls. As a boy, he helped support the family by selling cigarettes from a stand made of cardboard.

## Career Highlights

Tran continued to nurture his entrepreneurial spirit when he reached adulthood. In his twenties, he sold water buffalo and Singer sewing machines; he even managed bars and stores during the time that Vietnam was undergoing radical political changes. "What was important to me," he wrote in his self-published autobiography, *Chapters of My Life*, "was how political events would affect my business."

He was able to start a bicycle factory, which expanded to 700 employees after a gasoline shortage spiked the demand for an alternative to automobiles. In 1976, however, a year after the communist government took over his town, Tran had to relinquish his business to the military. While supporting a wife and six children, he continued work at the factory for $1.50 a day.

Waiting to remove his family from Vietnam at any cost, Tran sent his two oldest sons, Phu and Hung, with relatives to escape in a fishing boat. Soldiers shot at their boat, causing it to sink. The boat was finally towed to shore and Tran's sons, only 10 and 8 years old, were imprisoned. Upon their release, Tran had them try to escape again. This time, the boys made it safely to Malaysia. Tran and the rest of his family—his wife and their remaining four children—prepared to leave as well. With only a few hundred dollars in his pocket, Tran finally arrived in San Diego, California, where the entire family was reunited in July 1979.

Tran first got a job as a television repairman at $6.25 an hour. When the shop closed, Tran vowed to never work for anyone else again. Instead he began selling produce from the back of his station wagon. Rising at 2 a.m. to buy fruit and vegetables from farmers, he traveled daily from Escondido to Los Angeles. He also began taking classes at the local college.

Like other budding Vietnamese American entrepreneurs, Tran recognized the economic possibilities in Westminster in Orange County, which would later be dubbed Little Saigon. The Trans eventually moved to the area, and in 1982, Tran officially launched a wholesale business, Delta Food Company Shortly thereafter, he leased a store on the main thoroughfare, Bolsa Avenue, with $45,000 borrowed from friends and family.

Little Saigon Supermarket was one of the first modern grocery stores of its kind in Westminster. Soon customers were lined up outside, waiting 40 minutes for an available parking spot. In 1984, Tran opened a second supermarket in nearby Garden Grove. Calling it Vanco Foods, after his home town in Vietnam, he also established Vanco Trading, Inc. as the parent company of all his enterprises.

Among Tran's business advisors was attorney James Albert Davidson, an African American professional who had established strong ties with Asian American business leaders in Orange County. Davidson encouraged his clients to diversify into various businesses. "He motivated us to think about using research instead of just going into a business based on hearsay, which is what most of us in the Asian community do," Tran's oldest son, Phu, now known as Robert, said to the *Los Angeles Times* (26 October 1992). Robert, like some of his siblings, have management positions with Vanco Trading.

Tran's ventures also include Thuy's Bakery and Thuy's Food to Go (Garden Grove), AA Buffet (Buena Park), and Noodle 2000 (Alhambra). In 1998, another Vanco Foods was opened in Fountain Valley, also in Orange County and within a three-mile radius of the other supermarkets.

In 2000, Vanco Trading had $20 million in revenues, an 11 percent increase from the previous year, and 1,000 employees. Tran also founded Tran Du Foundation to fund community causes. In recognition of his accomplishments, he was honored as Business Person of the Year by the United States Congress.

## Sources

Cziborr, Chriss. 19–25 March 2001. "Minority Firms Feel Tech's Downward Pull." *Orange County Business Journal*: 1+ .

Earnest, Leslie. 18 August 1999. "Lessons and Insight on Southland Businesses; Big Trouble in Little Saigon; Merchants Are Squeezed by Competition, Generation Gap." *Los Angeles Times*: C1+ .

El Nasser, Haya. 12 June 1991. "Some Find Prosperity, But Not All." *USA Today*: 3A.

Lee, Cristina. 26 October 1992. "East Meets West with Black Attorney's Help." *Los Angeles Times* (Orange County Edition): D4.

"Role Models" KSCI Web site. www.kscitv. com/rolemodels.asp [accessed November 29, 2001].

Tran, David Du. *Chapters of My Life: An Amazing Story of a Vietnamese Who Has Become a Millionaire from His Empty Hands!* (self-published).

# Gerald Tsai

Gerald Tsai. Photo courtesy of Gerald Tsai

**Full Name at Birth**: Gerald Tsai Jr.

**Born**: 10 March 1928, Shanghai, China.

**Education**: Boston University, B.A. in economics, 1949; Boston University, M.A. in economics, 1949.

**Positions Held**: Junior security analyst, Bache & Company, 1951–52; stock analyst, Fidelity Management and Research, 1952–58; manager, Fidelity Capital, 1958–60; vice president, Fidelity Investments, 1961–65; executive vice president, Fidelity Investments, 1965–66; Tsai Management and Research Corporation, 1966– ; founder and manager, Manhattan Fund, 1966–68; executive vice president, CNA Financial Corporation; chief executive officer, Primerica, 1986–88; chairman of the Executive Committee of the Board of Directors; Primerica Corporation; chairman, chief executive officer, and president, Delta Life Corporation, 1993–97; chairman and president, Tsai Management, 1998– .

**Summary**: Gerald Tsai defined the role of the independent, growth-oriented money manager in the 1960s—also referred to as the "go-go" years by financial writers of the time. His investment acumen is well-known by longtime Wall Street observers.

## Early Years and Higher Education

Tsai spent his youth and most of his teenage years in the bustling metropolis of Shanghai, China. When he was 17, he was sent by his father, a district manager for Ford Motor Company, to Wesleyan University in Middletown, Connecticut. "Shanghai was a big city," he said in an interview published in *Newsweek* in 1968, "and you could stand in the middle of Middletown, look past Sears and J.C. Penney's and that was it."

From Wesleyan, Tsai transferred to Boston University where he gained his bachelor's degree, and three months later, his master's in economics. He worked a short time at a textile company, and then returned to Boston for his master's in business administration.

## Career Highlights

Tsai first got hands-on experience in the securities field while a junior analyst at Bache & Company. After a year, he joined a then-small Boston mutual fund company, Fidelity Management and Research, as a junior stock analyst in 1952. At Fidelity, Tsai found himself in a corporate culture that encouraged independence and risk-taking. According to *Newsweek*, slow-growing New York Stock Exchange blue-chip stocks were abandoned by Fidelity for investments in technology and other high-yield areas.

Tsai thrived in this competitive environment, which cast money managers as financial celebrities. "I liked the market," he stated to *Newsweek* in 1968, "and I also felt that being a foreigner didn't have a competitive disadvantage. If you buy GM at $40 and it goes to $50, whether you are an Oriental, a Korean, or a Buddhist doesn't make a difference."

Tsai, with his profitable investment decision-making ability, rose through the ranks of Fidelity and by the age of 28 was head of a new fund—Fidelity Capital. "He has a great sense of market timing," stated Edward Crosby Johnson II, Fidelity founder. "But he also can go through a mass of analytical material and get right to the point." During his tenure at Fidelity, the company's funds grew from $239 in 1955 to $1.5 billion a decade later.

Tsai left Fidelity in 1966 for New York, where he launched his own mutual fund— the Manhattan Fund—on February 15. That day alone investors, responding to Tsai's success at Fidelity, bought an unprecedented $247 million worth of shares. The Manhattan Fund then spurred the founding of many other growth funds by other money management companies. *Newsweek* (13 May 1968), in fact, acknowledged: "And no man wields greater influence in the world of funds than Gerald Tsai Jr."

With the escalating conflict in Vietnam and general financial instability, the stock market experienced great fluctuations during the late 1960s. In the middle of a huge downturn, Tsai sold his Manhattan Fund to the insurance conglomerate CNA Financial Corporation for $27 million in CNA stock in 1968. This marked the end of Tsai's direct involvement in mutual fund management, yet he continued making savvy business investments. He bought a seat on the New York Stock Exchange and began trading under the name G. Tsai & Company. He became executive vice president of CNA, only to sell his shares in 1973. Within five years, Tsai had acquired a small insurance company, Associated Madison, for $2.2 million and positioned the firm as an innovator in selling life insurance through the mail. In 1981 American Can Company, an established manufacturing company, purchased Associated Madison for $162 million. With Tsai as the new CEO, the company—with a new emphasis on financial services—was renamed Primerica.

In 1988, Primerica—after a series of risky acquisitions—was sold to Commercial Credit Corporation for $1.5 billion. Tsai remained as chairman of the Executive Committee of Primerica's Board of Directors until 1991. Within two years, he had raised enough capital and attracted enough investors to purchase a 48 percent share of the Memphis-based annuity company, Delta Life Corporation, for $26.8 million. He served as Delta Life's chairman, CEO, and president until the company was sold to AmerUs Life Holdings in Des Moines, Iowa, for $163 million.

Now chairman and president of his own company, Tsai Management, Tsai is a director of Saks Incorporated, Rite Aid Corporation, Sequa Corporation, Triarc Companies, Inc., Zenith National Insurance Corporation, Satmark Media Group, IP Network.com, and United Rentals. He also serves as a trustee of Boston University, Mount Sinai-NYU Medical Center, and NYU School of Medicine Foundation Board. His philanthropic gifts include $3 million to the Norton Museum of Art in Pasadena, California.

He and his wife Nancy have a home in Palm Beach, Florida.

### Sources

"AmerUs Life Holdings Announces Agreement to Acquire Delta Life Corporation." AmerUs Group. http://www.amerus.com/invrel/newsroom/97-08-14.html. [accessed February 22, 2001]

"Fresh Face in Money Management." 20 February 1965. *Business Week*: 54–56.

Nocera, Joesph. 1994. *A Piece of the Action: How the Middle Class Joined the Money Class*. New York: Simon & Schuster.

Pouschine, Tatiana, and Carolyn T. Geer. 15 April 1991. "Be Careful When You Buy from Gerry Tsai." *Forbes*: 84–87.

Stodghill, Ron II. 11 May 1992. "You Thought Gerry Tsai Was Retired? So Did He." *Business Week*: 102–103.

"Tsai and the 'Go-Go' Funds." 13 May 1968. *Newsweek*: 79–83.

# John Tu

**Born**: 1941, China.

**Education**: Technische Hochschule, Darmstadt, Germany, B.S. in electrical engineering, 1970.

**Positions Held**: Engineer, Motorola Company, Wiesbaden, Germany, 1970–72; gift store proprietor and real estate developer, Scottsdale, Arizona, 1972–74; president, Tu Development, Los Angeles, California, 1975–82; cofounder and president, Cam-

John Tu. Photo courtesy of Kingston Technology President, Mr. John Tu

intonn Corporation, Santa Ana, California, 1982–86; vice president, general manager of Digital Division, AST Research, Irvine, California, 1986–87; president, Newgen Systems Corporation, Fountain Valley, California, 1987– ; cofounder, chief executive officer, president, Kingston Technology, Fountain Valley, California, 1987– .

**Summary**: John Tu, who gained his engineering education in Germany after spending his early years in Taiwan, cofounded a memory chip company with partner David Sun in southern California. When 80 percent of Kingston Technology Company was sold in 1996 for $1.5 billion, Tu and Sun made labor history by giving generous bonuses to their employees—in some cases sums that equaled three times their salaries. The partners, known for their "whole-life approach" to doing business, eventually reacquired their company in 1999.

## Early Years and Higher Education

Tu was born in China during the turbulent years of World War II. His father, edu-cated at the University of Lyon in France, was the minister of cultural affairs for the Nationalist government, while his mother had been a student at the national acting school.

As the conflict between Mao Tse-tung's communist forces and the Nationalist Army intensified, Tu's family joined the exodus to Taiwan in 1949. In Taiwan, Tu was a rebellious student. He often skipped class, choosing instead to go to movies or play pool with friends. Finally confronted by his parents, Tu expressed his frustration with the Taiwanese educational system. Surprisingly, his parents were sympathetic, according to an article in *Transpacific* (March–April 1996). Tu desired to change his ways, but acceptance to a good Taiwanese college was now impossible. He traveled instead to Bremen, Germany, where his uncle operated a Chinese restaurant.

Because he had once been affiliated with the Catholic church, Tu sought a priest for help in obtaining his education. A priest who had spent three decades in China helped get Tu accepted into a German-language school. However, before Tu could be accepted into a German university, he was required to serve an apprenticeship for two years. As part of this apprenticeship, he was sent to a shipyard in the northern German town of Kiel, where he lived in a loft fueled only with rationed coal, without a bathroom or shower.

After two years of service, Tu enrolled and majored in electrical engineering at Technische Hochschule, in Darmstadt, Germany. He finally gained his degree in 1970.

## Career Highlights

After graduation, Tu worked as an engineer at Motorola Company in Wiesbaden, Germany. However, he soon realized that he did not want to stay in Europe. "Though I was fully assimilated into German culture,

I knew that the Germans would not completely accept me," he told *Transpacific*. "No matter how good you speak the language, no matter how close friends you are, they will always treat you like an outsider."

As a result, Tu resettled in Scottsdale, Arizona, where his sister and brother-in-law resided. There, he opened a gift store and later developed a real estate business. When his sister relocated to Los Angeles, Tu followed. Tu continued with his commercial development company until he met David Sun, an engineer originally from Taiwan, in 1981. At the time, Sun was working at Alpha Micro Systems, an Orange County-based high-tech company that manufactured add-on products for Digital Equipment Corporation (DEC).

Together they decided to launch their own company, Cadmintonn Corporation in Santa Ana, California, with a one-megabyte DEC-compatible memory board designed by Sun. Cadmintonn was officially started in 1982 with Tu as president and the only full-time employee. For nine months, the company continued without a sale—until DEC contacted them in 1983 and asked Tu to fly to Boston to give a presentation. Tu, described by associates as a pessimist, feared the worst. Thinking that DEC might sue them for patent infringement, he delayed a meeting. Finally, in April 1993, nine staff members of DEC descended on the tiny offices of Cadmintonn, now manned for the meeting day by friends and relatives.

As it turned out, DEC wanted to purchase Cadmintonn's 1 MB board design for a new product awaiting shipment. DEC offered Cadmintonn $250,000, and Tu and Son accepted. "A lot of people later said that I jumped too fast," Tu stated to *Transpacific*. "'You should have held out for $2 million.' But this is what I always say to

people: Never be greedy. Chances are there's some competitor that will [step in]."

The $250,000 in capital marked a new phase in Cadmintonn's corporate history. DEC customers who wanted to upgrade their computers bought Camintonn's memory products for less money and better service. By the end of 1984, the company was selling $800,000 of products a month; by 1986, annual sales had reached $10 million. Their success was being monitored by other high-tech companies: in 1986, Cadmintonn was sold to AST Research for $4 million in cash and $2 million in AST stock. Both Tu and Sun received corporate positions within the Irvine, California-based AST with Tu serving as vice president and general manager of the Digital Division.

A personal financial setback—caused by the stock market crash of October 1987 and a few bad investments—led the partners to consider striking out on their own again. Within a year, they left AST to launch Kingston Technology Corporation in Fountain Valley, California, to manufacture a memory module using an alternative chip that was more readily available than one that was in short supply. The response to their new computer upgrade product was instantaneous. By 1988, sales exceeded $12 million and rose to $142 million in 1991 with the introduction of such products as SX-Now!, a line that upgraded a 286 processor with a 386 processor. A sister company, NewGen Systems, also headquartered in Fountain Valley, was also established to produce high-resolution, high-speed laser printers. Soon Kingston became the world's largest independent manufacturer of memory products with manufacturing facilities in the United States, China, Taiwan, Ireland, and Malaysia. By 1996, the company was producing approximately 2,300 products and doing $1.2 billion in business.

Even more remarkable than Kingston's financial success is their "whole-life approach" to business. Their mission statement—"Courtesy, Compassion, Modesty, Honesty, and Respect"—has been exemplified in both their treatment of workers and customers. Most deals with vendors have been sealed with a handshake, rather than legal paperwork. Low pricing and constant new product introductions—only possible through a simple decision-making process—have captured and retained customers.

However, nothing would prepare either the 450 Kingston employees, the business world, or the general public for Tu and Sun's announcement after 80 percent of the company was sold in 1996 to Softbank Corporation of Japan for $1.5 billion. Employees learned that a $100-million trust fund had been established for them: they would receive $38 million to be disbursed based upon their salary, performance, and time with the company, while the other 60 percent would be reserved for future bonuses. Later, the Kingston cofounders initiated an innovative program to fund and support their employees' own entrepreneurial efforts.

The partners' generosity was met with worldwide publicity. Their unusual way of doing business was further noted when they traded the final $333 million payment owed to them by the financially troubled Softbank for a seven-year loan. "It's very simple; this is about David and me, what we are about. We wanted to create a win-win situation," Tu told the *Orange County Register* (2 December 1997). "Everybody told us we were crazy. Even our own accountant said that nobody in the world would do this deal." Eventually, in 1999, the two bought back Kingston from Softbank for $450 million, a third of the price originally paid to them.

The high-tech downturn did eventually touch Kingston in March 2001, when the company laid off 19 of 2,200 workers for the first time in its 14-year history.

Tu and his wife have a son and daughter.

## Sources

Arterian, Susan. 3 February 1992. "Staying One Step Ahead of the Pack: Ex-AST Managers Hit $140 Million in Sales in Just 4 Years." *Orange County Business Journal*: 1+ .

"Doing the Right Thing." 20 May 1995. *The Economist*: 64.

Huffstutter, P.J. 20 May 1999. "Kingston Plans a New Round of Big Bonuses." *Los Angeles Times* [Orange County Edition]: 1.

Kingston Technology Company, Inc. Web site. www.kingston.com. [accessed December 1, 2001]

Laabs, Jennifer J. February 1997. "Kingston Employees Get Huge Bonuses." *Workforce*: 11.

Lansner, Jonathan. 2 December 1997. "Kingston Technology Co-founders Pass Up a Guaranteed $333 Million Payoff." *Orange County Register*.

Miller, Greg. 16 August 1996. "Japan's Softbank to Buy 80% Stake in Kingston." *Los Angeles Times*.

Newcomb, Peter. 13 October 1997. "David Sun/John Tu." *Forbes*: 300.

Star, Marc. March–April 1996. "John Tu: User Friendly." *Transpacific*: 52+ .

Strickland, Daryl. 7 March 2001. "Kingston Technology Lays Off 19 Employees." *Los Angeles Times* [Orange County Edition]: C3.

# W

## An Wang

**Born**: 7 February 1920, Shanghai, China.

**Died**: 24 March 1990, Boston, Massachusetts.

**Education**: Chiao Tung University, Shanghai, China, B.S. in electrical engineering; Harvard University, Cambridge, Massachusetts, M.S. in applied physics, 1946, and Ph.D. in applied physics, 1948.

**Positions Held**: Research fellow, Harvard Computation Laboratory, 1948–50; founder and chairman, Wang Laboratories, 1951–90.

**Awards, Honors**: National Inventors Hall of Fame, 1988.

**Summary**: An Wang, who earned his doctorate in applied physics from Harvard University, built a billion-dollar calculator and mini-computer company from a scientific patent he filed in 1949. He was once rated as the fifth wealthiest man in the United States.

### Early Years

An Wang, whose name means "Peace King," was raised during the Cultural Revolution in China. Wang's father, an English-language schoolteacher, relocated the family to Kun Sun, a town 30 miles from Shanghai, in 1926. The eldest of five children, Wang was two years younger than his fellow classmates when he began school that same year. "It is a little bit like being thrown in the water when you don't know how to swim," wrote Wang of the experience in *Lessons: An Autobiography* (Wang 1986). "You either learn how to swim—and fast—or you sink. You might hate the unpleasantness of the experience, but you gain a little confidence in your ability to deal with difficult situations."

In school Wang excelled in mathematics. When he took an entrance exam to a prestigious junior high school, he received the highest score. In junior high school he became involved with the school newspaper, and became familiar with the challenges of typesetting—an issue that he would grapple with again in his future business endeavors. During this time tensions heightened between Japan and China; by 1931, Japanese military forces had seized Manchuria and were repeatedly bombing Shanghai.

## Higher Education

After graduating from Shanghai Provincial High School, Wang entered Chiao Tung University in Shanghai, his father's alma mater. There he studied electrical engineering with an emphasis on communications. He also edited a scientific digest, based on information from American magazines such as *Popular Mechanics* and *Popular Science*. Japan's encroachment into China unfortunately interrupted his studies, forcing his university to move into an international zone for safety. In August 1937, Japan invaded Shanghai, changing the course of Wang's future.

In the summer of 1941 Wang signed up for a project to design and build transmitters and radios for Chinese government troops for the Central Radio Corporation. He was sent into the mainland to a city called Kweilin, where he oversaw the invention of a hand-powered generator that operated a mobile radio transmitter.

He eventually entered a two-year training program in the United States for Chinese engineers. Boarding a DC 3 military plane on April 1945, Wang traveled a circuitous route through India and the Suez Canal and across the Atlantic Ocean before arriving in Newport News, Virginia, in June 1945. He opted to pursue graduate studies at Harvard University instead of serving an apprenticeship at a corporation; he completed his master's degree in applied physics in 1946 and went on to complete his doctorate in the same subject in 1948.

## Career Highlights

In the late 1940s, computer science was in its infancy; in fact, only one electronic computer was operating in the United States. It was during this era that Wang joined Harvard Computation Laboratory under Howard Aiken, a pioneer of computer development. Wang was responsible for discovering a way to record and read magnetically stored information without mechanical motion. With his experience in building radios in war-torn China, Wang learned to depend on simplicity. "Even when components are abundant and cheap," he writes in his autobiography, "I still believe that the simplest solution to any engineering problem is the best solution. The fewer the components, the fewer the opportunities for something to go wrong" (Wang 1986).

As a result, Wang devised a way for electricity to be used to read and rewrite information from doughnut-shaped "cores." This concept, called *magnetic core memory*, later became the basis of modern computer technology.

Wang decided to patent his invention and met with a young lawyer, Martin Kirkpatrick, in September 1949. On October 21, 1949, he officially filed his patent. That same year, he married Lorraine Chiu, a Shanghai-born student of English literature at Wellesley College in Massachusetts. After his fellowship at Harvard ended, Wang opened his own business in an office in the South End District of Boston with $600 in savings, no orders, no contracts, and no office furniture. He named his business Wang Laboratories with the intention that it would expand in the future. The Wang family was also growing: Son Frederick was born in 1950, followed by another son, Courtney, and then a daughter, Juliette.

In addition to manufacturing and selling memory cores, Wang also offered research and development services. In 1953, Wang entered a consulting agreement with IBM; six years later IBM purchased Wang's core memory patent for $500,000. The company was incorporated in 1955 with Wang as the president and treasurer. Lorraine Wang and his attorney Martin Kirkpatrick comprised the first board of directors. The balance sheet was a single handwritten piece of notebook paper.

Wang continued to pursue government contracts while also developing machine tool control units. One device was used for the first digitally programmed scoreboard at New York's Shea Stadium. A phototypesetter called the Linesec was developed for Compugraphic Corporation. In 1964, Wang Laboratories' sales for these typesetters exceeded $1 million. But more sales were yet to come.

With Wang's development of a user-friendly electronic desktop calculator, Model 300, sales rose from about $2.5 million in fiscal year 1965 to $3.8 million in 1966. In 1967, sales exploded to $6.9 million. The staff also increased from 35 employees in 1964 to 400 in 1967. To finance growth and retire short-term debt, Wang, known to his employees as "The Doctor," decided to take the company public in 1967. The stock sold for $38 a share, and the corporation received a market capitalization of $70 million. (The Wang family, however, continue to maintain a controlling share.)

"Since I had been warned that I might encounter discrimination because of my company's name, I was pleased by all this demand for the stock, which evidenced the respect the business community had come to feel for a company bearing a Chinese name," Wang writes (Wang 1986).

With semiconductors driving down the price of calculators, Wang Laboratories began to explore other lines of business, namely computers. It developed the first screen-based word processing system in 1971 and was able to compete against larger competitors like IBM and Digital Equipment by "keeping prices low, offering

a wide array of peripheral equipment, and providing custom-made programs for buyers," according to *Fortune* (3 February 1986). A larger facility, which eventually became the company's headquarters, was established in Lowell, Massachusetts.

As Wang himself amassed great personal wealth, he and his wife donated to many nonprofit organizations, including the Boston's Metropolitan Center.

In the 1980s, the rise of the personal computers threatened Wang Laboratories' future in word processing and data processing. In 1985, 1,600 workers were laid off, and salaries of top executives, were slashed. Wang returned from semi-retirement to the day-to-day operation of his company at age 65. His oldest son Frederick took over as the ailing company's president in 1986, but was replaced in 1989 after a $424.3 million loss was reported. That same year the senior Wang underwent surgery for cancer of the esophagus. He passed away on March 24, 1990 at the age of 70.

After more financial difficulties, Wang Laboratories emerged from Chapter 11 bankruptcy in 1993 with a renewed focus on desktop and network services. Renamed Wang Global, it was eventually acquired by Getronics, one of Europe's largest service providers in the field of information and communication technology.

## Sources

Beam, Adam. 18 April 1986. "An Wang." *Business Week*: 222.

Louis, Arthur M. 3 February 1986. "Doctor Wang's Toughest Case." *Fortune*: 106–110.

Madden, John. "Getronics Buys Wang Global for $2B." *ZDNet*. zdnet.com/eweek/stories/general/0, 11011, 1014576, 00.html. [accessed May 31, 2001]

Perry, Nancy J. 25 April 1988. "Lasting Fame, Honorable Invention." *Fortune*: 327.

Wang, An, and Eugene Linden. 1986. *Lessons: An Autobiography*. Reading, MA: Addison Wesley.

## Don J. Wang

Don J. Wang. Photo courtesy of Don J. Wang

**Born**: 1944, Tainan, Taiwan.

**Education**: National Chung Hsing University, Taipei, Taiwan; B.A. in agricultural chemistry, 1969; Utah State University, Logan, Utah, M.A. in nutrition and food science, 1972.

**Positions Held**: Real estate investor, Houston, Texas, 1976; founder, United Oriental Capital Corporation, 1981–87; founder, chairman of directors, president, and chief executive officer, MetroBank National Association, 1987– ; chairman, New Era Life Insurance Company, 1989– ; Houston, Texas; founder and chief executive officer, Metrocorp Banshares, 1998– .

**Awards, Honors**: Humanitarian Award, National Conference for Community Justice, 1999; Asian Chamber of Commerce Award, 1999.

**Summary**: Don Wang was instrumental in the revitalization of the city of Houston during the region's economic slump in the 1980s. First intending to help immigrant entrepreneurs, he launched a venture capital firm, and later invested in a bank and an insurance company, both of which have experienced tremendous growth in the state of Texas.

### Early Years and Education

Don Wang was raised in Taiwan after World War II, and gained his bachelor's degree in agricultural chemistry from National Chung Hsing University in Taipei. He later came to the United States and gained his master's degree in nutrition and food science from Utah State University. He planned to pursue his doctorate degree and teach food processing in Taiwan, but then changed his mind to go after another dream—business.

### Career Highlights

Wang, like other Asian immigrants, came to Houston after the end of the Vietnam War. "In the '70s, oil made Houston boom, but it also brought in immigrants," said Wang in an interview with economic observer Joel Kotkin (December 2000). "When the oil crisis came, everything dropped, but it actually was our chance to become a new city again."

It was during this time that many Asians acquired real estate in Houston and launched businesses related to food processing, distribution, and electronics assembly, according to Kotkin. Wang himself, after dabbling in jobs at a gas station, iron mill, and motels, bought a Houston motel property with a $50,000 down payment. Later, he began investing in apartment complexes.

Recognizing the need of fledgling immigrant businesses to attract venture capital to grow their businesses, Wang established United Oriental Capital Corporation with partner David Tai, in 1981. Funded by the U.S. Small Business Administration, United Oriental Capital Corporation was designed to provide startup capital to minority businesses. His company lent $500,000 to Vietnamese shrimpers in Galveston Bay for new boats and $300,000 to a food processing company that eventually grew into a $20 million-a-year business.

Wang then followed his own entrepreneurial instincts. With venture capital and investments from friends, he began MetroBank in 1987 with $3 million in assets. In the beginning, MetroBank served primarily Asian customers who valued the financial institution's sensitivity to their cultural values. However, MetroBank soon expanded its focus to include Latino communities seeking loans for their small- and medium-sized businesses. The bank also works in the international trade financing arena; through an Overseas Chinese Credit Guarantee Fund sponsored by the government of Taiwan, MetroBank is the tenth largest issuer of overseas Chinese loans in the world.

By 1997, assets had grown to $370 million; in 1995 alone, according to *Asia, Inc.* (March 1997), loans and deposits increased by more than 40 percent. The institution now has multiple full-service banking facilities in the greater Houston and greater Dallas metropolitan areas with assets of more than $520 million. A loan production office has also been established in New Orleans, Louisiana. In 1998, Metro-Corp Bancshares was incorporated to serve as a holding company for the bank. It went public the same year at $11 per share.

Wang has also diversified his business interests. In 1989, he was approached by a relative, Bill S. Chen, to invest in a new insurance company, New Era, which originally specialized in buying blocks of insurance policies from insolvent insurers. With Wang as the company's chairman, New Era was immediately successful and made a profit by its third quarter. It now offers a wide array of life and health insurance products to customers throughout the United States.

Wang has also been active in civic affairs. He served as president of the Taiwanese Chamber of Commerce of North America in 1992 and currently sits on the Advisory Board. He has served as a board member of the Greater Houston Partnership since 1994. His other philanthropic affiliations include the Hope Shelter/Abused Children Program and the Chinese Community Center. He is the chairman of the Chinese Senior Estates/Senior Housing Project and cochairman of the Asian and Pacific Islander Division of the United Way.

In recognition of his contributions, Wang received a Humanitarian Award from the National Conference for Community Justice and an Asian Chamber of Commerce Award in 1999.

Wang and his wife Ming have a daughter and a son. His sister Helen F. Chen is one of the directors of MetroCorp Bancshares.

### Sources

Bradshaw, Tangela M. July 1997. "Don Wang: Serving the 'Underserved.'" *Texas Business.*

Kotkin, Joel. December 2000. "Movers and Shakers." *Reason Online.* ⟨http://www.reason. com/0012/fe.jk.movers.html⟩.

"Meet Houston's 25 Power People." April 2000. *Inside Houston*: 26.

Résumé provided by Don J. Wang, March 2002.

Shlachter, Barry. March 1997. "Lone Star Banker." *Asia, Inc.*

Yip, Pamela. March 21, 1993. "'Head Men' Have Clout in Communities." *Houston Chronicle*, B1.

# Vera Wang

Vera Wang. Photo by Nigel Barker

**Born**: 27 June 1949, Manhattan, New York.

**Education**: Sarah Lawrence College, Bronxville, New York, B.A. in art history, 1971.

**Positions Held**: Editorial staff, *Vogue*, New York City, New York, 1972–74; senior fashion editor, *Vogue*, New York City, New York, 1974–87; design director, Ralph Lauren Women's Wear, New York City, New York, 1987–89; founder, chair, and chief executive officer, Vera Wang Bridal House Ltd., New York City, New York, 1990– .

**Summary**: Vera Wang, a competitive ice skater in her teens, made her mark in fashion as a *Vogue* magazine editor and design director at Ralph Lauren before introduc-ing her line of classic, minimalist bridal and evening gowns. The head of Vera Wang Bridal House Ltd. in New York, she often dresses film actresses for special engagements such as award and wedding ceremonies.

## Early Years

Wang and her younger brother Kenneth were raised in Manhattan's exclusive Upper East Side in New York City. Their parents, Cheng Ching and Florence Wu Wang, built a multimillion-dollar oil and pharmaceuticals company, U.S. Summit Company, after emigrating to the United States from China in the 1940s. Her mother Florence, who molded a strong sense of fashion in her daughter, had also been a former translator at the United Nations.

When Wang was seven years old, she received a pair of ice skates from her parents for Christmas. After taking a turn around a pond in Central Park, she was hooked, and dedicated herself to the sport—even waking up at 6 a.m. to practice before school. Wang combined this training with her ballet lessons at the Balanchine's School of American Ballet.

## Higher Education

Wang excelled in ice skating to the point that she competed in junior pairs skating at the U.S. National Championships with partner James Stuart in 1968 and 1969. She even had aspirations to skate in the Olympics, but did not make the 1968 Olympic team. Although Wang was enrolled at Sarah Lawrence College, she dropped out to move to Paris and study art history and languages at the Sorbonne. She eventually reenrolled at Sarah Lawrence, changing her focus from premed studies to art history.

## Career Highlights

After graduation, Wang eventually landed a job at *Vogue* magazine, where she did "everything from Xeroxing messenger slips to packing and unpacking for photo shoots," according to *People Weekly* (20 July 1998). Although she had a college degree, the magazine was first more concerned whether or not she could type. In time, Wang demonstrated her ability in the fashion editorial world. "Vera had all the ingredients of a star," stated Polly Allen Mellen, one of Wang's supervisors at Vogue, to *People Weekly*. "You could tell that immediately."

By the age of 25, Wang had become fashion editor for the Condé Nast magazine. She explains in her March 2001 essay in *Vogue*: "I came to find that fashion and figure skating were not unrelated: Expressing myself visually was not so different from expressing myself physically. And when I realized that skating could no longer be my life, *Vogue* became my life. They used to tease me and call me Vera Vogue, but I was a real *Vogue* person. Not just a little—more than I even wish to talk about anymore, because I gave my youth to the magazine, and even though I sometimes suffered, I loved every minute of it."

As fashion editor, Wang helped set up provocative photo shoots, which sometimes ended in disaster. For instance, a sitting with model Christie Brinkley and a Doberman resulted in a destroyed designer dress. However, these risks also had their payoffs, too, and Wang established herself not only as a trendsetter, but also a player in the social scene at nightclubs such as Studio 54.

After 13 years as fashion editor, Wang moved into fashion design as a designer director for Ralph Lauren, responsible for 10 lines of clothing and accessories. While at Ralph Lauren, she became reacquainted with businessman Arthur Becker. In 1989,

she was in the middle of planning for her June wedding to Becker when she became aware that there was nothing appropriate for a bride in her forties. "There was one basic look at the time: froufrou," Wang stated to *People Weekly* regarding the fussy bridal styles. To *The New York Times* (2 November 2001), she further elaborated: "I didn't see anything that was my own sense of modernity."

As a result, she spent $10,000 to have a beaded dress custom-made. Later, spurred by a $4 million loan from her father, she decided to provide another option for brides seeking classic and chic gowns by opening her own boutique. In March 1990, she rented a two-story space in the posh Carlyle Hotel in Manhattan. While a $1 million renovation of the salon was underway, she and her associate, Chet Hazzard, formerly of Anne Klein Design Studio, sold dresses out of a hotel suite. In September 1990, the doors of Vera Wang Bridal House Ltd. were officially open—with the fanfare of a six-page article in Wang's former magazine, *Vogue*. At first, Wang sold mostly other designers' dresses, but soon began offering her own bridal gowns, which gained her a strong reputation for the use of luxurious fabrics, exquisite detailing, and contemporary interpretation of classic lines.

Although her workmanship was top-notch, it took Wang time to make a profit. In 1991, she had sold 1,000 ready-to-wear gowns worth $1 million and an additional $1 million in custom-made dresses, but was still not making money. Growth eventually developed. By 1993, Wang's boutique had a staff of 27 salespeople, seamstresses, and stylists. Customer service was emphasized, in addition to strong branding—Wang spent $200,000 in advertisements that year.

By 1998, Vera Wang Bridal House had 200 employees and $20 million in annual sales. Currently, according to *The New York Times*, the price of her one-of-a-kind wedding dresses starts at $26,000, while her ready-to-wear bridal dresses start at $1,700. In addition to her original bridal salon, a second retail store dedicated to bridesmaids collections was opened on Madison Avenue. Her line of products is also sold in high-end stores such as Saks Fifth Avenue, Barneys New York, and Nordstrom. A business office is located on West 39th Street in Manhattan.

Her label has been further elevated by celebrities who have chosen to wear Vera Wang dresses to award ceremonies and their own wedding ceremonies; they include Sharon Stone, Holly Hunter, Meg Ryan, Elisabeth Shue, Mariah Carey, Uma Thurman, and Helen Hunt.

The popularity of Wang's wedding gowns has spawned many imitators. But it is Wang's 30 years of experience in fashion, as well as her service, that sets her apart from her competitors. Interestingly, her early experience in ice skating has also played a role in her work. "I can't design a gown without thinking of how a woman's body will look and move when she's wearing it," Wang wrote in *Vogue* (March 2001).

Wang further expanded from her bridal gown lines to eveningwear, ready-to-wear clothing, and accessories. In 2001, her book *Vera Wang on Weddings* was released by HarperCollins. In addition to introducing new collections of shoes, handbags, and eyewear, Wang, like other designers, is diversifying into fragrance and tableware products such as crystal and china. She has even designed dresses for the Barbie fashion doll. In 1992 and 1994, Wang's life came full circle when she designed U.S. skater Nancy Kerrigan's outfits for the Olympics.

Wang, her husband, and their two daughters, Cecilia and Josephine, live in a Park Avenue apartment. They also own homes in Pound Ridge, New York; Palm Beach, Florida; and Southampton, New York.

## Sources

"Chic to Chic." 20 July 1998. *People Weekly*: 129.

Coleman, Lisa. 26 April 1993. "A Designing Woman." *Forbes*: 118+ .

Cruz, Clarissa. 16 November 2001. "Vera Firma: Designer Vera Wang Shoots from the Hip on All Things Wedding." *Entertainment Weekly*: 122.

Givhan, Robin. 22 January 1997. "A Little Something in Wed: Vera Wang Borrows Nothing for Her Bridal Creations." *Washington Post*: C1.

"The Look of Vera Wang." December 2000. *Instyle*: 142.

Richardson, Lynda. 2 November 2001. "A 24/7 Superwoman, Living La Vida Loca in Style." *New York Times*: 2.

Thomas, Barbara. 3 February 1999. "Getting Married: What to Wear; Profile: Vera Wang; Visionary in White." *Los Angeles Times*: 1+ .

"Vera Wang and Arthur Becker." 13 February 1995. *People Weekly*: 78.

Vera Wang Web site. www.verawang.com [accessed December 24, 2001].

Wang, Vera. March 2001. "Vera Wang." *Vogue*: 130, 136.

# Yick Wo

**Born:** c. 1800s, China.

**Died:** Unknown.

**Positions Held:** Laundryman, c. 1863–85.

**Summary:** Barred from prospecting for gold and other skilled trades in the 1800s, many Chinese immigrants found themselves in the laundry trade. Yick Wo was one such Chinese American, but notable in that he successfully challenged discriminatory business laws in San Francisco. Winning his case in California's Supreme Court in

1886, Wo set a legal precedence that has been cited in hundreds of cases since.

## Early Years

Not much is known of Wo, other than he came to California in 1861 at the height of the Gold Rush. While many newcomers from Canton, China, hoped to make riches in what they called *Gum Saam*, Gold Mountain, they instead discovered racial hostility and barriers to prospecting. As a result, many Chinese immigrants turned to other professions, including farming, cigar-making, sewing, and washing clothes, at that time considered "women's work," to make a living. By 1870, approximately 2,000 Chinese laundries soon populated San Francisco, according to the U.S. Census.

Wo apparently opened his own laundry business in 1863, two years after he arrived in the United States. He operated his shop in the same San Francisco wooden building for 22 years. Despite the longevity of Wo's laundry business, dealing with city officials was anything but smooth. Ordinances were upheld to close laundries from 10 p.m. to 6 p.m. to allegedly reduce the number of fires due to high night winds. At that time more than 95 percent of all laundries were housed in wooden buildings.

In 1880, another ordinance decreed that laundries in San Francisco County had to be approved by the Board of Supervisors. Out of the approximately 320 laundries within the county, about 240 were owned and operated by Chinese immigrants. Those who continued to operate without the Board of Supervisors' approval would be subject to a possible $1,000 fine and six months in jail.

## Career Highlights

Wo's laundry had passed previous inspections from the board of fire wardens. However, when he applied to have his license renewed in 1885, the Board of Supervisors denied his request, along with those of nearly 200 other Chinese applicants. In contrast, only one of the 80 non-Chinese laundry operators was refused a license. Wo disregarded the ordinance and continued business as usual with his equipment—stoves, washing and drying machines, and irons—all of which had been previously deemed in good condition and "not dangerous to the surrounding property." Found in violation of the 1880 ordinance, Wo was arrested, ordered to pay a fine, and imprisoned in the county jail.

Believing that he and his countrymen were being unfairly discriminated against, Wo petitioned the California Supreme Court in *Yick Wo v. Sheriff Hopkins* on August 24, 1885. Represented by attorney Hall McAllister, Wo maintained that the San Francisco Board of Supervisors exercised arbitrary power in granting licenses to only certain businesses "without regard to the competency of the person applying." The filed legal brief also mentioned the significant economic impact of the Chinese laundries; their businesses represented $200,000 in investments and $180,000 in annual payment for rent, licensing, taxes, gas, and water.

The case, which was argued together with another case involving a Chinese American laundryman (*Wo Lee v. Sheriff Hopkins*), was finally resolved on May 10, 1886. The California Supreme Court sided with Wo and his Chinese American colleagues. In their reversal of Wo's conviction, the judges determined that the laundry ordinance was administered in a discriminatory manner and violated the Constitution's Fourth Amendment: "Nor shall any State deprive any person of life, liberty, or property without due process of law; nor deny to any person within its jurisdiction the equal protection of the laws."

As stated by Justice Matthews in the court opinion, "For the very idea that one man may be compelled to hold his life, or the means of living, or any material right essential to the enjoyment of life, at the mere will of another, seems to be intolerable in any country where freedom prevails, as being the essence of slavery itself."

In fact, *Yick Wo v. Sheriff Hopkins* became a landmark case that was subsequently cited in civil rights cases in the 1960s. Not much is known of Wo after the court rendered its opinion in 1886, although an elementary school in San Francisco was named after the famed laundryman.

### Sources

Kim, Hyung-chan, ed. 1992. *Asian Americans and the Supreme Court: A Documentary History*. Westport, CT: Greenwood Press.

Sing, Bill. 17 July 1984. "The Chinese Laundry: A Revival." *Los Angeles Times*: 1.

"Victory of the Chinese Laundrymen." 11 May 1886. *San Francisco Chronicle*: 8.

*Yick Wo v. Sheriff Hopkins*, Supreme Court of the State of California, 10 May 1886.

## Charles Woo

Charles Woo. Photo courtesy of Charles Woo

**Born**: 1951, Hong Kong.

**Education**: University of California, Los Angeles, California, B.S. and M.S. degrees in physics.

**Positions Held**: Cofounder and chief executive officer, ABC Toys, Los Angeles, California, 1979–1989; cofounder and chief executive officer, Megatoys Los Angeles, California, 1989– .

**Awards, Honors**: World Trade Hall of Fame, World Trade Center Association, 1996; Historymakers Award, American Museum, 1997; Distinguished Community Service Award, Anti-Defamation League, 1999; Business Leadership Award, Asian Business Association, 2000; Outstanding Entrepreneur Award, Asian Business League, 2001; Community Service Award, League of Women Voters, 2001; UCLA Alumni Award for Excellence; Professional Achievement Award, 2001; Pinnacle of Leadership Award, Los Angeles Area Chamber of Commerce, 2002.

**Summary**: Charles Woo, an immigrant from Hong Kong, is credited with creating a billion-dollar wholesale toy industry in a revitalized manufacturing district in downtown Los Angeles, now referred to as "Toytown." Through his companies, Woo designs and manufactures toys in Asia and Mexico and sells them in the United States; he and his family also own buildings within Toytown where 500 toy importers and distributors do business.

### Early Years

Woo's family has had a long connection with the United States. His great-grandfather came to California from China with his brothers during the Gold Rush and established a business in Marysville, a town north of Sacramento, to buy gold from the miners, and eventually returned to Guangdong, a southern province of China, as a wealthy man.

Woo's grandfather did not fare as well in his attempts to succeed in America. He traveled to Mexico but could not cross into the United States because of the Chinese Exclusion Act of 1882. Woo's father, Pak Wah Woo, moved from China to Hong Kong in 1949 where he launched an import-export business in construction machine parts. In Hong Kong he purchased a warehouse in which merchandise was stored as it came off the ships.

When Woo was an infant, he contracted polio, which left both legs paralyzed. Yet this affliction did not deter him from his dream of attending school in the United States.

## Education

In 1968, Woo came to Los Angeles intending to attain his doctorate in physics at the University of California, Los Angeles (UCLA). He gained his bachelor's and master's degree in the subject, with the school's highest honor, but before he completed his doctorate, he became involved in the family business. His father and mother, Ping Yee, had followed Woo and his three brothers to southern California. They had been operating a Chinese restaurant at Redondo Beach, but were investigating more promising ventures, including Chinese arts and crafts. Woo suggested importing toys from Hong Kong and Taiwan.

"Toys seemed to me to be the perfect commodity," he was quoted in a *Los Angeles Times* article published in 1993. "They turn over rapidly, and people buy them even when the economy is bad. I was just going to take a summer off to help get the business off the ground, but it kept growing bigger and bigger, until there was no going back."

## Career Highlights

In 1979, Woo and his family—including brothers Peter, Jack, and Shu—opened ABC Toys in a declining warehouse district in downtown Los Angeles. ABC Toys was one of the first wholesale toy merchants in the area. In fact, large companies like Mattel dominated the toy industry, and smaller importers were in operation usually only during the Christmas season.

Securing a $40,000 line of credit from a Chinatown bank, the family rented a warehouse for $400 a month. With *guanxi*, or connections, with toy manufacturers in Asia, they imported inexpensive toys and sold them to flea market vendors and swap meet retailers in southern California. The company had no employees outside the family for the first year of operation.

ABC Toys eventually was able to expand nationally and establish a wholesale business to major distributors targeting "mom-and-pop" stores. Soon the company tripled and quadrupled in orders and revenues. Woo realized the potential of the affordable area in which his company was located and its proximity to the ports of Los Angeles and Long Beach. Envisioning a specialized merchandising district as was typical in Hong Kong, Woo began purchasing real estate and buildings in the area and leasing them to other wholesalers and exporters, predominantly Asian and Latino immigrants. Toytown was born.

Not content to just import generic items, Woo began to work with overseas factories in producing specially designed products. A Santa Claus figure with electronic music, and a stuffed doll carrying an ice cream cone were among bestsellers.

Seeing the potential for further growth, Woo and his older brother Peter launched their own enterprise, MegaToys, in 1989. Within a decade, MegaToys had $30 million in sales and 100 employees. By the year 2000, Toytown consisted of 500 different toy importers, warehouses, and distributors; 6,000 people worked in the district, which at the time supported revenues at approximately $500 million. Sixty percent of the $12 billion in toys sold to American retailers were handled in Toytown and the adjacent industrial area, according to a report submitted to Rebuild L.A. Customers come from all over the world, including the East Coast, the Midwest, Mexico, South America, and Asia, to do business in the district. Manufacturing, in turn, has moved into China and other parts of Asia.

"So the dynamics of the market keep changing," Woo said in an interview, "and the business situation changes all the time, but the opportunities are always there. Sometimes we have to be here, trying to find out what the consumer taste is all about, and then we do the design work, and we would go overseas to the manufacturer and sort of supervise the production."

Woo is also active in civic and political affairs. He was the 2001 Chairman of the Los Angeles Area Chamber of Commerce, as the first Asian American chair in its 113 years of existence. He served two terms as president of the Toys Association of Southern California. He is currently the president of the Los Angeles City Workforce Investment Board, overseeing the nation's second largest job training program. When the Democratic National Committee held its convention in Los Angeles in 2000,

Woo served as a vice chair of the mayor's host committee. He was chairman of Asian Rehabilitation Services, Inc., on the boards of the Los Angeles Library Foundation, YMCA Metropolitan Los Angeles, and LA's BEST, a nationally renowned after-school program. He is the chair of CAUSE-Vision21, a non-partisan organization that provides voter education and registration services, as well as leadership development program in the Asian American community.

In his limited free time, Woo pursues his hobby of physics, the field of his academic studies. He, his wife Ying, and two children make their home in Rancho Palos Verdes.

## Sources

Kotkin, Joel. November 1999. *The Future of the Center: The Core City in the New Economy* (Policy Study No. 264). Los Angeles: Reason Public Policy Institute.

Micklethwait, John, and Adrian Wooldridge. 26 June 2000. "Toy Story." *Fortune.*

Newman, Morris. 24 April 1995. "Toy Companies Animate Industrial Sector in Eastern Downtown L.A." *Los Angeles Business Journal.*

Schoenberger, Karl. 5 October 1993. "Expatriate Entrepreneurs: Well-Educated Chinese Pour Their Energy into Business." *Los Angeles Times*: D10.

Torres, Vicki. 21 January 1997. "New Games in Town." *Los Angeles Times.*

Woo, Charlie. 29 May 1994. "Action Figure." *Los Angeles Times* (City Times): 22.

# Y

## Elaine Yamagata

**Full Name at Birth**: Yoko Yamao.

**Born**: 21 February 1922, Walnut Grove, California.

**Education**: Kobe College, Kobe, Japan, teaching license, 1942; Columbia University, classes in English and accounting, c. 1940s.

**Positions Held**: Teacher, Seichin High School, Okayama, Japan, 1942–43; interpreter, Tientsin camp, Tientsin, China, 1946; translator, Hyogo Military Government, Japan, circa 1946–49; interpreter and secretary, Atomic Bomb Casualty Commission, Hiroshima, Japan, 1949–51; New York representative, Green Hill Trading, Inc., 1951–55; cofounder and vice president, A & A Trading Company, New York City, New York, 1955–68; vice president, A & A International, Inc. (now a subsidiary of Tandy Corporation), Fort Worth, Texas, 1968–81; president, A & A International Inc., Fort Worth, Texas, 1981–89.

**Summary**: A second-generation Japanese American raised in a farming community in California, Elaine Yamagata helped her husband establish an international trading company, A & A International, Inc. in New York City in the 1950s. Their company, which originally specialized in importing audio goods from Japan and other parts of Asia, was eventually acquired by the Tandy Corporation and made into a subsidiary which was worth $1.5 billion at the time of Yamagata's retirement in 1989.

## Early Years

Yamagata was the eldest daughter of the only Japanese doctor in the town of Walnut Grove, California, just south of Sacramento. Her parents, Dr. Enichi and Matsuyo Yamao, had come to the United States from Hiroshima, Japan, in 1921. Her father was initially intending to study at Johns Hopkins University, but because of monetary constraints, went to Walnut Grove to take over a medical practice. In the 1920s, Walnut Grove and outlying communities had segregated elementary schools: one for European Americans, and another for Japanese and Chinese children.

After attending school every day, Yamagata had to make time to attend Japanese-language school, practice the piano, and do the grocery shopping for the entire family. One of her Japanese schoolteachers, Dr. Terami, had a doctorate in mathematics from the University of California; he was instrumental in encouraging Yamagata to read a variety of books.

In spite of her many responsibilities, Yamagata says she had an idyllic childhood. In an interview with Akemi Kikumura of the Japanese American National Museum (5 November 1989), she remembers ringing the church bell of the Japanese Methodist church every Sunday.

Yamagata attended Courtland High School, approximately nine miles away from her home. This school was desegregated, and Yamagata flourished both academically and socially. She performed in musicals, and was the president of both the Friendship Club and Epworth League.

When she was 16 years old, Yamagata's parents returned to Japan in 1938 so that Dr. Yamao could continue his advanced medical studies at Okayama Medical School. Although Yamagata did not want to go to Japan and be away from her homeland, she accompanied her family, hoping to someday return to America. She graduated third in her class from a Catholic high school, Seichin, in Okayama.

## Higher Education

Yamagata attended Kobe College, where she studied English and music. She lived in a dormitory and described her college life as "the happiest time of my life. I was blessed with good friends, and the dormitory was a very happy place." (Interview with Nancy Araki, Japanese American National Museum, 1996.) While Yamagata was in college, Japan bombed Pearl Harbor, and many of the American professors were sent back to the United States. Yamagata had dual citizenship; as a second-generation Japanese American, she was considered a Nisei; the Japanese military police would monitor the Nisei in Japan on a regular basis.

## Career Highlights

After gaining her teaching license, Yamagata taught music at her former Japanese high school in Okayama. During this time, she met Tadashi "Tad" Yamagata, the son of a Japanese Methodist minister who had been working in international trade before the war broke out. They married in 1943, and Tad went on to Beijing, China, to pursue a steel and scrap metal business with a Japanese friend. Yamagata eventually joined her husband, and together, they moved about 10 times throughout China in three years. Eventually Tad opened a steel mill in Tientsin, China, which was eventually taken over by the Chinese military weeks before the war in the Pacific ended.

Hearing of a need for English-language interpreters in a concentration camp in Tientsin, Yamagata worked as a translator for American doctors in the hospital. By this time, she had a three-year-old son and was pregnant with her second child. She gave birth in the camp in 1946; after three months, the Yamagata family returned to Tad's hometown in Japan, Bofu. There the couple opened a small gift store targeted to Australian occupation soldiers. After international trade eventually opened up, Tad moved to Kobe to work with Green Hill Trading Company Ltd., while Yamagata worked as a translator in the personnel department of the Hyogo Military Government. She later spent some time as an interpreter and secretary to a radiologist in Hiroshima with the Atomic Bomb Casualty Commission.

Finally, in 1951, as a result of her husband's job transfer to New York City, Yamagata returned to the United States.

Together they opened the New York office of Green Hill Trading Company Ltd.—a Japanese and British international trade company. They first imported stainless utensils and exported coal, but under Tad's leadership, the company began handling optical equipment. While her husband was visiting customers, Yamagata was responsible for correspondence, telephone sales calls, and bookkeeping from their home office. It was unusual for a woman of Japanese ancestry to be involved in international trade in the 1950s. "I guess that caught their [customers'] attention, which was good for us," explained Yamagata.

In 1955, the Yamagatas had received a shipment of bicycles from Japan that turned out to be so defective that their customers, including Macy's and Gimbals department stores returned them. On the other hand, the optical and audio business with Radio Shack was booming. As a result, with $10,000 seed money from Radio Shack, $10,000 from a friend, and a $10,000 investment of their own, the Yamagatas launched their independent enterprise, A & A Trading Company (A & A stood for Asian and American).

A & A specialized in importing electronics equipment from Japan. In the 1950s, vacuum tubes dominated the audio market, but the introduction of the semiconductor was making way for transistor radios. The fledgling Sony Corporation, in fact, introduced their first pocket transistor radio in 1955. While Japan-made products were initially viewed during the postwar period as being of substandard quality, Sony and trade companies like A & A were soon changing the reputation of Japanese audio equipment.

In 1963, despite the growing demand for audio merchandise, Radio Shack—with its nine retail stores and mail-order business—found itself in financial trouble. It even owed A & A approximately $400,000 at this time. Charles Tandy of the Fort Worth, Texas-based company, Tandy Corporation, seeking to diversify from leather manufacturing and hobby stores, purchased Radio Shack and made it profitable within two years.

Recognizing the need to import goods from Asia, Tandy acquired A & A in 1968; the Yamagatas eventually had to move to Fort Worth. Relying heavily on her bilingual strengths, Yamagata continued on as vice president of the Tandy subsidiary. When Tad retired in 1981, she served as president until August 1989. At the time of her retirement, the company was making $1.5 billion in annual sales.

The Yamagatas have two sons, Harvey and Mark; both work for A & A International. The subsidiary is the procurement center for the approximately 7,000 Radio Shack retail stores across the nation.

Yamagata has been active with the Fort Worth Japanese Society, Van Cliburn Piano Competition, and the Japanese American National Museum.

### Sources

Interview with Elaine Yamagata (Akemi Kikumura, Japanese American National Museum, 1989 November 5).

Interview with Elaine Yamagata (Nancy Araki, Japanese American National Museum, 29 March 1996).

Interview with Tad Yamagata (Nancy Araki, Japanese American National Museum, 5 November 1989).

Interview with Tad Yamagata (Nancy Araki, Japanese American National Museum, 27–28 March 1996).

## Tsuru Yamauchi

**Full Name at Birth**: Tsuru Kamigawa.

**Born**: 25 December 1890, Shuri, Okinawa, Japan.

**Died**: 1990, Hawaii.

**Positions Held**: Cofounder of Aala Tofu Company, Honolulu, Hawaii, 1940–58.

**Summary**: Tsuru Yamauchi, a "picture bride" from Okinawa, Japan, helped her husband Shokin establish Aala Tofu Co. in Honolulu, Hawaii, in 1940. The tofu (soy bean curd) company, which originally dates back to 1923, eventually made its way to the mainland United States; this offshoot merged with a Japanese spice manufacturer, House Foods, to create Hinoichi Tofu.

### Early Years

Yamauchi was born to the Kamigawa family, which had samurai roots, in the town of Shuri, located near Okinawa's current capital, Naha. Yamauchi's parents were strict and insisted on speaking in the dialect of Shuri, which was much different from other dialects within this small island west of the main island of Japan.

When Yamauchi was three, the family moved to the countryside in an area called Itoman. Yamauchi's father had been well educated, but faced economic pressures in supporting their many children—a total of 12 (at least five, however, died in childhood). Because Yamauchi and her older siblings all had to work to help support the family, they did not attend school.

Yamauchi assisted her parents in their sewing business. They sewed by hand various styles of kimonos and coats. Next door to them was a shop that made and sold fresh tofu, or soy bean curd. In Okinawa, tofu was made by taking uncooked dried soy beans—very inexpensive vegetables shaped like large peas—and soaking and grinding them in a mortar. They would then be squeezed; all residue (*okara*) would be removed before the mashed consistency was boiled and then poured into a barrel. Once set, the tofu would be cut into blocks. Some soy would be used for bean paste, *miso*, a soup base.

"You never waste tofu," Yamauchi said in an oral history interview (Michiko Kodama, University of Hawaii Ethnic Studies Oral History Project) published in *Uchinanchu: A History of Okinawans in Hawaii* (1981). In fact, every part of the tofu product, even the residue, was eaten by the Japanese.

When Yamauchi was about 13 years old, she learned how to make tofu. Grinding the beans by hand early in the morning, she sold tofu as a sidewalk vendor later in the day. She also tended her own agricultural field, growing potatoes, turnips, and even hay, which she harvested to make mats.

At the age of 18, Yamauchi was being primed for marriage. Her parents and her future in-laws arranged the match, and, Yamauchi had to send her photo to her prospective mate, the son of sugar cane growers who had moved to Hawaii. Her name was entered in the Yamauchi family register in 1908, and she went to live with her in-laws in the countryside of Okinawa for a year. She eventually left on a boat to meet her husband, Shokin Yamauchi, in 1910.

### Career Highlights

Yamauchi's early years in Hawaii were spent living in a workers' camp in a sugar cane field in an area called Waipahu. She worked in the fields, and while pregnant with her first child, she secured a position as a cook. Maintaining her own household and working proved to be a harsh life at times; in an oral history interview with Michiko Kodama, Yamauchi said that many times she did not even have enough time to put on her sandals.

In 1919, Yamauchi returned to Okinawa with her four children. She gave birth to her fifth child there, but her third child died in the Spanish flu epidemic. Yamauchi lived with her family in Okinawa for four years, before returning to Hawaii in 1923. Her children, who were attending school in Okinawa, were brought back to Hawaii one at a time.

Yamauchi and her husband then secured domestic work at the Honolulu Military Academy. As their household expanded further, Yamauchi worked at a pineapple cannery where she made 30 cents an hour. During the off-season, she skinned fish at a tuna factory for 20 cents per hour. Her husband, Shokin, meanwhile, did yard work at a landing pier, a position he retained for 15 years.

Advised by friends to establish their own business, the Yamauchis learned of a tofu shop that was for sale. Haruko Uyeda Tofu had been originally established in Honolulu as H. Iwanaga Daufu in 1923, according to William Shurtleff of Soyfoods Center. The Yamauchis renamed the enterprise Aala Tofu Company as it was located in the Aala district, in the neighborhood of a Japanese theater. Tsuru Yamauchi learned that making tofu in Hawaii was a little different than in Okinawa. The dried soy beans were first boiled before the pulp-like residue, *okara*, was removed. Yamauchi woke up at two o'clock in the morning to begin grinding the beans. She and her son Shoan hand delivered the tofu to a dozen markets and stores. Their other products included *age* (fried bean curd), *konnyaku* (yam cake), and finally *okara*, which was fed to pigs.

Yamauchi and her son were working at the Aala Tofu Company when they heard about the bombing of nearby Pearl Harbor from a taxi cab driver. They saw the destruction and smoke, and quickly evacuated the area. Aala Tofu Company was reopened three weeks later. Because of limited foodstuffs, the tofu sold well. To supplement their tofu business, they opened a *saimin* (noodle) shop in 1942.

After Yamauchi's son was drafted into the U.S. Army, the noodle shop was eventually closed, and Yamauchi and her husband focused on tofu production. After returning from World War II, Shoan Yamauchi rejoined the family enterprise until 1946, when he moved to Los Angeles and purchased Hinode Tofu Company in the Little Tokyo district. The company eventually became Matsuda-Hinode Tofu Company in 1963, and in 1983, on Osaka, Japan-based spice company, House Foods, purchased an interest in the company, which was then renamed House Foods/Yamauchi, Inc.

In 1997, House Foods, which does not make tofu in Japan, opened a new $21 million plant in Garden Grove, California, that was designed to produce 150,000 pounds of tofu a day. Demand for tofu, high in protein but low in fat and cholesterol, has risen steadily in the United States. By the mid-1990s, domestic sales of tofu had increased to $130 million from only $40 million in 1979.

Yamauchi, who continued to work at Aala Tofu Company until her late sixties, passed away in 1990. Becoming a naturalized American citizen in 1959, she had been involved with community-based organizations with connections to Okinawa: the Itoman Nisei Club and Kanegusuku Sonjinkai.

## Sources

Apodaca, Patrice. 13 March 1997. "Curd Is the Word." *Los Angeles Times* (Orange County Edition), 1.

Kodama, Michiko, ed. 1984. *Uchinanchu: A History of Okinawans in Hawaii.* (second printing). Honolulu, HI: Ethnic Studies Oral History Project/United Okinawan Association of Hawaii.

*Tofu History.* http://www.tofufest.org. [accessed September 5, 2001]

# Janet Yang

**Born**: 13 July 1956, Queens, New York.

**Education**: Brown University, Providence, Rhode Island, B.A.; Columbia University, New York City, New York, M.B.A.

**Positions Held**: Staff, Foreign Language Press, Beijing, China; founder and president, World Entertainment, San Francisco, California, c. 1980s; production development executive, MCA/Universal Studios, Hollywood, California, 1985–89; vice president of production, Ixtlan, Santa Monica, California, 1989–96; president, Ixtlan, Santa Monica, California; partner and producer, Manifest Film Company, Culver City, California, 1996– .

**Awards, Honors**: Emmy Award, 1995; Golden Globe Award, 1995.

**Summary**: Janet Yang is one of the pioneering Asian American female producers in the film and television industries. Currently a partner of Manifest Films, Yang was the former president of Oliver Stone's production company, Ixtlan, where she served as executive producer of the critically acclaimed movie, The *Joy Luck Club*, and a television movie, *Indictment: The McMartin Trial*, that earned her both an Emmy and Golden Globe.

## Early Years

Yang was born in Queens, New York, to immigrants from mainland China. Her father, T.Y., had come to the United States in 1947 and developed a career in engineering. Yang's mother, Anna, emigrated to America to study and eventually worked for the United Nations.

Yang was raised among primarily Jewish Americans on Long Island, New York. Regarding her early experience of Asian American media images, she observed in an article in the *Los Angeles Times* (13 May 1998): "As a child, I never saw an Asian in films or TV unless he was the butler."

When she was 15, Yang visited China with her mother—thereby peaking her interest in her ethnic heritage. She studied the Chinese language for a summer at Middlebury College. After graduating from the exclusive private high school, Philip Exeter Academy, Yang decided to pursue her interest in Asian Studies.

## Higher Education

Yang gained her bachelor's degree from Brown University. After her undergraduate education, Yang worked in Beijing, China, for one and a half years with the Foreign Language Press. She then returned to New York to enter Columbia University's business administration graduate program.

## Career Highlights

While working toward her M.B.A., Yang launched World Entertainment, a distributor of films from Hong Kong and China. The San Francisco-based company served as the North American distributor of works by Chinese filmmakers such as Zhang Yimou and Chen Kaige. At this time, the early 1980s, most Americans were unfamiliar with movies from China.

One day, while eating at a Chinese restaurant in New York's Soho district, Yang was approached by a film director who wanted her to appear in his latest film. The director was Oliver Stone; the film, *Year of the Dragon*. Although Yang declined the acting offer, the two began a long friendship that would eventually culminate in a productive working relationship years later.

With her Chinese-language and cultural expertise, Yang found herself a hot commodity. MCA/Universal recruited her to work with Steven Spielberg's Amblin Entertainment. In 1986, she served as Spielberg's liaison in China during the filming of *Empire of the Sun*, a movie that takes place during World War II. On the set Yang met another female film executive, Lisa Henson, the daughter of puppeteer Jim Henson who would eventually rise to the presidency of Columbia Pictures and form an important alliance with Yang.

In addition to her direct involvement on the Spielberg film, Yang also worked in conjunction with Universal, Paramount, and MGM/UA to export movie classics like *Love Story* and *Roman Holiday* to the Chinese markets. "I had to interpret Hollywood to China and China to Hollywood, which is not an easy task," she said at an executive luncheon with the Women in Film in 1994.

While at MCA/Universal, Yang befriended Kathleen Kennedy, one of Spielberg's long-time executives and one of the few high-ranking women leaders in the entertainment industry. MCA/Universal, in fact, was known for its male-dominated corporate culture; its headquarters was even referred to as the "Black Tower."

According to the *San Francisco Examiner* (18 June 1995), Kennedy's management style embodied a spirit of collaboration and open communication, a contrast to the industry's competitive nature. "Kathy showed me that our work was about making movies, not power and politics," Yang expressed to the *Examiner*. During Yang's affiliation with Universal, she also initiated the production of *Dragon: The Bruce Lee Story*, the biopic of the legendary Chinese American martial artist.

In time, however, Yang sought a more independent work environment. Learning about Oliver Stone's new production company, she wrote him a long letter persuading him to hire her as a producer. "I loved Oliver's movies," Yang told the *Examiner*. "He had independence and clout. He had a strong interest in Asia."

In 1989, she was named vice president of production of Ixtlan. Her early films with the company included *South Central* (1992) and *Zebrahead* (1992). Stone, known for his political and artistic risk-taking with such works as *Born on the Fourth of July* and *JFK*, encouraged Yang to rethink her role as "an outsider." "Oliver made me realize being an outsider has less to do with skin color than state of mind," Yang said at the 1994 Women in Film luncheon. In this context, being an outsider involved "questioning and challenging, disagreeing and debating."

So when Yang brought Amy Tan's novel, *The Joy Luck Club*, to Ixtlan as material for a film, Stone was supportive, in spite of the story's cinematic limitations. "We figured eight rules [of filmmaking] were broken by *Joy Luck Club*," Yang was quoted in the *Hollywood Reporter* (31 March 1994). "Asians don't sell and neither do females. You can't have subtitles, flashbacks, or voice-overs. You must have a clear protagonist and antagonist, and a clear linear structure."

*The Joy Luck Club* (1993) starred Ming-Na Wen and was directed by Wayne Wang, gave many Asian American professionals an opportunity to showcase their talents. The film was also well-received by critics. Yang served as executive producer of the HBO movie *Indictment: The McMartin Trial*, starring James Woods and Mercedes Ruehl, for which she received both the 1995 Emmy and a Golden Globe Award for Outstanding Made for Television Movie.

Her Ixtlan producing credits included *Killer* (1995) and *New Age* (1994). *The People vs. Larry Flynt*, released in 1996 by Columbia Pictures, proved to be Yang's most controversial project during her tenure with Ixtlan. While it opened to excellent reviews, the biopic following the life of porn entrepreneur Larry Flynt was highly criticized by feminists like Gloria Steinem. Although the film garnered Academy Award nominations for director Milos Forman and actor Woody Harrelson, the $35-million film did not perform well at the box office.

The president of Columbia Pictures at this time was Lisa Henson, and in September 1996, she and Yang joined forces to launch a production company, Manifest Films Company, based at Columbia Pictures (later acquired by Sony Pictures Entertainment) in Culver City, California.

Women in the entertainment industry need to work together, according to Yang. "What I have found, almost uniformly at this point in time, is an abundance of support from other women. There's immediate networking. There's enough there that we don't feel one person is taking someone else's job away and enough so that we can really help each other. And there's still enough to go around," she stated to *Executive Female* (13 March 1997).

The partners had a three-year first-look deal with Sony, but their film projects ended up being released by other studios. Among them were *Savior*, set during the Bosnian war, and *Zero Effect*, a comedic detective movie starring Bill Pullman. *The Weight of Water*, a complex psychological thriller directed by Kathryn Bigelow, was released by Lion Gate in 2000.

Yang is also an advisor for the Coalition of Asian/Pacifics in Entertainment (CAPE), and serves on the board of directors for Independent Feature Projects/West and Women in Film.

## Sources

Cohen, Karen. 6 October 1993. "'Joy Luck' Producer's Parents Tell Story of Her Career." *Rossmoor News*.

Collins, Scott. 1 March 1997. "The Many People vs. 'Larry Flynt.'" *Los Angeles Times*: F1+ .

"Henson to Leave Post at Columbia Pictures to Start Own Company." 22 July 1996. *Wall Street Journal*: B5.

Honeycutt, Kirk. 31 March 1994. "Yang Finds Way on Road to Ixtlan." *Hollywood Reporter*.

"Interview: Universal's Janet Yang Foresees Real Profits on Vast Chinese Frontier." *Variety*: 482.

Iwata, Edward. 18 June 1995. "The Hot Movie Executive." *San Francisco Examiner*: B1+ .

Lacher, Irene. 2 March 1997. "A New Kind of Networking." *Los Angeles Times*: 1+ .

"Profile: Janet Yang." Coalition of Asian/Pacifics in Entertainment Web site. www.cape-usa.org/yang.html [accessed December 8, 2001].

Seger, Linda, and Johanna Goodman. 13 March 1997. *Executive Female*: 52+ .

Thomas, Kevin. 13 May 1998. "Asian American Filmmakers Ride in on New Wave." *Los Angeles Times*: 4+ .

# Jerry Yang

**Full Name at Birth**: Chih-Yuan Yang.

**Born**: 1968, Taipei, Taiwan.

**Education**: Stanford University, Stanford, California, B.S. and M.S. in electrical engineering, 1990.

**Positions Held**: Cofounder and Chief Yahoo, Yahoo! Inc., Santa Clara, California, 1994– .

**Summary**: Jerry Yang, who came to California from Taiwan when he was 10 years old, cofounded Yahoo! Inc., the first online navigational guide to the World Wide Web in 1994. The company has since become a leading global Internet communications, commerce, and media company that serves 200 million customers each month.

## Early Years

Yang and his younger brother Ken were born in Taipei, the capital of Taiwan. When Yang was two years old, his father passed away, and so his mother, Lily, had to raise her two sons on her own while working as an English professor at a university in Taipei. During the 1970s, the United States was shifting its diplomatic relations toward China and away from Taiwan. Yang's mother, concerned that her two sons would eventually be drafted into the Taiwanese army, moved her family to the United States and settled in San Jose, California, in 1978. Yang was 10 years old.

Yang eventually attended Piedmont Hills High School in San Jose. He played on the tennis team and was elected student body president his senior year. He was also class valedictorian.

## Higher Education

Yang was offered scholarships to attend the University of California, Berkeley, the California Institute of Technology in Pasadena, and Stanford University. He ultimately chose Stanford because it was close to his family in San Jose. Yang had to take part-time jobs on campus, including working as a sorter in one of the university libraries. There, according to *Fortune* magazine (6 March 2000), Yang became familiar with the Dewey decimal system and sorting methods in general. "That's where I first learned about how systematically information was categorized," he stated in the *Fortune* article. This information would prove to be useful in launching his pioneering enterprise in the future.

Yang graduated from Stanford with bachelor's and master's degrees in electrical engineering in four years. He then entered the university's Ph.D. program, specializing in computer-aided design (CAD) software.

In 1992, he went on a six-month academic exchange program in Japan, where he became friends with another Stanford doctoral student, David Filo, originally from Louisiana. When they returned to the school, they found the scientific world in early stages of the development of the World Wide Web, in which information could be accessed on computers all around the globe. Widely used to browse this information was a software program called Mosaic. For fun, Yang and Filo used Mosaic, along with their own software, to access statistics on professional basketball players for a "rotisserie" team they had assembled. Soon the hobby became more of a serious pursuit as they created Internet categories and subcategories. Initially called Jerry's Guide to the World Wide Web, the site was renamed *Yahoo*, an acronym for "Yet Another Hierarchical Officious Oracle." According to the Yahoo! Web site, the cofounders also were taken by the definition of yahoo: "rude, unsophisticated, uncouth."

Soon thousands of Internet users were accessing the Yahoo! site. In the fall of 1994, Yahoo received its millionth hit, and it became quite apparent that Yang and Filo had an incredible business opportunity in their hands. Eliciting the help of another Stanford student, Tim Brady, they incorporated Yahoo! (including the exclamation mark) in March 1995. Considering various offers of venture financing, the fledgling company finally partnered with Menlo Park, California-based Sequoia Capital, which had also funded Apple Computer, Atari, Oracle, and Cisco Systems. Sequoia's initial capital investment was $2 million for a 19.2 percent share of the company, which moved into offices in the suburb of Mountain View, California.

From their company's inception, both founders knew that they did not want to become the company's chief executive officer (CEO). Yang and Filo gave themselves each the title "Chief Yahoo," and set out to establish their corporate management team. Tim Koogle, also a Stanford alumnus and veteran of Motorola Corporation, became the corporation's first CEO in 1995. In April 1996, the company, which had 49 employees, launched a successful initial public offering. Priced at $13 per share, the stock opened at $24.50 per share and closed at $33 on opening day. The first international office was established in Japan; more than 22 other world properties followed, placing offices throughout Asia, Europe, Latin America, Canada, and the United States.

Yahoo!—which depends largely on advertising—did not immediately reap large profits. In fact, according to *Marketing* magazine (30 October 1997), Yahoo! registered its first profit of $222,000 on revenues of $17.3 million in fall of 1997. However, its early domination as an Internet navigation tool was widely recognized and its stock was highly valued. In fact, Yang, who at one time shared 34.6 percent of the company with cofounder Filo (*Forbes*, 5 October 1998), was reportedly worth $3.7 billion in 1999.

Beginning in 1997, Yahoo! began to acquire a number of Internet-related businesses, in addition to launching various new products including Yahoo! Shopping and Yahoo! Mail. As one of the first Internet search engines, Yahoo! enjoyed steady growth. In an interview with *Fortune* magazine's Brent Schlender, Yang explained that Yahoo!'s strength includes the speed in which the Yahoo! page appears onscreen as well as the flexibility of its product. "If you use Yahoo! for mail, fine; if you use it for chat, great; if you use it for finance, who cares, as long as we get you into Yahoo!, because chances are, we can keep you there a little longer," he stated.

In 1999, revenues rose to $588.6 million with a $61.1 million profit, at least 100 million users, and 2,000 employers. The following year proved to be even more successful: revenues hit $1 billion. However, the dot-com business experienced a serious downturn in 2001, and Yahoo! itself was not immune. In light of weak performance in the beginning of the year its CEO Tim Koogle stepped down. Approximately 420 employees, or 12 percent of its total workforce of 3,500, were laid off. A new chairman and chief executive officer, Terry Semel, was named in May 2001.

Chief Yahoo Yang continues as director of the company and is instrumental in guiding the future direction of the company—the second largest Web service after America Online with 1.1 billion page views a day. He and Filo have also been involved in philanthropy; they endowed a $2 million chair at the School of Engineering at Stanford University.

He and his wife Akiko, also a Stanford alumnus, reside in Los Altos, California.

### Sources

"Chief Yahoo." 30 October 1997. *Marketing*: 23.

Iwata, Edward. 12 April 2001. "Yahoo! Sees Weak Profit, Plans Layoffs." *USA Today*: B1.

Pickering, Carol. 5 October 1998. "A Tale of Two Startups." *Forbes*: S85.

Schlender, Brent. 6 March 2000. "The Customer Is the Decision-Maker." *Fortune*: F84+ .

Schlender, Brent. 6 March 2000. "How a Virtuoso Plays the Web: Eclectic, Inquisitive, and Academic." *Fortune*: F79+ .

"Yahoo! Key Milestones." Yahoo! Media Relations. http://docs.yahoo.com/info/pr/milestones.html [accessed September 13, 2001].

## Shirley Young

**Full Name at Birth**: Shirley Young.

**Born**: 25 May 1935, Shanghai, China.

**Education**: Wellesley College, B.A. in economics, 1955; New York University Graduate School of Arts and Sciences, 1956–57; Honorary Doctorate of Letters, Russell Sage College, 1982.

**Positions Held**: Project director, Alfred Politz Research, New York City, 1955–57; market research manager, Hudson Paper Corporation, New York City, 1957–58; research associate, Grey Advertising, Inc., 1959–69; director of marketing and research, Grey Advertising, Inc., 1969–71; executive vice president of planning and strategy development, Grey Advertising, Inc., 1980–83; president of Grey Strategic Marketing, Inc., 1983–88; chairperson of Grey Strategic Marketing, Inc., 1988–90; consultant, consumer market development, General Motors, Detroit, 1983–90; vice president of consumer market development, General Motors, 1988–96; vice president for China Strategic Development and Counselor for Asia Pacific Operations, 1996; president of Shirley Young Associates, LLC.

**Awards, Honors**: Top 50 women in business, *Business Week*, 1992; Outstanding Business Leaders Award, Northwood University, 1998.

**Summary**: Shirley Young applied her expertise in brand development and consumer motivation to help one of the Big Three automakers in Detroit, General Motors, recover its domestic market share and also expand sales overseas, specifically in Asia. One of the few influential women in the automotive industry, she has been a leading authority on doing business in China.

### Early Years

Shirley Young was born in Shanghai, China, one of three daughters of a career diplomat with the Nationalist Chinese government. Her family left China when she was two, and they continued to move throughout the world from one diplomatic assignment to another. In 1942, her father, Clarence Young, was assigned to serve as the Consulate General in the Phillippines, a nation that Japan invaded during World War II. Young's father, who refused to acquiesce to the Japanese military forces, was imprisoned and then executed.

Young's mother, Juliana Koo Young, now had to support her three young daughters on her own. She opted to take Young and her sisters to the United States after the war ended.

"When we got here, we realized that we were the beneficiaries of the American way, and that was to be received with open hearts and a helping hand for those in need," stated Young in a speech she made upon receiving the Outstanding Business Leaders Award from Northwood University in 1998.

"And as a result, each one of us three girls went on full scholarship to wonderful schools and got our start in life and became Americans."

### Higher Education

Young received her bachelor's degree in economics from Wellesley College in Massachusetts in 1955. Intent on making a contribution to the world economy, she got a job as a project director with the Alfred Politz Research in New York City, while also attending graduate school at New York University. She then worked as a market research manager for Hudson Paper Corporation for a year before joining Grey Advertising, the well-known Madison Avenue agency, as a research associate.

In her new position, Young honed her natural ability to observe people and define problems. She developed the method, "Market Target Buying Incentive Studies," which identified consumer decision-making motivations and pioneered the use of attitudinal studies in market research. Her accomplishments led to several promotions; in 1983, she became president of Grey Strategic Marketing, and then in 1988, chairperson.

While at Grey, Young began consulting with General Motors (GM) in 1985, and was able to initiate a program for roadside assistance and toll-free hotline for Cadillac owners. In 1988, she joined GM full-time as vice president for consumer market development. The challenges for Young were clear from the beginning: sales for the Detroit automaker had fallen steadily in the 1980s due to increased competition from imports. Even GM's own studies revealed that consumers were reluctant to buy its cars because of quality concerns.

Young decided to face consumer concerns straight-on. In charge of GM's $40 million advertisement campaign, she initiated a strong market campaign representing the slogan, "Putting Quality on the Road." Now safety and features would be emphasized over image and lifestyle. She also created a distinct market identity for each car division so that a Cadillac, "standard of luxury worldwide," could be differentiated from a Buick, "a premium American motorcar."

"A lot of this job," she stated in an article in *Business Week* (June 11, 1990), "is what I call persistent evangelism."

Named among the 50 top women in business in *Business Week's* June 8, 1992 issue, Young indeed has been recognized for her influence in a very male-dominated industry. But her work at GM did not end with "evangelizing" to the U.S. auto market. In fact, in 1996, she became the vice president for China Strategic Development and Counselor for Asia Pacific Operations. In this capacity, she would help forge the largest foreign joint venture in her birthplace, China.

This globalization of the car market is essential, according to Young. "Eighty percent of the growth in the automotive industry is going to take place outside of the United States, and 40 percent of that growth is going to take place in Asia," she stated in a speech at Northwood University.

With this globalization in mind, Young began her own New York-based business advisory company while continuing as a senior advisor to General Motors–Asia Pacific and consultant to the Interpublic Group of Companies for Asia. She has served on the boards of Bell Atlantic, Dayton Hudson, and Bank America, and as trustee of the Associates of the Board of the Harvard Business School and Wellesley College. Living part-time in China, she is an honorary professor of Tsinghua University and Tong Ji University and honorary trustee of Jiaotong University. She is the former chairman of the Committee of 100, a national Chinese American leadership group, and presently chairperson of its Cultural Institute. She is a founding member of the Committee of 200, an international organization of leading businesswomen.

"Have a dream, have a goal, and always try to decide how you are going to make a contribution in the work you are doing," Young said in an interview with Asian Connections. "But keep your eye on that dream, because in the end, somehow you always end up doing it, although I would have never imagined ending up in a company like General Motors doing what I wanted to do."

Young is married with three sons.

## Sources

Interview with Shirley Young (Mario Machado), www.asianconnections.com [accessed January 16, 2001].

Lander, Mark. 11 June 1990. "Shirley Young: Pushing GM's Humble-Pie Strategy." *Business Week*: 52–53.

Young, Shirley, acceptance speech given at Outstanding Business Leaders Award, Northwood University, 1998.

# Henry C. Yuen

Henry C. Yuen. Photo for Gemstar-TV Guide International, Inc.

**Born**: 7 April 1948, Shanghai, China.

**Education**: Wah Yan College, Hong Kong, graduate, c. 1966; University of Wisconsin, Madison, Wisconsin, B.S. in mathematics, 1969; California Institute of Technology, Pasadena, California, Ph.D. in applied mathematics, 1973; Loyola University, Los Angeles, J.D., 1979.

**Positions Held**: Math professor, California Institute of Technology, Pasadena, California, 1973; professor, New York University Courant Institute of Mathematical Science, New York, New York, 1974; research scientist and technical fellow, TRW, Inc., Redondo Beach, California, circa 1975–91; private lawyer, c. 1979–89; cofounder, Gemstar International Group, Ltd. (later renamed Gemstar–TV Guide International, Inc.), Pasadena, California, 1989– ,

president, Gemstar-TV Guide International, Inc., Pasadena, California, 1994–2000; chief executive officer, Gemstar-TV Guide International, Inc., Pasadena, California, 1994–2002.

**Awards, Honors**: Best Entrepreneur (with Daniel Kwoh), *Business Week* magazine, 1990; National Entrepreneur of the Year, Ernst & Young, LLP, *USA Today*, the NASDAQ Stock Market, Inc., and the Center of Entrepreneurial Leadership, Inc., 1996; Distinguished Alumni Award, California Institute of Technology, 1999.

**Summary**: Scientist and lawyer Henry C. Yuen, who holds multiple patents, coinvented a video cassette recorder programming device in 1989, which formed the foundation of his billion-dollar new media empire. His company, Gemstar-TV Guide International, Inc., seeks to make its interactive television program guide as a standard for millions of households across the United States.

## Early Years and Higher Education

Yuen was born in Shanghai after World War II, but spent most of his formative years since the age of two in Hong Kong. His father (known as Chen Fan or Qian Fan) had been trained as an attorney, but eventually became involved in filmmaking. (Fan's most critically acclaimed work was *True Story of Ah Q*, an adaptation of a classical Chinese novel by Lu Xun, produced by Shanghai Film Studio. In 1982 the film was nominated for a prize at the Cannes Film Festival.)

In high school in Hong Kong, Yuen was a star forward on the soccer team; he also practiced Wing Chun martial arts. When he was 17, he moved to the United States, where he studied mathematics at the University of Wisconsin in Madison.

After receiving his bachelor's degree, Yuen headed for Pasadena, California, to work on and obtain his doctorate in applied mathematics from California Institute of Technology.

### Career Highlights

Yuen taught for two years: first at California Institute of Technology, and then at the New York University Courant Institute of Mathematical Scienes. He then left academia to pursue a career as a research scientist at the global technology company, TRW, Inc., for approximately 15 years. At TRW Yuen specialized in the mathematical description of ocean waves—information that was later applied in global weather forecasting. While at TRW, Yuen obtained his law degree from Loyola University in Los Angeles and worked as an attorney advising Asian businesses in his spare time. One of his clients was Mary Lau, the sister of the Hong Kong tycoon Thomas L.H. Lau.

One day in 1989, Yuen, an avid Boston Red Sox fan, attempted to record a baseball playoff game on his videotape recorder (VCR). When the game was over, he discovered that he had made some kind of technical glitch and had recorded a screen full of electronic snow. Recognizing a need for some kind of device to facilitate recording of TV programs, Yuen and some friends, including TRW coworker Daniel Kwoh, and college classmates Wilson Cho and Louise Wannier, used mathematical codes to create VCR Plus+ in 1989. Working out of a law office, they officially launched the company, Gemstar. Originally priced at $60 each, the VCR Plus+, a simple electronic gadget that connects to a VCR, was designed to enable the user to record a program by punching a number assigned to that program.

The success of VCR Plus+ was dependent on two factors: financing and the inclusion of those program numbers in television listings. Mary Lau, Yuen's legal client, agreed to put up $50,000 of seed money to manufacture the units in Asia. (Later, her brother Thomas would own 24 percent of the company.) Gemstar then went to work to convince newspapers to publish the numbers; *The New York Times*, concerned by its falling subscriptions, finally agreed to participate. After only six months in business, more than 100 newspapers followed suit, and soon these media outlets were paying Gemstar royalty fees for publishing the numbers. Yuen had also approached *TV Guide* to print his codes, and as a part of the negotiations, he agreed to sell 20 percent of his company for $20 million. The deal fell through—and would have some ironic implications in the future.

Gemstar was able to further exploit licensing opportunities by making deals to TV and VCR manufacturers who wanted to incorporate the VCR Plus+ in their product packages. As stated in *Forbes* (27 May 1991), timing was key: "there was only a brief opportunity to get TV watchers hooked on these program numbers, and Gemstar seized it." In its inaugural year, Gemstar sold literally millions of VCR Plus+.

Up to 1991, Yuen was still working at TRW, while Daniel Kwoh had quit to work on VCR Plus+ full-time. Eventually Yuen left TRW to devote all his attention to his new enterprise; he became president and chief executive officer in 1994. A year later, Gemstar went public and was valued at $250 million. "Science is like solving puzzles," Yuen said in an article in *Fortune* (14 August 2000). "I find law is a little more like playing chess. Business is the most exciting. There are no rules. It's a free-for-all."

From the start, Gemstar did break conventional rules. Instead of paying high fees for a booth at the Consumer Electronics Show, Yuen and his chief financial officer, Elsie Ma Leung, purchased a house on a golf course in Las Vegas. Potential customers were transported to the house to examine new products and make deals.

Gemstar was not content with its one best-selling product. The company developed other devices, such as Index Plus, which tracks videotape recordings through an indexing and addressing system. Although Index Plus failed to catch on with consumers, it became clear to Gemstar and Yuen that their future lay in interactive electronic program guides, also known as IPGs or EPGs. According to one scenario, viewers would see this IPG first when they turn on their television set. As in the case of Web portals like Yahoo!, the IPG would help viewers navigate through hundreds of available channels. Consumers could buy products and "interact" through these IPGs.

This concept was not a new one. Already at least two companies, VideoGuide and StarSight, had begun some work in creating these guides. Yuen sued StarSight for allegedly infringing on one of his patents. In 1996 he purchased VideoGuide and a year later, acquired StarSight. Gemstar's future domination of the IPG market caught the attention of cable television leader John Malone and News Corporation chairman Rupert Murdoch. Malone's Liberty Media controlled a cable channel that offered scrolling listings, while Murdoch's News Corp. owned *TV Guide*. Seeing an opportunity that would be mutually beneficial, the two media leaders joined together to form United Video Satellite Group and embarked on a $2.8-billion hostile takeover of the Pasadena-based Gemstar in 1998. Yuen, however, refuse to give up his company—and his then 90 patents—without a fight. He went directly to the stock-

holders, arguing that the value of Gemstar must be worth much more than what was being offered. The board was finally convinced; soon after the unsuccessful takeover bid, Gemstar's worth soared to $10 billion. Yuen further strengthened his empire with licensing deals with Microsoft Corporation and AOL for use of Gemstar's technology in its Internet applications. He also formed @TV Media, a joint venture with NBC and Thomson, the manufacturer of RCA television sets, to sell advertising on his IPGs.

Yuen, who had sued *TV Guide* for alleged patent infringement six years previously, made an effort to acquire the magazine in 2000. At that time, *TV Guide's* business was languishing, and Malone's cable company was being purchased by ATT. As a result, Malone and Murdoch finally acquiesced to the merger. According to the $14-billion deal, News Corporation owned 43 percent of the new company, Gemstar-TV Guide International. Yuen remained chief executive officer but served as "co-president" with chief financial officer Elsie Leung in Pasadena; Joe Keiner, a former News Corporation executive in New York; and Peter Boylan, a Liberty Corporation executive in Tulsa, Oklahoma. Yuen, who owned about 10 percent of the company, was eventually replaced as CEO in 2002, in a $22 million payout deal.

The Justice Department's antitrust division initially cleared the merger in 2000, but it was reopening the investigation in 2001. Critics, especially cable companies, have maintained that the combined company would form a monopoly over IPGs. Competitors, including Scientific-Atlanta, Inc., EchoStar Communications Corporation, and Pioneer Corporation, have filed lawsuits against Gemstar over licensing difficulties.

In addition to IPGs, Yuen has his eye on the future of electronic books. He purchased two leading manufacturers of e-books, NuvoMedia and Softbook, and their patents in 2000.

Yuen, who is divorced, has two sons, Philip and Gerald.

## Sources

Churbank, David. 27 May 1991. "Success Formula." *Forbes*: 334.

Gemstar-TV Guide International Inc. http://www.gemstartvguideinternational.com [accessed August 28, 2001].

Gunther, Marc. 14 August 2000. "Henry Yuen Wants to be Your TV Guide." *Fortune*: 200+ .

"TV Guy." 12 March 2001. *Business Week*: 66+ .

Vogelstein, Fred. 7 August 2000. "Meet the Bill Gates of TV." *U.S. News & World Report*: 50+ .

# Appendix: Distinguished Asian American Business Leaders Arranged by Field

## Agriculture/Horticulture

Kanetaro Domoto
Charles Kim
Chin Lung
Shoji Nagumo
George Tanimura

## Automotive

Shirley Young

## Chemicals

Donna Fujimoto Cole

## Consulting

Rajat Gupta

## Cosmetics

Andrea Jung

## Defense

Jeong H. Kim
Joanna Lau

## Electronic Goods (Consumer)

George Aratani
Amar Bose
James Chu

James J. Kim
Noel Lee
An Wang
Elaine Yamagata
Henry C. Yuen

## Energy/Environmental

Larry Asera
Doan Lien Phung

## Fashion Industry

David Chu
Ellery J. Chun
William Mow
Josie Natori
Vera Wang

## Financial Services/Insurance

Ramani Ayer
Phyllis Campbell
F. Chow Chan
Lilia Clemente
Helen Young Hayes
Chinn Ho
Benjamin Hong
Josephine Jimenez
Masayuki Tokioka
Gerald Tsai

Don Wang

## Food Service/Industry

F. Chow Chan
Roger H. Chen
Andrew Cherng
Eddie Flores Jr.
Sue Ling Gin
Supenn Harrison
Mercedes del Rosario Huang
Gennosuke Kodani
Tri La
Loida Nicholas Lewis
Wing Chuai Ngan
Ted Ngoy
Indra K. Nooyi
Charlie Shin
David Tran
David Du Tran
Tsuru Yamauchi

## Health Care

Cora M. Tellez

## High-Technology Products and Services

Pauline Lo Alker
Kavelle R. Bajaj
Dado Banatao
Sabeer Bhatia
James Chu
Vinita Gupta
Rose Hwang
James J. Kim
Jeong H. Kim
Kija Kim
Steve Y. Kim
Lata Krishnan
David K. Lam
Joanna Lau
David S. Lee
Christine Liang
Sean Nguyen

Ko Nishimura
Scott D. Oki
Cecilia Pagkalinawan
Doan Lien Phung
Safi U. Qureshey
John Tu
An Wang
Jerry Yang
Henry C. Yuen

## Household Services

Yick Wo

## International Trade

Rioichiro (Ryoichiro) Arai
George Aratani
James J. Kim
John J. Sie
Kay Sugahara
Elaine Yamagata
Shirley Young

## Media/Publishing

Yen Ngoc Do
Fritz Friedman
Chinn Ho
Chris Lee
Sonny Mehta
Ismail Merchant
Scott M. Sassa
John J. Sie
Janet Yang
Jerry Yang
Henry C. Yuen

## Real Estate

Eddie Flores Jr.
Sue Ling Gin
Chinn Ho
Frank Jao
Lilly V. Lee
George Ow Jr.
Leslie Tang Schilling

## Retail

C.K. Ai
Ellery J. Chun
Robert C. Nakasone
Joe Shoong

## Shipping

Kay Sugahara

## Sports

Paul Isaki
Kim Ng

## Tourism

Robert Iwamoto Jr.

## Toys

Pedro Flores
James J. Kim
Robert C. Nakasone
Charlie Woo

## Venture Capital

Dado Banatao
Lilia Clemente
Steve Y. Kim
Scott D. Oki

# Index

Page numbers in **bold type** refer to main entries.

# About the Author and Contributors

NAOMI HIRAHARA is an independent writer and editor. A past recipient of a California Community Foundation's Brody Arts Award, she was the English section editor of *The Rafu Shimpo*, a Japanese American daily newspaper in Los Angeles and a Milton Center Fellow in creative writing at Newman University in Wichita, Kansas. Hirahara is the author of *An American Son: The Story of George Aratani, Founder of Mikasa and Kenwood*. Her unpublished novel "Summer of the Big Bachi" was a finalist for Barbara Kingsolver's Bellwether Prize in 2000. She received her degree in international relations from Stanford University and studied at the Inter-University Center for Advanced Language Studies in Tokyo.

TAKESHI NAKAYAMA is a freelance writer and editor based in Walnut, California. He was a former editor of *The Rafu Shimpo* newspaper in Los Angeles. He earned his bachelor's degree in history from California State University at Los Angeles.

JOYCE NAKO is a freelance writer, editor and researcher based in Moreno Valley, California. Her articles and stories have been published in various newspapers, literary magazines, and academic journals including *Amerasia Journal* (UCLA Asian American Studies). She was the assistant editor for *Moving the Image: Independent Asian Pacific American Media Arts* (1991) and *Green Makers: Japanese American Gardeners in Southern California* (2000). She also was a 1994 Rockefeller Foundation Fellow at UCLA Asian American Studies.

JOHN SAITO JR. is a freelance writer and editor based in Los Angeles, California. He was a former editor of *The Rafu Shimpo* newspaper in Los Angeles. He earned his bachelor's degree in English from Loyola Marymount University.